International Guide
to
Children's Theatre
and
Educational Theatre

International Guide
to
Children's Theatre
and
Educational Theatre

A HISTORICAL AND GEOGRAPHICAL SOURCE BOOK

Edited by Lowell Swortzell

GREENWOOD PRESS

New York • Westport, Connecticut • London

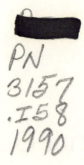

PN
3157
.I58
1990

Library of Congress Cataloging-in-Publication Data

International guide to children's theatre and educational theatre : a
  historical and geographical source book / edited by Lowell
  Swortzell.
    p. cm.
  Bibliography: p.
  Includes index.
  ISBN 0–313–24881–8 (lib. bdg. : alk. paper)
  1. Children's theatre—Handbooks, manuals, etc. 2. Drama in
education—Handbooks, manuals, etc. I. Swortzell, Lowell.
II. Title: International guide to children's theater and educational
theater.
PN3157.I58 1990
792′.0226—dc20   89–12059

British Library Cataloguing in Publication Data is available.

Library of Congress Catalog Card Number: 89–12059
ISBN: 0–313–24881–8

First published in 1990

Greenwood Press, Inc.
88 Post Road West, Westport, Connecticut 06881

Printed in the United States of America

The paper used in this book complies with the
Permanent Paper Standard issued by the National
Information Standards Organization (Z39.48–1984).

10 9 8 7 6 5 4 3 2 1

74649664

For Vera Roberts,
teacher, friend and mentor,
who, from the time we met performing in a play
when I was fifteen-years old, has guided
my life with inspiring wisdom and warmth.

Contents

Illustrations

Acknowledgments

This book could not be international in scope had I not received the help of those artists and educators far and wide who generously responded to requests for articles, information, programs, and photographs and who met deadlines even, in several cases, in the midst of internal strife and full-fledged wars. Perhaps the best insight into the spirit prevailing among contributors can be seen in the example of one who promised to supply materials with this caveat, "I'll do my best to reply on time, but, Sir, you must understand there is a revolution going on here." Even a revolution, however, did not prevent the promise from being kept, any more than it stopped theatre for young people from being produced. This book, like the art it documents, owes its existence (and my ever-deepening gratitude) to those who possess such unflinching faith and courage in the work they do. Their names are to be found throughout the entries and in the contributors section, but a few must be singled out for special thanks at the outset.

Professor Ann Shaw, former President of ASSITEJ/USA and Vice President of ASSITEJ, from the beginning gave guidance and shared her own collection of international resources which proved invaluable. The present President of ASSI-TEJ/USA, Professor Harold Oaks, also has been encouraging on several occasions. Martha Coigney, Director of the International Theatre Institute of the United States, Inc., provided helpful advice on diplomatic procedures when it seemed impossible for one country to get its article beyond its borders. Those who solved particular problems include: Maria Luisa Barredo, Secretary General, ASSITEJ/Spain; Maria Navarro Blanco, President, ASSITEJ/Spain; Benvenuto Cuminetti, President, ASSITEJ/Italy; Janine Flory, Executive Secretary, ASSITEJ/Australia; Morton Harrie, ASSITEJ/Sweden; Henryk Jurkowski, President, UNIMA, Poland; Heribert Kloh, Executive Secretary, ASSITEJ/Federal Republic of Germany; Galya Kolosova, Executive Secretary, ASSITEJ/USSR; Kazuto Kurihara, President, ASSITEJ/Japan; Halina Machulska, President, ASSITEJ/Poland; Janos Meczner, Acting Secretary, ASSITEJ/Hungary; Rose

Marie Moudoues, President, ASSITEJ/France; Ha Nhan, ASSITEJ/Vietnam; Orna Porat, Director General, ASSITEJ/Israel; Michael Ramlose, ASSITEJ/ Denmark; Eddy Socorro, President, ASSITEJ/Cuba; and, Hya-Joo Sohn, General Secretary, ASSITEJ/Korea. Special thanks also go to Joyce Doolittle and Hélène Beauchamp, Canada; Andreas Michaelides, Cyprus; Pam Ritch and Seabury Quinn, United States; John Hodgson and Tony Jackson, Great Britain; and, Stig Eriksson, Norway.

For informative materials I have adapted, I thank Vibeke Gardmand and Biba Schwoon, Denmark; Olli Pellikka, Elina Rainio, and Nena Stenius, Finland; Bernard Goss and Bernadette Tsui, Hong Kong; Istvan Nanay, Hungary; Marco Baliani, Walter Cassani, Giovanna Marinelli, Graziano Melano, Franco Passatore, and Brunella Reverberi, Italy; Akio Araki, Yasuo Fukushima, Shin Shikata, Shoji Takahira, and Hiroyuki Tomita, Japan; and A. M. Lesaoana and Sebolelo Mokhobo, Lesotho.

I wish to express my appreciation to colleagues in the Program in Educational Theatre at New York University for their support: Professors Nellie McCaslin, Robert Landy, Steven Hart, the late Stephen Palestrant, and, most of all, Nancy Swortzell, whose help stretched from office to home where she often extended hospitality to visitors from abroad. Without her patience, sacrifices, and understanding, this volume could not have grown to its present size.

For university funds which in part enabled me to travel to Australia and China, I am indebted to Professors Roger L. Cayer and Elmer E. Baker, Jr. of the Department of Communications and Communication Arts, School of Education, Health, Nursing and Arts Professions, whose interest in this project has been a source of encouragement.

I save Dr. Leslie White for last because her contribution is greatest, as research assistant, correspondent, and typist who gave order to my files and life for the last four years. When this near-impossible task couldn't be handled with her usual ease and humor, she was the first to demand and then find a solution. If only the United Nations could obtain her vast organizational skills, this world would be a saner, safer place in which to live.

Introduction: "A Very Great Invention"

When Mark Twain voiced his belief that "children's theatre is one of the very, very great inventions of the twentieth century" he could not foresee what subsequent decades would achieve. His conviction was based on a visit in the early 1900s to the Children's Educational Theatre in New York City, the first American theatre intended specifically for children and adolescents. This innovative concept had been largely devised to attract immigrant youth throughout the city by offering them plays that improved their English and briefly freed them from the ghettos in which they lived. Deeply impressed by what he saw, Twain went on to predict that children's theatre's "vast educational value—now but dimly perceived and but vaguely understood—will someday presently come to be recognized." This testimonial almost from the time it was made until the present day has inspired and reassured workers in the field. It, moreover, appropriately sets the stage for this book, which, by surveying theatre for young people and related aspects of educational theatre as they are practiced today throughout the world, proves just how correct Twain was.

Certainly, contemporary practitioners fully perceive, even if they cannot always make others understand, the educational value of theatre in the lives of young people. They recognize that theatre alone brings all the arts together into full, immediate, and dynamic performance and creates for its audiences experiences that can be unrivaled in urgency and excitement. They also know that those young people who participate in dramatic activities in schools and in recreational and religious centers can be stimulated to use their own inherent creativity as well as to relate to others in the united effort of larger group collaborations. Thus they see the benefits that come through self-exploration and self-expression, through interaction and socialization, and through the disciplines integral to all art forms. Whether in informal games or in full formal productions, participation in theatre ironically demands both independence of thought and suppression of will, limitless imagination and constant control, commitment to one's individual contribution and responsibility to that of the group's.

These seemingly contradictory notions are nonetheless true because theatre, by its illusionary nature, always must remain a paradox, whether it takes place in an open field in Africa where the spectators become the participants in an improvised play, as Augusto Boal would have them, or in Moscow in a magnificent theatre where spectators sit in upholstered chairs viewing a scripted and long-rehearsed musical production, as Natalia Sats would have them. Both experiences have the potential to enlighten and entertain, as does the work of every country and company mentioned in this book, each in its own specific way. Only through understanding our own accomplishments, along with those of others, will we ever come close (or at least closer) to learning the mysteries of the multilayered paradoxes that make theatre an endlessly fascinating art to work in and watch.

Children's theatre and educational theatre, no less than that for adults, thrive in paradox. When Stanislavsky was asked early in the century the difference between adult and children's theatre, he replied that there was none. Then after a doubtless well-timed pause for maximum effect, he added that theatre for young people must be better! A challenging paradox! Children's theatre is at once the youngest and the oldest of theatrical arts, a fact this book demonstrates time and again. Youngest in the sense that conscious attention has been given to creating a theatre specifically for youth only in the current century; oldest in that children have been part of theatre from its beginning. A historical paradox! It is specialized in its appeal to certain age groups, yet it is mainstream too because at its best it entertains audiences of all ages. An aesthetic paradox! So far, it is the most neglected of theatre forms but also the most important as the training ground and laboratory for the development of future audiences without whom the adult theatre may not survive. A fatalistic paradox! It can be naive, silly, and childish, or it can be fanciful, complex, and child-like, sometimes all of these within the same performance. A stylistic paradox! It demands of its practitioners experience and comprehension far more specialized and sensitive than that required by the adult theatre, but few training programs exist in the world and all too often a high percentage of those working in the field do so because they have been unable to succeed in the adult theatre. A professional paradox! It should not be compromised by considerations of the box office or by censorship of educational authorities, but it *is* almost daily, even hourly. A financial and philosophical paradox! It can be an artistic embarrassment, yet in many countries theatre reviewers do not cover productions or lend support to raise artistic standards. A critical paradox!

The field will march into the next century still debating these concerns and asking itself such perennial questions as: Is theatre, by educating its audiences, lessening its effect and value as an art? Should children perform for children, or should young audiences see only professional adult actors if they are to develop professional tastes and standards? Should dramatic activities in which young people engage be developmental, as part of a creative process, or should they lead to a finished product with the ultimate goal of a public performance? Is audience participation essential, what children's theatre is all about, as one critic put it, or is it cheapening an art form by turning it into fun and games, as I have accused it? These and dozens more quandries plague and stimulate practitioners who regularly strengthen their positions through their lack of agreement and the intensity of their persuasions, with the result that their work constantly improves. Paradoxes, we learn—because the muses who made them knew exactly what they were doing—can be wonderfully productive!

Since the 1950s children's theatre has become a full-time profession for hundreds of teachers, writers, directors, actors, managers, designers, and puppeteers the world over, as it is for hundreds—perhaps even thousands—more an avocation in community and educational enterprises to which they are avidly devoted. Through local and national organizations they discuss and debate the questions just mentioned or the latest ones of the day. Leaders come together every three years for a World Congress organized by the Association Internationale du Théâtre pour l'Enfance et la Jeunesse (ASSITEJ). Here they not only talk and argue, but also see productions by the world's leading companies and come away overjoyed or angry, or both. The membership of ASSITEJ currently consists of forty countries and provides the real and symbolic evidence that children's theatre is a worldwide movement, populated by dedicated artists and educators who are forging an art form against tremendous odds, many of which are subsequently spelled out herein.

One purpose of this volume is to document the history of this movement in each country, to define its current state of artistic achievement, and to project its foremost needs for the future. No previous book has undertaken this task. Only one, in fact, has examined international theatre for young audiences at length, and that did so largely in production photographs with only brief descriptions of the history and repertory.

International Guide to Children's Theatre and Educational Theatre is intended as a reference work, organized alphabetically from A (Australia) to Z (Zimbabwe). Each entry begins with a historical overview that describes the first important plays and productions as well as influential dramatists, directors, designers, performers, and pedagogues. Representative companies, usually three or four, are then described, giving their history, organization, and an account of several significant plays from the current repertory. In the final section a survey is made of contemporary children's theatre in general, discussing its basic operation, its artistic and educational goals, and the major problems faced in achieving them. Where it has been provided by the country, a bibliography of plays and books about children's theatre is also included.

When this volume was first planned it was to have featured the work of only twenty representative countries, but thanks to the wide response to the need for such a study, twenty-five more were added, making the range and distribution truly international. Now readers may track patterns of development, compare and contrast methods of administration, and draw inspiration from the artistic goals and accomplishments of their own and other countries.

The amount of information provided depends entirely on that supplied by representatives of each country. Although cooperation has been generous, there remain several nations for which no correspondent could be found; consequently those nations do not appear here even though theatre is known to flourish in them. These few omissions are regretted, and attempts will continue to be made to obtain materials so that they might be added to any future editions.

The final bibliography contains the major works, in English, on theatre for young people and educational theatre, including a list of doctoral dissertations that may not be known outside the United States, but that add significantly to research in the field. The bibliography is proof, if it is needed, that children's theatre is an academic discipline to be studied. The index gives names of major figures mentioned in the Introduction or in more than one entry in the book itself; it provides cross references to generic aspects of the field in topics such as creative drama, shadow-puppets, and theatre-in-education (TIE). It does not list companies and names of individuals, since in a volume of this length these run into the thousands.

In five years of preparation this book has changed considerably because of the steady arrival of new information that needed to be included. When, as often happened, all resources seemed to have been exhausted and a country was about to be crossed off the list, a telephone call, telegram, or large envelope was received that changed (and enlarged) the contents yet again. One chapter was sent by diplomatic courier, another was carried to a second country where it was then hand-delivered to an embassy in Washington, D.C., and then mailed to me. Children's theatre, it seems, is subject to international intrigue and intervention as much as any other. Another paradox, perhaps? Yes, for the reader soon will discover the presence of politics in these pages. Entries openly discuss the doctrinaire nature of some children's theatres, those in which plays are performed to project particular values that express official government policy or that advocate those of others parties. As becomes clear here, the potential for political propaganda, although not developed in many countries, is widely understood and effectively used in others.

However circuitous their arrival, the articles are accurate, written by either the country's president of ASSITEJ or someone officially delegated by the president to represent that office. In the case of countries that are not members of ASSITEJ, the writer is working directly in children's theatre or educational theatre and, therefore, is an authority speaking from personal and professional experience.

Where the work of countries could not be described in the specified format requested by the editor, contributors were asked to create their own outlines, and in one form or another most supplied the required materials. Some sent reprints of newspaper articles, or programs, press releases, publicity brochures, government pamphlets, or personal letters and asked me to take from them information of interest. In other cases several countries submitted outlines that again had to be assembled by me. Each entry is signed at the end by the person or persons responsible for its contents. Authors and translators of articles may be identified further by consulting the list of contributors and translators at the end of the volume.

Each contributor was asked to respond in English, but this was not always possible, and a half-dozen entries have been translated, mostly by colleagues and graduate students at New York University. Although the translators have exerted great care in the accuracy of their translations, it was necessary for me to rewrite each article to make it conform to the general style of the book. Indeed, to varying degrees, this has been true of all articles; the effort, it is hoped, results in clarity and uniformity, which in dealing with forty-five countries, east and west and in between, did not always appear possible to achieve.

As the entries arrived they soon revealed that many writers, in outlining children's theatre, were in fact describing the educational theatre practices in their countries, for except in the Soviet-bloc nations (where there is a strict division between the two) they often are inseparable. And so the book becomes another guide, and again the first on an international basis, to the growth and current state of international educational theatre.

The writers prove that Mark Twain was doubly right in his prediction, for in heralding children's theatre as a great invention, he was also correct in foreseeing educational theatre. And today we are perceiving and understanding its "vast educational value" better than ever before. Drama both as a method of teaching and as a subject to be taught is firmly fixed in the educational systems of Great Britain and in various regions of Europe, Canada, and the United States. With more and more research documenting drama's effectiveness in the classroom as well as on the stage, educational theatre and TIE have become recognized disciplines in which experts work throughout the world (many of whom are discussed in this volume).[1]

And so this guide examines both areas, the paradox and the paradigm, two fields that often merge and yet remain separate as they bring theatre into the lives and minds of young people. An account of how this relationship developed follows in the general historical overview.

Readers who traverse the global pathways charted here may be astonished by the extent, diversity, complexity, and maturity of this "very great invention." Especially so if up until now they have thought of children's theatre mostly as a place to see *The Wizard of Oz* and other childhood classics. Even its own authorities may be surprised to learn of recent developments, such as the Moscow Theatre for Young Spectators' currently acclaimed production (April 1989) of the long-suppressed dramatization of Dostoyevsky's *Notes from Underground*, which contains full frontal nudity! No, Toto, we're not in Kansas any more! Of course, theatre for young people remains in Kansas, and happily so, but it also flourishes in vastly varying forms almost everywhere else in the world, as readers who turn these pages will discover when they follow not the yellow brick road, but the immense international highway just ahead.

A BRIEF HISTORICAL SURVEY

Drama through the centuries has dealt with all periods of human life—the seven ages of man Shakespeare called them—and therefore has included children and young people as characters from the beginning, just as theatre long has witnessed them as players on the stages of the world. Likewise, popular theatre has attracted young people as playgoers from the time of the Greeks onward. Even earlier, children had participated as performers in Egyptian ceremonies—young girls as dancers and boys as acrobats—while others watched at festivals and celebrations that in design and execution took on an undeniably theatrical look. Staged in long processions as carefully planned as modern-day parades and at Abydos even acted out in specially written texts, these performances were rituals that would excite any child in their use of movement, color, and pageantry. To what extent their meaning was made clear to young people depended then, as it does today, on the quality of writing and presentation and on the discussion that followed in which children, parents, teachers (where there were teachers), priests, and officials asked and answered questions to explore and explicate their significance.

In this same manner theatre has been central (and remains so) to all tribal cultures in which symbolism is manifested in masks, body makeup, special costumes, and properties that are given life through music, mime, and dance. Once words are added, be they chanted, sung, or spoken, drama has begun.

Much the same pattern of development may be witnessed in the growth of children, since they, too, pass through similar stages in their personal uses of play. First comes their fascination with objects that move or take on human characteristics, then arrives their early response to rhythm and enjoyment of verbal patterns even before words are understood, and their later attraction to masks and makeup, and to dressing up as someone else; these inclinations are part of most childhoods. Even more theatrical is the child's love of games, which in structure resemble short plays that require participants to perform roles and go through prescribed actions (which often parallel a beginning, a middle, and an end) in order to discover objects or outcomes that determine the winner (or hero). When children are declared to be ''it'' in a game, they become performers, the seeker in Hide and Seek or the king in King of the Mountain, and through words and actions they take on characters different from themselves. The joy of pretending and of role playing becomes an essential part of learning through imitation—of experiencing, for instance, what it is like to be grown up by wearing high heels, Mommy's best hat, or her favorite lipstick and speaking her most characteristic words. Children in everyday life are constantly making theatre: at holidays, birthdays, weddings, and even funerals when they participate in ceremonies staged according to family, religious, and cultural traditions that often use special settings, decorations, and clothing, as well as specific roles for the celebrants to play. A child's development, therefore, is often inherently theatrical whether or not formal playgoing is part of it.

But for many, actual theatre performances have been part of childhood, at least since ancient Greece. Plato, in summarizing tastes of the theatregoing public, contended that an audience survey would show young children voting for puppet and magic shows, older boys and girls for comedy, and educated men and women for tragedy. He himself resisted the inclusion of theatre in his idealized republic because he feared the harm that could result if characters and ideas miscarried (he advocated that only virtuous acts be described by writers and even banished Homer and Hesiod for their vivid misrepresentations and outright lies). But his very scorn is evidence of the effectiveness of theatre and asserts forever the communicative potency of drama in the lives of young people. Moreover, Plato recognized the good to be derived from dramatic literature, music, and imitation when honest examples prevail, for then, he admitted, the craft of the poet becomes light, winged, even holy.

Greek drama, both tragedies and comedies, include children as important, although often silent, characters. The most familiar perhaps are Medea's ill-fated offspring, used by their mother to deliver poisoned gifts to Jason's bride before being slaughtered and flaunted by Medea in the culmination of her jealousy and revenge. (They have been made the focus of Susane Osten's *Medea's Children*, a Swedish play of the 1980s that presents them as contemporary youths while their elders remain classical figures.) The sacrifice and burial of little Astananx in *The Trojan Women* is essential to the power of that tragedy. Earlier Euripides had used children in *Alcestis*, although the lamentation of Eumelus as he stands with his younger sister over the corpse of their mother does not sound like a child speaking: "Your death, O Mother, destroys our house." Historians have suggested that children mimed these roles while adult actors delivered the lines. Melessus, the young child of Andromache, pleads for his life but again sounds like an adult in miniature. Antigone and Ismene appear as children to telling effect in the final moments of *Oedipus*, when Creon presents them to their blinded father. In comedy, the little daughters of Trygaeus openly insult their father's scheme to fly to the gods on the back of a beetle in *Peace*, by Aristophanes. And young boys figure prominently as actors and dancers in *The Wasps*; a child appears in *Lysistrata*, another in *Plutus*.

In Roman comedy, Plautus, in his prologue to *Poenulus*, describes the noisy audience as hungry, social, restless, a body almost impossible to silence. He especially begs crying children and their scolding nurses to remain at home, but clearly, as the plea proves, they didn't!

Pantomime emerged as an art form during the first century B.C., developed by acrobats, jugglers, and imitators who long had been performing in the public squares of Greece and Italy. In Roman cities the tradition flourished as never before when troupes of players, often including children, performed on hastily erected stages in the open air. Their repertory consisted of comic and tragic dances, usually based on classic legend, with musical accompaniment. Part dance, part athletics, and part drama, pantomime underwent many changes, eventually growing into an elaborate theatrical art, investitured with ornate scenery and costumes, but still using children as cherubs, cupids, and other mythological figures.

When theatre reemerged in Europe in the Middle Ages it did so as "one-man shows" given by itinerant storytellers and balladeers who visited courts and town squares to eke out their livings by appealing to the aristocracy and peasants alike with their stories of great heroes. These epic adventures became the literary foundations and later cultural heritages of many Western countries. And once the church fathers realized that stories of the Bible, which congregations could neither read nor understand in Latin, could be made accessible when dramatized and performed as part of the Easter and Christmas services, medieval theatre was under way. At first performed by priests, these liturgical lessons later became popular enough for entire towns to participate in as they were developed into plays drawn from the Old and New Testaments, or from the lives of patron saints. Original allegories such as *Everyman* were intended for the moral as well as the religious instruction of viewers.

In the heyday of medieval theatre Hell was depicted as an enormous mouth of a monster and stood at the far right-hand side of the stage (with Heaven to the left at the opposite end). A highlight of every performance occurred when the mouth opened and, through smoke and simulated flames, the Devil emerged followed by his minions, little evil imps who cavorted gaily in wild abandonment. Their mischievous pranks quickly earned them laughs and no doubt especially pleased the parents in the audience because they were portrayed by the town children. Their performances in these local and seasonal celebrations correspond to today's Christmas and historical pageants in which countless young people still are introduced to the theatre both as players and as playgoers.

A child in the Middle Ages also could act a speaking role, as in *The Brome Abraham and Isaac*, with its portrait of a complex boy who is psychologically maturer than his father, or take part in reenactments of the Slaughter of the Innocents, the Noah legend, or many other biblical stories. In secular drama young people performed in interludes such as the allegorical *Play of the Weather*, by John Heywood, first published in 1553. *A New Interlude for Children to Play, Named Jack Juggler, both Witty and Very Pleasant*, composed sometime between 1553 and 1558, mixed classic and native elements by taking for its basic structure a Plautine farce of mistaken identity, to which were added characters typical of the English countryside: the Vice, Jack Juggler, Dame Coy, Alice Trip-and-Go, and the foolish knave Jenkin Careaway. *Jack Juggler* was the first published play expressly written for children to perform and is still playable today.

In the tenth century a farsighted religious figure, Hrothswitha of Gandersheim, a teacher in a school in Saxony, decided to accomplish several academic tasks at once by giving her students short plays to enact. Taking elements from Terence, whose plays she knew well, together with her own penchant for the pious, she wrote in Latin, thereby improving the language skills of her pupils as they spoke her lines. And because she told stories of Christian martyrs, religious instruction was also vividly provided, along with such other benefits as the improvement of students' voice, diction, poise, concentration, and socialization. True educational theatre had arrived in her classroom, and all those who practice it today should acknowledge and honor Hrothswitha as their patron saint.

The Italian renaissance, with its stimulation from the classical past, reinterpreted the rules of Aristotle in forging a theatre of its own, one that resulted in no drama of consequence, but in magnificent staging that witnessed new technical heights: great transformation scenes, changing from architectural grandeur to pastoral beauty in short order as audiences watched in wonder. When music and dance were added to this scenic magic, masques and operas became the favorite form of entertainment of the aristocracy. But other social orders were no less fortunate because the same tradition that earlier had produced the wandering storyteller now gave rise to the improvised theatre performed by families who traveled the length of Italy and eventually (over 200 years) throughout most of Europe, even as far as Russia, playing what is now known as *commedia dell'arte*.

The antics of Harlequin and his fellow clowns enthralled children everywhere, including the young Molière, who apparently observed performances in Paris and the provinces and later borrowed both characters and comic devices for his own plays. *Commedia*'s lively form of theatre emphasized rapid pace, buffoonery, and vivid physical action, ingredients readily appreciated by the young. To say that the greater portion of *commedia* was ribald and inappropriate for children is not to deny its unquestionable appeal to them. In fact, elements of the tradition still flourish in British Christmas pantomimes, in the art of mimes such as Marcel Marceau, and in the styles of film comedians such as Charlie Chaplin, Buster Keaton, Laurel and Hardy, and their contemporary counterparts Steve Martin and Robin Williams.

Carlo Gozzi (1720–1806) created a number of fairy-tale plays, several of which remain alive as sources of popular operas, *The Love of Three Oranges* and *Turnadot*, in particular. But it is *The King Stag* that is most often produced for young audiences. Here Gozzi mixed elements of fantasy with the Italian tradition of *commedia*, and even included passages intended to be improvised, along with aspects of *The Arabian Nights*, Chinese fables, and Indian mythology, with its magical effects and transformations. Andre Serban directed a critically acclaimed production of *The King Stag* at the American Repertory Theatre, Cambridge, Massachusetts, in 1985, which he followed with another of Gozzi's fairy-tale plays, *The Serpent Woman*, in 1988 and 1989, also given in special performances for young people.

Tudor England contributed importantly to the traditions of theatre in education, particularly in the teaching of Roger Ascham and Nicholas Udall. In *The Schoolmaster* (1570) Ascham, who himself had been tutor to young Elizabeth I, advocated the use of dialogues as teaching tools; his students could master Latin and enhance their appreciation of classical literature by performing short scenes from Aristophanes, Terence, and Plautus. At the same time, they also improved their diction, movement, and physical grace. Performing, he insisted, benefited both mind and body. Udall, teaching at Eaton and Westminster, recognized that it also could be enjoyable, and wrote plays in English for his students to act, the most notable of which is *Ralph Roister Doister* (ca. 1540). Plotted in the Roman mold, this first English comedy introduced native characters speaking everyday, middle-class dialogue that is mirthful and reflective of its happy characters, who bear names such as Gawyn Goodluck and Merygreek.

As actors and audiences, young people played significant roles in the development of the Elizabethan theatre, first at schools and universities and then at both public and private playhouses. Christ Church, Cambridge, was the scene of the first production of *Gammer Gurton's Needle*, a lively farce in verse by "Master S.," performed about 1560 and still valid for young audiences today. While John Lyly, a university wit, never intended his eloquent plays for child audiences, he meant them to be acted by child players, the boys of St. Pauls, the company for which he wrote a number of florid, mythological dramatizations, such as *Campase* and *Midas*. His *Endymion, the Man in the Moon* is a fairy-tale romance in which the hero Endymion sleeps for twenty years until a magic spell is broken by a kiss from his beloved Cynthia, goddess of the moon. The great appeal to the sophisticated audiences of these highly artificial plays presented in the private theatres is often credited to the charm of the young actors performing them.

And youths also were performing on the public stages where all female roles were played by boy apprentices who, under the tutelage of master actors, portrayed the great heroines of Elizabethan dramatists. The tragic figures of Lady Macbeth and Ophelia and the worldly Cleopatra were all created by boys, as were those high-spirited portraits of Kate, the beautifully wise Rosalind, and Olivia. Perhaps it is difficult for modern theatregoers to visualize a performance of *Romeo and Juliet* in which both lovers were played by male youths, but this in fact was the case and with total acceptance by audiences. The search for talented boys to fill female roles was so competitive among companies that youths were even kidnapped and conscripted as performers.

In *Hamlet*, Shakespeare took an opportunity to criticize the children's companies, whose popularity was rivaling his own: "There is, sir, an aery of children, little eyases, that cry out on the top of the question, and are most tyrannically clapped for't: these are now the fashion, and so berattle the common stages." Even so, Shakespeare, recognizing the emotional impact of child characters, peopled his own tragedies and histories with memorable youths: Macduff's luck-less lad; the sons of Edward IV in *Richard III*; Mamillius, the bright young prince in *The Winter's Tale*; and Falstaff's wise boy page; among others. Of his plays, *A Midsummer Night's Dream* remains the most often seen by young people today, with its mixture of lyric romance, fairyland magic, and robust low comedy.

But it was not uncommon to find entire families in attendance in the Elizabethan playhouse for tragedies and histories as well as comedies, since one of the characteristics of Shakespeare's audience was its youth.

Mme. de Brinon's plays as enacted by the girls at Saint-Cyr, the school for French nobleman's daughters that opened near Versailles in 1686, so bored Mme. de Maintenon, the school's founder as well as the King's morganatic wife, that she implored Jean Racine to write a new play with a religious theme. Retired as a dramatist for the previous twelve years, Racine nevertheless complied with *Esther*, the first of two biblical offerings by the young ladies, which was an immediate success. Louis XIV recognized in the noble Esther a flattering portrait of Mme. de Maintenon herself. Even more successful, *Athalie*, performed in 1691 by girls between six and nineteen years of age, remains highly favored today among Racine's critics.

Almost a hundred years later, in 1784, another French noble woman experimented with children's drama, producing pantomime and short plays of an incessantly moral nature, collected under the general title *Le Théâtre D'Education*. Mme. de Genlis guided her students, among them her own daughters, in fully costumed and staged performances for audiences that included the Duke of Chartres and other courtiers. Her theatre, however, having no Racine to write for it, never achieved the distinction or artistry of Saint-Cyr. Additional pragmatic scripts appeared in succeeding decades, penned in the name of educational drama by Arnaud Berquin, Maria Edgeworth, and Hannah More.

Perhaps more than any other before it, the literature of the nineteenth century concerned itself with young people; it was, after all, the age of Lewis Carroll, Hans Christian Andersen, Charles Dickens,and Mark Twain, each of whom was drawn to the theatre, although, unfortunately, not as playwrights. Theatre in the 1800s offered few works strictly intended for children but many that appealed to families. Popular stories and novels found long life on the stage, where they were seen by generations of young audiences. Joseph Jefferson played *Rip Van Winkle* for more than thirty years; Frank Mayo became so personally identified with the role of Davy Crockett that it remained his for the rest of his life, just as Edmund Dantes permanently belonged to James O'Neill in *The Count of Monte Cristo*. The works of Charles Dickens were most often dramatized; as many as twelve versions of *The Cricket on the Hearth* played simultaneously in London. In America, where they were not protected by copyright laws, Dickens' works served as the basis of a repertory of pirated plays: *A Christmas Carol, Oliver Twist, The Old Curiosity Shop, Great Expectations, Nicholas Nickleby,* and *A Tale of Two Cities*.

Lewis Carroll's Alice first came to life on the stage in the winter of 1876, and continues to be the subject of a variety of dramatizations, several of which have had long runs in the commercial theatre. Carroll himself carried on a life-long flirtation with the theatre, eagerly attending rehearsals, sending presents to actors, and advocating legislation to protect stage children that would guarantee them "a healthy and innocent occupation which they dearly love."

The century also witnessed a phenomenon not beheld since Shakespeare's "little eyases" had trod the boards: the triumph of the child actor, so widely acclaimed in one instance that he drove adult actors temporarily from their roles. In England, Master Betty, whose full name was William Henry West Betty, brought Shakespeare's major heroes to life in the season of 1804/05, at the age of thirteen, earning public approbation as "The Young Roscius." As "Betty-mania" swept London the leading players of Covent Garden and Drury Lane could no longer attract audiences and for this one season surrendered their fame to the talents of this bright and beautiful child. John Howard Payne, an American imitator of Betty's, although considerably older—all of seventeen—played a repertory of tragic roles in 1809 to critical acclaim; as a dramatist, his first play was presented in New York when he was fourteen. In the 1850s British and American audiences clamored to see an exhibition of even greater prodigious precocity when little Kate and Ellen Bateman, aged seven and nine, respectively, interpreted Hamlet, Shylock, Portia, and Richard III (with Ellen wearing an artificial moustache); they were especially admired together as Macbeth and Lady Macbeth. Other prodigies undertook roles closer to their own ages, one of which was the popular character Little Eva in the numerous dramatizations of Harriet Beecher Stowe's *Uncle Tom's Cabin* that held American and European stages from 1852 through the first decade of this century. Cordelia Howard, the first young actress to move the public to tears in this role, was able to put into Eva, according to one critic, "the very life, and soul, and spirit" of the character.

In the late nineteenth century the psychological relationships between children and adults were probed in a number of Ibsen and Strindberg plays that, although not intended for young people, definitely were about them. Both dramatists studied the guilt of parents whose offspring had died in mishaps: Ibsen's hero in *Little Eyolf*, for example, appears only in the first act as a delicate lad walking on crutches, but his subsequent drowning haunts his parents and measurably alters their lives. Youngsters appear briefly but importantly in *Peer Gynt, The Pillars of Society, A Doll's House*, and *An Enemy of the People*. Strindberg, to an even greater degree than Ibsen, explored the bonds of familial affiliation and in several plays that have been played for young audiences looked at childhood in particular. *Swanwhite* (1901), influenced by Maurice Maeterlinck's marionette plays along with medieval folklore, is a fairy-tale play filled with magic and miracles in which love eventually prevails over the evil forces that surround Swanwhite. In *The Adventures of Lucky Per* (1892) Strindberg presented another allegory on the importance of love in the lives of the young in the story of Per, whose father had locked him away from the world to protect him from evil. But intrigued by the mysteries outside his window Per escapes only to face a series of disillusioning adventures that finally bring him to the brink of suicide. He is saved by the love of a young girl whose devotion has made her loyally follow him despite his many mistakes and rebukes.

The twentieth century has lavished unprecedented emphasis on the creation of drama and theatre that fully belong to children and young people. As early as 1903 in New York City The Children's Educational Theatre established its programs, offering five seasons of plays, no longer "hand-me-downs" from the adult theatre, but specifically written for young audiences. Under the direction of Alice Minnie Herts Heniger this theatre played to thousands of city children, many of whom were immigrants otherwise confined to ghettos with only the culture of the streets available to them. Financial problems brought on by an ordinance forbidding Sunday performances ended, in 1909, an endeavor that, however short-lived, proved the value of formal theatre production for children.

In England, James Barrie did much the same when *Peter Pan* first took flight in 1904 to become the play seen by more children in English-speaking countries than any other. In one famous passage, certainly the best known in child drama, Peter enlists the aid of the audience to save the life of his friend, Tinkerbell: "She says she thinks she could get well again if children believed in fairies. Do you believe in fairies? Say quick that you believe! If you believe, clap your hands! Oh, thank you, thank you, thank you! And now to rescue Wendy!" Audience participation, later to become a vogue among writers of plays for young people, was never better used than here, where in order for the play to proceed the spectators must intervene with their resounding testimony of faith. In 1936, the year before his death, Barrie's last play was produced, the widely overlooked *The Boy David*, a poignant portrait of the biblical David, his slaying of Goliath, and, finally, his visionary dreams of the future of Israel.

Bernard Shaw, looking back in old age, said he had written *Androcles and the Lion* (1912) as an antidote to *Peter Pan* in order, he insisted, "to show what a play for children should be like. It should never be childish; nothing offends children more than to play down to them; all the great children's books, *The Pilgrim's Progress, Gulliver, Robinson Crusoe*, Andersen, *Arabian Nights* and *Grimm's Fairy Tales* were written for adults." His stated intention to create "a sample of what children like in contrast to Barrie's *Peter Pan*," which appeared to him to be "a sample of what adults think children like," probably was an afterthought, for Shaw nowhere else expressed interest in child drama. In any case, *Androcles* did not excite either young or old for long, and closed after eight weeks. Shaw's *Androcles* should not be confused with Aurand Harris' play of the same name, which is one of the most frequently produced plays for young people of this century.

Maurice Maeterlinck, the Belgian playwright, advocated a drama that expressed inner thoughts instead of outward motion. In *The Blue Bird* (1908) he fabricated an allegorical fairy tale that held professional and amateur stages for several decades. With a cast of more than 100 characters the protagonists Tyltyl and Mytyl seek the elusive Blue Bird of Happiness, journeying along the way to the Land of Memory where they visit their dead grandparents, to the Palace of the Night, to a graveyard, and to The Kingdom of the Future. Preoccupied with themes of death, blantantly didactic with characters bearing such names as Loving One's Parents, *The Blue Bird* now appears a dated curiosity of interest largely for its extravagant theatricality.

In Moscow the young Natalia Sats opened a theatre for children in 1920 with an adaptation of Kipling's *Mowghli*, and so began a career that made her famous throughout the world. The daughter of the composer for the Moscow Art Theatre who wrote the score for the original Stanislavky production of *The Blue Bird*, she grew up in an artistic household that nourished her love for both theatre and music. In 1935, when she asked Sergei Prokofiev to write a symphonic tale that would introduce children to the instruments found in an orchestra, she inspired "Peter and the Wolf," which the composer dedicated to her and which she narrated hundreds of times, including performances in Japanese and in English during her company's visit to New York in 1986. When she returned from political exile after World War II she created The Moscow State Musical Theatre, which moved into a spacious building of its own in the early 1980s, where a company of more than fifty singers maintains a repertory of operas and musical entertainments for children and young people.

Until the late 1930s, when an active market was created for the publication of play scripts, few authors specialized in child drama. One notable exception was A. A. Milne, celebrated for his *Pooh* books, who dramatized another childhood favorite, Kenneth Grahame's *The Wind in the Willows*, into a successful stage version titled *Toad of Toad Hall* (1932). His short fairy-tale romance *The Ugly Duckling* is still seen in community theatres; *Make Believe* (1918), in which a group of children seemingly improvise several short plays, enjoyed popularity in London and New York.

Beginning in 1935 with her dramatization of *Jack and the Beanstalk*, followed by *The Indian Captive* (1937) and *The Emperor's New Clothes* (1938), the American dramatist Charlotte Chorpenning wrote a series of more than twenty plays that prevailed for more than three decades in American theatres for children. A former student of George Pierce Baker's famous 47 Workshop at Harvard University, Chorpenning directed student-performed productions of her plays at the Goodman Memorial Theatre, an adjunct of Chicago's Art Institute.

As prolific a dramatist but neither as verbose nor as conventional as Chorpenning, Aurand Harris has contributed nearly forty plays, the most famous of which, *Androcles and the Lion*, is the most performed and translated of any modern American script. In 1987 he was invited to China, where he directed his version of *Rags to Riches* in Shanghai.

Such international exchanges of artists and companies has become a hallmark of the 1980s, as annual festivals are held in which numerous companies perform and particpate in discussions and workshops.

The influence of Walt Disney's animated films spread onto the stage soon after the release of *Snow White and the Seven Dwarfs* (1938) and *Pinocchio* (1940), affecting styles of production design and performance. The worldwide popularity of the Disney characters, songs, and treatment of stories soon became the cultural foundation for millions of children who grew up seeing these brightly colored, often sentimental versions of fairy tales and popular stories. In the late fall of 1940 Disney released his most experimental effort, *Fantasia*, which mixed classical music and animation in a program played by the Philadelphia Orchestra under Leopold Stokowski that included a Bach toccata and fugue, along with selections from Tchaikovsky, Stravinsky, and Beethoven. Twenty-five years later the film became popular all over again during the "pop" and drug cultures, when psychedelic art prevailed. But never since *Fantasia* has the Disney Studios attempted another "art" film.

The relationship between children's film and theatre has not yet been studied at length, but it is nonetheless clear that animation as an acting style in live performance takes its inspiration from Disney and other creators of cartoons. It is also evident that Disney's artists were influenced by children's theatre, at least in the case of *Pinocchio*, for they attended as many as seven performances of the production Yasha Frank staged for the Children's Theatre Unit of the Federal Theatre Project in Los Angeles in 1938, at the time they were planning the film. Frank created a vigorous physical style of performance that incorporated the skills of numerous vaudeville entertainers who were out of work because radio and movies largely had replaced vaudeville's popularity and because the Great Depression of the 1930s had ravished the American economy. With a large cast, full orchestra, and excellent designs and special effects this production, written in sing-song doggerel and fast-moving scenes, became a hallmark in American professional children's theatre production. When it transferred from California to New York City it became a Broadway "hit" that closed suddenly when Congress voted to end the Federal Theatre in June 1939. An attempt was made by commercial managers to continue *Pinocchio*, but the expense of the large enterprise proved too great without government backing.

In Russia, Yevgeny Schwartz, Soviet author of books and plays as well as longtime editor of Leningrad's State Children's Publishing House, used the stories of Andersen and the Grimms in the creation of his "fairy-tale" plays. Operating on several levels of meaning, from innocent fantasy to political satire, these were originally intended for production in adult theatres, but they have come to belong to the canon of child drama by virtue of their fanciful plots, original theatricality, and vivid humor. *The Naked King* (1933) blends three Andersen tales into a comical but doggedly anti-fascist protest of totalitarianism that Soviet censors kept from production until 1960. *The Shadow* (1940), again freely using Andersen, spins the romance of a poor scholar who sends his shadow to woo a princess for him, only to have the princess fall in love with the shadow and place it beside her on the throne. *The Dragon* (1943) also uses Schwartz's favorite theme of tyranny, which resulted in its suppression after one Moscow performance in 1944 before it was finally acclaimed in 1962. Other noted plays of Schwartz include his treatments of *The Snow Queen* and *Little Red Riding Hood*, the latter having been widely produced outside Russia.

The involvement of young people in opera and musical drama, a custom that dates back to Renaissance masques and court performances and later finds notable expression in *Bastien and Bastienne*, composed when Mozart was twelve, flourishes in this century as never before. Kurt Weill and Bertolt Brecht composed

Der Jasager (He Who Says Yes) in 1930 as a "school opera," to be performed entirely by students, with a score that calls for instruments and musical skills to be found in the average high school orchestra. Collaborating with Paul Hindemith, they also wrote a radio play for children, *The Flight of Lindbergh* (1929), in which a large chorus personifies the pilot on his pioneer flight and comments didactically on its significance. Hindemith alone turned his attention to children in short pieces such as *Back and Forth* (1927) and *Let's Build a City* (1930). Carl Orff and Gunild Keetman experimented with children's appreciation of music in a series of exercises beginning in the 1930s. Benjamin Britten's *Let's Make an Opera* (1949) calls for audience participation in a play-within-a-play framework. Earlier Britten composed *Paul Bunyan* (1941) with a libretto by W. H. Auden, which, after long neglect, has been performed and recorded in recent years. More popular, his *Noye's Fludde* (1958), a miracle play to be sung by children and adults, has been heard in churches, city parks, and Times Square, where hundreds of children from throughout the city played the animals boarding the ark. Gian Carlo Menotti's one-act opera *Amahl and the Night Visitors*, first seen on television in 1951, has proved stageworthy in introducing thousands of children to music drama. Menotti followed this with a series of short operas, the most notable of which are *Martin's Lie* (1964), *Help, Help, the Globolinks!* (1968), and *Chip and His Dog* (1979). William Schuman's *The Mighty Casey* (1953) has been sung by all-child casts. New York City's Metropolitan Opera Studio performed *The Happy Prince* in 1967, based on the Oscar Wilde fairy tale and composed by Malcom Williamson, which, following the tradition of Benjamin Britten, calls for child soloists, actors, and chorus.

In 1984 a *Directory of Opera/Musicals for Young Audiences* listed hundreds of titles of published works and for the first time established the extensive repertory available to audiences of all age levels. In England the National Youth Music Theatre presents offerings at the Sadler Wells Theatre in London, such as their 1989 productions of *Le Petits Rats* and *The Tailor of Gloucester*, based on the Beatrix Potter story. Opera for Youth, an American organization founded by Emily Hamood, through its publications and conferences, advocates opera for and by youth and serves as a network for practitioners in the field.

Drama as a classroom subject and activity began to emerge early in the twentieth century in England and the United States through the efforts of a number of teachers who began to experiment with its uses. Caldwell Cook published *The Play Way* in 1917, based on work he had done teaching at a boys school, in which he emphasized performance and play as keys to learning. Peter Slade, working in Birmingham, discussed his methods in *Child Drama* (1958), which further convinced teachers of the need for play to hold a central position in education. Rudolf Laban, European choreographer, designer, and teacher who, after expulsion from Nazi Germany, arrived in England, pleaded much the same argument for movement in *Modern Educational Dance* (1948), with an impact still being realized today among instructors of both drama and dance. Brian Way, in *Development Through Drama*, first published in 1967 and still widely read, advanced the field with his work at London's Theatre Centre and later through lectures and demonstrations given at home and abroad. Dorothy Heathcote developed her methods in Newcastle schools, and largely through demonstrations and films of her work in classrooms greatly influenced a generation of drama teachers in the English-speaking world. Her colleague Gavin Bolton gave voice to current educational theories underlying practices in England in *Towards a Theory of Drama in Education* (1979) and *Drama in Education* (1984). John Hodgson chronicled much of the movement in *The Uses of Drama* (1972) and other works. Richard Courtney outlined the intellectual background to drama in education in his seminal study *Play, Drama and Thought*, first published in 1968.

In America, Winifred Ward, a teacher in Evanston, Illinois, developed what she termed "creative dramatics" in the 1930s and became the leading American spokesperson of the field for the next thirty years in a number of books and courses taught at Northwestern University and workshops conducted throughout the country. She had studied with Hughes Mearns, a professor of education at New York University whose *Creative Power* (1958) testified to his belief that creative expression was inherent in every child and needed only to be released through the stimulation of an imaginative teacher. What Mearns did for the creative writing movement in education, Ward and her numerous disciples performed for dramatic activities in the classroom. They emphasized participation as a process that existed in its own right, and not as a means of formal play production. In the field of children's theatre Ward was also a leader, establishing The Children's Theatre of Evanston and spearheading the formation of a professional organization to spotlight work throughout the country, particularly in colleges and universities. After Ward, others began to emerge: Agnes Haaga and Geraldine Brain Siks at the University of Washington, Kenneth Graham at the University of Minnesota, and Jed Davis at the University of Kansas. Nellie McCaslin at New York University, through her numerous publications, widely influenced educational theatre in America, as did Viola Spolin with her *Improvisation in the Theatre* (1963), a text that advocated the use of games, play, and spontaneous experimentation in education and the training of actors.

Educational theatre in the United States, firmly established by the 1960s, first began in limited instances in the nineteenth century and attracted national attention when George Pierce Baker began teaching playwriting at Harvard University in 1903. Among his students were the founders of the modern American theatre, a generation of dramatists who led the professional theatre to its greatest achievements: Eugene O'Neill, Philip Barry, Sidney Howard, S. N. Behrman, among others, and the widely produced playwright for young people, Charlotte Chorpenning.

The interest in children's theatre in various parts of the world led to an exploratory meeting in 1964; from this gathering of specialists and observers emerged the Association Internationale du Théâtre pour l'Enfance et la Jeunesse (ASSITEJ), which held its first Congress in Prague in 1966 under the leadership of Léon Chancerel of France, Gerald Tyler of Great Britain, and Sara Spencer of the United States. The organization's goal is to promote greater international understanding of what clearly has become a professional field and a major subdivision of theatre itself. Meeting every two years at first and later every three years, ASSITEJ has held a series of Congresses in Amsterdam, Montreal, Albany (New York), West Berlin, Madrid, Lyon, Moscow, and Adelaide. At these Congresses leading speakers and companies have been featured, often with analytical discussions taking place after performances. Problems that face companies have been addressed, texts of plays distributed, and, perhaps most important of all, a network between countries has been established to disseminate information and exchange artists and productions. These connections have enabled the field to define its activities and declare its artistic goals. ASSITEJ provides visibility to companies and individuals who daily face challenges of making their work better known at home and abroad. Although much more needs to be accomplished, ASSITEJ is the established voice and official agent to bring about a lasting, full-fledged identity to theatre for young people everywhere.

MAJOR TRENDS AND CONCERNS THROUGHOUT THE WORLD TODAY

Of a book of this length, a number of logical questions well may be asked, such as what, if any, patterns emerge, what commonalities and differences exist between countries, and what major concerns become apparent in the reports that follow? In other words, what is the world picture as we approach the end of the first century of professional and educational theatre for young people? And what are the political, social, academic, and artistic implications? I have isolated twenty-one recurring trends and concerns that should answer most of these questions and no doubt raise a few of their own. These are not presented in any order of frequency of appearance (no scientific tabulation was made); they simply impress me as the most often cited and significant problems expressed herein. Readers will find additional insights that they consider to be important, and they are encouraged to do so, as well as to challenge those presented here.

Mixed Audiences

Clearly, there is a worldwide artistic movement toward audiences of mixed ages, often with entire families attending plays together. So much evidence appears here in fact that it brings into question the use of labels such as "children's theatre" and "theatre for young people" when the more comprehensive term of "family theatre" or "theatre for family audiences" now appears to be more accurate. No longer do parents necessarily believe that their adult sensibilities will prevent them from appreciating performances at which they were once considered to be outsiders. Now plays, like books young people read, need not to be identified by age levels when they clearly appeal to audiences of various ages, including adults; moreover, the pleasure of seeing them as a family allows valuable opportunities for discussion, exploration, and explication (if needed) later on.

Size of Audience

Playwrights, directors, and producers always have voiced concern over the size of audiences at school and public performances. But today more than ever they insist that these numbers be realistic. Such restrictions also limit the amount of income and may make additional performances necessary to include the total number of students as well as to meet expenses. What bothers companies most is that whatever total capacities they set, school authorities tend to ignore the figures by bringing still more spectators. Large school auditoriums encourage this practice, which always results in a loss of artistic effectiveness. Companies find it difficult to educate producers to recognize that in limiting numbers, they are acting in the production's best interests and, therefore, in that of the audience.

Audiences in Remote Areas or Without Access to Live Theatre

The responsibility of bringing theatre to all children within a country is world-wide, sometimes dictated by government subsidy, sometimes supported by special grants, but always accomplished through the desire of the profession itself to serve rural and remote areas where plays and other cultural activities may be limited or otherwise nonexistent. A universal pioneering spirit is demonstrated here that takes performers to even the most inaccessible regions on a regular basis. Not only can young people see plays, but adults do also, for the appearance of any company is a cultural event of interest to everyone in a village or town. Companies do not generally view themselves as missionaries imparting art to the underprivileged, but instead are dedicated to creating works of interest that involve audiences in stories that relate to and reflect their lives. Such specialized touring is expensive, and costs seriously limit size of casts and scale of productions. Conditions can be difficult when companies travel long hours in order to keep engagements, often serving alike as performers, stagehands, and leaders of follow-up activities. Arriving at a school for early morning performances can mean little sleep the night before and little rest afterward if the distance to the next stop requires more time on the road. But such hardships quickly become the customary way of life for touring actors, whose pay often is as low as their energy and dedication must be high. To them, the field owes particular tribute for yearly enlarging its geographical boundaries, increasing the size of its audiences, and seeing that live theatre belongs not just to the city child. It is clear, however, that most believe that additional funding and commitment need to be given to this essential cause.

Handicapped Audiences

Just as rural children increasingly are included in the total audience, so, too, are the handicapped, sometimes seeing productions intended for general play-goers and sometimes attending performances designed especially for them. In the United States The Little Theatre for the Deaf, an offshoot of the National Theatre for the Deaf, to cite one important instance, plays for both hearing and nonhearing audiences in performances that are simultaneously spoken and signed. The hearing-impaired have long responded to theatre as a source of both enter-tainment and education, with excellent work being achieved in schools and in colleges such as Gallaudet College in Washington, D.C. Special signed perfor-mances during the run of a play are now common in many theatres in major cities. But, here again, more attention needs to be given to these special audi-ences, not only so they can attend performances, but also so they may experience dramatic activities in workshops and classrooms as part of their education and personal development. This means, of course, greater funding and the availability of more training for specialists to supervise appropriate programs.

Bilingual and Foreign-Language Companies

Although the development of bilingual companies necessarily occurs in those countries in which more than one "official" language is spoken, their effec-tiveness is also noted as a means of teaching foreign language and respect for the languages of others in countries in which only one is spoken. We expect to find companies performing in both French and English in Canada, but we may be surprised to learn of the great success of the English-speaking company in Austria, so effective in fact that the same producer, at the request of teachers and school authorities, now also offers tours of productions spoken in French. Such presentations promote greater familiarity with the country's dramatic lit-erature as well as language, introducing students to Molière, for instance, as well as to voices from the contemporary French theatre. Bilingual theatre is mentioned prominently in the accounts of Czechoslovakia, Finland, and Switz-erland, as well as in Austria and Canada.

In the United States, where English often is replaced in classrooms by Spanish, Chinese, and various native American languages, the need for bilingual theatre is particularly felt. But so far, only a few attempts have won widespread rec-ognition. The most successful of these is *Maggie/Magalita*, Wendy Kesselman's intergenerational play about a young girl fully assimilated into New York life who must suddenly relate to her grandmother when she arrives from their native country speaking only Spanish. Her embarrassment gradually gives way to un-derstanding and respect. Throughout the play English and Spanish are used such that audiences can understand both equally well. The play was presented in a major professional production off-Broadway and has been seen in various re-gional theatres throughout the United States, yet its success so far has not resulted in other scripts of note. Much good work goes on by individual teachers who dramatize folktales and fairy tales as a means of bringing together language and literature of various backgrounds.

If the field is to serve a need for which it is particularly well equipped, it must generate much greater effort. As *Maggie/Magalita* proves, bilingual plays need not be of interest merely as vehicles of instruction, but also as plays of genuine dramatic distinction.

Movement Toward Child Art Centers

In the accounts of the European countries readers may note references to child art centers in which a playhouse designed specifically for young audiences is a major component. Such centers also normally offer art studios and galleries, concert halls, dance and movement spaces, rehearsal areas, and scenic and costume workshops. Sometimes restaurants, snack bars, and meeting rooms are available, as well as executive offices, libraries, photography laboratories, and equipment and supply centers. The benefits of bringing all the arts together under one roof fosters greater collaboration and understanding both for young people and the artists.

Other arrangements may include an art gallery, such as that adjacent to the Children's Theatre Company of Minneapolis, or a museum, such as that which is attached to the Children's Theatre of Nashville. Theatres located in universities, as many are in the United States, can offer the facilities of the campus to augment the theatregoing experience. Theatres in Russia often sponsor clubs that publish newsletters and magazines announcing activities such as art exhibitions of members' works, special workshops, and social events. The center thus becomes a place not just to see a play, but also to return to again and again to follow artistic pursuits and to visit with friends who hold similar interests.

Some centers maintain their own libraries that allow audience members to read scripts of plays they attend as well as to take home books on related subjects. They also may have schools attached so that young people learn basic theatre crafts to further enrich their interest in the performing arts. Puppet and marionette performances, along with mask making, mime, and storytelling, all appropriately belong among the offerings of an art center, just as do programs in creative or developmental drama, acting, speech arts, and dance and movement.

Theatres designed especially for young people basically follow the same principles as for adult theatres, except that special consideration must be given to sight lines for viewers who are shorter and weigh less (many children cannot hold down a regular theatre seat). Other considerations include adaptations in bathrooms, lobbies, cloakrooms, and meeting areas, which must accommodate a wide range of sizes and needs. But today architects and interior designers are more aware of these specifications than ever before and are creating playhouses that make theatregoing increasingly attractive to young audiences.

Actor Training

The need for specialized training in the field has been recognized and met to widely varying degrees. In the USSR, for example, entire conservatories are devoted to training actors for careers in professional theatre for children; they place special emphasis on physical grace, athletic skills, and acting techniques ranging from comedy to tragedy. Specialized programs also exist for directors and other practitioners. Such widespread and thorough training, however, is not common elsewhere, for in most countries professional training exists for the adult theatre but seldom specifically for those who want to act for young people.

An attitude prevails in some countries that acting for young people is easier than performing for adult audiences because children are inexperienced and, therefore, less discriminating. But those who do act attest that however little formal knowledge they may possess about the craft, children are among the most demanding, as well as appreciative, theatregoers any player faces. Acting for young people requires great energy, both vocal and physical, along with concentration and control. Often because performance time is shorter and the action heavily intensified, it also demands quick transitions, fast development of character, and sharply defined motivations. Within less than half the time required in the adult theatre, the actor is expected to create, build, and extend a character to the fullest degree suggested by the script and desired by the director. To meet this goal, actor training must be made widely available, with seasoned directors able to operate schools in conjunction with their theatres. More extensive research must take place on the essential differences between adult and children's theatre acting techniques and on the perceptions of young people as they relate to production and performance.

The secrets of good acting often are elusive even to those giving the performances, for good acting always remains, in part, a mystery, the paradox of creating an illusion of truth that is not the truth. That, to some extent, explains its fascination and its greatness as an art form. And that is all the more reason to constantly advance new theories and training programs, which so far have barely begun in children's theatre outside the Soviet Union.

Issue-based Plays

A direction away from dramatizations of traditional literature, folktales and fairy tales and toward a repertory rooted in contemporary problems and issues easily can be traced through these pages. Topics such as divorce, child abuse, crime, peer and parental pressure, suicide, decision making, and alcoholism and drug abuse are among a myriad of present-day subjects for plays seen in such diverse places as Sweden, Canada, Australia, Soviet Union, Federal Republic of Germany, and the United States, to name only a representative number. In others the standard repertory remains firmly in place, but the presence of topical plays also is solidly established, especially in works intended for older audiences, aged ten and above.

In most countries, however, traditional titles, once the staple of professional children's theatre, have given way to topics of immediate interest, including not only those just mentioned, but also others of local concern, such as questions facing the community on governance, politics, and ethical and moral issues. Although some plays may treat these subjects broadly, others take specific stands and point out possible solutions for audiences to discuss that ultimately should lead to appropriate courses of action.

Certainly, the type of play known as TIE, which originated in England and spread to Australia, Canada, and the United States, operates as a forum for ideas to be explored in the performance itself and in the activities that follow. During these, discussion often takes place between the audience and the actors, who remain in character throughout, or in dramatic workshops and sessions conducted by teachers after the company has departed.

Clearly, theatre for young people in the past three decades has become a platform from which playwrights, directors, and actors express their beliefs in a more direct manner than ever before and, in the case of TIE, actually provide the opportunity for young people to engage in decision making on topics that concern them or, according to the theatres, should concern them.

Politically-Based Plays

Given the extent of issue-based plays and their tendency to take on major questions and even sensitive problems, the inclusion of political views and ideologies follows as no surprise. And so we read here of companies that espouse specific credos or political missions, in some cases boldly stated, in others more subtly suggested. To many producers, "children's liberation" is in itself a cause to be pursued as vigorously as the freedom of men and women. Political advocates who hope to induce children and young people to join their ranks see theatre as an effective method of recruitment. In some countries it is not common for a company to intentionally become an instrument of propaganda rather than a source of entertainment or even of genuine artistic purpose.

If, on the other hand, children are to be considered as political beings, then theatre has every right to address them, and does so effectively in such countries as Sweden and Italy. Some theatres readily admit that they manipulate audiences, a right that they see as their major reason for being. In other countries such practices would create a public outcry in the belief that children must not be subjected to political proselytizing of any sort, since they are not yet prepared to make decisions about complex issues and ideas. Even in countries in which freedom of speech is constitutionally guaranteed, lines would be drawn against treating young people as ideological pawns.

Still, advocacy groups find theatre, film, and television effective means of reaching large numbers of potential constituents. The rise of TIE brought with it definite political tendencies since the movement started in Coventry, a center of radical viewpoints that from the beginning found their way into numerous projects. Discussion of problems as part of the performance quite naturally leads to suggestions or implications for solutions, a fact that suggests that issue-based theatre necessarily must become political if it is to fulfill its mission. Each company then must decide for itself to what degree its underlying beliefs will be evident in text, performance, and follow-up activities.

No reader can deny that "politicization" of children's theatre has taken place, to some extent, in every country; in many it is the major reason for the existence of the most vital companies. This revelation may not be willingly accepted by traditionalists, who should remember that the fairy tales and folktales that they advocate often are, in themselves, political and psychological instruments, as Jack Zipes and Bruno Bettleheim have effectively reminded us. To this extent, children's theatre always has been political, but only in recent years has it openly begun to take greater advantage of its provocative possibilities.

The Development of Playwrights

The following statement, made in the article on France, best voices a commonly shared realization of the past decade: "Today we seem to have rediscovered (or perhaps only now discovered) the importance of the quality of the text (for both children's and adult theatre)."

The domination of the stage director as the key figure in the creative process prevailed in much of Western adult theatre in the sixties and seventies and found a counterpart in children's theatre, in which a number of strong talents emerged who mostly used the script as the starting point for their own experimentation. Some of this work proved remarkable: John Clark Donohue in Minneapolis, with his highly pictorialized style; Zinovi Korogotzki in Leningrad, with his varied inventive theatricalism; and Volker Ludwig in West Berlin, with his contemporary dynamics. Their individual styles made them and their companies internationally famous; indeed, their names often became better known than the plays they directed and certainly better known than that of their playwrights. Even when they served as their own dramatists, it was the total production, not their texts, that most impressed viewers.

Plays were also created by teams or with entire companies developing texts in collaboration throughout the stages of research, scripting, and production. In TIE, specifically, the group concept became essential to its philosophical beliefs, which often resulted in vivid ensemble playing and clearly communicated commitment to each work. In education, too, team efforts were encouraged as a means to stimulate classes to work together on projects of interest to the school and community. Such productions were so styled to the individual talents of their creators and their particular companies that they seldom proved effective when produced by others.

In time, creativity by committee, however nobly dedicated in intention, revealed such artistic limitations as a lack of unity, personal point of view, and a uniform style of expression. Missing were the playwrights, who, toward the end of the seventies, began to reclaim their position as the theatre's essential artists.

Awards to dramatists further increased their stature. In the United States, for example, the National Endowment for the Arts recognized Aurand Harris with its first Creative Writing Fellowship to a playwright for young people. The Children's Theatre Association of America began to choose the best play of the year, both to honor current writers and to serve as an incentive to future ones. Numerous regional and local awards, prizes, and citations also helped to enhance the position of dramatists in other parts of the world.

Publication of plays as books for children, although still negligible, began to appear in greater numbers in the 1970s. *All the World's a Stage*, edited by Lowell Swortzell and cited by *The New York Times Book Review* as one of the "outstanding books in 1972," went through three printings. *Six Plays by Aurand Harris*, edited by Coleman Jennings in 1977, further launched a series of anthologies that continues to this day. Joan Aiken, the noted British author of children's fiction, wrote three plays that were published in handsome illustrated editions. Carol Korty offered a variety of folk plays in hard-cover library editions. Miriam Morton, an expert on Russian culture, edited an anthology titled *Russian Plays for Young Audiences* (1977). In 1979, the International Year of the Child, the Boston Public Library hosted an international conference on poetry and drama that brought writers and educators together to hear presentations by John Ciardi, Phillip Lopate, and Lowell Swortzell, who celebrated the appearance of published plays in libraries throughout the world. Through such efforts the commonly held belief that young people find plays difficult to read began to erode.

With the break from traditional subjects and the popularity of contemporary plays, dramatists who never before considered writing for young people found an audience and the freedom to make use of any form or idea that interested them. Established playwrights in Great Britain and the United States, such as Robert Bolt, John Arden, Wendy Kesselman, Mark Medoff, William Gibson, and David Mamet, began to write for young people, proving that a dramatist can work successfully for both adults and children.

Greater incentives through larger grants and awards still need to be developed because even after almost a century of growing productivity, the chances of making a living by writing plays for young people remain distressingly unrealistic, with the exception of those writers in the communist-bloc countries, who draw salaries comparable to those of playwrights for adults. By combining writing with directing or teaching, a number of dramatists have fashioned careers for themselves in Western countries. This is particularly true in Canada and the United States, where universities and colleges offer degree programs in children's theatre and often produce the premiere performances of original scripts. Still, all too few playwrights for young people can live on their royalties alone.

While conditions for dramatists continue to improve—in recent years their royalties have increased along with their recognition—still more encouragement needs to be given through travel grants, commissions, and production grants that enable them to be present at rehearsals and first performances of new scripts. Here they can benefit from working directly with directors and actors in the day-to-day creative process of mounting productions. Funding must be found to give dramatists time to write and for workshops, courses, and internships. Frequent competitions to attract new talent must be held, along with symposia such as those conducted every two years by Dorothy Webb at Indiana University–Purdue University in Indianapolis, which attracts writers and leaders from across the United States.

Separate Identities for Theatres That Specialize in Education

Perhaps the enormous impact and success of TIE practices in the past quarter-century have created a need to distinguish between those companies whose primary purpose is educating audiences and those that intend to entertain them. Some companies maintain that they perform both functions, inasmuch as all good theatre, to some extent, accomplishes both. But the contributors to this book, particularly in the English-speaking countries, where TIE is most deeply rooted, separate the two types of work, not to pit them against each other, but merely as a means of clarifying their functions and forms. They see the two as being of equal importance while sharing different goals for the same audience. But the problem remains of communicating these differences to the public at large (as well as, to some extent, explaining them to the field itself, which tends to separate the two altogether without knowing why). Communicating a clear definition of purpose still eludes the field as it completes nearly a century of work.

Recognition of Theatre for Children by Children

From the outset ASSITEJ has focused its energies on professional uses of theatre for young people rather than on amateur, community, and school efforts. Other organizations fill this gap in most countries, but as of now they do not have the international unity, history, or prestige of ASSITEJ. Often national festivals are held to emphasize works by young people, with some noteworthy examples to be seen in Yugoslavia, Austria, and Ireland, among others. The Ninth Congress of ASSITEJ, meeting in Adelaide, Australia, was presented in conjunction with the biannual Outreach Festival of Youth Theatre, the major festival showcasing Australian productions by teenagers. Here delegates saw an impressive variety of works, including Voltaire's *Candide*, an original full-length opera, comtemporary problem plays, and original works by young playwrights, all performed by youth groups representing a number of cities and schools throughout the country.

For many, the accomplishments of these performers proved to be eye-openers, revealing high levels of expression that young people can achieve when carefully trained and strongly directed. As also happened, when weakly directed, they can be embarrassing if they cannot meet the artistic demands placed on them, as opponents to young people acting are quick to point out. But often in such cases it is not the cast that is at fault, but the director who fails to take full advantage of the talent and the production's artistic opportunities. The unprepared teacher who discredits students should be discouraged from continuing to direct at all costs!

Even though the sentiment prevails in these pages to keep amateur and professional organizations separate, just as it does in the adult theatre, the excellent work that goes on in schools needs to be better known and respected. Skilled directors working in nonprofessional companies and educational settings are as significant in their field as professional directors are in theirs. Yet they seldom achieve recognition outside their own regions, except from young people with whom they work who realize how much they have gained and remain, often for the rest of their lives, deeply indebted.

The rewards of amateur productions for audiences, too, can be considerable, for casts normally can be larger than professional budgets permit, affording the proper number of townspeople, guests at a ball, and cheering crowds that are always missing in small professional companies. Young people playing young people also bring greater authenticity in age and appearance than do older actors and provide stronger points of audience identification. Companies such as the Children's Theatre Company in Minneapolis have met such considerations of verisimilitude by casting children as children and adults as adults. In Russia "travesty actresses" specialize in playing children throughout their careers, but this practice is seldom found elsewhere, except in the tradition of casting a woman in the title role in *Peter Pan*. Even here, some audience members are sensitive to questions of age and sex, as voiced by one five-year-old watching the television production of *Peter Pan*, starring Mary Martin, whose disenchantment was revealed by the exclamation, "Daddy, that's not a boy. That's a lady and she's *old*!" Clearly, this viewer expected to see a real boy who won't grow up rather than someone who already has, and a long time ago at that.

Radio Drama

Radio drama plays a large role in the lives of young people in numerous countries, and reaches larger audiences than live theatre. In countries such as the United States, where dramatic radio programming has all but disappeared, it may come as a surprise to read here of the great number of radio plays for young people being broadcast to regions that seldom see live performances. Those who grew up in the thirties and forties require no help in remembering the great pleasure to be derived from radio drama that demands the listener's full concentration and use of imagination, something that television never does. The fact that numerous companies have wide listening audiences for full seasons of regularly scheduled broadcasts should inspire others to investigate this dimension of children's theatre as a far-reaching and vital means of introducing children to theatre.

The Alternating Fate of Fairy-Tale Plays

The fairy tale, once the basis of the repertory, has undergone serious reexamination by educators and, consequently, by children's theatre producers in the past twenty-five years, and as the century comes to a close it still stands as a subject of debate that promises to continue indefinitely.

Those opposed, to state the case as simply as possible, cry for contemporary relevance in plays so that young people can identify with current crises and problems of everyday life. To them, the fairy tale represents a throwback to the past, to the safe (both for the viewer and the box office) form of children's theatre, from which they want to make a complete break. They believe that the quaint, cute, and charming circle of Cinderella and her cohorts is an artificial world from which children should be protected. It is arcane, and to some even immoral, to perpetuate myths that were created, they contend, by people whose lives were so wretched that merely in order to survive they had to hold onto the hollow hopes of fairy godmothers, of finding treasures, and of living happily ever after—the pipe dreams of self-delusion.

With social unrest in many parts of the world in the 1960s, this type of "saccharine" brainwashing became the subject of criticism. At the same time, protests developed against the great amount of cruelty in many of the tales: beheadings, fingers chopped off to gain rings, wolves devouring old ladies, and so on. The disapproval leveled by parents at violence in movies and on television was also targeted against the most fundamental tales.

Fairy tales survived such attacks, as they have for centuries, but their significance nonetheless was reexamined. Then came the counterargument from Bruno Bettleheim, a noted Freudian child psychologist whose book *The Uses of Enchantment: The Meaning and Importance of Fairy Tales* (1976) received major public attention from educators, librarians, and parents. He contended that fairy tales survive because they are needed by everyone to work out desires, fears, guilt, and relationships that are psychologically sound and basically comforting despite the graphic descriptions of blood and gore.

The light and dark sides of the tales have continued to be explored by others. Jack Zipes viewed them as radical tracts of political protest in *Breaking the Magic Spell* (1979). Stephen Sondheim and James Lapine, in their prize-winning Broadway musical *Into the Woods* (1987), examined the traditional use of the tales to produce a variety of wish fulfillments in their happy first act and showed that in real life it doesn't work out that way, in their sombre and cynical second act. The musical was heavily attended by children and subsequently adapted as an elaborately illustrated picture book for young readers.

Suddenly, after Bettleheim, fairy tales not only were acceptable, but also officially approved as essential to a child's psychological maturity and social adjustment. Once more respectable, the tales soon became familiar in children's theatres from which they had been banned only a few seasons before. And to make them more relevant, they often were adapted as "audience participation" plays so that children could become actively involved in the story by interacting with the principal characters.

In America, fairy tales even fostered a new performance style, Story Theatre, which was developed by Paul Sills using improvisational techniques defined by his mother, Viola Spolin. This part-narrated and part-performed style of presentation first attracted audiences in Chicago and then became a Broadway success in the 1970 season. More important, it encouraged a host of imitators who began to adapt a wide range of literature to its special features.

Today, although fairy-tale plays are no longer considered out of date or harmful, the questions still arise in these pages as to which companies should include them and how they should be presented. Those who present fairy tales in traditional formats are frowned on by the avant garde, who tend to use the tales largely as points of departure for their own deconstructive purposes, which are certain to be contemporary and controversial. The fate of the fairy tale continues to be widely weighed as playwrights, directors, and producers must decide which of the many uses of enchantment they will make of them.

Establishment Theatres Versus Independent Theatres

Establishment theatres, those commercial or heavily subsidized companies that offer traditional repertories, often are portrayed in these pages in a critical, even negative, light, as representative of the past, as spending great sums on spectacle instead of new plays, and as offering "dull" acting and directing that results in giving children's theatre a bad name with the public. As always in anti-establishment protests, the strongest cries come from the struggling young writers and directors, who contend, and often correctly, that their own work is innovative and in the vanguard of the field. Indeed, the greatest amount of experimentation today does take place within the ranks of the young (and often politically motivated) companies as well as in certain college and university groups.

Obvious financial factors compel the older groups to present large productions of familiar titles usually aimed at holiday consumption. If experimentation exists here at all, it consists of updating the story (but leaving the title clearly recognizable), securing a well-known personality to play a key role, or adding technology derived from rock concerts. This type of production can lapse quickly into the pitfalls of formula, which results in the lack of excitement complained about in these pages. Yet, when kept fresh and expertly performed, traditional offerings can make suitable introductions to the theatre for millions of children. For decades, Christmas pantomimes or "pantos" throughout the British empire and countless productions of *The Nutcracker* ballet in the United States and in Europe have successfully served this purpose. Ought not there be a few places in every country where children may see traditional theatre well performed in elaborate professional productions?

Not according to the writers represented here. For the most part, they consider those who produce this kind of theatre to be "the enemy" and firmly believe that they should be stopped before they do greater harm. Producers of smaller, younger avant garde companies often disassociate themselves from this type of production by moving to the opposite extreme and negating production values altogether. Believing that the message matters above all else, they work with what they have, simple props on a bare stage or against a house curtain. Although this practice simplifies touring problems and fully focuses audience attention on the acting and the text, it also denies the play a strong visual statement that should be part of every production. Audiences need to see ideas as well as hear them, and the ideas should be viewed in a variety of theatrical expressions that a bare stage alone cannot evoke. Lighting, too, must be part of every professional mounting if mood and atmosphere are to be guaranteed. Many touring groups cannot afford their own lighting equipment and must use the resources available at each stop, which may offer little or nothing of artistic consequence. They may be as guilty of denying their audiences a valid theatrical experience as establishment theatres are of overindulging theirs.

The reader certainly cannot argue with those writers who acknowledge the independent theatres as the major sources of artistic growth. Through experimentation and real risk taking they are willing to place a company's very existence in the balance. These innovators resent the establishment, especially when it makes money or, even worse, is granted large sums of national or local subsidy to carry on the work of the past while they piece together budgets from smaller allocations or receive none. This resentment nowhere has been articulated so forcibly as here; in fact, in several countries the separation of the establishment and independent theatres appears to be complete.

Readers should remember that contributors are either officers of ASSITEJ or those appointed by them, and that their entries respresent "official" viewpoints. In countries that are not members of ASSITEJ the authors are major figures in the field and as such are representative of their profession. They include far more voices from independent theatres than from the establishment, a fact that indicates where leadership in the field currently resides. The question, then, of the "generation gap" in children's theatre, the traditionalists versus the reformers, now can be debated on an international scale, with the challenge of fostering what is best in both to be met in future conferences and surveys such as this.

The Influence and Importance of Individuals

As the brief historical overview already has demonstrated, the advancement of both children's and educational theatre can be charted through the work of a number of leaders whose influence often spreads far beyond the boundaries of their own countries. Certain names recur in the entries that follow, proving that this pattern continues in the present day. Names such as Natalia Sats, Léon Chanceral, Peter Slade, Brian Way, and Winifred Ward have become synonymous with various aspects of theatre and drama as practiced in the Western world through the 1960s. Their contributions are documented here and in the volumes cited in the Bibliography. Many others who deserve mention if space allowed are also described in these works and are well known internationally. ASSITEJ has helped to provide leaders the attention they deserve among their colleagues through its meetings, elections, and Congresses.

Certain names emerge in these pages as the major influences of recent years, and they are not always directly involved in the field. A dramatist such as Athol Fugard, a psychologist such as Bruno Bettleheim, and a field worker such as Augusto Boal may have influenced children's theatre the most, if we are to count their citations in the Index. Certainly their plays, theories, and practices are widely recognized among today's leaders as being of special importance in their work.

Many within the field, likewise, are important. Brian Way, Dorothy Heathcote, and Gavin Bolton have explained and illustrated their work in most quarters of the world in lectures, workshops, and special courses. Volker Ludwig has toured with his GRIPS Theatre Company throughout Europe and far beyond. Suzanne Osten and Per Lysander have described their approach to child drama with Young Klara, as have many other writers and directors during professional tours and in appearances at festivals and conferences. Stressed in the various accounts that follow is testimony of the importance of the individual in the creation and growth of a company, in the transmission of an idea, and in advancing the artistic and academic goals of all those working in the field. Such significant individuals must continue to be encouraged and be given the opportunity to be heard.

Increase of Theatre and Drama in School Curriculum

Readers from educational theatre will be gladdened by evidence given here of the addition of courses and entire drama programs for both students and teachers. Through the efforts of numerous leaders the benefits of developmental drama, improvisation, and theatre games have become recognized by school authorities. Throughout Great Britain and in many places in the rest of the English-speaking world drama is entrenched not as an extra curricular activity, but as a full-fledged academic subject, one that is often required for certain age levels. Several states in the United States have mandated the inclusion of drama in the curriculum for elementary schools, while others require college students who are preparing for careers as teachers to take courses in drama, language, and speech arts.

This growth results from decades of effort on the part of all those who believed in the importance of drama in the classroom to convince others of its academic and developmental worth. Resistance to the formal implementation of drama in the curriculum still prevails throughout large parts of Europe, where the structure of educational systems often does not provide the flexibility to include nontraditional subjects. Yet here, too, courses can be made available if parents and teachers use the examples and models developed by British and American pioneers and then adapt this work to the needs of their own educational systems. The accomplishments of those described throughout this book should inspire others to pursue drama in the classroom wherever it is not yet established.

Publications and Research

With the development of the field came increased publications about its work in textbooks and theoretical studies. The establishment of the Children's Theatre Press in the United States in 1935 provided a forum for printing new plays and important works by leaders in the field such as Winifred Ward and Charlotte Chorpenning. Eventually, established publishers of scripts began to include plays for young people in their catalogues and proved that there was a growing market for reading and producing them. Samuel French in London and New York leased performance rights of a number of dramatists writing expressly for children: Nicholas Stuart Gray, Aurand Harris, Charlotte Chorpenning, and, in more recent years, David Wood. In European countries plays often appeared in magazines and in special editions for schools and libraries. Canada, in particular, can claim a distinguished record for publishing plays by Canadian dramatists and establishing a body of drama about Canadian life. *Plays Magazine* in the United States, under the editorship of A. S. and Sylvia Burack, has published royalty-free plays suitable for school assembly and classroom production for several generations. Significantly, this magazine made its way into school libraries where thousands of young readers encountered their first plays. Recently in the United States, as has been noted, a spate of play anthologies have been published. The Bibliography fully documents the most important works and proves the rapid growth of publications in English in this field. Research is also listed, along with major doctoral dissertations.

However extensive this Bibliography, additional study needs to be undertaken and disseminated. The work of ASSITEJ and of developmental theatre in Third World countries remains little known to the general public and is available largely through newsletters rather than in permanent volumes to be found in libraries. Special collections, such as that of the International Theatre Institute in New York City, need to be made available to students and researchers throughout the world. Funding for research and publication must be found if the field is to continue its self-documentation and the expansion of its dramatic literature.

Festivals and International Exchanges

The concept of a festival to celebrate and promote theatre is shared by producers and educators throughout the world. To some playgoers, any worthwhile production is a festival in itself—an event and special occasion to be cherished.

But when several productions are brought together in a season of, for example, Shakespeare or Shaw, as they are each year in England and Canada, then they truly constitute a festival with a particular emphasis and identity. Most are summer events related to tourism, but some, such as that of the Royal Shakespeare Company in Stratford-upon-Avon, England, and the New York Shakespeare Festival in New York City, have developed into year-round institutional theatres of major importance in the cultural life of their countries. And in these pages we can see to what a great extent producers of children's theatre now are attracted to this idea.

International festivals are of special importance in allowing viewers to see the works of several countries in a short period of time and in one place, as well as to attend symposia at which they may ask questions and share ideas with representative directors and actors. After the success of the first such international gathering of companies in Vancouver, Canada, similar festivals quickly developed in Toronto and several American cities. Now each spring nine or ten companies from Europe, Japan, and Australia join Canadian and American groups and are seen in participating cities extending from Vancouver to Philadelphia. So under the auspices of international festivals, the outstanding work of the Kaze-No-Ko and Himawari companies of Japan, for instance, have been enjoyed by thousands of children in North America. Once additional festivals are developed, companies may be booked for several months each summer in following the international festival circuit. They will then have year-round employment divided between their seasons at home and abroad.

The festivals also serve to stimulate the field by the controversy they may stir. In Philadelphia several years ago a performer from Holland offering a one-man show that involved audience participation earned the ire of at least one critic for manipulating children who sincerely hoped to assist him on stage. This resulted in a much needed reexamination of the ethics of players and the artistic power they wield over young audiences. Festivals also may inspire those artists who see the work of colleagues and gain inspiration and ideas for their own future efforts. Performers are quick to surmise which plays attract the most interest, just as they are eager to learn about working conditions and professional trends outside their own countries.

International festivals often include, in addition to productions, free activities such as makeup demonstrations, performances by clowns and storytellers, arts and crafts activities, and concerts. The publicity a festival attracts is far greater than any one production can gain by itself; moreover, it demonstrates to the public that theatre for children is not just a home-grown effort, but a full-fledged professional field operating throughout the world.

Likewise, local, state, and regional festivals draw together artists who share common interests. The support of audiences for favorite companies and productions generates enthusiasm and promotes the common cause of all participants.

Another attractive enticement to teachers is a "One-Day Theatre Festival" during which students see a performance, tour backstage, discuss the play with the cast and director, participate in workshops, and become acquainted with various aspects of play production. Sometimes a class may also perform a play they have prepared in advance, and receive suggestions and commentary from members of the professional staff. Such day-long visits can become regularly scheduled events in the school calendar and important sources of additional income for producers. They also bring professional theatre and education into collaboration and closer understanding.

Young Playwrights Festivals

The success of these programs that involve children and young people as dramatists is firmly established in Australia, Great Britain, and the United States, where festivals present professional and semi-professional productions of works by playwrights ranging in age from eight to twenty. They examine subjects such as sexual identity, parental pressure, and disillusionment in the nuclear age, and, for the most part, do not believe in happy endings or bromides as acceptable answers to their probings.

Such festivals long have taken place within various schools, but it was not until the Young Playwrights Festival at the Royal Court Theatre in London that their true worth could be evaluated. Here an annual national call brought scripts from throughout the country, from which a handful were selected for production by the resident company in a program advertised as part of the Royal Court's regular season. Although he did not originate this concept, Gerald Chapman advanced its standing through a number of excellent productions that attracted strong critical attention. One viewer impressed with a bill of four plays was Stephen Sondheim, the Broadway composer and lyricist, who, while in London attending rehearsals for one of his musicals, read a glowing review that led him to the Royal Court. He responded with the suggestion that a similar festival should take place in New York City and was influential in importing Chapman to supervise its implementation.

The New York Festival, likewise, impressed young people, teachers, parents, and even cynical critics, whose initial enthusiasm guaranteed the continuation of the program, which now receives hundreds of scripts each year. The Festival conducts workshops in schools to stimulate young authors and to provide them with basic considerations they should keep in mind while structuring and writing plays. Adult playwrights serve as mentors to their young counterparts, sometimes guiding them through revisions and into productions or staged readings by professional actors. Scripts are submitted from throughout the United States in what has become a full-fledged national festival. Readers may well want to investigate the British and American festivals as models for encouraging young playwrights in their countries.

The Three Major Obstacles/Objectives

Major impediments revealed here that deter the growth of international theatre for young people today will come as no surprise to anyone working in the field; they are the constant struggle for financing, recognition, and respect.

Financing

Even in nations in which theatre is generously supported by government subsidy, the fight for funding is an ongoing pursuit of authorities to increase annual allocations, or at least maintain them at current levels. Almost every budget is hard won through written requests, spoken arguments, and documented justification of service to schools and communities. Rarely is box office income sufficient to meet costs of operation, and it should not be expected to be adequate when children seldom pay for their tickets or, at most, give only modest amounts. Funding must come from other sources, and if not from cultural agencies, then from those that support education, health, and welfare. But each of these avenues can be blocked by bureaucracy, by unenlightened administrations, and by an agency's own limited budgets. Sometimes funding from the private sector can be more direct but no less unencumbered; it requires time-consuming preparation of proposals and grant applications. In many countries fund raising for the arts has become a field in itself (and an art as well), a fact that children's theatre practitioners often only slowly come to recognize and master. More expertise is needed everywhere so that sources and procedures can be better identified and greater amounts secured for productions, commissions, special projects, research, and dissemination of information. Even so, chances are that the struggle will become no less difficult, a limitation the field must continue to face and surmount.

Recognition

A cry for recognition can be heard here again and again, for the belief that companies are underpublicized is commonly shared by practitioners around the world. The battle to promote productions and projects in newspapers, television, and radio is made all the more difficult when children's theatre must compete for the same space and air time as adult theatres, with their substantially larger budgets and professional staffs. When denied access to press and electronic media children's theatres rely heavily on mailing lists to reach their patrons and on schools to supply their audiences. As a result, their work becomes known only to teachers and remains unfamiliar to the general public. In some instances full seasons of plays come and go without being noticed outside the school system. No artist enjoys working in a vacuum, and many desert theatre for young people, hoping to find the recognition that their talents deserve elsewhere.

Although this situation does not prevail in the Soviet bloc countries, where artists in children's theatre receive comparable salaries and hold equal stature with those in adult theatre, recognition for much of the rest of Europe and the

Western world is difficult, if not impossible, to obtain. There are exceptions, of course, in several world-famous companies such as the Paper Bag Players in New York City, the Unicorn Theatre in London, the GRIPS Theatre of West Berlin, the Young Klara of Stockholm, and the Kaze-No-Ko of Tokyo; from their examples others may gain hope that their work, too, will come to be recognized through adequate coverage in the media.

Respect

Hand in hand with recognition goes the desire for respect, for the field itself and for all those who labor in it. Just as teachers in many parts of the world have long been taken for granted by society in general, so are most artists, producers, and educators in theatre for young people. They feel the lack of respect not just from the public, but also from the profession itself, from those in the adult theatre who view children's theatre as "child's play" in comparison to their own work, and so do not take them seriously.

Perhaps most disheartening is the lack of respect from critics who refuse to see and write about children's theatre on the assumption that it is mediocre or worse, or that they are not qualified to review it. This last excuse usually means that they simply are not interested. True, few newspapers have sought critics with appropriate training, nor are they willing to set aside space for this purpose on a regular basis. Consequently opportunities are lost for the public to learn about the quality of available productions and to develop aesthetic standards, as well as to heighten those of companies and individual artists. Constructive criticism has served these purposes in the adult theatre world for more than two centuries, and clearly, those who work for children believe that the time is here for the same benefits to come to their audiences and to themselves.

CONCLUSION

However depressing some of the foregoing trends may be, I cannot end this Introduction on any but an optimistic note. Of course, I recognize the distressing facts and figures of financial difficulties that have resulted in crippling setbacks in many countries, and at the end of the 1980s threaten the future existence of drama in the schools of Great Britain. I further realize that in the United States the number of professional children's theatre companies has decreased by half in the last twenty years. But I also know that the pioneering efforts to create theatre worthy of young people have woven throughout the world in this century a cultural and educational fabric strong enough to endure even the most stringent economic dangers. The evidence is here page after page, country after country, as it is in the undaunted energy and artistry at work today. Theatre for young people is entrenched within each nation and collectively is a solidly-established, world-wide movement already busily planning its second century. Through increased research, the return and rise of the playwright, and the involvement of more and more young people as participants, the field can surmount its problems and continue to redefine itself in its search for an ever-increasing variety of goals and forms. Then what Mark Twain called "a very great invention" will indeed, as he prophesied, "someday come to be recognized." The accomplishments documented in this volume demonstrate that day could be soon.

NOTE

1. Readers who are not familiar with the terminology of the field, such as "children's theatre," "child drama," "developmental drama," "drama-in-education," and "theatre-in-education," should consult the definitions provided in the first entry in which Michael FitzGerald of Australia has conveniently defined them.

International Guide
to
Children's Theatre
and
Educational Theatre

Australia

HISTORY

As in many other countries, the history of professional theatre for children and young people in Australia begins after 1945, even though one company, the Australian Children's Theatre, founded by Joan and Betty Rayner, had toured productions throughout the country since the 1920s. In 1955 only one organization in Australia performed programs related to school studies: the "Shakespeare in Jeans" Company of the Young Elizabethan Players. During the sixties a number of children's theatres emerged, including Pageant and the Australian Theatre for Young People in Sydney, Children's Arena Theatre in Melbourne, Patch Theatre and the Children's Activities Times Society in Perth. Today the Arena Theatre, Patch Theatre, and Australian Theatre for Young People still exist, and in place of the others a number of groups have appeared. By 1975 there were over twenty full-time companies engaged in tours to schools and performing for children and young people.

Theatre-in-education (TIE), which is well established in Australia, has a relatively short history and distinctly British origin. The TIE movement found its way to Australia in the early seventies in the work of Barbara Manning and her Salamanca Theatre Company, which remains one of the country's finest. Also attracted to Australia were some of the English TIE founders, such as Roger Chapman, who set up Magpie Theatre Company in 1977 based at the State Theatre in Adelaide and who went on to become the founding director of the Carclew Youth Performing Arts Center, and David Young, who at first was artistic director of Arena Theatre in Melbourne and then of the Toe Truck in Sydney and who later took over at Salamanca on Barbara Manning's retirement in 1984.

In 1975 the Theatre Board of the Australia Council, the federal government's arts advisory and funding body, gave, for the first time, general grants for youth programs to five major adult theatre companies: the Melbourne Theatre Company (Victoria), the National Theatre Company (Western Australia), the Queensland Theatre Company (Queensland), the State Theatre Company (South Australia), and the Tasmanian Theatre Company (Tasmania).

During the seventies drama-in-education (DIE) grew as education departments began to include drama as a subject in the school curriculum. Some departments supported existing TIE teams or set up their own, and the youth theatre movement flourished. Writing in 1977, Anne Godfrey Smith, in her report "Youth Performing Arts in Australia, 1975–1977," saw two main growth points: TIE and youth theatre.

Today there is a wide range of theatre available for young people that, to a great extent, reflects local concerns. The TIE movement, although it is of British extraction and has benefited enormously from British talent, is natively oriented, for its plays are predominantly written by Australians and are about Australian issues. And as ethnic diversity is a feature of our society, it is not surprising that TIE companies have attempted to reflect this in their work. Youth theatre and DIE also reveal local interests because, invariably, the young people involved play a major role in the creation of the programs.

Children's theatre tends to be an exception. In 1986 there were only one or two full-time professional companies in the country. However, a number of adult theatres include children's theatre as part of their repertory, and many TIE and youth theatre companies present an occasional production, as do a number of independent groups. The repertory of children's theatre always has been indebted to British theatre, but the work of such playwrights as Anne Harvey, Dorothy Hewitt, and aboriginal Jack Davis have contributed enormously to the development of an Australian style.

No comprehensive statistics exist to show the development of young people's theatre over the years, but an idea perhaps may be gained by the fact that in 1974, seven companies received general grants from the Theatre Board for youth activities and that by 1981 the number had risen to seventeen. In 1986 the Board funded eleven TIE companies and twelve professional-salary grants for youth theatres. The total number is larger, since some companies of both kinds are funded only by their respective state departments for the arts or temporarily manage to operate by their own resources.

Notable people who have been influential and instrumental in the development of young people's theatre include those mentioned above as well as playwrights Richard Tulloch, Peter Charlton, David Holman, and Graeme Pitts; directors Andrew Ross and, in the youth theatre movement, Errol Bray; the South Australian Magpie Theatre Company's exemplary leadership in design through Richard Roberts and Ken Wilby; and pedagogues Christine Westwood and John Lonie.

Landmark productions include *Eureka*, written and directed by David Young at Arena Theatre Company, Melbourne; *I'll be in on That*, written and directed by Anne Harvey, Salamanca Theatre Company, Hobart; *Strike at the Port*, group devised and directed by Richard Tulloch, Toe Truck Theatre Company, Sydney; and *Wolf Boy*, written and directed by Peter Charlton, Arena Theatre, Melbourne. Also noteworthy are the plays of aboriginal writer Jack Davis, *No Sugar* and *Honeyspot*, directed by Andrew Ross, and *Mesh* and *Memo*, by Graeme Pitts, directed by Don Mamouney, Sidetrack Theatre Company, Sydney, which are the first successful plays that deal with multicultural issues. Also deserving mention is the Salamanca Theatre Company of Hobart, noted for its integrated program of arts activities based on the play adaptation (Richard Meredith) and direction (Richard Davey) of *Annie's Coming Out*, a book by Annie McDonald and Rosemary Scrossley. The project director was Bernard Rosenblatt, a theatre educator from Cemrel, Inc., in St. Louis, Missouri.

Of major importance is Carclew, the Youth Performing Arts Center established in 1976 in Adelaide, which works on a local, national, and international level to promote the quality and viability of performing arts for young people through-out Australia. The only center of its kind in the country, Carclew's Council includes senior representatives of the departments of education and the arts, both of which give full support to its programs. Carclew publishes *Lowdown*, Australia's national magazine of youth performing arts, operates a youth radio project in conjunction with a public radio station, and operates the Odeon, South Australia's only theatre devoted entirely to performances for or by young people. Carclew also mounts special projects and seminars from time to time and is the umbrella organization for the national and prestigious Come Out Youth Performing Arts Festival held biannually in Adelaide since 1975. "Come Out" is a showcase of visual, creative, and performing arts by, for, and with young people.

Also of national significance, the Australian Youth Performing Arts Association (AYPAA) was established in 1975 under the inspired leadership of Margaret Leask and Joan Pope. This group was the early driving force in the promotion and development of theatre for children and young people at the national level, along with the Australian center for Association Internationale du Théâtre pour l'Enfance et la Jeunesse (ASSITEJ). In 1981 the name AYPAA was dropped to become ASSITEJ Australia, which has since operated from Carclew. The Salamanca Script Resource Center was established in 1980 in Hobart; together with the Carclew Scripts Directory, set up in 1978, it aims to service Australian writers and performers by listing all Australian material, published and unpublished, for performance by and for young people.

CONTEMPORARY YOUNG PEOPLE'S THEATRE

Five main terms are used in discussing theatre for children and young people—theatre-in-education, drama-in-education, children's theatre, youth theatre, and young people's theatre; the following is an attempt to clarify them. These definitions are only a rough guide because many companies' activities cannot be labeled neatly or exclusively with any one of these terms, as they cut across them.

Theatre-in-Education

TIE is a form of theatre developed during the 1960s in England whose primary function is to educate through entertainment. It is a learning theatre through which audiences, young and old, may comprehend problems related to their social environment and possible solutions to such problems. Scripts are usually based on school curriculum or relevant social or historical issues, and teachers are often provided with follow-up work for their students based on the topics discussed in the productions. The audience is invited to participate both actively and passively, sometimes actually determining the outcome of a play by their involvement and at other times discussing the issues raised during or after the performance. On occasion and where applicable, TIE plays are presented for adults. Because TIE performances usually take place in classrooms, sets and lighting must be minimal in order to make the plays as portable as possible. Adult actors are used, many of whom possess teaching experience and skills.

Drama-in-Education

Whereas TIE plays are generally tightly scripted theatrical events, DIE is a workshop rather than a performance-based activity, drawn extensively from children's play. It allows participants to discover for themselves, through action and in the company of others, solutions to problems they encounter. The emphasis is on learning by doing, on experience and activity for the participants. Although utilizing many of the techniques of theatre, DIE lacks the element of the actor/audience relationship that is essential to TIE.

Children's Theatre

Unlike TIE and DIE, which are strongly concerned with education, children's theatre is chiefly concerned with entertainment. And unlike TIE and DIE, children's theatre is often presented in theatres during school holidays, and can therefore be more lavishly produced, sometimes with elaborate stage effects. Children's theatre may be presented by adult subsidized theatre companies, usually at Christmastime, or by companies whose usual work is TIE.

Youth Theatre

In youth theatre the actors are young people (ranging from primary-school age to about twenty-five) working under the guidance of experienced adult tutors and directors. Frequently they write or improvise their own plays and are responsible for many of the technical aspects of production. As well as performances, there are workshops designed to teach theatre skills and foster the participants' personal development.

Young People's Theatre

This blanket term includes TIE, children's theatre, and youth theatre, the areas of concern of professional theatre companies in Australia. It does not include DIE, which is usually conducted by classroom teachers or specialist drama teachers in primary and secondary schools as well as by one or two companies attached to education departments. In DIE, drama is often taught as a subject in its own right in addition to being utilized as a teaching method. Companies in the other three categories usually are not part of the education system, but work with it as appropriate and on most occasions.

THE AUSTRALIAN SYSTEM AND PROFESSIONAL YOUNG PEOPLE'S THEATRE

There are six states (Queensland, New South Wales, Victoria, Tasmania, South Australia, and Western Australia) and two territories (Australian Capital Territory and Northern Territory) forming the Commonwealth of Australia. Each state and territory has its own arts, educational, and other youth-related bodies that can provide funds and resources for professional companies. These are paralleled by arts, educational, and other youth-related bodies at the federal level, including the Australia Council, the Ministries of Education, Youth Affairs and Foreign Affairs, the Schools Commission, and the Special Minister of State.

No professional young people's theatre company can exist without government subsidy. This subsidy can contribute toward general grants (for one year's program) or project grants. Subsidies can be drawn from one or some or all of the available resources at both federal and state levels. Subsidy goes toward basic operational costs. A mean subsidy from all sources for an average-sized TIE company is $A185,000. One or two exceptional companies receive more, up to $A250,000. Few receive less than $A100,000.

Companies depend on box office to a marked degree for continuing operations. Exceptionally, in the two states of South Australia and Tasmania support from education departments for respective state TIE companies enables free performances in schools. All companies have to compete against one another and against other theatre art forms (dance, drama), other art forms, and prevailing federal and state policies for the limited money available. Young people's theatres are considered by some exponents as the "Cinderella" of the performing arts.

THE CURRENT SITUATION

A predominance of TIE companies may be noted—some twenty-one in all—whose characteristics are small teams of approximately four actors, performing mainly in schools, touring extensively in metropolitan and country areas, and presenting original productions on themes relevant to young people's experiences, needs, and development.

An increasingly vigorous and creative youth theatre movement can be documented (i.e., work that is created and performed *by* young people *for* young people under professional teaching and guidance). There are now some fifteen youth companies throughout Australia.

There is currently a dearth of children's theatre, since few professional artists perform classic, traditional, and new pieces; only one or two full-time professional children's companies now operate. However, today more major adult companies include a children's theatre production as part of their repertory. An encouraging development is that the number of groups of individual artists who present children's theatre on an occasional basis is increasing, along with a burgeoning of dance-in-education and dance for young people.

Important recent trends include expanded attention toward work that reflects multicultural themes and issues as well as an emphasis on aboriginal arts, which in theatre focuses on music, sound, and movement, as well as themes of significance such as racism, tolerance, and the need for greater awareness and development. Attention is also given to the work of young playwrights, especially those of school age. Increasing commissions are granted to professional artists (directors, designers, writers, choreographers, musicians) to work in all aspects of young people's theatre.

The total population of Australia is 15.4 million, of which 6.3 million, or 41 percent, are under twenty-five years old. Approximately eleven million persons, or 70 percent of the population, live in cities, thus discounting the myth that Australians are rural dwellers. On the contrary, Australia is predominantly an industralized, modern urban society, and well over half of the population, or more than 9 million, live in the five coastal cities of Sydney (3.3 million), Melbourne (2.9 million), Brisbane (1.1 million), Adelaide (970,000), and Perth (969,000). Nearly 21 percent, or at least one in every five persons, are born overseas. The largest ethnic groups come from the United Kingdom, Italy, Greece, the Netherlands, and Yugoslavia, but increasing numbers now come from Central and South America and Asia, including Vietnam, Laos, and Kampuchea. The aboriginal population is some 160,000.

Australia is 4,000 kilometers east to west and 3,180 north to south, excluding Tasmania. In traveling around the country there are climactic and geographical differences but no marked variations in standards, types and styles of living, language, or culture. Two-thirds of the country is desert or semi-desert.

The Theatre Board of the Australia Council allocates about 12 percent of its total budget of $A12.4 million to young people's theatre. It has been the main source to date for the maintenance and development of young people's theatre in the country. Two states in particular, South Australia and Tasmania, are progressive in their policies, resources, and funding for young people's theatre; the others are less so.

SOME MAJOR CONCLUSIONS

A wide range of activity exists, with at least one major company (TIE and youth) in each state and territory.[1] The companies provide a number of community services, foster Australian writing, and achieve high standards in some of their work.

Funding bodies have marginally increased both the real value of their funding to young people's theatre and the proportion of their total budgets that has been allocated to young people's theatre.

In 1980, for the first time, the Theatre Board published a policy statement on young people's theatre. The policy enables the Board to assist the development of young people's theatre in a wide variety of ways. Only one state, South Australia, has done likewise. The establishment of Carclew in 1976 as a youth arts resource center, with subsequent refinement in 1980 as a youth performing arts center, makes it the only center in any state in the Commonwealth with a unique funding, resource, and service role, including the development of policy.

Relations between funding bodies are growing. The staffs of federal and state arts funding bodies hold regular consultations with each other and subsidized companies. Federal and state funding groups have made efforts to establish a rapport with the companies and have improved their procedures for the assessment and documentation of their work.

Inasmuch as only about one-sixth of the school population is reached by subsidized companies, inadequate budgetary provision of young people's theatre clearly remains a problem. Also, the precarious financial position of companies forces them to economize in salaries, training, and production costs, with the result that they have difficulty attracting suitable artists. Their sets, costumes, and props are frequently minimal, their cast sizes below average, and their training programs inadequate. Given this, it is difficult for the companies to present continuing work of a high standard; consequently their prestige, in the eyes of the theatre world and the funding bodies, is lowered, and it becomes still harder to attract funding and suitable artists. A vicious circle thus impedes development.

The need to raise money at the box office may mean that a company cannot afford to visit a small school or one in a poor area; or it may mean that a company plays to an excessively large audience and thus reduces its effectiveness; or that the company cuts its rehearsal period short so as to maximize its performing time.

The further development of young people's theatre is hampered by a lack of documentation, research, and evaluation, and by the fact that there is no training course in Australia that adequately equips actor-teachers for TIE or actors for children's theatre work. Lack of communication between young people's companies and mainstream theatre, education departments, teachers, and the general public also remains a problem. To date, government funding has concentrated on TIE, rather than on children's theatre or youth theatre. Moreover, there is too little coordination between funding bodies responsible for theatre in schools and a resulting tendency to shirk the responsibilities of funding. TIE in particular suffers because of bureaucracy between education funding sources and arts funding sources. By and large, the area of young people's theatre receives little attention from theatre critics and the media on either a state or national level.

REPRESENTATIVE COMPANIES

Arena Theatre Company Ltd., Melbourne

The Arena Theatre Company was founded in 1966 when there was no theatre available for children in Melbourne. Through the Toorak Players (an amateur dramatic society) the first play for children was presented at Arena Theatre in South Yarra and went on to tour primary schools. In 1968 the company, then known as Children's Arena Theatre, or CAT, became fully professional, presenting theatre in both primary and secondary schools throughout Victoria.

Since then Arena has been committed to offering high-quality and challenging theatre to young people in schools, which it performs in many styles and approaches. Even though each artistic director has brought his or her own philosophy and form to the productions, the aims of creating theatre of relevance and innovation, as well as a firm commitment to young people, have remained central.

The company employs a full-time artistic director, administrator, and administrative assistant. Financial, marketing, and programming decisions are primarily the responsibility of the administrator and the artistic director in consultation with the Board of Management. Artistic decisions are made in a cooperative form with the actors. Rehearsal processes concentrate on shared responsibility for the final product by all those concerned with the production.

In 1986 Arena Theatre Company created five projects for young people: *What's the Difference?*, a play about equal opportunities for young people presented to senior secondary students; *Our Antigone*, a performance/workshop of a required text; *Made Together*, a fantasy for junior primary children written in conjunction with a group of physically disabled children; *The Dumb Waiter*, an in-house production for secondary students of Harold Pinter's classic play; and *Stacks On!*, a play about safety and decision making for upper primary students (currently on tour).

Canberra Youth Theatre Company, Canberra

The Canberra Youth Theatre Company began as part of Canberra's Children's Theatre, Inc., in 1971 and then became the main component of Reid House Theatre Workshop during 1972. The Jigsaw TIE Company developed out of Reid House in 1975. Both companies moved to Gorman House in 1981. In 1983 the Canberra Youth Theatre Company separated from Jigsaw and began to operate as its own entity.

The basic structure of the company is three full-time staff members—artistic director, administrator, and production manager—as well as one part-time associate director (two days per week) and three part-time tutors (approximately two hours per week). The artistic director and the administrator hold the executive positions in the company, and the administrator is also responsible for financial management. In the final analysis, however, the artistic director has ultimate responsibility. The Management Committee meets once a month, and it is to the Committee that the administrator and the artistic director are responsible. The Management Committee is responsible for the overall management of the company.

The associate director works with the artistic director on determining the direction of the company. The associate director also supervises workshops, as does the artistic director. The production manager is responsible for all maintenance, set construction, lighting and sound design, and the tutors' technical workshops. The staff of four hold meetings once a week during which everyone contributes to the agenda and discusses issues from all areas. For the most part, there is collective agreement on company policies.

Three major productions were presented in 1986: *Sunset Boulevard*, a music/theatre piece dealing with images of women in the rock-and-roll industry (a young women's project); *Legends*, a play written by John Romerill, Jennifer Hill, and Chris Anasstiades about a group of young people (fifteen- to sixteen-year-olds) and the awakening of their awareness of their own identity, individuality, and group consciousness; and *The Young Playwright's Season*, four short plays written by young people. The latter two productions were performed by Canberra Youth Theatre Company in workshop groups.

In addition, the company mounted a short piece on women and the media called *Can I Say Something . . . !*, devised and performed by four of the older workshop participants. The 1987 season included three short monologues written and performed by Pauline Caddy, a nineteen-year-old writer-actress and one of the company's tutors.

Magpie Theatre Company, Adelaide

Magpie Theatre, the young people's section of the State Theatre Company of South Australia, was organized in 1977 with the mission of presenting professional theatre in schools, playhouses, and communities throughout the state of South Australia.

Over the years Magpie Theatre has been responsible for commissioning and devising numerous new works, as well as for performing pieces by acknowledged authors from the repertory of plays for young people. The research that the company does in conjunction with writers takes place not only with young people in schools, but also with teachers and parents in rural and metropolitan areas. Magpie has a policy of performing in schools free of charge, which allows its work to be immediately accessible to all young people. Through good theatre that is entertaining, thought-provoking, age specific, and geared to the concerns and interests of its audience, the group supports, challenges, and encourages young people in their efforts to more fully understand themselves and the experience of others.

The company consists of a permanent ensemble of five actors, a director, an administrator, a stage manager, and a designer. As an integral part of the State Theatre Company of South Australia, it has the benefit of the expertise of personnel in the workshops, wardrobe, and financial offices.

A recent season included *Sparks'll Fly* by Graeme Pitts, for upper secondary grades; *Soloman and the Big Cat* by David Holman, for the primary level; a summer holiday attraction; a tour of *Soloman* to the Far North, including workshops and a community cabaret; and Theatreful of Fantasy (*Soloman*).

Salamanca Theatre Company, Hobart

The Tasmanian Theatre-in-Education Company, founded in 1972 as a branch of the Tasmanian Theatre Company, left its parent organization and became incorporated in its own right in 1977, changing its name to Salamanca Theatre Company to suit its new address in Salamanca Place, Hobart. Barbara Manning was the founder of the company and executive artistic director until 1984. The company provides its services free to Tasmanian schools; its style, variety, and approach have remained reasonably consistent, with company-devised works dominating its history. The staff has increased over the years from two actors and a director to the current company strength.

Salamanca Theatre Company is governed by a seven-member Board of Directors. Five directors are elected annually, one is an actors' representative, and the executive artistic director is the seventh member. Both the actors' representative and the executive director have full voting rights at Board level. The executive director is responsible to the Board for the running of the company and has the final say on all decisions that affect policy and practice, subject to the approval of the Board, but the general practice is for decisions to arise from company meetings by consensus approach.

The company's current repertory includes *Susumu's Story* by David Holman, for grades 5 and 6, primary schools; *Jobo's Journey* (company-devised), for special schools; and a new participation play on the peaceful resolution of conflict (company-devised), for grades 2 and 3, primary schools.

BIBLIOGRAPHY

Australia Council Occasional Papers Program Review Board. *Theatre Board: Support for Young People's Theatre*. Sydney: Australia Council, 1982.

Australian Youth Performing Arts Association. *National Theatre-in-Education Study*. Sydney: Australian Youth Performing Arts Association, 1980, 3 parts.

More Tricks Than We Have: A Program About Theatre-in-Education. Produced for Toe

Truck Theatre by Lyn Tuit, directed by Karl Zwicky. Sydney: Tasmanian Film Corporation, 1982.

Salamanca Theatre Company. *Annie's Coming Out: A Study of a Residency Program.* Tasmania: Education Department, 1982.

Anne Godfrey-Smith. *Youth Performing Arts in Australia, 1975–1977.* Sydney: Australian Youth Performing Arts Association, 1977.

Mark Radvan. *Youth Theatre.* Sydney: Australian Youth Performing Arts Association, 1980.

PLAYS

Hewett, Dorothy. *Golden Valley.* Sydney: Currency Press, 1985.

———. *Song of the Seals.* Sydney: Currency Press, 1985.

Lonie, John, ed. *Learning from Life: Five Plays for Young People Selected and Introduced by John Lonie.* Sydney: Currency Press, 1985. The plays include *If Only We Had a Cat*, Richard Tulloch; *Wolf Boy*, Peter Charlton; *Until Ya Say Ya Love Me*, Magpie Theatre Company; *Wasting Away*, David Young; and *Hey, Mum, I Own a Factory!*, Magpie Theatre Company.

One Act Plays: Series 2. Melbourne: Australian Theatre Workshop, Heinemann Educational Australia, 1983. The plays include *Karen*, David Allen; *To a Trainee Accountant*, Michael Dugan; *The Actor*, Michael Dugan; *Urbs Urbis*, Tony Nicholls; and *Year 9 Are Animals*, Richard Tulloch.

Romeril, John. *Legends.* Melbourne: Cambridge University Press, 1986.

NOTE

1. Australia Council/Occasional Papers; Program Review Series (Maacle: Theatre Board: Support for Young People's Theatre, 1982).

Michael FitzGerald

Austria

HISTORY

Austrians have always been enamored of the theatre. William M. Johnston, in *The Austrian Mind*, thinks of Austrians as consumers of art: "Among people loath to make decisions, spectacle and amusement gladdened daily life."[1] And they have always insisted on excellence, as he further observes: "Although the public might feel indifferent to politics and nonchalant about morals, it demanded the utmost from each actor and musician."[2] Naturally, a population that thinks of art and drama as important parts of its life also will want to educate its children to enjoy theatre. At court, from the beginning of the seventeenth century until late into the eighteenth century, not only professional actors performed, but also the children of courtiers and of the ruling house. The one-act *opera buffa* by Christoph Willibald Gluck, *Il Parnasso Confuso*, performed at Schoenbrunn in 1765, was sung and danced by several archdukes and archduchesses, among them Marie Antoinette, aged ten, and Leopold, aged eighteen, who was to become Holy Roman Emperor but who then served as conductor and cembalo player.[3]

Since World War II few statistics are available regarding theatre for children and young people. The state-subsidized theatres, such as Burg, Oper, and Volksoper, still give, as they always have, some performances especially for children, usually around Christmastime. These are beautifully mounted costumed plays acted and sung by first-rate actors and singers. Children and young people can see some performances at special rates, but these are few in number. The Burg sponsors a day each year called "Theatre to Touch," when children are invited to inspect the scenery and sound installation, and meet the actors and stage-workers, and are entertained by clowns, tightrope walkers, and musicians. In 1984 the Burg presented a popular play by Jerome Savary titled *About the Fat Pig Who Wanted to Become Thin*. The Volksoper mounted a new but conventional and much-admired production of *Hansel and Gretel* in 1986. The Volksoper also started a series, Children and Conoisseurs, which encourages children to compose and/or play an instrument. The company has, too, presented four operas for children, among them *Help! Help! The Globolinks* by Gian Carlo Menotti.

In 1932 the Theatre for Schools was founded by Hofrat Dr. Hans Zwanzger, who changed the name to Theatre for Youth two years later. He wanted to present on stage those plays that young people read in school and to organize performances at cut-rate prices in three theatres. The idea was good, but the results were not always successful: some teachers failed to cooperate, money was limited, and attendance was poor. Only a few performances could be scheduled, and the quality of the productions suffered. When Austria was annexed to Germany in 1938, the name of the Theatre for Youth was changed again; this time it became Organization for Hitler Youth, and soon other events superseded those of the theatre.

After World War II Zwanzger again started the Theatre for Youth (TFY). But 1945 was not an easy year for Austrians. The Burg and Opera theatres had been bombed, and the companies operated in other locations under great difficulties. Some theatres kept their actors busy clearing rubble; actors as well as audiences went hungry. Still, performances were given because people were starving not only for food, but also for art. When America, in devising the Marshall Plan to help Europe, asked Austria what it needed most urgently, expecting to hear various foods enumerated, the Austrians replied that their number one priority was to restore the opera house.[4]

In October 1945 TFY opened with productions of *Clavigo*, *Medea*, and *Sappho and Nathan*, performed in various theatres. In 1945/46 the company played to an audience of 169,000 youngsters, but by November 1982, fifty years after its inception, nearly 500,000 saw its performances each season. (These figures include visits to concerts and other entertainments such as ice shows.)[5] Plays offered by TFY include dramatized fairy tales and myths for the younger children and classic plays by Grillparzer, Raimund, Nestroy, and Shakespeare, along with modern plays about problems related to everyday life, for older audience members.

COMPANIES AND REPERTORY

TFY plays in three theatres, two of which it owns: the Renaissance Theatre, with 800 seats, and the Theatre im Zentrum, with 300 seats. The group rents another theatre with 1,000 seats for two productions. Three different subscriptions are offered: one for six- to ten-year-old children, with five productions a year; one for ten- to fourteen-year-olds, with four productions per season; and one for fourteen- to nineteen-year-olds, with two productions—totaling eleven plays. Apart from its own productions, the company sponsors, at special prices, about sixty offerings each season in seven to nine different theatres.

The range of the TFY repertory may be seen in its choices for the 1987/88 season:

For younger children: *Prince and Fairy* (Voerosmarty)

Hans in Luck (Bauschmid)

The Singing, Dancing Loewenneckerchen (Fussenegger)

The Emperor's New Clothes (Drude)

The Fairy with the Coppernose (Tordon)

For ten- to fourteen-year-olds: *Lost and Found* (Phantasy)

Tom Sawyer (Twain/Wiens)

The Exchange Student (Noestlinger/Weger)

The Adventurous Simplicissimus (Becker/ Freitag)

For older children: *The White Illness* (Capek)

It Ain't a Beautiful Country (Mitterer)

These were company productions. The subscription also included the following sponsored productions, which were offered according to age groups: *Wild Honey* (Frayn), *Loyalties* (Galsworthy), *An Afternoon with the Saengerknaben, A Chorus Line* (Hamlisch), *Cats* (Lloyd Webber), *Easy Game* (Schnitzler), *Le Bourgeois Gentilhomme* (Molière), *The Tempest* (Shakespeare), *Hansel and Gretel* (Humperdinck—opera), *The Good Fairy* (Molnar), *The Talisman* (Nestroy), *Dream Girl* (Rice), *The Broken Jug* (Kleist), and *Pravda* (Brenton/Hare).

These plays were in the repertory of various theatres in Vienna, and were approved by both the educational authority and the artistic director, who sanctions productions as proper for viewing by children. Many of the plays are well-known classics and serve to introduce young people to the world's greatest dramatic literature. Some in-house productions are commissioned by TFY, mostly from Austrian writers (e.g., Gertrud Fussenegger, Renate Welsh, Helmut Butterweck, and Felix Mitterer). The great Austrian playwright Carl Zuckmayer wrote his last play, *Der Rattenfaenger*, for TFY.

An illustration of the goals TFY wants to achieve in its plays may be found in a true story dramatized under the title *It Ain't a Beautiful Country*, by Felix Mitterer. In a village in the Tyrol one of the most respected citizens is a cattle dealer who made his town famous by opening it up to international winter sports. It is 1938 and many of the citizens reveal themselves to be followers of Hitler; soon proof of being "aryan" is necessary in order to continue doing business. To the great surprise of his neighbors, the cattle dealer cannot comply. The man who up to now has been considered the village hero is suddenly isolated, threatened, and finally shipped to a concentration camp and killed. Each production offers a study guide with questions for teachers to ask about problems inherent in the play, such as "How do the villagers react?" and "Can children be taught to avoid inhumanity in the future?" Most commissioned plays underscore universal subjects, such as the generation gap, use of drugs, hostile feelings toward immigrant workers, AIDS, or tolerance toward people who look and act differently from the norm.

How are the plays chosen? TFY has three directors who respectively supervise finances, educational policy, and artistic management. Plays are selected by the educational and artistic directors in conjunction with an advisory council composed of members who support TFY, such as those representing the Ministry of Education and the countries of Vienna, Burgenland, and Nieder-Oesterreich. In addition, teachers and parents have a voice in the choice of plays. The advisory council often faces problems because children, parents, and teachers may possess different ideas, different politics, and different world views. The organization of parents consists of such disparate groups as Catholic Family Society, Social Democratic Society, Society of Parents of pupils whose attendance at school is obligatory (up to age sixteen), and Society of Parents whose children are enrolled in higher education. Although it is not surprising that Catholics and Socialists may disagree on a play, it is the job of the educational advisor to find a compromise between different points of view.

Two dramaturgs read plays, and for approximately every fifty scripts present a resume of ten texts to the educational and artistic directors. These two decide whether the plays meet the standards of TFY: to acquaint children with problems of today's societies, as well as those of the past; to make them aware of the problems in their own lives; and to enhance their literary awareness.

After performances the actors and the artistic and educational directors lead discussions with audiences and answer questions. A questionnaire designed to stimulate young people to reflect on what they've seen is distributed. It is important to note that TFY does not go into schools, but performs for children who voluntarily come to the theatre. TFY does not view itself as a continuation of school, but as a third major factor in the youngsters' lives: home, school, and theatre. Some goals are sociopolitical, as TFY tries to attract audiences from the social strata that would normally have no opportunity to visit the theatre, such as children of immigrant and transient workers. TFY also tries to interest handicapped children, although the directors admit that their facilities are not yet adequate to accommodate this audience.

TFY is a member of the Buehnenverien, a labor organization that can be compared with Actor's Equity (the performers' labor union in the United States and Great Britain). The company employs three directors, twenty-one actors, two dramaturgs, two stage managers, one musical director, four puppeteers, and various behind-the-scene workers, including ticket-takers, wardrobe people, hairdressers, scene-builders, firemen, lighting experts, carpenters, seamstresses, locksmiths, makeup people, and property people. The yearly budget of TFY is approximately 100.000.000 schilling (approximately 8 million U.S. dollars). Of this money 55 percent to 60 percent comes from ticket sales and the rest is obtained from subsidies.

Dr. Reinhard Urbach, the current artistic director, recently discussed some of the difficulties he faces. He wishes that children could participate in plays instead of just watching them, but this would necessitate an audience size of no more than seventy and space other than a proscenium stage. The economic base for such an undertaking currently does not exist. Urbach would like to make drama a voluntary subject in schools and instigate role playing and creative drama within the normal curriculum. Training for teachers has been offered, but so far few have demonstrated interest.

Urbach favors Austrian membership in ASSITEJ but refuses to become its director in order to avoid the jealousy of the smaller independent companies who already feel dominated by TFY, calling it "the giant." TFY is willing to provide space and a dramaturg for ASSITEJ. Urbach has written a position paper in which he pleads for a theatre that is directed for young people, not for grown-ups, teachers, and parents, a theatre of fantasy that assists young people in the art of living. On the other hand, he states that theatre for children should not be geared *against* parents and teachers, even if plays may contain seeds of protest against the world of grown-ups.

TFY should educate children to attend the theatre, Urbach urges. Children should not be viewed as "tomorrow's audience," but as today's, an audience that in time should want to become tomorrow's audience. Urbach pleads for a truly Viennese TFY; instead of importing plays from foreign countries and then giving them local Viennese color, he hopes that Austrian playwrights will write for the children and young people of their country.

Urbach contends that if we take children and young people seriously, we must also take the theatre we make for them seriously; this requires excellent playwrights, directors, and actors. But theatre for children is not valued as highly in either salaries or recognition as is the theatre for adults, and it will be necessary to challenge both audiences and artists to overcome this discrepancy. He believes that quality will improve once fewer plays are in the repertory and when staff and actors no longer have excessive demands made on them. Children, he says, like actors, need to be trained to concentrate because theatre is not as easy to watch as television, where they can switch channels whenever they become bored.[6]

The training of actors and staff for children's theatre is also one of the main concerns of Ladislav Povazay, who founded Moki, a mobile children's theatre, in 1973 for children from five to thirteen years old. Povazay had studied in Prague, where, as in other Eastern bloc countries, professional training is available for practitioners of children's theatre. He directs his own troupe with the help of another Eastern bloc refugee, Stefan Kulhanek. Both men claim that children's theatre demands special skills. For instance, actors not only must be able to act, sing, and dance, but also should be able to walk tightropes, juggle, perform acrobatics, and be skilled in pantomime. It is also vital, in their view, to have children participate—a difficult task that requires actors to depart from a written script and to improvise new dialogue whenever necessary. In their play *Tony Ratcatcher* the children can decide the fate of the protagonist, whether he should live or die. Povazay says: "That was super. The children had the feeling that they themselves had written the play . . . but these techniques necessitate special plays and creative author/actors."[7]

Povazay thinks it is difficult to have the entire audience participate, but he provides opportunities to incorporate actions so that children drawn from the audience can perform. In one of his plays a king and queen bring in two clothes hangers that turn into characters when the children dress them by taking costumes from a large chest placed on stage. Povazay is an idealist with a great sense of humor that no doubt helps him, since his subsidy is small. He receives only 400.000 to 500.000 schilling (30,000 to 35,000 U.S. dollars) from the same people who back TFY; this is augmented by ticket sales, which range from 36 to 45 schillings ($3.00 to $3.80). His company consists of about twenty-six persons, some of whom are employed only for special performances. Ninety percent of the plays performed by Moki are written especially for the company, many of them by Povazay himself; plays sometimes remain in the repertory for several hundred performances. Although the theatre is dedicated to children, 26 percent of its audience is composed of adults. Moki gives approximately 350 performances a year, wherever it is invited.

Moki's artistic goal is to incorporate educational, psychological, and socio-logical aspects of significance to young children. Problems discussed include environmental issues, dehumanization in a computer-dominated society, and stress that comes from pleasing grown-ups. Nightmares that ensue from pressures at home and school are analyzed at the end of performances. Another subject Povazay tackles successfully is obesity (40 out of 200 children in Austria are overweight). *TomCat Dicky, Cat Fatty and Rosalinde* shows what happens when fat cats encounter the mouse Rosalinde, who is agile, mobile, and thin. Povazay's plays are not censored, but sometimes his strong commitment and involvement in schools call for restraint in dealing with controversial subjects.

Moki does not have its own theatre, although it maintains office and rehearsal space. The company plays on rented stages, at youth centers, in schools and physical activities facilities, in churches, and, during the summer, even in mead-ows. The actors, scenery, and sound equipment are transported by bus, usually driven by Povazay himself.

Because Povazay cannot offer his actors adequate salaries and cannot pay them for rehearsal time, he frequently employs young people who are still in acting school. Some of them, after a few years with Moki, try to found theatres of their own. Anna Hnilicka is the latest to desert Moki and start her own company, presenting *The Selfish Giant* by Oscar Wilde. She has also begun a training program for children, doing role playing, improvisation, movement, makeup, and some elementary aspects of backstage work. "It's not just a game," says Hnilicka. "With ideas contributed by the children, a story is created which is shown at the end of each course."[8]

There are a few other independent groups. Lilarium is a puppet theatre that presents a fairy tale each Friday and Saturday. The Appletree, a group connected to the Rudolf Steiner school, also offers traditional fairy tales with marionettes. In Linz, one of Austria's larger cities, A Child's Theatre was founded in 1978; they are, along with TFY, the only youth companies in Austria that own their own theatres. Salzburg is home to a mobile children's theatre that travels to schools. Another group, Dandelion, played *Conference of the Birds* by Jean-Claude Carriere in 1986/87 and has since presented a musical with a peace theme. They also plan a future project to be performed in two languages, Turkish and German.

Educators Angela and Volker Waldegg, who work in a children's home in the "City of the Child" (a Viennese suburb), give classes for six- to eighteen-year-olds. At first the Waldeggs worked exclusively with handicapped youth, but now there are small groups of nonhandicapped children, gathered according to age, who have worked together under the leadership of professionals. In the winter of 1985 they produced *Carnival in Venice*, which they toured to Venice. Unlike most groups, this one is more interested in creating theatre than in the product or end result; children select themes of interest and develop them not only from a theatrical approach, but also from a psychological point of view.

FESTIVALS

Austria holds several annual festivals for children that include an emphasis on children's theatre. One of the oldest and most popular is Noekiss; here, for the past fifteen years, 500 to 700 children have met on the last two weekends before school starts. The location is an abbey in Lower Austria that backs the festival by providing space and voluntary helpers. The church becomes a center for performances by various companies and puppeteers, Moki among them. In 1987 a clown, a group from the wine country, one from Graz, and another from Bruck an der Leitha entertained the children. With the help of the Austrian Amateur Theatre Association, children are also encouraged to create their own plays and act them out. It is Noekiss' ambition to become a showplace for different forms of modern children's theatre in which actors, authors, directors, and dramaturgs can exchange information and ideas.

Children take classes in a relaxed atmosphere at the Carinthian Summer Festival, which each year produces an opera. About 100 children take part, of whom 50 percent are repeaters. Director Gerda Froehlich believes that the festival's major achievement is that the children and parents who participate continue to pursue their musical endeavors together during the rest of the year. Kurt Pahlen, musical director of the Carinthian festival, provided a similar opera at the festival for children in Bregenz. In August 1984 the theatre in Baden (a small town about one hour from Vienna) gave a two-week course called "We Make an Opera." One hundred fifty children presented *Der Utzenmutz*, which played not only in Baden, but also in The Vienna Konzerthaus—an opera performed by children for children. On this occasion music was provided by the youth orchestra of Dornbirn, a city that regularly presents opera and ballet productions performed by children for children.

FOREIGN-LANGUAGE THEATRE

Children's theatre in Austria has an added dimension in its two foreign-language theatres. The older and much better known is the English Children's Theatre. In 1959 Ruth Brinkmann, a young American actress, came to Austria as a tourist. She met and married an Austrian director and settled in Vienna. Because she spoke no German at the time (she now doubles as a German actress), her husband had the idea of starting an English theatre, which they opened in 1963. Vienna's English Theatre became a success and now owns its own space. The year 1966 saw the first school production by the English Theatre, organized through the initiative of Ruth Brinkmann and the Vienna Board of Education; it was seen by 800 high school students. The production met a favorable response and has become an annual event that extends throughout the country under the auspices of the Ministry of Education. The theatre tours widely between October and May, playing to some 200,000 students in 109 Austrian communities, including towns "in the Tyrol and in Vorarlberg that have never known any other live theatre."[9]

Nicholas Allen joined the English Theatre in 1967 and has been actor, author, manager, and organizer of the school tours. The Viennese Board of Education endorses the English Theatre for Young People (ETFYP) and encourages high school students studying English to see English-language productions performed by professionals whose mother tongue is English. Because a large percentage of Austria's income is derived from tourism, Austrians need to speak English idiomatically to attend to their many visitors.

The ETFYP is a self-supporting, nonprofit organization that uses only English-speaking professional actors and actresses. Allen has said that their proficiency as actors is important to him, but not as important as their rapport with young people. He says that his auditions are usually spent talking with the four young men and four young women he will engage, two each for the tours for thirteen- to fifteen-year-olds and for sixteen- to eighteen-year-olds. There is no tour yet for children younger than thirteen years old because their English, which is an obligatory school subject, is not yet proficient enough to understand the plays. However, in 1987 Allen began to include twelve-year-olds in his audiences with *Dick Whittington and His Cat*, written as an English Christmas pantomime. Allen's next venture is to write a Krimi (detective story) that has three different endings, the ending used for a particular performance to be chosen by the audience.

The aims of the English Theatre are to improve the children's English, to help them understand English culture, and to augment their world view. Artistically, the English Theatre simply wants to produce good theatre. One special goal evolved by necessity: to educate children to become a good and interested audience. According to Allen, in the beginning it was most difficult to stop children from running, eating, and generally creating havoc. Allen rewrote most of the plays after what he deemed a catastrophic experience with a play called *A Slight Accident*, which was met with a total lack of comprehension.[10] He also interspersed songs to give the children the opportunity to sing along; these songs, like the texts of the plays, are printed by the Ministry of Education. The money needed to finance operations is earned by charging about 50 schillings for a ticket. Allen has formed a company of Friends of the English Theatre for Youth in which each "friend" pays a membership fee for such privileges as attending general rehearsals, meeting the actors, and discussing trends in English literature.

Sets and costumes are simple, as they must be to allow as many as five performances a day. Actors are paid competitive salaries and receive hotel accommodations and per diem. In each text an appendix lists the vocabulary used in the play and gives comprehensive questions and points for discussion. Teachers also prepare students in advance for performances. Some of the plays shown by the English Theatre during the past seventeen years include *The Importance of Being Earnest*, by Oscar Wilde; *The Glass Menagerie*, by Tennessee Williams; *Man of Destiny*, by George Bernard Shaw; *Lovers*, by Brian Friel; *An Inspector Calls*, by J. B. Priestley; *The Happy Journey*, by Thornton Wilder; *Of Lovers and Fools*, by Shakespeare, arranged by Vogel; *A Slight Accident*, by James Saunders; *Look Back in Anger*, by John Osborne; *Arms and the Man*, by Shaw; *The Canterville Ghost*, by Nicholas Allen and Wilde; *Relatively Speaking*, by Alan Ayckbourn; *Robin Hood*, by Allen; and *King Arthur*, by Allen.

Because the English Theatre's concept of a children's theatre performed in a foreign language is admired by other European countries, they have toured widely in Italy and Switzerland. Two years ago the English Theatre started a tour that performs in French; as in the English tours, there are four French actors, two men and two women, and one musician, subsidized by the Ministry of Education. Still in its beginning stages, this tour travels only from October to March (unlike the English tours, which go until May). The French tour plays only one or at most two performances a day, and has been well received by teachers and students. Even though the first play, a work by Molière, was widely enjoyed, audiences asked that the next play be in contemporary French. A play by the late Jean Anouilh was planned for 1988.

CONCLUSION

As one can see, theatre is an important part of the children's lives in Austria, and they have a large selection of performances from which to choose. The leaders in the field are well-known and well-versed professionals. Dr. Ernest

Novotny, educational director of TFY, started as a teacher of upper-level pupils, then taught teachers, and finally became an inspector of schools; after retirement he became educational director of TFY. Dr. Urbach, artistic director of TFY, was chief dramaturg at the Bergtheater before starting his new job. Povazay, director of Moki, had intensive training in his native Czechoslovakia in children's theatre. Allen, director of the English Theatre's children's tours, worked his way up from an actor to tour leader and director.

When asked if this was his first year as a subscriber, a ten-year-old boy at a TFY performance of Butterweck's *The Cold Heart* replied: "No, I've gone since I was six years old. It was not an easy decision at first; I have to miss a lot of soccer games if I take the subscription. But, you know, here I learn about other people in other times and about life in other countries and I love it!"

ACKNOWLEDGMENTS

I wish to thank the people who have been generous with their time and have shared their ideas, knowledge and materials with me. They include: Hofrat Dr. Ernst Novotny, Theater der Jugend, Vienna; Dr. Richard Urbach, Theater der Jugend, Vienna; Nicholas Allen, English Theatre, Vienna; Ladislav Povazay, Moki, Vienna; Regierungsrat Franz Podborsek, Ministry of Education, Vienna; Dr. Alfred Fischl, Ministry of Education, Vienna; Ms. Friederike Teitelhofer, Austrian Institute, New York; and, Mr. Markus Rumpler, Noekiss Festival, Nieder Oesterreich.

BIBLIOGRAPHY

Buehne (Austria's theatre magazine), play reviews from issues in December 1984, October 1985, December 1985, January 1986, February 1986, June 1987.
Butterweck, Hellmutt. *The Cold Heart*. Private manuscript of the author, February 1986.
————. *The Miracle of Vienna*. Verlag Thomas Sessler, 1984.
Mitterer, Felix. *Dragonthirst*. Oesterreichscher Buehnenverlag, 1985.
Ossowski, Leonie. *Identifying with the Part*. Private manuscript, Theater der Jugend, 1985.
Povazay, Ladislav. *Piccolo, the Last Clown*. Private manuscript of the author, 1986.
Theater de Jugend, Vienna's English Theatre, Moki, Noekiss, pamphlets, plays, press clippings, and statements.

NOTES

1. William M. Johnston, *The Austrian Mind, An Intellectual and Social History, 1848–1938* (Berkeley: Univ. of California Press, 1972), 116.

2. Ibid., 125.

3. Hilde Haider Pregler, *The Theatre in Austria* (Austria: Federal Press Service, 1962).

4. Author's conversation with Dr. Mayer-Guenthoff, president, Association of Industrialists, December 1947.

5. These statistics have been published in a special issue of *Neue Wege* (*New Paths*) to celebrate the 25th anniversary of TFY. *Neue Wege* is a magazine published by TFY.

6. Interview with Dr. Reinhard Urbach, artistic director of TFY, September 11, 1987.

7. Interview with Ladislav Povazay, director of Moki, September 10, 1987.

8. Interview with Anna Hnilicka by Monica Mertl in *Die Buehne* (Austria's theatre magazine), November 1985.

9. Leaflet printed by Vienna's English Theatre.

10. Interview with Nicholas Allen, manager and tour leader of Vienna's English Theatre, September 10, 1987.

Elizabeth Gay

Brazil

HISTORY

In its forty-year history, children's theatre in Brazil has undergone many meaningful changes in its artistic, aesthetic, and linguistic development. The outcome of this evolution is the concept of children as thinking, sensitive, and intelligent beings who are not merely striving to be miniature adults. But even with this significant growth we have no centralized comprehensive sourcebook, nor do we offer formal programs for advanced study. Specific publications are scarce; most documentation consists of scattered articles published in newspapers or specialized magazines. This essay, therefore, is heavily dependent on interviews conducted with theatre groups and people who are important in the field of children's theatre, and is restricted primarily to the cities of Rio de Janeiro and Sao Paulo, although it does not ignore other parts of the country. Several states, like Rio Grande do Sul, Pernambuco, and Bahia, deserve further study.

Children's theatre in Brazil began in this century. It was primarily used to transmit patriotic messages or as a pedagogic tool. The records show small comedies and monologues written by adults to be declaimed by children. These first attempts at theatrical expression were mainly written to please the parents, who attended the recitations to be charmed by the declamatory skills of their little "artists." The children, however, understood neither the meaning of the individual words they spoke nor the meaning of the piece as a whole.

In the late 1940s the situation changed when the first theatrical productions performed specifically for children were presented. In Rio de Janeiro, Lucia Benedetti presented a new play, *O casaco Encantado* (*The Betwitched Coat*), in 1948. In Sao Paulo in the same year Tatiana Belinky and her husband, Julio Gouveia, were invited by the mayor's office to present the premiere of *Peter Pan* in Brazil. The couple continued staging plays for children and later branched out into television programming for young people.

MARIA CLARA MACHADO AND THEATRE TABLADO

Author and director Maria Clara Machado initiated a new concept in children's theatre when she altered the form of the dramatic language directed toward the child audience. The change was not merely theoretical, but was also introduced into professional usage with the creation of Theatre Tablado, a theatrical company and school through which Machado influenced three generations of actors. Founded in 1951 by Machado and a group of friends, Tablado operated in a space lent by the Patronato da Gavea, a social institution.

Machado had previously studied theatre in France and had also worked with a marionette company for five years. Then in 1953 she adapted *O Boi e o Burro no caminho de Belem* (*The Bull and the Donkey on the Way to Belem*), a marionette play she wrote, for a Christmas performance that proved very successful. Machado's talents were further recognized in a contest for children's plays held by the city of Rio de Janeiro, which she won twice, first with *O rapto das cebonlinhas* (*The Kidnapping of the Small Onions*) in 1953 and then with *A bruxinha que era boa* (*The Witch Who Was Good*) in 1954. She was only twenty-five years old at the time.

Her most well-known play, *Pluft, o fantasminha* (*Pluft, the Little Ghost*), followed in 1955. Pluft tells the story of a ghost who is afraid of people and afraid of growing up. Children identify with the story, which has been performed for three generations. Machado explains that because most children have fears of growing up and facing life, they need symbols and super heroes such as the ghost in her story.

Machado has written twenty-two children's plays, including some that are adaptations of classics. Her works are staged by professional and amateur groups both nationally and internationally. She has also published eleven books: five anthologies of her plays, four volumes of children's stories, one technical book (*One Hundred Dramatic Games*), and one on puppet theatre. In addition, she has written five plays for adults and several articles related to theatrical activities and to the child. Her plays have been translated into French, English, German, Dutch, Swedish, Russian, and Arabic, and she has been presented with two "Moliere" awards for her work. Her most popular plays are *Pluft, o fantasminha, O rapto das cebolinhas, A bruxinha que era boa, O cavalinho azul* (*The Little Blue Horse*), and *A menina e o vento* (*The Little Girl and the Wind*).

In 1956 she founded the magazine *Cadernos de Teatro* (*Theatre Copybooks*), which to date has published 115 issues. The periodical offers information that is helpful to teachers and new groups being formed, and also reports about theatrical activities around the country. In addition, it prints texts of plays from abroad.

Since 1964 Machado has taught an interpretation course that focuses on stage language, movement, and character composition. One of the trademarks of the course is the emphasis given to practice; the students participate in the whole production process, from script selection through performance. Many of today's drama teachers were members of the first classes of Theatre Tablado. Today there are twelve separate sections of Machado's course; each teacher has a certain amount of autonomy and can modify the course according to his or her preferences and style. At the end of the year each group stages a performance that can range from a Greek play to experimental theatre.

Despite numerous invitations Machado has never professionalized her school. In order to do so she would be forced to transform the program excessively, making it bigger and more bureaucratic. In order to maintain her independence she prefers her small school with its family-like atmosphere and amateur status, in which the casts for the plays are chosen by the students in the classes.

SAO PAULO: THE "TESP" EXPERIENCE AND TELEVISION THEATRE

In Sao Paulo, beginning with the staging of *Peter Pan* in 1943, Tatiana Belinky and Julio Gouveia initiated a new kind of children's theatre by producing a work that was considered both educational and formative, but not didactic. Drawing on this initial experience, they, along with some friends, founded the Teatro Escola de Sao Paulo (Theatre School of Sao Paulo, or TESP). TESP, a semi-amateur theatre group, specialized in plays for children and teenagers. The group performed from 1949 to 1964, when it ceased activities.

From 1948 to 1951 TESP performed every weekend in different theatres in Sao Paulo. In areas in which there was no theatre, they performed in libraries, movie houses, social clubs, and hospitals, reaching audiences of all social and economic classes. They always played to full houses, since the city provided the transportation, picking up the children in city parks. The city also provided scenery and lighting equipment as well as technicians and stagehands.

In 1951 TESP was invited to give a presentation for TV TUPI of Sao Paulo, which had just been established. The broadcast was an instant success, and the group was asked to create children's programming for the network. The first show, called "Fabulas Animadas" ("Animated Fables"), was a one-act piece based on fables and national and international folklore. After this came the series "O sition do picapau amarelo" ("The Yellow Woodpecker Ranch"), based on a book by Monteriro Lobato, who wrote for young people.

All the programs in the children's series were broadcast live. Gouveia was the producer and director, Belinky wrote the scripts, and the actors were all members of TESP. The texts were based on national and international children's literature, classic and modern stories, and fantastic, realistic, or historical works. The programs were geared toward emphasizing reading: each piece began with a narrator taking a book off a shelf, saying its title, and reading the first line of the story.

With their work, Belinky and Gouveia promoted both children's theatre (which was still in its infancy) and literature through a new medium. Because television was still experimental, it did not yet have a large following to encourage the development of more artistic programming primarily aimed toward children. Through TESP and the production of television theatre a new generation of actors and directors was influenced, and they, in turn, developed works related to theatre and education.

Belinky has continued working in the field of theatre and education. She founded the child/youth division of the Comissao Estadual do Teatro de Sao Paulo (Sao Paulo Theatre State Committee), where she has worked for many years. She writes reviews of theatre and literature for television and is a reviewer of children's theatre in Sao Paulo. About theatre, she comments: "Theatre, when it is done well, has a tremendous strength . . . and the people who work with children's theatre have a huge responsibility."

1960–1970: THE DREAMS AND COLLECTIVE CREATION

The dignity obtained for children's theatre by Maria Clara Machado is an essential cornerstone in the field. Her ground-breaking efforts led to the idea that work with children and their psychic and affective world is an important and significant profession. The mission of children's theatre was furthered in the 1960s by changes that reflected the concerns and desires of the times.

Two Argentinians, Ilo Krugli and Pedro Domingues, arrived in Rio de Janeiro during the sixties and introduced puppet theatre to Brazil. They gave several courses in making and handling puppets that stimulated the creation of centers for actors looking for new forms of theatrical expression. The sixties were a fruitful time for innovations in adult theatre, music, dance, and the plastic arts, all of which contributed to changes in children's theatre. The result of this mixing of influences was an explosion, at the beginning of the 1970s, of several children's theatre groups, each searching for new forms of expression and communication.

Vento Forte

Vento Forte (Strong Wind), a group led by Krugli, is a good example. The company was created in 1974 for the Festival de Teatro Infantil de Curitiba (Children's Theatre Festival of Curitiba), for which they performed *Historia de Lencos e Ventos* (*Story of Kerchiefs and Winds*). After the Festival, Vento Forte traveled to Rio de Janeiro to perform the piece, and remained there. Krugli began a kind of colorful revolution with the play. It was an innovative work, different from anything being done at the time, in that it integrated the use of several languages, live music, dance, theatre, puppets, and several animated objects. A chalk line became a river; pieces of fabric were transformed into a storm; and Krugli was searching for ways to use the expressive energy of the human body.

In 1978 the group began to tour around Brazil and abroad, and was invited to participate in several festivals. They also moved to Sao Paulo, believing that they could more easily expand in that city. In their fourteen years of existence they have staged twelve children's plays and won numerous awards. Most of their plays are written by Krugli, although some are only basic outlines, like the piece "As quatro chaves" ("The Four Keys"), which has been in the repertory for five years. The play includes a childbirth scene, and the audience participates in building the puppets that are "born" in this delivery. The actors and audience also make bread, which everyone eats together at the end of the performance.

The Vento Forte theatre, built by the company, was a project of communal architecture. It has large sheds, three theatres, open spaces for outdoor performances, and a bandstand for music. The company's performances are expressive, both visually and musically, and are based on movement. They tell small stories in which the pieces connect like those of a puzzle. The actors use a form of interpretation that is nonclassic and spontaneous, and this gives the impression that the action is being created on the spur of the moment.

The group currently continues to produce creative theatre that is nonconformist and noncommercial. Their goal is to build a sensitive theatre, beyond the commercial and industrial spheres, and to preserve their craftsman-like values while trying to bring theatre to the general population. Vento Forte offers different courses and workshops, spreading their ideas and giving rise to other independent works. The plays developed by Krugli and Vento Forte use a poetical language that is lyrical and moving, emphasizing sensitivity to find humanity's roots. Children's theatre has a special meaning to Krugli: "I believe that the theatre we create is not only for children, that would be too limiting. What we do has different interpretations which reach the adult, the adolescent, and also the child."

Hombu

When Vento Forte moved to Sao Paulo, another group, Hombu, was formed in Rio de Janeiro. The five founding members had worked with Krugli but preferred a company with no central leader. The writing, direction, and staging of works would be a collaborative effort. The group utilized puppets and live music, and all actors played an instrument or sang.

Hombu presented its first play in 1977. *A gaiola de Avetsiu* (*Avatsiu Bird Cage*) was inspired by a native tale called "Hombu," which means "come to see us" in the language of the Crao Indians. The company took this as its name. The play tells the story of birds locked in a cage that discover they can free themselves through their singing. The piece played for two years, during which time it toured through most of Brazil.

In 1979 they staged *Fala palhaco* (*Speak, Clown*), also created and directed collectively; the play's theme was the group's own difficulty in staying together and making theatre. This production toured the country for several years and then traveled to Europe; it also won several awards. *Ou isto ou aquilo* (*Or This or That*), presented in 1981, was different from Hombu's previous plays in that it was a staged version of the poems of Cecilia Meireles. In 1983 the company staged an adult play that was not well received and left them with a large debt. In 1984 they were invited to an international festival in New Orleans to present *A gaiola de Avatsiu*. The next year they participated in the Lion Festival in France. On their return to Brazil the group began to disintegrate. Financial difficulties finally forced the members to look for jobs in other fields.

Hombu developed important works in its ten years of existence, and the company's demise signaled the end of an era during which it was possible to survive in the theatrical profession with little more than a group of people committed to an idea.

Navegando

The company called Navegando (Sailing) was an outgrowth of work developed by the group's director, Lucia Coelho, through her experience as an arts teacher at Colegio Bennett in Rio de Janeiro. After taking courses with Krugli and Domingues, Coelho introduced puppets and masks in her arts classes and then began to stage amateur performances in her school. At the beginning she staged historical plays and works by Maria Clara Machado; however, she was always exploring new ways to present and express her views.

Her work changed in 1965, when, together with other teachers, she founded Teatro Amador Benetense (Benetense's Amateur Theatre, or TAB), an independent theatre school where the collective model was followed. Students experienced all phases of mounting productions and chose their own style of staging and presentation. Coelho noticed that many of her students, when given the chance, went beyond the text and introduced improvisation, theatre games, and play into their productions. Coelho kept track of these experiments and later wrote a book about them.

Motivated by the work done in her school and her desire to reach larger audiences, Coelho went on to found Nucleo de Artes da Urca (Arts Center of Urca, or NAU). At first NAU was a children's school, with one division dedicated to mounting productions. The school offered theatre courses taught by former members of TAB. This school was the origin of Navegando, and the group's first production, *Ta na hora, ta na hora* (*It's Time, It's Time*) was presented here.

Navegando continued to present this piece for two years, traveling throughout the country and winning several awards in the process. Some of their later pieces are as follows: *Duvide o do* (*Doubt the Do*), 1979; *Passa passa tempo* (*Pass, Pass Time*), 1980; *Cara ou coroa* (*Heads or Tails*), 1982; *Dito e feito* (*Said and Done*), 1984. This last play was inspired by Brecht's *The Caucasian Chalk Circle*. Except for the last title, these plays were all written by Coelho and Caique Botkay, who also composed the music and wrote the lyrics for all the songs that are included in the works. Navegando developed a style of production that emphasized light, color, form, sound, and movement, and that reached children through their senses. The use of puppets also characterizes the work of this company.

Manhas e Manias

Many members of Manhas e Manias (Whims and Fixed Ideas) came from Tablado, Maria Clara Machado's theatre company, but brought with them different influences such as work in experimental group theatres and in the Sao Paulo circus school, where they learned acrobatics and magic tricks. The company adopted a circus style, in which the emphasis was on action. Much less verbal than other companies, the group preferred to use elements of surprise and magic to reach its audience. The company's first production, *Recordacoes do futuro* (*Remembrances from the Future*), was performed for adults.

While looking for a theatre in which to present the play, Manhas e Manias was invited to prepare a children's play. They adapted the adult play, which, with some changes, became the first in a series of productions titled "Shows de Variedades Manhas e Manias" ("Variety Show of Whims and Fixed Ideas"). In this piece the actors combined magic, acrobatics, clowning, music, dance, and humor. The style was loose and spontaneous, with maximum use of the body and movement and a minimum of spoken words.

This production won the group several awards, and with it they traveled throughout Brazil. Then they decided to become involved in children's theatre, for which they prepared their second work in 1981, *Brincando com fogo* (*Playing with Fire*), also a collective creation but under the direction of Jose Lavine, one of the founders. The same circus elements of humor and play were utilized, but they deepened the emotional content by showing a child's world day by day, and underscoring the child's fears and fantasies. In the piece they refused to take a protective or paternalistic attitude toward childhood.

The group left Rio de Janeiro for Sao Paulo, where they obtained a six-month contract with Centro Cultural Sesc Pompeia (Cultural Center Sesc Pompeia). During this time they presented performances almost daily, and also developed courses and workshops and staged plays with the students. It was an intense time for the company, in terms of creativity and accomplishment.

In addition to the emergence of new companies, the sixties and seventies were important in that new concepts of dramatization arose as well as advances in the fundamental search for methods of making theatre meaningful. All the groups discussed above were involved to some degree with the concept of collectivism, and they experimented with it by transforming themselves into small family units that lived and worked together. They divided equally their profits and losses and organized their productions around a central group. This model worked because then it was possible to stage a production with little money. Of the four groups, only Vento Forte is still active, which is not a chance occurrence: this was the only group to own its own theatre. The other three groups disbanded when their sixties idealism and lack of economic foresightedness came into conflict with the fiscal realities of the late seventies and eighties.

THE 1980s

Feliz Meu Bem

The group called Feliz Meu Bem (Happy My Sweetheart) was founded by a diverse group of people who had as their common goal the development of a children's theatre company. Both author and director Tonio Carvalho and scenographer, actor, and director Vicente Maiolino (together with others who gradually became part of the group) were looking for different ways of narrating and combining puppets, music, and poetry. They tried to work directly with the audience's emotions, believing that children have the capability to establish a rapport with any situation presented onstage.

In 1981 Feliz Meu Bem presented *As tres luas de junho e uma de julho* (*The Three June Moons and the One of July*), in which they mixed puppets and live actors in order to recover and understand the Brazilian spirit. The play was based on old native festivals held in June, which today are celebrated only in the country, and was presented in streets and village squares. *As sete quedas do meu pobre coracao* (*The Seven Falls of My Poor Heart*), about the destruction of the Seven Falls Waterfall, was presented in 1983. The group managed to create a playful production without being either didactic or demagogic.

In 1984 they presented *O misterio do boi Surubim* (*The Mystery of Bull Surubim*), inspired by the poet Fernando Pessoas and the folk tales of Bumba-Meu-Boi. In the same year the group also produced an open-air Christmas play in which the birth of Christ was juxtaposed with the birth of a child in the circus. The 1985 production of *A idade do sonho* (*The Dream Age*) had as part of the scenery an enormous window through which came the wishes of one girl, repressed until now by her aunts. In 1986 the company presented *O ouro das estrelas* (*The Gold from the Stars*).

As it was developing, Feliz Meu Bem intuitively realized that it had to experiment with its format if it expected to ensure its existence. Some members began to perform outside the group; not all worked on the same plays; others became involved in puppet theatre and stopped performing live roles. They produced a play written by a northeastern author, reinforcing the idea that it was necessary to encourage communication among the different states and groups. One group within the company currently works primarily with museums, for which it performs a piece called *Visitacoes Animadas* (*Animated Visits*), based on the museum's collection.

Tapa

The seeds for Teatro Amador Producoes Artisticas (Amateur Theatre Artistic Productions, or Tapa) began in 1974 in meetings at the Pontifical Catholic

University, a university in Rio de Janeiro where the members participated in theatre courses and staged amateur plays. Tapa became professional in 1979 with a children's play, *Apenas um conto de fadas* (*Only a Fairy Tale*), directed by Eduardo Tolentino, organizer and creator of the group. Since it began Tapa has worked in three areas: adult theatre, children's theatre, and adolescent theatre. Its goal is mainly educational and the scripts are generally taken from national classics that examine and explore the country at different periods in its history. The company performs in schools and promotes discussions with the students.

After *Apenas um conto de fadas* the company presented works including *O anel e a rosa* (*The Ring and the Flower*), 1981; *Tempo quente na floresta azul* (*Hot Time in the Blue Forest*), 1982; *Pinoquio* (*Pinocchio*), 1984; *Beto e Teca* (*Beto and Teca*), 1985; *Joao e Maria* (*Hansel and Gretel*), 1987. Today Tapa has about 100 members who perform in both Rio de Janeiro and Sao Paulo. Its children's unit has won several awards and traveled throughout the state.

PUPPET THEATRE

Though not specifically geared toward children, puppet theatre is used by many children's theatre companies, and puppets are an essential and important part of the history of children's theatre in Brazil. Although it appears simple, working with puppets is extremely difficult and delicate, and the actor has to develop movements that are studied and harmonious. Festivals have been fundamental in the promotion of this art, the first coming in 1966 in Rio de Janeiro. In 1973 the Associacao Brasileira de Teatro de Bonecos (Brazilian Association of Puppet Theatres) was founded. Traveling festivals stimulate the creation of puppet companies, create centers in each city they pass through, promote interchange among states, and encourage foreign groups to visit. Nowadays only the Puppet Festival can boast international participants. This exchange serves to fill part of the void that exists because there are no specialized puppet theatre courses or schools in Brazil.

PROBLEMS

Despite the increase in the number of performances presented in Rio de Janeiro and Sao Paulo, where it is possible to find at least thirty children's plays being staged each weekend and where the number of opening nights reaches eighty per year, the quality of some of the work is questionable. Many of these plays are staged purely for commercial reasons. Others present distorted views of children or develop themes that are simplistic and insulting. These productions do not take into consideration the intelligence and critical capabilities of the child.

In the theatrical field itself there is also prejudice toward children's theatre: it is seen as a lesser art form, easier to make and produce, and without economic rewards. In many instances children's theatre becomes simply a bridge to reach the more lucrative field of adult theatre. In addition, there are no theatre buildings designed to fit the unique specifications of a juvenile audience, and not all theatres allow simultaneous productions of adult and child plays. When they do, they restrict rehearsal time and the use of technical facilities.

Finally, there is a tremendous lack of media coverage for children's theatre. Articles in newspapers and reports on television are rare, and publicity is almost impossible to attain for smaller productions. This has generated an increase in "superproductions" that hire famous actors and invest thousands of dollars in scenery and costumes but do not take such care with the content or style of the presentation. The lack of specialized reviews is also a problem, since they could speak to the problems outlined above.

CONCLUSION

It becomes difficult to establish only one conclusion about the course of children's theatre in Brazil, since there is no study proving its impact on young audiences. During the twenty years of dictatorship in the country, theatre suffered economic and political restrictions: the speeches became metaphoric, there was no place for experimentation and boldness, investigation of new forms froze. Children's theatre, however, was spared these limitations because it did not have the same commitment to political and economic realities. Most of the workers in this area had no great expectation of surviving solely in children's theatre. Because it was not politically threatening to the government, as adult theatre was, it could be more daring and experimental. Its creativity resulted in a scenic boldness never seen before. Several groups developed important and innovative investigations into the uses of language, combining puppets, masks, shadows, music, and other resources that the adult theatre had not utilized for a long time. Ironically, given the time, children's theatre had the freedom to develop its most creative work.

Denise Crispun
Translated by Sulamita Scharfstein Donnolo

Canada, English-speaking

HISTORY

Professional theatre for children in English-speaking Canada is a relatively young art form in a relatively young nation that challenges practitioners by the vast distances between its low-population centers.

The first company was founded in Vancouver, British Columbia (B.C.), when Joy Coghill and Myra Benson established Holiday Theatre in 1953. Within a few years their weekend and holiday entertainments were expanded to include small touring shows of fairy tales and children's classics by authors such as Charlotte Chorpenning and Nicholas Stuart Grey. Later plays by Marge Adleberg, Brian Way, and Jean Anouilh were added for high school audiences. A trouping arm composed of professional pioneer artists toured live theatre under difficult physical conditions, often to first-time audiences, throughout B.C. During its twenty-two years of existence Holiday Theatre was transformed several times. In 1966 it merged with the adult regional Playhouse Theatre and was renamed Holiday Playhouse. Later, under the same administration, it was again renamed; it now became Playhouse Holiday theatre.

Under Gloria Shapiro-Latham, the Playhouse Theatre Center (1971) began experimenting with theatre-in-education (TIE) techniques, which had originated in England. Playhouse Holiday's weekend shows in the city had been dropped from the repertory in 1973. Then in 1977/78 financial and artistic pressures forced the company to cease operations after a TIE presentation for a group of teachers. By this time three new children's companies had begun to serve the needs of B.C.'s younger audience: Carousel, Green Thumb, and Kaleidoscope (these companies are discussed later).

The Manitoba Theatre Center (MTC), Canada's first regional theatre, opened in Winnipeg in 1958 and until 1972 included children's theatre as part of its production mandate. MTC premiered James Reaney's *Names and Nicknames*, directed by John Hirsch and Robert Sherrin. There is currently no regular policy on theatre for the young.

Anne of Green Gables, by Norman Campbell and Donald Harron from the novel by L. M. Montgomery, opened the Charlottetown Festival on Prince Edward Island in 1965 and has drawn large audiences ever since. Unlike forty-five-minute school-touring plays that are performed in gymnasiums, *Anne of Green Gables* can afford to be longer, with more elaborate theatrical design and production features.

Toronto had no professional children's theatre until Susan Rubes started what became the Young People's Theatre. The Globe Theatre (1966) in Regina began exclusively as a company for the young and is still a vibrant group that runs an adult subscription season as well.

Founded in 1966, Actor's Showcase, Winnipeg, has served the province since its inception. There are annual tours, often the only live theatre that reaches rural communities in Manitoba. The repertory varies from new Canadian scripts and international works to issue-related plays, including the long-running *Feeling Yes, Feeling No*, about sexual abuse, written by Dennis Foon.

The Citadel Theatre and Theatre Calgary added children's touring companies to their regional theatres: Citadel-on-Wheels (1968) and Caravan Theatre, later Stagecoach Players (1977). Citadel produced many of Brian Way's participation plays (*The Hat, The Decision, Clown I*, and *On Trial*) as well as works by Canadian playwright Isabelle Ford. The company traveled to isolated Arctic regions, presenting a variety of Canadian scripts, including those of Rex Deverell, Len Peterson, and Paddy Campbell. Theatre Calgary formed Caravan Theatre under Joel Miller in 1968; it produced its first touring production, *Hang On to Your Lid*, by John Murrell, under the direction of David Lander. A new artistic director, Rick McNair, who later went on to become artistic director for the adult stage of Theatre Calgary, changed the name of the company from Caravan Theatre to Stagecoach Players. McNair wrote his own scripts for young audiences, including *Dr. Bernardo's 5 Pioneers, Chagall*, and *Beowulf*. Both Stagecoach Players and Citadel cited financial reasons for the demise of their children's companies in 1985.

In the 1970s the following companies were founded (some of which are still active today): Alberta Theatre Projects, Calgary, Alberta (1972); The Carousel Players, St. Catherine's, Ontario (1972); The Mermaid Theatre, Wolfville, Nova Scotia (1972); Prairie Theatre Exchange, Winnipeg, Manitoba (1973); Kaleidoscope Theatre, Victoria, B.C. (1974); Green Thumb Theatre, Vancouver, B.C. (1975).

The emergence of more than a dozen theatres for young people in this decade was the result of Canada's favorable economic climate, increased government support, and the availability of trained students who had graduated from university drama departments. A new touring company, added to the Bastion Theatre, Victoria, B.C., in 1971, offers a two-show tour to elementary and secondary schools throughout the province and includes both traditional and new scripts.

Artistic and administrative directors Elizabeth and Colin Gorrie have devoted their talents to Kaleidoscope, a company founded by Paul Littich. This versatile group, which uses a blend of creative movement and sound, tours to schools and performs with symphonies and in theatres throughout B.C. and other parts of Canada.

Alberta Theatre Project (ATP) was founded in 1972 by Paddy Campbell, Doug Riske, and Lucille Wagner to produce historical plays about southern Alberta. The works have been presented to schoolchildren bused to the Canmore Opera House in Heritage Park, Calgary. ATP was the first Canadian company for young audiences to have its own home, where child audiences experienced a professional proscenium stage with traditional design, sound, and lighting.

In its early years ATP had unique interests—the Canadian prairie experience (*Jake and the Kid*, by W. O. Mitchell) and social issues such as the exploitation of the Canadian Indian (*Cyclone Jack*, by Carol Bolt). Other premieres included *Under the Arch*, book and lyrics by Paddy Campbell and music by William Skolnik; *A Very Small Rebellion*, by Jan Truss; and *The Devils' Instrument*, by W. O. Mitchell. During her ATP-funded residency as a children's playwright, Sharon Pollack wrote *The Wreck of the National Line Car* and *Chautauqua Spelt E-N-E-R-G-Y*. As the adult season expanded, ATP eventually eliminated children's shows altogether. What had begun as a quality company for children evolved into a regional theatre for adults, which moved into the new Calgary Center for the Performing Arts.

Carousel Theatre in Vancouver mounts touring plays for young audiences and also performs in its permanent space, Waterfront Theatre, which it shares with two other groups. Artistic director Elizabeth Ball values this home base and sees it as an important part of helping to develop a theatre-going habit for her young audience.

During the 1970s TIE became more widely used in Canadian schools and was incorporated into existing programs by such companies as Playhouse Holiday, Carousel Theatre, and Theatre Direct in Toronto (founded in 1976). Theatre Direct, committed to TIE principles, produced *Friends*, by Tom Bentley-Fisher (with Patricia Grant), about day-care practices, and *Getting Wrecked*, by Tom Walmsley, about drug abuse. The company generally produces its own scripts and tours schools with historical dramatizations (*All for Beaver Hats: The Story of the Canadian Fur Trade*) and explorations of social issues (*How I Wonder What You Are*, which deals with the mentally handicapped).

Jabberwock and Sons Full Theatre Company (1980) tours schools, libraries, and community centers in Ontario, Prince Edward Island, and Nova Scotia. It incorporates dance, story-telling, masks, music, and puppetry into its presentations, one of which was *Cart Before the Horse*, a tongue-in-cheek look at transportation. Persephone Youtheatre, Saskatoon (1982), tours to schools and community centers throughout Saskatchewan with fantasy and socially relevant plays (*Pride Saskatchewan*, about teenagers and marijuana).

CURRENT STATE OF CHILDREN'S THEATRE

The state of contemporary children's theatre in English-speaking Canada is healthy, with a wide range of organizational and operational styles. Money to finance companies comes from some or all of five sources: ticket sales/tours, federal Canada Council grants, provincial cultural service departments, private foundations, and contributions from individuals and corporations. The larger a theatre's budget, the more time and staff it spends on generating funds from all five sources.

Some companies run school tours and a season at home in a permanent theatre space. Young People's Theatre (YPT) is the largest operation of this kind. The 1977/78 subscription season (October-May) in Toronto offered *A Christmas Carol*; four chamber concerts; *Jacob Two-Two Meets the Hooded Fang*, by Mordecai Richler; *Willing the Squowse*, by Ted Allan; *Getting Through*, from England's Theatre Center; *The Effect of Gamma Rays on Man-in-the-Moon Marigolds*, by Paul Zindel; *Parasols*, by Quebec's Theatre de las Marmaille; and *The Prince and the Pauper*, by Mark Twain. During this same season YPT toured *Hilary's Birthday*, *Skin*, and *A Midsummer Night's Dream*.

Some companies offer only schools tours, as is the case with Quest Theatre, Calgary (1984). It is a modest operation with a committed staff of three, including artistic director Duval Lang. Many small companies have no permanent theatre space and undergo grueling tours to rural areas with a repertory of one to three plays. These companies are usually staffed by ten or fewer persons, including the actors. And yet theatre for young audiences constitutes 25 percent of all professional theatre performances in Canada. For the personnel involved, working in the field of children's theatre is a labor of love, donated to the thousands of children who delight in seeing live plays with their heightened reality and imaginative possibilities.

Companies offer a variety of pre- and post-performance materials, and some give workshops for students and teachers related to the play and drama, in general. *Feeling Yes, Feeling No*, requires a team of actor-teachers who spend several sessions with parents, teachers, and students both in preparation for and as follow-up to the theatre experience itself.

A positive and exciting phenomenon in Canada is the emergence of International Children's Festivals of Theatre and Arts across the country. In 1972, under the chairmanship of Joyce Doolittle, the Canadian branch of ASSITEJ organized a highly successful international children's theatre festival in Montreal to coincide with the biannual ASSITEJ Congress. Plays from many nations were performed, including works from Russia, Romania, United States, and Canada. ASSITEJ has offered opportunities for worldwide exchange of ideas in theatre for young audiences. Joyce Doolittle, professor at the University of Calgary, Alberta, and a tireless worker for children's professional theatre, was Canada's ASSITEJ representative from 1969 to 1979, during which time she became the international organization's vice-president. She has nurtured and disseminated ideals and information in the field as author, editor, and theatre artist that have benefited individuals and companies both in Canada and abroad.

In 1976 the Vancouver Heritage Festival Society launched its first Children's Festival as the cultural contribution to the U.N. conference on Human Settlements. Well received, the festival continues to grow annually and to act as a showcase for a variety of nations' performances for children. Presented in red and white tents in Vanier Park, it has included since 1987 an international symposium on arts programming for young audiences, with speakers, panelists, and resource people under the auspices of the Canadian Institute of the Arts for Young Audiences. Producer Ernie Flavell is now looking for a permanent home for this high-quality art, music, and theatre celebration.

The success of the Vancouver Children's Festival spawned similar festivals in Edmonton (1981), using six stages in the downtown core; in Toronto (1982), which produced a seven-day festival for children three to sixteen years old; and in Calgary (1987), where the goal was to present the arts so that they would become an integral part of the audience's lives. Some companies travel across Canada in May and June to perform the wide festival circuit. Both Canadian audiences and children's theatre professionals benefit by comparing and contrasting their work with that of successful companies from all over the world.

One aspect of theatre for young audiences that needs further professional attention is the area of criticism. Critics from the media have little or no training in children's theatre, which results in superficial reviews of productions. Artists and audiences would be better served with educated and sophisticated criticism.

REPRESENTATIVE COMPANIES

The Globe Theatre

Ken and Sue Kramer founded the Globe Theatre (1966) with the major purpose of touring participation plays in Saskatchewan schools. For six years they produced works by Brian Way such as *The Dog and the Stone* and *The Rescue*; these participation plays, developmentally appropriate to the age groups for which they were presented, were performed by small casts on flat floors close to the audience. Starting in 1968 the Globe gradually began producing plays for adult audiences as well. In 1972/73 the company included Rex Deverell's *Shortshrift* in its season, and Deverell was appointed playwright in residence, the first appointment of this kind in Canada. He has continued to write his prairie plays with social relevance for both youth and adult audiences.

After performing in the Saskatchewan Arts Center for three years, the Globe acquired an abandoned bank building in downtown Regina, which became its permanent home in 1973. Under artistic director Ken Kramer and associate director Brian Way the Globe is a unique example of a company that continues to successfully serve its two diverse audiences (youth and adult) with quality theatre and a thriving artistic ensemble.

Young People's Theatre

YPT, now a center for performing arts in Toronto, was founded in 1966 by Susan Rubes to present plays on weekends and holidays in theatres and gradually expanded to touring in schools. By 1970 multiple companies presented plays for specific age groups. The repertory included bright minimusicals such as *The Popcorn Man*, by Dodi Robb and Pat Patterson. From 1966 to 1970, as was the vogue, Brian Way's participation plays were part of YPT's elementary school repertory, replaced in later years by Canadian plays by Carol Bolt (*Tangleflags,*) Betty Jane Wylie (*The Old Woman and the Peddlar,*) Len Peterson (*Almighty Voice,*) and the popular social-issue scripts of Dennis Foon.

In 1976 Rubes leased the historic 1881 railway stablehouse and then raised money to renovate it as a theatre of 468 seats. After five successful seasons a second theatre, The Nathan Cohen Studio, with 175 seats, was added. YPT also boasts school matinees as well as family evenings, a theatre school, and a summer camp. The repertory now includes classics (*The Taming of the Shrew*), musicals (*Jacob Two-Two and the Hooded Fang*, by Richler), and new Canadian works (*The Village of Idiots*, by John Lazarus).

Peter Moss, artistic director of YPT since 1980, has leaned heavily toward "family plays" for the over-twelve age group: *Dracula, Look Back in Anger,* and *Of Mice and Men* have been some of his choices. These are not considered traditional children's theatre fare in Canada, but Moss sees his mandate as a call to produce professional theatre for families. One of his goals is to overcome the image of theatre *only* for children. He increased the theatre's season to sixteen plays and mounts two productions in each theatre simultaneously, one that performs during the day and one in the evening. The theatre's budget now amounts to $2.2 million, and it receives subsidies from all levels of government that total 37 percent of its operating costs. Ten percent of its budget comes from private contributions and the remaining money is earned at the box office. Future prospects for YPT include moving into television and video work, with Carol Bolt as dramaturg for a TV Ontario program.

Mermaid Theatre

In the Maritimes, Wolfville, Nova Scotia, the Mermaid Theatre was born of a $12,000 grant from the federal Opportunities for Youth program in 1971. Founded by Evelyn Garbary and later joined by administrator Sara Lee Lewis and designer Tom Miller, Mermaid produced plays written by writer-director Garbary (*The Invisible Hunter, Glooscap's People, The Brothers, The Journey,* based on Indian Micmac legends indigenous to Nova Scotia). From its inception the theatre has been closely tied to Miller's designs. His puppets, masks, and costumes are strong images and often provide the primary ingredient in the company's style. Actors who work for Mermaid must have skills in mask, mime, and movement.

Mermaid is a touring company, performing in Nova Scotia schools and community halls as well as in Europe and the eastern United States and across Canada. After Garbary's departure in 1982 Graham Whitehead became artistic director. He is the company's writer-adaptor and, along with composer Steven Naylor, has collaborated on scripts for *Just-So Stories, Peter and the Wolf*, and *The Red Ball*. Whitehead's works incorporate original live or recorded music and, for the younger viewers, multimedia components. Mermaid's budget has grown in recent years to over $500,000.

Green Thumb Theatre

Opposite in style and content to Mermaid is Green Thumb Theatre of Vancouver, B.C. Cofounded in 1975 by Dennis Foon and Jane Howard-Baker, its mandate was to develop and produce original Canadian plays for young audiences. The issue-related script has become Green Thumb's focal point—*New Canadian Kid, Mirror Game*, and *Raft Baby*, all by Foon. The company leans toward works that confront significant social issues (e.g., living below the poverty line in *One in a Million* by David Holman). However realistic the dialogue and believable the characters, these plays don't offer easy solutions to life's problems, although comedy often helps the story move along.

Offering strategies for the prevention of sexual abuse of children, *Feeling Yes, Feeling No*, first mounted by Green Thumb in 1983, was sponsored in its schools tour by the Vancouver Foundation. Subsequently the production (as well as many of Green Thumb's other pieces) has been produced by fifty-three companies in five countries and has been translated into French and Spanish. The National Film Board has made films for children and teachers of *Feeling Yes, Feeling No*. In 1985, author Foon was presented with the British Theatre Award for Best Theatre for the Young. Green Thumb, meantime, has toured Canada, the United States, Europe, and the Pacific Rim, quickly growing into a significant children's theatre company while retaining its vision and artistic quality.

PLAYWRIGHTS

Canadian playwrights who write for youth emerged after the 1960s when companies had firmly established themselves, for with this sense of permanence came the need to put the work of Canadians on stage. Playhouse Theatre produced Eric Nicol's *Beware the Quickly Who* (1965), about a boy's and a nation's identity; this was a Canadian Centennial Commission. The tradition of original scripts for radio has been strong in Canada, and several radio dramatists also write stage plays for children; they include Betty Lambert, who wrote *The Riddle Machine* for Holiday Theatre; Dodi Robb and Pat Patterson, who wrote *The Dandy Lion*; Len Peterson, with *Almighty Voice* for YPT; and W. O. Mitchell, whose *Jake and the Kid* was produced by Alberta Theatre Projects.

As a result of the federal Canada Council's subsidy of professional theatre for young audiences in 1971, more children's theatre companies emerged and more plays were written for these companies to perform. The federal Local

Initiatives Program gave birth to the Playwright's Co-op, now the Playwrights Union of Canada. The publication of these plays for children has made subsequent performances possible, although Canadian children's theatres tend to produce more new scripts than old, often because members have the opportunity to write and tailor scripts to the needs and resources of their company. Established playwrights for the adult theatre also write for children, as is the case with Sharon Pollock's *Prairie Dragons* (1987), about two young girls growing up on the prairies in 1916.

The Chalmers Children's Play Award for the best play performed in Toronto carries a cash prize (although of less value than its adult counterpart) and is judged by theatre professionals. Past awards have been presented to Marcel Sabourin's *Pleurer Pour Rire* in 1983; Jim Betts' *Mystery of Oak Island Treasure* in 1984; Colin Thomas' *One Thousand Cranes* in 1985; Duncan McGregor's *Running the Gauntlet* in 1986; and Dennis Foon's *Skin* in 1987. The major publisher of children's plays is Playwrights Canada in Toronto.

BIBLIOGRAPHY

Canadian Children's Literature (Nos. 8 and 9) (1977).
The Canadian Theatre Review (Nos. 10 and 41) (Spring 1976).
Davis, Desmond. *Theatre for Young People*. Don Mills, Ontario: Musson Book Co., 1981.
Doolittle, Joyce, and Zina Barnieh. *A Mirror of Our Dreams*. Vancouver, B.C.: Talonbooks, 1979.

PLAYS

A Collection of Canadian Plays. Vol. 4. Edited by Susan Rubes. Toronto, Ontario: Simon and Pierre, 1975.
Eight Plays for Young People. Edited by Joyce Doolittle. Edmonton, Alberta: Newest Press, 1984.
Kids Plays. Toronto, Ontario: Playwrights Canada, 1980.
Six Fantasy Plays for Children. Edited by Joyce Doolittle. Alberta: Red Deer College Press, 1988.

Zina Barnieh

Canada, French-speaking

HISTORY

Since 1973 children's drama and theatre have developed at an impressive pace in Quebec. The production of scripts and performances has consistently increased; the companies have grown to become independent entities; and festivals have been organized regularly. Slowly but surely, this theatre has developed original forms of writing and staging and has expanded the concept of audience to include both the three-year-old and the teenager. Consequently it has circumscribed a specific artistic field, identified audiences to be reached while remaining attuned to the exacting demands of dramatic writing and theatrical realization.

Children's theatre in Quebec first developed within the administrative structure and according to the artistic policies established by adult theatre companies.[1] Les Compagnons de Saint-Laurent, le Théâtre-Club, and les Apprentis-Sorciers, although different as to their artistic choices, have shared common attitudes toward children's theatre; they considered producing only when they had achieved financial stability and had moved into their permanent theatre spaces. They gave their children's theatre sections specific names and chose scripts in accordance with their main stage repertory (Léon Chancerel for les Compagnons, improvisations and adaptations of Guignol texts for les Apprentis-Sorciers). The performances, presented mainly on weekends, aimed at entertaining their spectators. To the companies' great satisfaction, audiences grew and the number of performances doubled. Thus, from 1950 to 1965, children's theatre gradually took its place in the developing *québécois* theatre.

A serious problem that faced actors and directors during those fifteen years was the lack of worthwhile scripts, which prompted les Apprentis-Sorciers to promote improvised theatre, and le Thèâtre-Club and la Roulotte (city of Montreal's itinerant summer stage inaugurated in 1953) to adapt tales of Perrault and Andersen. The first original script to be produced was Luan Asslani's *Les Trois*

Désirs de Coquelicot (The Three Wishes of Coquelicot)[2] (Thèâtre-Club, 1960[3]),
featuring a young hero whose encounters with elves and fairies teach him a sense
of generosity toward others.

The first company to devote itself entirely to young audiences was le Théâtre
pour Enfants de Québec (TEQ, 1965–1970). Ably directed by Pauline Geoffrion,
it resolutely adopted a policy favoring the creation of original plays. Beginning
as a division of l'Estoc, a small experimental theatre, TEQ soon acquired full
autonomy and commissioned Monique Corriveau, a well-known author of children's novels, to write puppet plays. In her five resulting scripts, recurring
characters and story lines appear that are clearly inspired by existing children's
literature and by the nascent television series for the young. So as to widen the
spectator's experience, Geoffrion included performances by live actors in the
TEQ's season; she attracted professional performers and provided them with
opportunities for extensive regional and provincial touring. Authors Roland Lepage, Patrick Mainville, and Pierre Morency wrote for TEQ and the latter's
Tournebire et le Malin Frigo (Tournebire and the Cunning Fridge, 1969)[4] remains exemplary of that period: it calls for audience participation, shows heroes
in courageous adventures against mysterious enemies, features robots, and is set
in an absent-minded professor's laboratory.

Despite a strong management and a successful artistic policy, TEQ's subsidy
was not renewed by the Ministry of Cultural Affairs in 1969. Geoffrion refused
to compromise, and TEQ closed its doors. Its experience, however, was not
wasted. From 1973 on, autonomous companies and theatre collectives would
form and opt more and more for scripts and performances specifically created
for young audiences. Before this decisive turning point two established companies integrated the production of children's plays into their adult-oriented
structures: Le Théâtre du Rideau Vert (Montreal), which did so quite successfully, and Le Théâtre du Trident (Quebec city), which proved itself incapable
of a true commitment, despite François Depatie's efforts.

Le Théâtre du Rideau Vert dedicated itself to children's plays with exemplary
enthusiasm from 1967 to 1978. Its magnificent opening presentation was that of
Maeterlinck's *L'Oiseau bleu (The Blue Bird)*; afterward it offered not less than
twelve productions in four seasons, five of which were of new scripts by Roland
Lepage and Marcel Sabourin. In 1970 André Cailloux became artistic director
of the youth section. From then on puppet shows by Nicole Lapointe and Pierre
Régimbald and productions of André Cailloux's scripts[5] were programmed each
year, and were given on weekends as well as on schooldays. Magic and the
supernatural appeal to Cailloux: objects appear and disappear, characters are
constantly and mysteriously transformed, space and time are manipulated with
great ease in story lines that, in essence, remain close to the fairy tale. Lapointe
and Regimbald worked on the actual tales of Perrault and Grimm, with their
hand and string puppets constantly contributing an atmosphere of delightful
festivity.

This first period of achievement shows how eager theatre artists were to share their art with young audiences and to what extent fairy tales constituted the lot for young spectators. It soon became evident that this form of theatre could survive, grow, and arrive at an interesting level of performance only if it became artistically and administratively independent.

In 1973/74 several events contributed toward bringing together the most active builders of "le nouveau théâtre pour la jeunesse." A writers' workshop was organized by Monique Rioux in which authors, actors, and children together created characters and plots that spoke of the children themselves. *Cé tellement "cute" des enfants (But Children are so "Cute,"* 1975),[6] by Marie-Francine Hébert, was directly influenced by these workshops. A pioneering play, it shows children playing in back alleys on a school holiday and failing to conform to their elders' idealized view of them. It uses realistic language and amounts to a social document and a political statement. In 1974 meetings were convened to discuss the ends, the means, and the qualities of children's theatre. Also, the first (of eleven) Festival *québécois de théâtre pour enfants* was held in Longueuil. In the same cooperative spirit the companies have since established their own theatre space, the *Maison québécoise du théâtre pour l'enfance et la jeunesse*, which opened in 1984.

Companies still active today were founded in or shortly after 1973: Théâtre de la Marmaille, 1973; Théâtre de Carton, 1973; Théâtre de l'Oeil, 1973; Théâtre de Quartier, 1975; Théâtre du Carrousel, 1975; Théâtre du Gros Mécano, 1976; Théâtre de l'Avant-Pays, 1976; Théâtre l'Arrière-Scène, 1976; Théâtre Petit à Petit, 1978. This new children's theatre movement broke with the past, especially as concerns the choice of themes, characters, and plots by advocating the belief that theatre is not merely superficial entertainment, but an art of experimentation and focus on progressive thematic content. They consider that young audiences are their best critics and their main source of inspiration.

THE REPERTORY

The most consistent trend in the writing of scripts can be described as political realism. The first of these plays were intended to make children conscious of pollution (*Tohu Bohu, [Hustle and Bustle]* l'Oeil, 1976) and of cooperation (*Le Toutatous [All to All]*, l'Oeil, 1978). Children themselves are active in *Un jeu d'enfants (Games Children Play*,[7] Quartier, 1979), in which they inquire about playground space in urban surroundings. *On n'est pas des enfants d'école (So You Think You're the Teacher)* by Gilles Gauthier[8] (Marmaille, 1979) stresses the fact that school is not the only place to learn and that school should encourage sharing and caring. *Pleurer pour rire, (Crying to Laugh*, Marmaille, 1981) by Marcel Sabourin,[9] considers as positive the free expression of emotions and of the sensual self, as does Théâtre de Carton's *Les enfants n'ont pas de sexe? (Is Sex for Kids?*, 1979).[10] Suzanne Lebeau, in writing *Les Petits Pouvoirs (Little Victories*, Carrousel, 1982),[11] questions the child-parent relationship, especially in those daily routines that can foster so much authoritarianism and tension.

At first linear and realistic, these plays of serious content grew to be more imaginative in their structure and fanciful in their sets and costumes. Visual stylization contributed to a lightening of tone in the writing but with no reduction of meaning.

Until 1975 participation plays were frequent. *Ti-Jean voudrait ben s'marier (Ti-Jean Would Like to Marry . . .* , Carrousel, 1974), by Suzanne Lebeau,[12] is an interesting example of this genre in its intelligent use of participation, folklore, and legends. This trend was increasingly criticized, however, and soon abandoned. *Une lune entre deux maisons (The Moon between Two Houses*, Carrousel, 1979) by the same author,[13] brings the spectators into sympathy and complicity with the characters. This last play, particularly successful internationally, was written for three- to six-year-olds, as were *Trois Petits Contes (Three Short Tales*, Gyroscope, 1980), by Louise LaHaye,[14] which happily mixes theatre with elements of a drama workshop, and *Coup de fil (Give a Ring*, Carton, 1986) by Diane Chevalier, which tells of the love of Danièle for her five-year-old son and of her longing for a love of her own age!

Poetic plays and theatre of the fantastic have not been too common in Quebec's theatre for the young. This style of writing appealed to Françoise Depatie, who directed his own plays: *Luclac dans l'inifni (Luclac in Inifinity [sic]*, Trident, 1975), about the zodiac signs and mathematics; *Le cadran et le cerf-volant (The Dial and the Kite*, Trident, 1974), about time and space; *En écoutant le coeur des pommes (From the Heart of Apples*, National Arts Center, 1976), on memory and the multiple self. Louise Bombardier, quite surrealistic in her approach, adapted a Tolkien short story about the artist—the suspicious one—in the city (*Le cas rare de Carat [Carat, the Unusual One]*, Gyroscope, 1979) and wrote *Dis-moi doux (Tell Me Softly*, Bêtes à coeur, 1974), about words and their emotional sounds.

Puppeteers have contributed excellent productions to children's theatre. *Regarde pour voir (Look and See*, l'Oeil, 1979)[15] shows how Lise and Jocelyn learn how to make puppets from secondhand materials and how to write and produce sketches. *Il était une fois en Nueve-France (Once Upon a Time in New France*, l'Avant-Pays, 1976), with the legendary hero Ti-Jean as main character, and *Une histoire de marionettes (A Puppets' Story*, l'Avant-Pays, 1979), on the art of theatre itself, were both written by Diane Bouchard. *La couleur chante un pays (Color of a Country*, l'Avant-Pays, 1981)[16] introduces its audience to 200 years of Canadian and Quebec paintings. This last production was aimed at the thirteen- to eighteen-year-old age group, who greatly enjoyed it.

Adolescents as a full-fledged audience have been catered to by Théâtre-Club, which produced classic plays for college students (1960–1963). In 1963 the Nouvelle Compagnie Théâtrale (NCT) was founded specifically to bring plays of the repertoire to students: Racine, Marivaux, Goldoni, Shakespeare, and Chekhov, among others, were presented as a complement to literature courses. In 1968–1969 the NCT opened its seasons to Quebec author Marcel Dubé and since then has considered contemporary authors as worthy of production alongside Molière, Ruzzante, and Strindberg. The NCT's style of production is quite coherent with its choice of repertory: actors, designers, and directors are chosen among professional artists of reputation.

To further enhance its selection of plays, NCT inaugurated Opération-Théâtre in 1971, commissioned authors to write plays about theatre (Jean Barbeau's *Le théâtre de la maintenance [Maintenance Theatre],*[17] 1972–1973), or invited companies presenting new scripts (Gros Mécano with *Titre provisoire: Romeo et Juliette [Working Title: Romeo and Juliette]* by Denis Chouinard and Shakespeare, 1984). To foster its well-established relationship with educators, the company regularly publishes *Les Cahiers de la NCT*, in which each play is studied from historical, sociological, theatrical, and literary points of view.

Contemporary creations aimed specifically at adolescents are essential: the thirteen- to eighteen-year-olds are not only students, but also people who are involved in social, cultural, and political realities. Authors and companies who have recognized this important truth have created several excellent plays. *Où est-ce qu'elle est ma gang? (Where Can I Find My Gang?*, Petit à Petit, 1982) by Louis-Dominique Lavigne,[18] underlined the gang phenomenon but, mostly, that the search for identity, for true relations to others, is basic to adolescence. *Sortie de secours (Emergency Exit*, Petit à Petit, 1984), by a collective of authors, shows youth running away from trying situations: no jobs, no dialogue, no understanding, no link to a society that bans differences and highlights "normality." *Au pied de la lettre (Literally Speaking*, Gros Mécano, 1981) by André Simard, spoke of the consequences of divorce and of new surroundings on two young characters. *Le sous-sol des Agnes (The Angel's Basement*, Carton, 1984) by Louis-Dominique Lavigne, used suicide as its theme. Most recently Alain Fournier's *Circuit fermé (Closed Circuit*, l'Atrium, 1986) touches on youth and prostitution. Theatre for adolescents chooses to speak loudly and clearly on youth's problems and preoccupations, with music and choreography as central theatrical elements.

Set and costume design, music, and lyrics have always been an integral part of theatre productions for young audiences. They have known a qualitative evolution from the timid attempts of 1974 to the quite effective realizations of 1985–1986. Michel Robidoux's music for *L'Umiak (Umiak, the Collective Boat*, Marmaille, 1984)[19] was widely acclaimed, as are the designs of Daniel Castonguay, who works mainly with Théâtre de la Marmaille, and Michel Demers, who is developing quite a modernistic style with Théâtre Petit à Petit and director Claude Poissant.

Theatre for young audiences can be said to present its spectators with experiences of life, of communication, and of artistic practice. In Quebec it has evolved in an exemplary way from 1950 to 1986. Its founders and builders have won the autonomy it needed to flourish by providing adequate administrative structures and personnel to carry out its tasks. Yet this form of theatre still runs up against the lack of a clear policy on ways to bring art to children. Should children and youth be exposed to the arts? In 1986 it is still the artists who stand out as the most ardent defenders of the democratization of artistic activity and its appreciation.

NOTES

1. Hélène Beauchamp, *Le théâtre pour enfants au Québec, 1950–1980* (Montréal: Hurtubise HMH, 1985). See also, by the same author, "Impressive beginnings—Petite histoire des grands événements en théâtre pour les jeunes au Québec," in *A Mirror of Our Dreams—Children and the Theatre in Canada*, eds. Joyce Doolittle and Zina Barnieh (Vancouver: Talon Books, 1979), 159–182; "Theatre for Children in Quebec—Complicity, Achievement and Adventure," *Canadian Theatre Review*, no. 41 (Winter 1984): 17–24; "Ecrire pour les jeunes publics—les multiples facettes d'une rélité d'apparence si simple," *Etudes littéraires* 18, no. 3 (Hiver, 1985): 159–179.

2. Luan Asslani, *Les Trois Désirs de Coquelicot*, suivi de *Le Retour de Coquelicot*, Montréal, Leméac, coll. "Théâtre pour enfants," 1973.

3. The date is that of the first stage production of the play. Most unpublished scripts are available at Centre d'essai des auteurs dramatiques, Montréal.

4. Pierre Morency, *Tournebire et le Malin Frigo* suivi de *Les Ecoles de bon Bazou*, Montréal, Leméac, coll. "Théâtre pour enfants," 1978.

5. André Cailloux, *Frizelis et Gros Guillaume* (1973), *Frizelis et la Fée Doduche* (1973), *L'Ile-au-sorcier* (1973), *François et l'oiseau du Brésil* suivi de *Tombé des étoiles* (1977), Montréal, Editions Leméac, coll. "Théâtre pour enfants."

6. Marie-Francine Hébert, *Cé tellement "cute" des enfants*, Montréal, Québec/Amérique, coll. "Jeunes Publics," 1980.

7. Théâtre de Quartier, *Un jeu d'enfants*, Montréal, Québec/Amérique, coll. "Jeunes Publics," 1980.

8. Gilles Gauthier, *On n'est pas des enfants d'école*, Montréal, Québec/Amérique, coll. "Jeunes Publics," 1984.

9. Marcel Sabourin, *Pleurer pour rire*, Montréal, VLB éditeur, 1984.

10. Théâtre de Carton, *Les Enfants n'ont pas de sexe?*, Montréal, Québec/Amérique, coll. "Jeunes Publics," 1981.

11. Suzanne Lebeau, *Les petits pouvoirs*, Montréal, Leméac, coll. "Théâtre pour enfants," 1983.

12. Suzanne Lebeau, *Ti-Jean voudrait ben s'marier . . .*, Montréal, Leméac, coll. "Théâtre pour enfants," 1985.

13. Suzanne Lebeau, *Une lune entre deux maisons*, Montréal, Québec/Amérique, coll. "Jeunes Publics," 1980.

14. Louise LaHaye, *Trois petits contes*, Montréal, Québec/Amérique, coll. "Jeunes Publics," 1981.

15. Théâtre de l'Oeil, *Regarde pour voir*, Montréal, Québec/Amérique, coll. "Jeunes Publics," 1981.

16. Diane Bouchard *et alli, La Couleur chante un pays*, Montréal, Québec/Amérique, coll. "Jeunes Publics," 1981.

17. Jean Barbeau, *Le Théâtre de la Maintenence*, Montréal, Leméac.

18. Louis-Dominique Lavigne, *Où est-ce qu'elle est ma gang?* Montréal, Québec/Amérique, coll. "Jeunes Publics," 1984.

19. François Camirand, Yves Lauvaux, Michel O. Noël, Monique Rioux, *L'Umiak (le bateau collectif)*, Montréal, VLB éditeur, 1984.

Hélène Beauchamp

China

Editor's Note: Two separate articles represent China which together provide an overview of past and present work.

HISTORY

China, a country with a long cultural history, was under feudal rule for many years. Because feudalism does not recognize children as full-fledged human beings with independent personalities, children's theatre remained largely undeveloped. It was not until the 1930s that theatre for young people began to take shape in China when Li Jinghui created a few "song/dance" dramas, including *The Night of the Shining Moon, The Little Painter*, and *The Sparrow and the Child*. These works quickly attracted attention from schools throughout the country, but there were no professional children's theatre companies in the country at the time to perform them.

On July 7, 1937, the Japanese invaded China and ignited the Second Sino-Japanese War. Many children lost their families, and in Shanghai some elementary- and secondary-school children were forced to hide in the French-controlled compound, where they enrolled in refugee facilities. To propagate resistance against the Japanese and to save the country that they loved, they formed the Children's Troupe under the leadership of Wu Xinjia, Xu Liming, Zhang Ying, and Fu Chenmuo, with the following anthem:

> Hi! Hi! We're a group of poor kids!
> Hi! Hi! We're a group of little kids!
> We're born and raised in hardship,
> We grow up under cannon fire.
> Unafraid of having no teachers,
> Not missing our parents,

We rely only on ourselves,
Learning hard and working hard.
Children, stand on your feet!
Children, stand on your feet!
In this great era of resistance,
Create a new world that belongs to us!

After seeing *At the War Front, Catch the Traitor*, and *Kick the Enemy Home*, the famous author Mao Dun said: "The Children's Troupe is a wonderful flower that grows out of the blood of our wartime resistance." The youngest actor in the company was only eight years old and the oldest was nineteen. To enhance China's effort in fighting its Japanese invaders, these young actors traveled extensively, performing in Nanjing (Nanking), Wuhan, and Shanghai.

Often audiences were deeply moved by the group's performances, and on one occasion an army officer in the audience rushed onto the stage and held one eight-year-old actor in his arms. With tears flooding his eyes, he said, "Who doesn't have parents? Who doesn't have a wife and children? The Japanese have invaded our country. We must fight our enemy!" The crowd joined him, thundering slogans: "Down with Japanese imperialism!" "Beat them back home!" The Children's Troupe spread the fire of resistance wherever it went, leading Vice-Chairman Zhou Enlai to say, "The children's spirit of resisting the Japanese invasion substantiates our nation's hope." During the difficult struggle of resistance the troupe was active in both cities and rural villages.

In 1941 the Children's Troupe performed *The Paradise March* and *The Bald Lord (Tu Tu Da Wang)* in Chongqing (Chungking). The content of these two plays reflected the will of the masses in their fight against the invaders and in their demand for democracy. It also reflected the eagerness of the people to have traitors punished and dictators exposed. Moreover, the plays raised the artistic standard of children's theatre to a new height.

During this time the Xinan Traveling Troupe was founded in Shanghai. Composed of teenagers who had lost their families in the war, this company, as they traveled to most parts of China with their productions, mobilized the population to join the forces of resistance.

In the development of China's children's theatre Dong Linken contributed significantly by founding the Kuaming Children's Troupe in 1939 while he was studying at Tong Ji University. This amateur company, whose performers were all elementary- and secondary-school students who acted in their spare time, also had a troupe anthem:

We are the master of the Chinese nation,
    We are the young vanguards of our
    resistance struggle,
We are not afraid of hardship, we work hard to save our country.
    Jump onto the stage, run into the street,
Expose our enemy's cruelty, and awaken our nation's soul.

The Kuaming Children's Troupe created *The Little Spy*, which shocked Kuaming City. Later the company presented *Child Refugees, Toll from the Ancient Temple, The Paradise March*, and *The Song of the Dancing Flowers*. Written by Linken and Tong Chen, *The Little Master* achieved great success and became one of the best loved children's plays of the 1940s. The liveliness and the sadness of the story often evoked strong emotions from the audience. *Watch*, adapted by Linken from a Russian novel, proved to be another favorite and was performed by many other theatre companies at the time.

The young actors of the Kuaming Children's Troupe spearheaded the development of theatre in schools and helped to advance the entire children's theatre movement. The popularization of young people's theatre had become a major goal in Linken's career, but in addition to organizing companies he wrote many plays for children. When he returned to Shanghai he founded The Lihua Press, which specialized in the publication of children's theatre literature.

Other companies established in the thirties and forties included the Boys and Girls Troupe, the Little Troupe, the China Youth Troupe, and the Shanghai Children's Theatre Association. Dramatists writing plays for children included Linken, Bao Lei, He Yi, Yao Shixiao, Zhang Shiliu, and Sun Yi.

The growth of theatre for young people extended beyond the boundaries of big cities. Military theatre companies, attached to many resistance troops, also performed for children. They followed wherever their units went, performing plays, songs, and dances as a means of informing the population and energizing the cultural life of both soldiers and civilians.

In 1947 Soony Ching Ling (Mme. Sun Yat-sen, 1893–1981), founded the China Welfare Institute's Children's Art Theatre, with assistance from Liu Housheng, Zhang Shiliu, and Ren Deyao. Linken's adaptation of *Watch* was chosen as the opening production of the Children's Art Theatre; it was followed by presentations of such plays as *Street Circus*, which exposed social cruelty against children, and *The Little Teacher, You Evil Fellow*, and *Opening Up Wasteland by a Brother and a Sister*.

Ling's contribution to the development of children's theatre in China was tremendous. When New China was established many of the children's theatre troupes mentioned earlier no longer existed; the China Welfare Institute's Children's Art Theatre is a rare survivor from that era. Ren Deyao, its director for more than forty years, has written and directed many plays, such as *Friendship, Ma Lan Hua, A Small Football Team*, and *Madam Soong Ching Ling and Children*. His works have made him the most famous children's playwright and director in China.

The Northeast Literature and Arts Troupe's Children's Group was also founded in 1947. In addition to performing in plays with mostly adult actors, such as *White-Haired Girl* and *Our Land Returns Home*, child actors in this company also wrote and performed in children's plays, including *Children Entertain Troops* and *Beat the Snake*. After the establishment of New China the Northeast Literature and Arts Troupe was renamed the China Youth's Art Theatre. In 1953 the Children's Group was renamed the China Children's Troupe. Three years later it was rebuilt as the China Children's Art Theatre and was the first national children's theatrical organization in China. Its first director was Ren Hong.

During the "cultural revolution" the China Children's Art Theatre was abolished by the "Gang of Four." Fortunately it was reinstated in 1980, with Zhou Lai as director and Luo Ying, Wu Ping, and Fan Jufen as deputy directors. Under the leadership of the Ministry of Culture the Art Theatre has created and performed several hundred children's plays in the past several decades, presentations that have been deeply welcomed by their child audiences. Plays have included *Ma Lan Hua, Little Wild Geese Fly Together, The Revolutionary Family, Yueh Yun, Newspaper Boys*, and *The Strange 101*. Foreign works also have been performed by the China Children's Art Theatre, including *In Behalf of the Revolution* (or *Lenin and the Second Generation), Twelve Months*, and *The Prince and the Pauper*, from Mark Twain's novel.

The China Children's Art Theatre and the China Welfare Institite's Children's Art Theatre have played an important role in setting the model for and advancing the development of children's theatre in China. They have existed the longest and are regarded by many as having achieved the highest artistic standards of all companies.

In 1960 the Liaonin Province Children's Art Theatre, the Xian City Children's Theatre, and the Wuhan City Children's Theatre were established. Although they created and performed numerous children's plays, they were, unfortunately, disbanded during the "cultural revolution."

CHILDREN'S THEATRE TODAY

After the fall of the "Gang of Four" the demand for children's theatre was high. In 1981 the Ministry of Culture established the Children's Art and Culture Committee, which is responsible for overseeing the development of artistic fields for children. To promote children's theatre, the Ministry of Culture organized national performances of forty-three children's plays. Thirty-three theatrical organizations from twenty-one provinces and cities participated in the event, which involved more than 2,000 persons.

Plays presented included *Zhu Siubin, Song of Happiness, Madame Soong Ching Ling and Children, The Little Detective, The Story of the Tiger and the Bear, San Mao Wants to Go to School, Golden Child, 3 + 2 × 5 = ?, Rosy Clouds at Dawn, Twinkling Stars*, and *The Ginseng Baby*. At the same time, the China Children's Theatre Research Society was founded, which later became a center for academic research in children's theatre; today it has more than 1,000 members.

This national event greatly furthered the development of children's theatre in China. Currently there are twenty-two professional companies, not including puppet show troupes. Activities in amateur children's theatre are also making excellent progress. In 1986 the Ministry of Culture organized a playwriting competition that prompted the writing of many scripts about life in elementary and secondary schools. The Ministry, in conjunction with the China Children's Theatre Research Society, also has organized three conferences on playwriting for children, which have fostered a group of children's playwrights. In the past two years children's playwrights have been most prolific, providing new works that include *Gan Luo Became an Envoy at the Age of Twelve, Fly, Sea Swallow, The Adventure of Pinocchio, The Six Nights of Having Tête-à-Tête with the Moon*, and *A Daily Record of the Class of '52*.

Because China is extremely attentive in nurturing its young, children's theatre is considered an investment in aesthetic education and the government promotes it by subsidizing the cost of tickets to children's plays. Depending on individual circumstances, theatres may receive from $54 to $110 of subsidy per performance for children's plays. Almost every play produced for child audiences has a "life span" of about 100 performances at a given theatre. Some may have 200 performances in the same theatre and the house will be full for most of them. Operating costs and salaries for the personnel who work in the field of children's theatre are provided by the government. Costs for medical care and most housing expenses are also absorbed by the government.

Workers in children's theatre in China are trying their best to advance their field because they strongly believe in what they do and they appreciate the government's underwriting of their activities. However, they would like to have increased contact with their colleagues throughout the world.

Luo Ying
Translated by Casey Man Kong Lum

*   *   *

HISTORY

Theatres designed especially for children did not exist in China before the founding of the People's Republic, although China has one of the longest and richest histories in theatrical culture in the world. "Children's theatre," as we know it, can only be considered a contemporary concept. This is not to say that children were totally ignored by the theatre in Old China. For example, Tang dynasty's (618–907) "southern theatre" ("Nanxi"), Song dynasty's (960–1279) "drum Lyric" ("Gu-zi-zu"), and Yuan dynasty's (1271–1368) drama ("Yuan-qu") did have works that were written about children and sometimes were played by child actors.

"Palace theatre" ("Gong-Ting-Xi") became very popular in the beginning of Qian Long's reign (1736–1795) in the Qing dynasty (1644–1911). And as Beijing opera began to move toward sophistication and maturity, important works were created, such as *Sanliang Educates Her Son, Split the Mountain to Save His Mother, and Ne Cha Stirs Up the Sea*. These works were based on folk legends, oral literature, or popular classic novels such as *Journey to the West* (also known as *Pilgrimage to the West*) and *The Canonization of the Gods*. Most of them depicted the qualities of wit, bravery and righteousness of children of ancient China. When child actors who specialized in playing these types of characters began to appear on stage, children's theatre in China had begun.

Toward the end of the Qing dynasty there appeared a number of very young actors who specialized in playing children and youthful characters. These included such famous figures as Chen Xiang in *The Jaded Lotus Lamp* and Xu Xige in *San Liang Educates Her Son*.

The real development of children's theatre in China began after the establishment of the People's Republic, for then the government paid special attention to the cultural enrichment of children. In the early 1950s it established children's art theatres in Beijing, Shanghai, Liaonin, and Heilongjiang whose mission was to create, rehearse, and perform plays for young children.

In 1947 the China Welfare Institute's Children's Art Theatre was founded and produced, in the early 1960s *Boat of Treasure*, a play written by the famous writer Lao She (1899–1966). Later on the theatre translated and produced the Russian play *In Behalf of the Revolution* (also known as *Lenin and the Second Generation*).

COMPANIES AND REPERTORY

Boat of Treasure was especially written for children and is the most famous and popular play of Lao She. After production at the Children's Art Theatre it was presented by several other children's theatres. This play has received popular support and critical acclaim from both children and adults, and its widespread presentation has helped to build a solid foundation for the growth of children's theatre in China.

Gradually the Children's Art Theatre developed its repertory. Among other works the group presented *Ma Lan Flower, The Story of Qiu Ueng's Encounter with Fairy*, and *Ma Liang and His Magic Brush*, a play that had great influence throughout the country. Some of the works were made into movies and achieved popular success in the fifties and sixties.

These plays helped to enrich the content of children's cultural life in New China and cultivated affection, sentiment, wisdom, and spirit in the youth of our country. For example, the fabled *Ma Lan Flower* uses the interaction between human characters and anthropomorphized animals, plants, and flowers to portray life experiences. Through this fascinating fable the difference between good and evil and the victory of good over evil are highlighted.

Adapted from a mythic legend, *The Story of Qiu Ueng's Encounter with Fairy* describes how Qiu Ueng struggles against injustice with the help of a flower fairy. Qui Ueng's incorruptible virtue and the fairy's fight for kindheartedness are praised and glorified in the play. In *Ma Liang and His Magic Brush*, a comedy based on folk legends, Ma Liang paints what are considered by the people to be beautiful, virtuous, and kind-hearted works. They become targets of the greedy and evil, but Ma Liang uses his magic brush to subdue the villains, often in comical situations.

These plays were an important means of developing the minds of the children. They reflected the aesthetic ideal and psychology of the nation after independence, its search for beauty and goodness, and its longing to glorify kindheartedness and humanity. Children's theatre became not only an important part of this national culture, but also a mirror for the cultural ideal.

Pushed by this cultural current of children's theatre, the Shanghai Children's Art Theatre and the Liaonin Children's Art Theatre (located in Shen Yang City) were founded and soon began to exhibit a growing influence throughout the country. These two theatres, plus the Children's Art Theatre in Beijing, are the only playhouses entirely devoted to children's theatre. However, works for young audiences are frequently presented by over 100 theatre organizations throughout China. Children's theatre is part of China's overall theatrical development, and this has helped to facilitate the growth of many other theatrical genres.

It is important to note that in the 1950s, famous literary works from all over the world were translated and published in China. These foreign works added new life and color to children's theatre. They included Pushkin's *The Wolf and the Sheep*, Grimm's *The Fisherman and His Wife*, Andersen's *The Little Match Girl* and *The Emperor's New Clothes*, and Chekhov's *Uncle Vanya*. Their influence radiated through adaptation into dramas, films, and introduction by regional theatres. Heilongjiang Province is among the most representative region in the development of children's theatre in China.

CHILDREN'S THEATRE IN HEILONGJIANG PROVINCE

The Heilongjiang Province is situated at the northeastern tip of China; adjacent are Siberia, Mongolia, and the Sea of Japan. The Heilongjiang, Songhua, Wusuli, Nun, and Mudan rivers run through its land. The population includes a great variety of minority ethnic groups, such as the Manchu, the Olunchun, the Owenk, the Dahur, and the Hezhen. Even though the culture in Heilongjiang Province is not as advanced as that in such areas as the Central Plains, it is nonetheless rich in its diversity. People who live in this part of China have long had the reputation of being openminded, emulous, and explorative. In fact, natives from this region have, on several historical occasions, conquered the Central Plains. The people are known for their ability to integrate and be absorbed into existing cultures.

It was within this unique northern cultural heritage that puppet shows and shadow plays began their evolution. When these two genres were being modified and introduced into urban areas, children were their primary audience. The Heilongjiang Puppet Show and Shadow Play Art Theatre was founded in 1960. Its enormous puppet repertory includes *Monkey Subdues the White-Bone Demon*, *Tunnel Warfare*, *The Story of a Hunter*, and *Battle with the Ox-Demon King*.

Some are adapted from classic Chinese literature or folktales while others are original works. The need of the child audience in New China helped to transform the puppet show into a major component of Chinese children's theatre.

Heilongjiang's shadow play originated in the "Luanxian Skin Shadow Play" from the Luanxian County, Hebei Province. Performed by moving figures controlled by strings, the puppets are made from dyed donkey skin (hence the alternate name "donkey skin shadow play"). Originally, candlelight projected the moving shadows onto a specially made screen, but today electric light is used instead. A shadow play is performed with music that is rich in northeastern regional characteristics, which possess the unique earthy qualities of enthusiasm, passion, and humor. Stories are adapted mostly from folk legends, which explains why, in the past, the primary audience for this genre was farmers and working-class city dwellers.

Because of advances in audio and visual media, the shadow play has lost much of the adult audience. However, it has had success in maintaining child viewers in many villages and small towns, where new productions are generally tailored to the interests of the young. For example, *The Bald-Tail Li* is based on the folk legend of the struggle between a white dragon and a black dragon along the Heilongjiang River. (Literally, Hei-long-jiang means the Black Dragon River in Chinese.) Other works include *The Flaming Mountain* and *Pigsy Carries the Bride* (in the Monkey and Pigsy series), adapted from the classic novel *Journey to the West*.

In 1964 the Youth's Beijing Opera Troupe of the Heilongjiang Province Theatre Institute presented *Three Youngsters*, a full scale children's opera written by Wu Jialai and Du Ping. The story is based on the real-life experiences of three youngsters who one day discovered a crack in a railroad track. They saw a train approaching, but the emergency signal wasn't working. Risking their lives, they stood on one another's shoulders to form a "sign pole." The top youth waved his red scarf and signaled the train to a screeching halt, thereby averting what would certainly have been a terrible disaster. *Three Youngsters* was a significant work in that it updated children's theatre in the region by introducing a story that reflected contemporary life. The continued use of topical issues and stories has had an influence well beyond the boundaries of children's theatre, for in many ways it helped to facilitate the modernization of China's ancient culture.

Development in the 1960s signaled a new era for children's theatre in general, an era of rejuvenation. During that period the China Welfare Institute's Children's Art Theatre presented *In Behalf of the Revolution*, a production that portrayed Lenin as a great and admirable man. The presentation achieved instant success and became popular throughout the country, including performances by the Harbin Drama Troupe that brought children's theatre in Heilongjiang to a new level of excellence.

All this changed during the "cultural revolution" when children's theatre sustained grave damage. In 1978 the China Children's Art Theatre in Beijing presented its first performance after ten years of turmoil. The play was *Newspaper Boys*, which told the story of the late Zhou Enlai and a group of newspaper boys during China's resistance against Japanese aggression. This production signaled the recovery of children's theatre in China, and once again performances for child audiences were common. In the early 1980s the Harbin Children's Art Troupe was founded, based on the tradition of the puppet show and shadow play.

The growth of children's theatre in China was not confined to the stage alone; it also found expression through film. In the late fifties and early sixties a number of narrative films, which received critical acclaim, were made for child audiences. These included *Flowers of Our Home Country, Little Soldier Zhang Ga, Kite*, and *Juvenile Criminals*. *Flowers of Our Home Country* portrayed young children in New China preparing themselves for the future. *Little Soldier Zhang Ga* depicted a witty boy's fight with Japanese invaders during the war. A Franco-Chinese production, *Kite* was an imaginative children's film integrating the images of Monkey King (from the novel *Journey to the West*) in dreams, in "real life," and on the stage. *Juvenile Criminals* was made in the early eighties by the Zhujiang (Pearl River) Film Studio in Guangzhou (Canton). It tells the story of how young criminals were saved and reeducated. These films are so-phisticated both artistically and in their social consciousness. They have raised children's theatre art to a higher level of expertise.

Youth theatre in China (which is differentiated from children's theatre as being for adolescents) began to take shape during the period of the May 4th Movement (1919), when Western drama was introduced into the country. Its development has gone through turbulent times, such as the Japanese invasion and the civil war that followed. Works influenced by and reflecting this turbulence had a significant effect both on youth theatre and on social life and theatrical art in New China.

In the early 1950s cultural life in New China was largely influenced by Russian culture. Among the first books read by secondary-school students in the big cities in the north was one about young Soviet anti-fascist heroes, which was adapted into several different plays that have been produced by many secondary school amateur theatre troupes in northern provinces and cities. Ostrovsky's *The Tempering of Steel* also has been widely seen.

Land revolution and agricultural collectivism were well under way by 1955–1956. Junior and senior high school students enthusiastically participated in the reform movement and returned to villages to cultivate the land. *The Chaoyang Valley*, written by Yang Nancun and performed by Henan Province's Henan Troupe, was a product of this era. It told the story of a junior high school graduate and the problems she faced, including love and conflicting ideals, after returning to her home village in Chaoyang, Shanxiang. The play, adapted into many theatrical genres and performed pervasively, was later made into a film and distributed across the country; it received widespread attention.

At the same time, drama troupes were formed in big cities such as Beijing,

Shanghai, Shen Yang, Harbin, and Changchun; the troupe's primary audience was college students and city dwellers. Works presented included Cao Yu's *Thunderstorm* and Ba Jin's *Home*. The anti-feudalism in these dramas was consistent with the thoughts and mood of the newly liberated youth. In the early sixties China experienced three years of natural disasters. Several dramas appeared that underscored these events: *Liu Jiemei Forgets His Roots* and *Liu Wenxue—A Boy Martyr*. Other works, such as *Lei Feng* and *For the Sixty One Class Brothers*, had a strong influence on the young throughout country.

Around 1962 four influential novels were published: Yang Mo's *The Song of Youth*, Luo Giangbin's *Red Crag*, Liang Bin's *Keep the Red Flag Flying*, and Qu Bo's *Tracks in the Snowy Forest*. They not only brought China's contemporary literary achievements to new heights, but also added new life and color to the youth theatre. They were adapted into drama, opera, and film and were widely performed. They still prove popular when revived.

In 1964 China organized a nationwide presentation of Beijing Opera with contemporary themes that aimed to revolutionize the opera and make it more responsive and sensitive to modern life. Many of the works mounted were by young artists, but none remains today; the Beijing Opera proved a rather rigid and inflexible art form and did not adapt well to the experiment.

While the Beijing Opera was being "modernized," five dramas made their mark on the youth theatre: *The Young Generation, Family Problems, Sentinels Under Neon Lights, Youth from Afar*, and *Don't Ever Forget*. They presented the ideals and hopes of the younger generation, and praised those who had moral character and who were willing to work to build the country and sacrifice for the people. Likewise, they skillfully depicted love and the life experiences of the young. The five dramas were well received by people from all classes across the country, but especially by young audiences. They represented a peak period in the youth theatre during the People's Republic, a period of bright artistic achievements and profound thoughts.

The plays were restrained because of the political environment in which they were created; playwrights had to use a certain "nonartistic" language at times, and to advocate theories of "class struggle." As a result, the plays have become dated, unable to transcend their time and become universal statements.

Although the social environment at large helps to create outstanding works, sometimes youth theatre itself is used to influence social currents. To be faithful to the time and to convey truth are, of course, two objectives in the arts. However, theatrical art in China had become a tool for political conspiracy and propaganda during the "cultural revolution," when plays became formulaic, unrealistic, superficial, and abstract. As a result, they became inevitable targets of contempt by the people.

After the "cultural revolution" responsible artists tried their best to revive theatre from the crisis it underwent. They proposed new theories for reform and creativity and for exploration through involvement. Led by a number of playwrights who write for the youth theatre, the "Explorative School" began to surface in Beijing, Shanghai, Nanjing, and Harbin. In their exploration of modernism in Western theatre, they created such dramas as *Station, Absolute Signal*, and *Wild Man*. The presence of this group stirred persistent debates over dramaturgical theory, but in the end the tide stirred up by the modernist theatre began to subside because the works were judged to be remote from Chinese artistic values.

Another group of young artists began to explore the treasure of China's national culture and, at the same time, to absorb new elements of contemporary culture. This group wrote such plays as *Black Stones* and *The Journey of Desire*. The works won unprecedented approval from both audiences and critics when they were presented in Beijing, where prominent theorists, led by Cao Yu, praised them for their realistic portrayal of the lives of contemporary youths. These plays once again remind us of the genuine artistic quality of the works presented by the youth theatres. They also put an end to the debates about what constitutes good theatre for youth. Moreover, from the point of view of artistic practice, they forged a union between the "Explorative School" and the "Traditional School," thereby moving Chinese youth theatre into a new phase of development.

Jia Fei and Lin Tao Pei
Translated by Casey Man Kong Lum

Cuba

HISTORY

Theatre for children in Cuba is a contemporary phenomenon, framed within a period characterized by new ideas about childhood (generated from important scientific discoveries and radical socioeconomic changes) and a recognition of the needs and rights of children. For centuries children were considered appendages of adults, not as beings in their own right. Art and literature directed toward children were shrouded in didacticism and aimed at preparing the future adult, not enriching the current child. Most art, however, was not directed toward children; culture was geared toward adults and sometimes reached the younger population, but not in any regular manner. This was the situation the world over, and in Cuba as well.

Theatre for children first came to Cuba when the Teatro Mecánico de Nueva Orleans (Mechanical Theatre of New Orleans) arrived in Havana in 1794[1] and when European puppeteers and jugglers passed through on their way to Peru and Mexico in 1798.[2] The review of the former stated that it was a moral performance about the destruction of Jerusalem, showing the dead emerging from their graves and life in hell, which was portrayed by 35,000 figures that moved about on a stage ten meters long (approximately thirty-three feet). The presentation included lighting and sound effects and a narrator who outlined the action. The Europeans were noted for traveling about the country (as did native puppeteers) performing their art for the delight of both children and adults.

The first example of theatre conceived specifically for children did not come until the first two decades of the twentieth century, at which time school theatre began. The pieces, written by teachers, were didactic and nonliterary; they lacked artistic value, and it is impossible to find even one example that deserves to be mentioned. These early works were the result of particularly poor imagination. In the 1930s, however, conditions began to change. Two theatre companies with child actors and adult directors showed concern for both the artistry of the plays and the age of the audiences for whom they performed, although they still adhered to the traditional didactic purposes of education. These were the Catalanian Pedro Boquet's (sponsored by the Sociedad Infantil de Bellas Artes [Fine Arts Children's Society]) and Roberto Rodríguez.

The Academia de Artes Dramáticas from the Escuela Libre de La Habana (ADADEL; Dramatic Arts Academy of the Havana Free School), the first Cuban theatre institution, opened in 1940. This school has had a great impact on Cuban theatre, and even though theatre for children was not a standard subject, some of its students became pioneers in the field. They adapted skills they had learned at the Academy and successfully mounted works for young people. Through the efforts of one of the school's professors, a playwriting contest was held in 1943; the prize was awarded to Modesto Centeno for his adaptation of *Little Red Riding Hood*.[3] The group built a small puppet stage where they produced programs for schools and local audiences; this work gave them the chance to test puppetry techniques.

Puppet performances for children also were fostered by the Academia de Artes Dramáticas (Dramatic Arts Academy, 1947), which took over from ADADEL (which had disappeared by this time). Among the companies who performed here were El Retablo del Tío Polilla (Uncle Moth's Puppet Stage, 1948), Camejo's Puppet Stage (1949), and Grupo Escénico Libre (Free Scene Theatre Group, 1949).

The only live theatre for children at the time was performed by Paco Alfonso's People's Theatre (the majority of the group's work was for adults). In 1943 the company presented the premiere of *Poema con niños* (*Poem with Children*) by Nicolás Guillén.[4] Throughout the 1940s and 1950s the idea of performing theatre expressly for children began to grow and prosper. During these years small companies presented works in a random manner; this grass-roots development provided the origins of professional theatre for children and young people. Many groups appeared and attempted to maintain a minimum level of stability, although most of them quickly disappeared. Among them were Teatro de munecos de Mayarí (Puppet Theatre of Mayarí) in the old province of Oriente, 1952; La Carreta (The Cart) directed by Dora Caravajal, 1952; Titirilandia directed by Beba Farías, 1955; and El Guiñol de los Hermanos Camejo (Camejo Brother's Puppet Theatre), 1955. This last company changed its name to Guiñol Nacional de Cuba (Cuban National Puppet Theatre) in 1956.

Another source of theatre for children and young people was la Sociedad Nuestro Tiempo (Our Time Society, 1955), a group composed of progressive intellectuals and artists who met regularly and occasionally performed works for children. Also, in 1953, María Antonia Fariñas began her attempts to introduce puppetry to the television networks. She wanted to produce a program geared toward children in which the characters were puppets, especially string puppets (she and her husband, Eurípides La Mata, had introduced string puppet techniques to Cuba). She was not successful with her plan because a commercial sponsor could not be found; no one wanted to underwrite a program for an audience that had no consumer purchasing power.

THE BEGINNINGS OF PROFESSIONAL THEATRE FOR CHILDREN

Almost immediately after the revolutionary victory in 1959, the first steps were taken to stabilize Cuban children's theatre. Ignacio Gutiérrez directed four productions with the Los Barbuditos Artistic Brigade, and within the Theatre Department of the Cultural Division of the Ministry of Education, Nora Badía resuscitated and revived some of the works and groups from the early 1950s. By means of government support for the performers, free performances for children were offered throughout the country. In 1961, as head of the National Department for Children's Theatre of the National Council of Culture, Badía underwrote children's theatre activities. The best puppeteers and actors were employed; training courses in production were instituted; the best students were chosen to participate; and in each province Puppet Theatre companies and La Edad de Oro Theatre companies (for live performance) were established.

In the capital city the Havana Puppet Theatre was founded in 1960. The Teatro Nacional de Guiñol (National Puppet Theatre), made up of former members of the Cuban National Puppet Theatre, began life with a performance of *Las cebollas mágicas* (*The Magic Onions*), by Brazilian author María Clara Machado. This production marked a forward step for Cuban puppet theatre because technicians and puppeteers from Moscow's Central Puppet Theatre, directed by Sergei Obratzov, acted as collaborators and advisors. They also conducted seminars in rod puppetry, a technique little known at the time. In 1970 the National Puppet Theatre and the Havana Puppet Theatre merged.

The year 1965 was significant for artists involved in theatre for children. Five years after the creation of government-subsidized theatre the National Exhibition on Children's Theatre was inaugurated, on October 1. This celebration was held at the Casa de la Cultural Checoslovaca (Czechoslovakian House of Culture) and featured current trends in children's theatre: sketches of set designs, examples of puppets, costumes, performances followed by public talk-backs and debates, analyses of the achievements in the field to date, and future plans as devised by practitioners in the field. There have been nine festivals since the first, and they have proved useful in that they allow evaluation of accomplishments, analysis of difficulties, and, particularly, appraisal of the importance of contact between theatre and audience.

CHILDREN'S THEATRE TODAY

Cuba has twenty-four state-subsidized theatre groups for children; seven are in Havana and the rest are distributed among the provinces. The division between puppet companies and actor companies has almost faded, as most companies work in both genres, sometimes incorporating live actors and puppets into the same production. There are, however, two groups that work exclusively with live actors: Centro Experimental de Teatro de Santa Clara (Santa Clara Experimental Theatre Center) and Grupo de Teatro de La Edad de Oro (Golden Age Theatre Group) from Camagüey. Seventeen of the children's theatre troupes have their own buildings in which they offer continuous programming for both general audiences and directed audiences.[5]

A common objective of the companies is to mount lightweight, movable productions that can be toured to schools, parks, town squares, and day-care centers. Those companies that have traveled extensively have gained considerable experience in the art of using space and have even developed their own theatrical language, which enhances this kind of production. Among these are the Joven Teatro de Marianao (Marianao Young Theatre), which regularly performs in all the schools and neighborhoods of its municipality; Los Cuenteros (The Story-Tellers Theatre Group), which has its headquarters in San Antonio de los Baños; and the Santa Clara Experimental Theatre Center, which has had great success with its production of *El porrón maravilloso* (*The Marvelous Jug*). Each company has a Management Council along with a Technical Council. They deal with the organization of the group, delegating work assignments, defining the group's development, and choosing the repertory.

Six companies stand out as representing the highest aesthetic level of achievement of the children's theatre groups. Four are from the provinces and two are from Havana: Grupo de Teatro Papalote (Kite Theatre Group) from Matanzas; el Centro Experimental de Teatro de Santa Clara (Santa Clara Experimental Theatre Center); Teatro Guiñol de Camagüey (Camagüey Puppet Theatre); Teatro Guiñol de Cienfuegos (Cienfuegos Puppet Theatre); and Grupo de Teatro Anaquillé (Anaquillé Theatre Group) and Teatro Nacional de Guiñol (National Puppet Theatre) from Havana.

The common task of all theatre activity for children in the country is to promote artistic works in which aesthetic values are supported by ethical and social values in order to contribute to the formation of the personality of Cuba's younger generation, keeping in mind the ideological principles of Cuban society. Despite permanent state subsidy and official recognition of the importance of children's theatre as a conveyer of pedagogical, ethical, and aesthetic values, there are still some artists from the adult theatre who question the place of theatre for children. This attitude, the result of tradition rather than substance, is disappearing as professional children's theatre becomes more and more pervasive.

The lack of specialized theatre criticism and professional and academic theatre education help to keep these prejudices alive. To date, there has only been one theoretical and practical seminar at the Instituto Superior de Arte (High Institute of Art) on the topic of theatre for children and youth. A School of Theatre for Children existed for two years (1969–1970), and many of its graduates went on to join the field as actors and directors of the early children's theatre companies. Currently the Theatre Art School within the High Institute of Art is working on the development of specialized curriculum and workshops that will advance the cause of children's theatre.

PLAYWRIGHTS, DIRECTORS AND DESIGNERS

The most representative Cuban playwrights, directors, and designers working in children's theatre are as follows: playwrights—Dora Alonso, Freddy Artiles, Bebo Ruiz, Ignacio Gutiérrez, Gerardo Fulleda, Yulki Cary, René Fernández, Dania García, Fidel Galbán, David García, and Francisco Garzón; directors— Fernando Sáez, Mario Guerrero, Yulki Cary, Enrique Poblet, Julio Cordero, Roberto Fernández, Raúl Guerra, Eddy Socorro, Félix Dardo, Ignacio Gutiérrez, and Pedro Valdés Piña; designers—Jesús Ruiz, Derubín Jácome, Zenén Calero, Yulki Cary, René Fernández, Armando Morales, Enrique Misa, and Mario Rodríguez.

REPRESENTATIVE COMPANIES

Papalote Theatre Group

This company was founded in 1962 by twelve actors (six men and six women), under the general direction of René Fernández Santana, who is also a playwright, designer, and teacher. Designer Zenén Calero also works with the group. They mount works that combine live performers with puppets (marionettes, human-sized, hand, etc.); theatrical versions of Afro-Cuban legends constitute the most important part of the group's repertory. Papalote has performed internationally at such places as the Bielsko-Biala Puppet Festival in Poland in 1984 (its production of *El gran festín* [*The Great Banquet*], by René Fernández was chosen as one of the ten best presentations at the festival) and the Iberoamerican Theatre Festival in Cádiz, Spain, in 1986 (with a production of *Nokán y el maíz* [*Nokán and the Corn*], by Diana Rodríguez).

They have performed other important children's plays, including *Historia de lo que ocurrió en un huerto escolar* (*The Story of What Happened in a School Playground*), *Cuatro actores narran la historia de un tomate grande grande* (*Four Actors Tell the Story of a Big Big Tomato*), *El día que la isla dejó de ser ordenada y limpia* (*The Day the Island Stopped Being Tidy and Neat*), all by playwright and director Fernández, and *La nueva mensajera* (*The New Messenger*) by Dania Rodríguez. Papalote performs in city parks and squares in Matanzas as well as in other municipalities throughout the province. It performs in its own Theatre Hall each weekend (Friday through Sunday).

Experimental Theatre Center

Working out of Santa Clara, the capital city of the Villa Clara Province, the company was set up in 1963. It is geared toward performing out of doors but also presents works on conventional stages. Artistic director Fernando Sáez, who has been with Experimental Theatre Center since its inception, is considered one of the country's outstanding directors. The group received a prize from ASSITEJ/ Cuba for its work in the Seventh Festival for Children in 1981. In 1984 its production of *El porrón maravilloso* (*The Marvelous Jug*, written by Rogelio Castillo and directed by Sáez) won the Grand Prize in the Eighth Festival for Children. *El caballo de ceiba* (*The Ceiba Horse*), an original work by Castillo and Sáez, presented for the Ninth Festival for Children in 1985, again won the ASSITEJ Prize and the company received a special acknowledgment from the jury. Company members Angel Victor Miguez and Carmen Pallas also received individual prizes for their acting in 1981 and 1983.

Other important plays presented by the group are *La caperucits roja* (*Little Red Riding Hood*), adapted by Ana María Salas; *El artista* (*The Artist*), by Carmen Pallas and Fernando Sáez; *Blancanieves* (*Snow White*), adapted by Sáez; *Caballito enano* (*Little Pony Horse*), by Dora Alonso; and *Margarita en el País de las Maravillas* (*Margarita in Wonderland*), by Sáez.

National Puppet Theatre

The group was founded in 1963 and has twenty-one actors and four artistic directors. Its current repertory contains twenty-two plays, ranging from adaptations of traditional stories such as *Little Red Riding Hood, El gato con botas* (*Puss in Boots*), *Blancanieves y los siete enanitos* (*Snow White and the Seven Dwarves*), and *El flautista de Hamelín* (*The Pied Piper of Hamelin*) to national narratives like *Los tres pichones* (*The Three Young Pigeons*) and *La lechuza ambiciosa* (*The Greedy Owl*), by Onelio Jorge Cardoso, and *Liborio, la jutía y el majá* (*Liborio, the Jutía and the Snake*), by Emilio Bacardí.

Well-known puppeteers Xiomara Palacios, Miriam Sánchez, Armando Morales, and Ulises García are members of the company, which performs in three distinct genres: puppet theatre, theatre with both live actors and puppets, and live theatre (with or without masks). The group presents regular performances for special audiences on Thursday and Friday of each week and for general audiences on Saturdays and Sundays (two shows each day). Little Concerts for Children are also presented every Saturday and include the participation of renowned guest musicians. Art exhibitions are hung in the theatre lobby, and the audience is encouraged to take part in these extra attractions.

Other plays in the group's repertory are *Pluft, el fantasmita* (*Pluft, the Little Ghost*), by María Clara Machado; *Los seis pingüinitos* (*The Six Little Penguins*), by Bulgarian playwright Boris Aprilov; *Viaje a las Galaxias* (*Trip to the Galaxies*), by Ignacio Gutiérrez; and *La nana* (*The Cradlesong*), which is Raúl Guerra's version of a play written by the Psychology Group of Bellevue Hospital in New York City. In 1969 the National Puppet Theatre toured to Czechoslovakia, Rumania, and Poland. It also participated in the First Festival of Theatre for Children held in Lima, Perú, in 1985.

Camagüéy Puppet Theatre

Though this group has been in existence since 1962, it was not until 1983 that it became a significant force. At that time the company redefined its artistic guidelines and developed its own distinctive style, which combines many kinds of puppets (table puppets, floor puppets, and finger puppets) with intensely physical and movement-oriented actors. The result is a merging of puppet theatre and dance, a search for images under "black light" effects, and original lighting design. The group is directed by Mario Guerrero, a graduate of the Theatre Institute of Leningrad.

Among the plays produced are *El niño y la flor* (*The Child and the Flower*), written by Guerrero and based on ideas from *The Little Prince; La calle de los fantasmas* (*The Street of the Ghosts*), by Javier Villafañe; *Balada para un pollito pito* (*A Ballad for Pollito Pito*), which is Guerrero's version of a traditional tale; and *El patico feo* (*The Ugly Duckling*), another Guerrero adaptation, this time of Andersen's original. The latter two adaptations received prizes for Best Play in the Eighth and Ninth Festivals of Theatre for Children, in 1983 and 1985, respectively.

IMPORTANT PLAYS

Espantajo y los pájaros (*The Scarecrow and the Birds*), is one of Dora Alonso's[6] most beautiful plays. Performed throughout Cuba, the play has also been seen in Colombia, Venezuela, Chile, and East Germany. Though written in 1962 and presented in a conventional structure, the play well defines the inner conflict of the characters, who symbolize the people's right to the fruits of work. An old couple place a scarecrow in their rice field, but the scarecrow does not know how to face responsibility and is demoralized in front of its enemies, the birds. A dove encourages the scarecrow to fight, thereby fostering an understanding of its importance and purpose in the rice field as a protector of the crops. After a fierce fight the scarecrow defeats the birds and the old couple enjoys a good harvest.

El pavo cantor (*The Singing Turkey*), by Freddy Artiles,[7] received La Edad de Oro Award (The Golden Age Award) in the Music and Literature Competition for Children and Young People in 1979. Artiles won this same prize in 1973 with his *El conejito descontento* (*The Unhappy Little Rabbit*). *The Singing Turkey* has been produced by the Santa Clara Puppet Theatre (1981), El Galpón Theatre Group of Havana City (1983), the Theatre Group for Children of Sancti Spíritus (1986), and the Popular Theatre Workshop of Quito, Ecuador (1982).

The play presents a picture of life in the Cuban countryside, where animals are engaged in building a social club for their community. A singing turkey refuses to do physical work because he is an artist, and so he isolates himself. Some wild dogs attack the industrious characters but fail in their action and turn against the defenseless turkey. After being captured the turkey realizes that he acted badly toward the other animals. With the support of the children in the audience the turkey defeats the wild dogs and then joins in the work and sings as a present to his new friends.

Okandeniyé, la dama del ave real (*Okandeniyé, the Lady of the Peacock*), the best of Yulki Cary's works, presents characters from Afro-Cuban folklore. Oshún, a beautiful Yoruban goddess and the queen of sensuality and freshwater streams, longs to have a peacock-feather fan. Not listening to the wise advise of the other gods and without waiting for the proper moment, she pushes ahead in her strong desire to possess it. The dénouement leads to a transformation in the main character, who, after admitting her mistakes, finally obtains her desire. The language of the piece evokes a poetic atmosphere.

El porrón maravilloso (*The Marvelous Jug*), Rogelio Castillo's[8] first play, was written for the Santa Clara Experimental Theatre Center in 1983. In it the countryside becomes the framework for a love story among some animals in the imaginary town of Mangunido. As the result of a misunderstanding, the animals are divided into two enemy groups: the Tinas (all females) and the Tones (all males). A magical jug appears and calls them to order, making them realize that without their mates, everything loses its beauty, and without procreation, the rhythm of life is interrupted. The use of the rural environment is enhanced by traditional folk music, sounds of guitars, decimas (stanzas of ten octosyllabic lines), and controversies.[9] At the end animals realize that the jug was not magical and they had been tricked into believing it was so in order that peace could reign in Mangunido once again.

Ruandi, by Gerardo Fulleda León,[10] is a song to freedom and equal rights among men. The action takes place in a nineteenth-century Cuban sugar mill where the little slave, Ruandi, wants to be free. Ruandi, inspired by his grandfather, Mingo, and with help from his closest friend, Belina (the landowner's daughter), along with his dog, runs away to the palenque,[11] where he finds freedom at last. The play is full of adventure, and Ruandi faces life-and-death struggles, which show that only those who take risks can achieve their goals. His escape is opposed by symbol-like obstacles, which he must overcome. Drumbeats announce Ruandi's arrival at the palenque, and one is left with the feeling that he will never be enslaved again. Along with a tight plot, the play contains high-quality poetic dialogue and skillful treatment of the boundaries between reality and fantasy.

Un niño de la patria (*A Child from the Homeland*), by Francisco Earzón,[12] is a trilogy. It contains *El pequeño buscador de nidos* (*The Little Searcher of Nests*), *El pequeño jugador de pelota* (*The Little Baseball Player*), and *El pequeño recogedor de caracoles* (*The Little Snail Picker*). The plays have been performed by companies in Cuba and abroad. The main character is a child named Raúl, who appears in three important historical periods: during the war against Spanish colonial power, during the struggle against Batista's tyranny, and during the fight against counterrevolutionaries in Escambray. Raúl symbolizes the youth of the nation, who played a significant role in the Cuban wars of independence.

BIBLIOGRAPHY

Artiles, Freddy. *Acting in Puppet Theatre*. La Habana: Dirección Provincial de Cultura, Col. Extramuros, 1980.

————. "De como los ninos encontraron su teatro" ("How Children Found Their Theatre"). *Conjunto*, no. 66 (October-December), 1985.

————. *Teatro y dramaturgia para ninos en la Revolución (Theatre and Playwriting for Children in the Revolution)*. Currently awaiting publication by Editorial Letras Cubanas (Letras Cubanas Publishing House).

Martínez, Juan C., and Mayra Navarro. "Punto de vista tema polémico" ("Point of View on a Polemic Theme"). *Tablas*, no. 2 (April-June), 1985.

Tablas, no. 1 (January-March), 1986. Issue devoted to the Ninth Festival of Theatre for Children in 1985, including twenty critical reviews about the plays performed.

NOTES

1. Papel Periódico de la Habana, nos. 25–40, March 27 to May 18, 1794.

2. Pascual Ferrer, Buenaventura. *Viaje a la Isla de Cuba*/carta/de 1798. Taken from *Las diversiones Habanaras a fines del siglo XVIII (Amusements in Havana at the end of the 18th Century)*. Cuban Folkloric Archives, vol. V (no. 2), 1930.

3. Centeno (1912–1985) devoted his professional career to theatre for children. He was one of the directors of the National Puppet Theatre until his retirement.

4. Guillen was a Cuban National Poet and former president of the Cuban National Union of Writers.

5. "General audience" means the regular public. "Directed audience" refers to groups who, as the result of a common interest, buy out certain performances. The theatre is closed to the general public during these performances.

6. Dora Alonso, *Espantajo y los pájaros* (Havana: Biblioteca del Teatro Infantil (Library for Children's Theatre), 1966).

7. Freddy Artiles, *El pavo cantor* (Havana, 1980).

8. Rogelio Castillo, *El porrón maravilloso*, Revista *Tablas (Tablas* magazine), no. 2 (June-April), 1985.

9. A challenge between two opponents expressed through songs.

10. *Theatre for Children*, ed. Freddy Artiles (Havana: Letras Cubanas, 1981).

11. Hidden settlements of slaves who ran away from their owners.

12. *Theatre for Children*.

Mayra Navarro

Cyprus

HISTORY

Children's theatre in Cyprus became an organized and permanent institution in 1976 with the founding of the Children's Stage of the Cyprus Theatre Organization. In the short time since then theatre for young audiences has become increasingly popular, attracting larger and larger audiences and laying the foundations for future generations of theatre-lovers. It also aroused the interest of Cypriot authors, who have begun to write plays for children.

During its first years, and on a rather experimental level, the Children's Stage presented adaptations of internationally known fairy tales, basing its policy on the belief that children love this form of literature. The first staged play was *Puss in Boots*, by B. Wayne, which proved to be a great success. The group proceeded to mount more complex works, and ultimately presented Rainer Hatchfeldt's *Mug Nog*, a GRIPS play from West Germany. This marked the first time that the protagonist of a children's play was neither studious nor obedient, causing the play to garner strong reactions, especially from parents. *Mug Nog* questioned the influence of parents on their children and censured their belief that they are always right.

In 1980 the Cyprus Theatre Organization held its first contest for children's plays and challenged Cypriot writers to exhibit their skills. The prize-winning play was staged in 1981, which gave the writers even more incentive to create works for the fledgling children's theatre. One common characteristic of these first plays is that they follow the format of the fairy tale, within which they use symbolism to reflect the lives and experiences of Cypriots in reflection on the forced division of the island. (Since 1974 40 percent of Cyprus has been occupied by the Turkish army. The Turks invaded the country in July and August of 1974, after a coup against the president of Cyprus; they then forced the island to be divided into two territories, uprooting 200,000 persons, or one-third of the population, in the process.)

As the interest in children's theatre increased, a second children's company was created: Vladimiros Kafkarides' New Theatre, which operates in conjunction with the Children's Stage of the Cyprus Theatre Organization. The founding of this second group has opened up more opportunities for Cypriot playwrights and helps in striving for higher standards. The plays, whether fairy tales or contemporary views of life, aim at enriching the children with feelings of love, friendship, and mutual support among the different people of the world.

THE CURRENT SITUATION

There are four children's theatre companies in Cyprus today, and on average, 20,000 children see each production presented by the various groups. Some performances are given in the mornings, so that children have the chance to watch plays in an organized way during school hours. The repertory changes continually, sharpening not only the children's imaginations, but also their knowledge of everyday situations and their analytical abilities. Solid foundations have been built, and the quality of Cypriot young people's theatres is constantly improving.

REPRESENTATIVE COMPANIES AND REPERTORIES

Children's Stage of the Cyprus Theatre Organization

The recent repertory has included *Puss in Boots; Two Maples*, by Yevgeny Schwartz; *Honey Pot, The Magic Gun, The Brave Frog*, and *Grey Town*, by Lev Ustinov; *The Penguin Goes to Town*, by A. White; *Mug Nog*, by Rainer Hatchfeldt; *The Last Travelling Pigeon* and *The Red Shoes*, by Robin Sort; *Max, the Whistler*, by Ludwig Kruger; *The Tale Telling Hare*, by Sergei Michalkov; *The Two Brothers and the Black River*, by Elli Peonidou; *The Town of Mice, The Laughing Moustache*, and *The Crazy Boy*, by Philisa Hadjihanna; *The Three Children and the Mermaid*, by Maroulla Rota; *The Fairy Tale of the Three Brothers*, by Panchio Panchief; *My Friend Monkey*, by Melpo Zarokosta; *Gaitanaki*, by George Sarri; *Once Upon a Time* and *Alice in Wonderland*, by Sophia Mouaimi; *Odyssevah*, by Xenia Kalogeropoulou; *The Ancient Boat of Kyrenia*, by Vasiliki Photiou; *The Scarecrow*, by Eugene Trivizas; *School for Clowns*, by F.K. Waechter; *Vassos and Vive*, by F. Ludwig; and *The Spaceman and Din*, by N. Papadopoulos.

New Theatre Children's Stage

The repertory has included *The Goldfinch* and *Mister Kikirikou*, by Kika Pulcheriou; *The Magic Key*, by Eugenia Petronda; *Puss in Boots; Snow White;*

The Bean and the Chickpea, by George Sarri; *Little Red Riding Hood; The Three Little Pigs*; and *Gatarpagan,* by S. Epaminondas.

Satiriko Theatre

In December 1986 some actors of the New Theatre split off and formed their own company called Satiriko Theatre. The group incorporated a children's theatre component that has produced the following plays: *Dili-dili,* by Vasilis Canstantinou, directed by Andreas Pantzis; *Pinocchio,* a free adaptation written and directed by Despina Bebedeli; and *The Adventures of Chipolino,* by J. Rontari, directed by Christos Ziakas.

Theatre One

Founded in November 1987 by director Andreas Christodoulides, the group presents some children's performances. Its first production was an adaptation of Oscar Wilde's *The Selfish Giant.*

Doros Kyriakides

Doros Kyriakides, an actor and a dancer, has been operating a children's company since 1987. Spectacle plays an important part in his works for young audiences, which have included *Where Is Evlambia,* by Sofia Mouaimi and Kyriakides, and *Love Boat,* by Toula Kakoulli and Kyriakides. Both plays were directed by Pitsa Antoniades.

Mobile Stage

An important experiment that, unfortunately, did not last long, Mobile Stage began in Limassol (the second largest town in Cyprus). It consisted of a few actors who presented plays for both children and adults. Some of the works presented were *Box-Little, Box-Tiny Box,* by Paul Mar; *The Marriage Proposal,* by Anton Chekhov; *An Unexpected Meeting,* by P. Anayiotos; and several one-act plays. The company also produced dramatized versions of Cypriot folktales, adapted by director Monica Vassiliou. The themes of the plays were accessible on many levels, allowing the group to perform the same works in both elementary and secondary schools. Because the company toured, they gave performances in even the remotest villages; this bold experiment, which contained the germ of a new approach to children's theatre, unfortunately ceased operations rather abruptly because of lack of funds.

Lowell Swortzell
(Prepared from materials submitted by the Cyprus Theatre Organization.)

Czechoslovakia

HISTORY

Children's theatre in Czechoslovakia went through several noteworthy steps in the first half of the century. Miroslav Disman, who is today an Artist of Merit, began in 1918 to deal systematically with theatre and children. During the thirties Miroslav Jareš made an impact with innovative plays and numerous productions in both Bohemia and Slovakia, sharing a fundamental purpose: to unite theatre with progressive ideas in education.

Initiative to carry out such a systematic program came from Milla Mellanová, a Prague actress and director who was influenced by Natalia Sats and her work at the Moscow Theatre for Children. Mellanová opened the New Theatre for Children in Prague on October 2, 1935; except during the Nazi occupation, it has been at the forefront of theatre for young people in Czechoslovakia ever since. At first the repertory was largely drawn from works by Soviet authors, but with the opening of a second theatre in September 1945, Václav Vaňátko's Theatre of Young Pioneers, native dramatists began to emerge. Vaňátko also developed an imaginative style of performance by combining elements of E. F. Burian's "synthetic theatre" with aspects of folk poetry and children's games.

New theatres also emerged in the postwar years in Brno, Ostrava, and Bratislava. Pressure from government authorities, who refused to give financial backing, nearly resulted in the closing of all theatres by 1947 but, with the popular victory of the Czechoslovak people, in February 1948 a new era was launched. A government-approved Theatre Law now included specialized theatres for children and youth and financially guaranteed their futures, so at last the importance of theatre in education was acknowledged by the state. New efforts began to find the true relation between the theatre and the school and to pursue the artistic qualities of socialist art. The aim soon became clear: to influence the young generation through theatre in the spirit of progressive ideas of mankind.

During the 1964 Congress in Venice, Czechoslovakia joined ASSITEJ and participated in discussions that resulted in the stated belief that theatre for children and youth must be of the highest artistic level and performed only by adults, be they professionals, amateurs, or students. The child audience was defined as being within the age range of mandatory school attendance; it is the mass audience of socialist society.

Prague's two theatres merged in 1949 under the leadership of Miroslav Stehlik, a well-known dramatist in the adult theatre who also wrote for young people. In the fifties the tradition began of naming theatres after important Czech people, the most famous being Prague's Jiří Wolker. Here delegates of the 1966 ASSITEJ Congress witnessed several outstanding performances and were introduced to the work of Vladimír Adámek, who had become artistic director of the theatre in 1957. Adámek also served as a founder of ASSITEJ and as a major spokesman for international theatre for young people. He claimed that professional theatres are the nucleus of children's theatres because only they nourish playwrights, conduct research gained in direct contact with young audiences and work with the best educators. Whenever possible, they summarize their findings on a theoretical basis.

In addition to the professional children's theatres throughout the country, the great majority of adult repertory theatres in the regional and district towns and cities of both republics also include plays especially staged for young people. Repertory theatres at Most, Olomouc, Uherské, Hradiště, Košice, Jihlava, České, Budějovice, Kladno, Příbram, Kolín, Liberec, Ústí nad Labem, Opava, Šumperk, Gottwaldov, Komárno, Karlovy Vary, and elsewhere can proudly point to their extensive work in this area, gained through many years of effort. Also, the Prague Magic Lantern has attempted to produce its first program for children. According to 1973 statistics, 6,420 performances were presented by professional repertory theatres for children and youth; these were seen by almost 2.5 million young spectators.

In recent decades the children's theatre repertory has become more and more international in its offerings, as long as individual plays achieve the primary artistic aim as defined by Adámek, who called for the enrichment of thinking and the aesthetic appreciation of young playgoers. By the late seventies theatre for children had become an integral part of Czechoslovak culture, always resisting what Adámek called trends that reduce children's theatre to amusement park entertainments or substitute creativity for mere playing with audiences. He was proud that theatres in his country had not allowed their productions to become text-book illustrations or tools of the teachers.

REPRESENTATIVE COMPANIES

Profiles of several companies reveal the energy and industry of children's theatre throughout the country. The first three companies discussed play in the

Czech language, whereas the latter three companies perform in the Slovak language.

The Jiří Wolker Theatre, Prague

Czechoslovakia's oldest theatre for children and young people, founded in 1935, the Jiří Wolker is noted for its progressive and avant garde character. Thanks to the inclusion of original works in strong stagings, the theatre has become a natural center for specialized productions. Guest engagements in partner theatres as well as at international festivals have brought the company many honors and awards in Venice, Nuremberg, Madrid, Zagreb, Belgrade, East Berlin, Dresden, and Sofia.

Since the late 1970s the director has been Artist of Merit Karel Richter, an actor who has been with the Jiří Wolker Theatre since its founding. The theatre has three directors, one conductor, one stage designer, sixteen actors and eleven actresses, and a permanent ten-member orchestra (it also stages a number of musicals and plays with music).

Each season the Jiří Wolker presents four to five new plays for children over six years old and young people under eighteen, in three age categories. Its changing repertory comprises up to twelve titles, and every year some 150,000 viewers see 270 performances of native and foreign classic and contemporary plays. The Jiří Wolker has a stage of its own with an auditorium that seats 600, as well as its own workshops and administrative offices.

In 1986 the group scored a success at the Berliner Festtage in East Berlin with its staging of the musical *The Prince and the Pauper*, based on the novel by Mark Twain and adapted by V. Hradská and A. Koenigsmark. Another recent success came with *Gaudeamus igitur*, an original musical drawn from World War II student experiences that expressed strong anti-fascist viewpoints.

A part of the Jiří Wolker Theatre is the Studio Ypsilon, founded in 1963, with Jan Schmid at its head. Studio Ypsilon's artistic program draws on the traditions of the Czechoslovak and Soviet avant garde of the interwar period, as represented in works by Burian, Honzl, Meyerhold, and Tairov. The Studio produces texts of its own creation, along with classics in a variety of styles. Great emphasis is placed on the text, as the foundation and stimulus of each production, which is explored through improvisation by both the author and all actors in the company.

The Studio Ypsilon has a record of more than twenty years of creative work, with performances given in Czechoslovakia, Belgium, France, West Germany, and Yugoslavia. Since their association with the Jiří Wolker, the Y-team (Studio Ypsilon members) has also represented Czechoslovakia in Poland, Italy, and East Germany, and has appeared successfully at the regular Czechoslovak festival of youth theatre.

In recent years the Y-team has added to its repertory the following stagings: J. Schmid's *You're a Good Boy . . .* , a stage montage from the life of the writer

J. Hašek; A. Dvořák—L. Klíma's *Honest Matthew*, a fantasy-like folk comedy treated in the spirit of the contemporary ideology; *The Evening Party*, a new play by J. Schmid that criticizes the petty-bourgeois attitudes of our time and their origins; a grotesque adaptation of Dostoyevski's social-satirical novel *The Crocodile*; and the Belgian satire by Michel de Ghelderode, *The Devil Who Promised Anything and Everything*, which attacks human weakness.

The Petr Bezruč Theatre, Ostrava

Originally an independent specialized theatre for children and young people, the Petr Bezruč is now attached to the Ostrava State Theatre. With Mojmír Weimann as artistic director, the company has three directors, one stage designer, one dramaturg, and nineteen actors and thirteen actresses. Its repertory features Czechoslovak and world plays of the fairy tale type, as well as plays for teenagers on modern subjects by contemporary authors. Recent stagings include adaptations of Lewis Carroll's *Through the Looking Glass and What Alice Found There*, directed by P. Palouš, which was addressed to young audiences but not to children.

The Theatre on a String, Brno

This company devotes part of its repertory to children and young people. Established in 1967 by a committed group of graduates of Brno's Janáček Academy of Arts as a platform for the kind of self-expression that was not possible in traditional theatres, it became professional after four years of existence and is now part of the Brno State Theatre. With Jaroslav Tuček as artistic director, the Theatre on a String is an open theatre whose basic ensemble attracts young actors from other theatres, including students, amateurs, musicians, visual artists, and writers. The theatre also runs a 100-member "workshop," the Studio of Children and Young Amateurs, for the seven-to-twenty-year-old age group. In its three-building complex, now under construction, the company will be able to expand all of its varied activities.

The underlying principle of the theatre's creativity is the search for topical subjects outside the province of traditional stage literature and through unconventional treatment of them to establish direct contact with the audience. The repertory draws for its inspiration on traditions of the folk and carnival theatre and the heritage of the Czechoslovak avant garde. The company strives to capture, in an unconventional way, the problems of our time and to establish dynamic communication with its audience. It has been highly successful with children in this respect, both in Czechoslovakia and abroad, where the messages, in their unusual presentation, manage to do away with the language barrier, as in Tálská's *The Queen Calls All Her Dwarves*.

The Trnava Theatre for Children and Young People, Trnava

A specialized theatre for children and young people in Slovakia, the company was established in 1974 largely by graduates of the University of Arts. It now performs not only in the town of Trnava, but also throughout Slovakia.

The staff, under Director Mikuláš Fehér, comprises twenty-seven actors, three stage directors, two dramaturgs, and one psychologist; their average age is thirty. The Trnava presents six new plays every season: two for children, two for teenagers, and two for adults. Since 1974 it has presented sixty-eight new titles and staged 210 performances every year. The group also performs outside Czechoslovakia and has attracted great attention with the play *Charlie*, presented in 1981 in Lyons, France, and in 1982 on its tour of Denmark. The theatre also has guest-performed in the USSR (Moscow and Leningrad). Stagings of *Night of Miracles*, by the Slovak playwright Uhlár, and *The Caucasian Chalk Circle*, by Brecht, also proved popular.

Apart from the Trnava, Slovakia also has stages at Spišská Nová Ves, a part of the J. Záborský Theatre of Prešov, and the Andrej Bagár Theatre of Nitra, which perform for children and young people. The Bagár has staged with great success Pushkin's fairy tale *Tsar Saltan* at the 1986 International Festival at Šibenik, Yugoslavia. The theatre is noted for its strong impact and its attractive and inspiring stage design, both of which have won international laurels, thanks particularly to the artistic leadership of the directors, Karol Spišák and Josef Bednárik.

THE REPERTORY

The Czechoslovak Center for ASSITEJ singles out the following plays as being the most significant in the current repertory: *Anička the Fairy and Straw Hubert*, by Vítězslav Nezval; *Princess Dandelion*, by Jaroslav Kvapil; *Golden Hair*, by Josef Kainar; *How Rumcajs Became a Bandit*, by Václav Čtvrtek; *The Firebird and Trixy the Vixen*, by Jan Jílek; *How the Devils Got Married*, by Václav Tomšovský; *Princess with the Golden Star*, by K. M. Walló; *Once There Was a Dragon*, by Lada-Koenigsmark; and *How the Devil Tried to Get the Princess*, by Božena Fixová.

Milada Kadeřábková

Denmark

HISTORY

Dansk Skolescenen (the Danish School stage), an association organized in the 1920s to introduce children to theatre, dominated the field for almost fifty years. Composed of both educators and theatre artists, it largely presented traditional offerings based on fairy tales, historical subjects, and dramatizations of popular books.

A new movement emerged in the mid–1960s, started because many in the field though a theatre should exist that dealt with the political, social, and psychological realities that children and young people experienced. Also, many were angry about the quality of offerings presented by Skolescenen, which some critics thought had grown old in pursuit of its major artistic goal: "to administer the cultural inheritance of Denmark." For the most part, they felt it was a close copy of the adult theatre and took little concern for the audience for which it performed. The new movement held the position that theatre should speak directly to its audience, who should no longer remain mere passive spectators, but become actively involved. Consequently performances were given for small groups averaging from 60 to 150, who had intimate contact with the players and the play. The "underground theatre" movement of the sixties produced one new creation after another, and when American theatre groups such as the Firehouse Theatre, The Open Theatre, La Mama, and the Bread and Puppet Theatre appeared here, they inspired the entire Danish theatre environment, including children's theatre.

An active Children's Theatre Association was formed in 1969, consisting of seven member companies whose hope was to make certain that every Danish young person would see at least one production each year. By the late seventies this association boasted thirty-five member theatres and touring companies with an annual audience of some 700,000. Beginning in 1979 these theatres were organized into two categories, either resident or touring companies, and their financial condition improved somewhat. Even so, subsidies still provide for only one performance per child per year, with an unequal geographical and social distribution. It would be better if each child could see at least two performances each year free of charge, and if children's and youth theatres were considered at least as necessary and important a part of a child's growth as school education and access to books in public libraries. Conditions may be improved by the anticipated revision of the Danish Theatre Law. And though it could always be better, Danish theatre for children probably benefits (along with Sweden) from the best financial circumstances in the Western world.

THE DANISH THEATRE LAW

The first version of the Danish Theatre Law dates from 1963, when Dansk Skolescenen was still responsible for presenting a classic and educational children's repertory. This version was based on actual practices and it gave a legislative framework to the existing theatrical activities. By 1968 Skolescenen had outlived itself. Now the tendency was to focus on the living conditions of children and youth. This concern led to the development of the new style of theatre that dealt with the lives of children and young people, their position in society and their thoughts and feelings.

Because this new style was developing quickly, it was necessary to find new forms of distribution. After 1970 theatre legislation included a new clause, section 16, which stated: "Grants can be given to performances of plays for children and young people, as well as for educational work on the theatre." Despite the wording, which delineated funding for the *performance* of plays, in practice, support was given for the *production* of plays. Initially, only 1,050,000 Danish Crowns was allocated for this purpose. Since then development has been rapid, and theatre for children and youth has become important enough to demand better conditions. Although these demands have been met, social attitudes have not really changed and the battles have been unpleasant.

In the current theatre law, again under revision, section 16 deals with regional theatre (mainly supported by municipalities), traveling and itinerant theatre for young audiences (supported by county authorities), and traveling and stationary theatre for children and young people (supported by the central state administration). In addition, there is support for a Committee for Children's and Youth Theatre, which, with the help of The Theatre Center, is responsible for gathering information and disseminating advice about children's and youth theatre in Denmark.

Regional theatres emerge in a particular location and have special links to that area. One or more local authorities, sometimes in cooperation with the county council, take the initiative to set up a regional theatre, and the state then contributes the same sum as the local funding agencies, technically known as a 50 percent state refund of the local expenses for regional theatre. One problem with this policy is that it does not give sufficient support to enable the theatre to stay in the region for the greater part of the year, since earnings must be supplemented through traveling activities. Another problem is that the local authorities estimate that their share of the financing is too high, since they seldom see the regional theatre in the municipality.

Section 16 also contains legislation for the total support by county councils of the traveling children's theatre and itinerant theatre (which can also be for young people). An executive committee comprising representatives from the county councils and relevant professional organizations grants support to a number of theatres according to recommendations from the five-member Theatrical Council (an advisory and support body elected through the Ministry of Culture). The problem with section 16 is, first and foremost, that the grants are not sufficient to meet the needs of the traveling and itinerant theatres and that the system is not binding on the county councils. Lesser problems are the size of the executive committee, the expenses associated with its work, and the risk of placing too many administrative demands on the theatres.

It is against this background that revision of theatrical legislation is taking place. The two theatre-membership organizations that deal with areas under section 16, the Children's Theatre Association (BTS) and the Association of Small Theatres (FAST), have presented their comments and requests to the revision committee, which has been set up by the Minister of Culture without representatives from the field. BTS and FAST want the total support for theatre for young audiences to be at least sufficient to provide two performances per year for each child. In addition, there are other theatrical activities that should be supported. As insurance for the future, the groups also want the legislation to underwrite continued theatrical development by supporting new initiatives and experiments. In this respect, they want the law to be formulated so as to meet the need of theatre producers for flexibility and dynamism, and thus become the catalyst for new thinking and developments in the theatre as the year 2000 approaches.

REPRESENTATIVE COMPANIES

Badteatret (The Boat Theatre)

Denmark's only sailing company was founded in 1972 when three architects had the idea of converting a turn-of-the-century barge into a playhouse. This is the only company that can be both a stationary and a touring theatre. Nine months of the year The Boat Theatre is anchored in Nyhavn, a historically restored and picturesque area of seventeenth-century houses in a central section of Cophenhagen. For two months in the summer and one in the autumn the theatre sails on tour to Helsingoer and a number of other ports on Zealand. Performing for all age groups, the company presents about 380 shows a year, almost always to sold-out houses.

Det Lille Teater (The Little Theatre)

Founded in 1966 as the first stationary theatre for children and situated in central Copenhagen, The Little Theatre stands close to the city hall and is part of an eighteenth-century warehouse, the interior of which has been restored to include ample technical facilities, rehearsal and workshop space, and a proscenium stage with fly gallery. Even so, the theatre lives up to its name, for the stage is small and the house seats only eighty children.

The Little Theatre produces three or four new productions each year. Three of these are aimed at children from three to seven years of age from nursery schools and kindergartens, as well as at their parents. The repertory varies widely, often combining live actors and puppets. In addition to these activities the company regularly hosts guest performances from other theatres, both from Denmark and abroad.

Bjorneteatret (The Bear Theatre)

The Bear Theatre consists of artists who have different creative backgrounds: musicians, architects, painters, ceramists, and schoolteachers. They use their knowledge in the plays that they create, which range from street theatre for all ages to short plays for children as young as one-and-a-half years old. Works in the repertory are widely different, depending on which members of the company have been involved in their creation. Of the six members, five are actor-puppeteers, who often dramatize stories drawn from their own lives in plays that dwell on such basic topics as waiting, enjoying oneself, aspects of daily life, and the sky and its connection to the people seen on stage. The group is experimental, looking for spontaneous contact with its audience, which includes parents as well as young people who together share an experience that the company hopes they will take home and discuss.

Dueslaget

Dueslaget was established in Ribe in 1972 and moved around the country during its early years before taking up permanent residence in Elsinore. A collective company, it strives for performances that appeal to adults as well as children. Besides performing in Elsinore, the group traverses all of Denmark, performing at elementary and high schools, offering an annual repertory of three plays. In addition to its regular season, Dueslaget produces plays on subjects of local concern. One such play, *Nitterdrengene (The River Boys)*, involved 110 persons, 60 of them on stage. The company has been supported by the Ministry of Culture but aspires to be designated a regional theatre subsidized by the municipalities of Zealand.

Teatret Artibus

An independent company founded in 1969 with a collective management, Teatret Artibus primarily performs for children and young people but produces for adult audiences as well. Located in Copenhagen, the theatre is subsidized by the Ministry of Culture to play in schools and institutions throughout Denmark. The staff consists of seven actors, one designer, one playwright-director, and two administrators. The recent repertory has included such works as *He Who Gets Angry First*, based on a German folktale that shows audiences how to fight trolls; *Three Strong Women*, drawn from a Japanese fairy tale expounding the theme that human strength is best found in work and peace; *Day of the Witches*, a play that describes a witch-hunt; and *The Adventurous Soldier*, a drama about the Thirty Years' War, based on the novel by Hans Jacob Grimmelshausen (1622–1676), which describes a young boy's experience with war.

Comedievognen

In its eighteen seasons Comedievognen has become one of Denmark's oldest experimental ensemble theatres, especially in developing new forms for children and youth. While the company owns its theatre, which is located in a suburb of Copenhagen, it also spends much of the year playing in schools and libraries and to theatre societies all over the country. A major characteristic of Comedievognen's policy is the size of its audience, which must be fewer than 200 (preferably 150) young people or 80 children. This guarantees close contact and greater interaction between spectators and performers.

The group consists of six actors and two administrators, plus a visiting director, designer, and composer, and technicians who are engaged for each production. Sometimes the company is augmented by additional actors. Of the four productions presented each season, some are written by the actors themselves, some are commissioned from Danish authors, and some are adapted from published works. The company has received both national and international awards and made guest appearances at the children's theatre festivals in Trieste in 1986 and Bologna in 1987.

THE DANISH CHILDREN'S THEATRE FESTIVAL

One of the biggest in the world, with more than seventy companies and 500 participants, the Festival offers more than 100 plays for one week each April. The vast organization of the Festival is managed by Teatercentrum (Theatre Center), whose aim is to allow every child in the area (the Festival changes locations annually) to see at least one performance suitable for her or his age. During the Festival the member companies of the Association of Children's Theatres conduct their annual seminar, which is dedicated to raising artistic standards in children's theatre. In 1987 forty-four professional companies participated, showing their offerings to those who book performances, including teachers, librarians, educators, and community leaders. About 10,000 children attend Festival performances, which attract spectators from throughout the country.

Lowell Swortzell
(Prepared from materials submitted by ASSITEJ/Denmark.)

Finland

HISTORY

The development of children's theatre in Finland is inseparable from the historical, social, and aesthetic dimensions of theatre as a whole, which, to a certain extent, has followed a different path than that in the other Scandinavian countries. The special flavor of Finnish theatre can be traced back to its more popular origins, to its strong social predominance among the arts, and to its contacts with Slavic theatre. Perhaps, unexpectedly, the joint influence of these factors has proved more of a burden to children's theatre than a foundation nourishing its development and originality.

In Finland, theatre has flourished for only just over a century. Until the 1860s this bilingual country was a periphery in which traveling Swedish, German, and Russian troupes toured. The founding of the first Finnish-language professional company in 1872, the precursor of the modern Finnish National Theatre, is generally considered to mark the birth of Finnish theatre. The specific conditions that made this possible were the awakening of national feeling, the rise of the labor movement in the cities, and, correspondingly, the spreading of the agrarian youth movement in the countryside. As their ideals of enlightenment involved great enthusiasm for acting, an idiosyncrasy of national character evidenced still by widespread amateur theatricals, the popular quality and social influence of theatre were immediately acknowledged.

Although Finnish theatre has always been aware of its national and educational vocation, it has not been so conscious of the continuity of its role and how to safeguard it. Powerful and original though Finnish theatre is acknowledged to be, it has lagged well behind other Nordic countries as far as the systematic development of children's theatre and the "preparation" of new generations of spectators are concerned. One possible explanation for the delay is that the lack of tradition in theatre has tended to support a strict, narrowly defined style.

Theatre has played such an important role in efforts to educate people that despite its freedom from the conventions of court theatre, it has been burdened with a solemn, "plushy" establishment tone.

The institutional theatres have long pandered to the tastes of the middle classes, and have turned attendance into a custom: instead of going to see a play, people "go to the theatre." The itinerant students and organ-grinders of old, the circus clowns, the acrobats, and the ballad-writers have been banished; puppet theatre and the music hall have never been accepted as real art. The link with early forms of folk theatre, and the theatre as a place of jokes and alternative images of reality conveyed by exaggeration and rough style have only reappeared quite recently.

Attempts to break the conventions have shown time and again how firmly Finns believe that realistic representation is in "our own tradition" and how quickly new international trends in twentieth-century theatre have been rejected here. The psychorealistic view has remained dominant throughout, inherited from the involvement of major Finnish theatre personnel and instructors with the Stanislavsky system. The conception of theatre as the dramatic form of world literature also has firm roots in Finland's institutional theatres. Only periodically have productions broken through the turgidness to become independent art forms, wherein various elements have been seen to support the theatrical experience instead of detracting from it.

The solemnity, psychorealism, and basic literary character of institutional productions is particularly ill-adapted to children's theatre. These traits have also reduced the interest of dramatic artists in children's theatre, as they have believed that plays for young people rarely provide an opportunity for total psychological character description, while they have had little training for more stylized expression. "Institutional" children's theatre is frequently hypocritical, affected, and condescending toward its young audience.

The financial support traditionally provided by society is a measure of the esteem in which theatre is held in Finland. A dense network of professional theatres, formed from the idealistic movements discussed above, appeared in this sparsely populated country with the help of extensive public subsidy. Every self-respecting town, no matter how small, has a "City Theatre" jointly supported by the local and state government, whereas the larger cities (Helsinki, Tampere, Turku, Vaasa) have several such theatres. All told, there are thirty-three institutional theatres in the country. The status of theatre takes concrete form in the steady flow of new, monumental playhouses built since the 1960s. Since the late 1960s nine brand-new theatres have been built, many old theatre buildings have been enlarged and renovated, and there are plans for several more. The new buildings tend to house two or three theatres, and the abrupt rise in production costs at the larger theatres has led, in turn, to increasing commercialization.

Since the early days of Finnish theatre the idea that financial assistance by society was essential to operation has been prevalent. Although this implies that theatre should be equally available to all citizens, including children and young people, public support for children's theatre has been restricted to a scanty annual subsidy for traveling companies. The coolness and slow awakening to the needs of children's theatre are, naturally, symptoms of general attitudes. The inferiority complex of a young culture requires prominent institutions to prop themselves up. The world encountered in children's theatre is prosaic and peripheral compared with the dramatic feasts served up by the "real" theatre. To the decision-makers, the general theatre-going public, and even most theatre people, the audience that attends children's plays seems like a remote "reservation of the dispossessed," made up of the more invisible members of society: youngsters and schoolchildren, housewives, kindergarten and school teachers. The independent companies that service these populations have been obliged to fight desperately for subsistence and to rely far more heavily on ticket sales, despite offering cheap children's tickets, to finance their productions than do the more highly subsidized institutional theatres.

CHILDREN'S THEATRE

As in the other Nordic countries, performances for children in Finnish theatres before the rise of independent theatre companies were generally limited to a single annual fairy tale play staged around the Christmas season. Finland was self-sufficient as far as these plays went, as it had its own storyteller in Zachris Topelius, a journalist and critic who wrote some thirty children's plays in the 1850s and 1860s based on Finnish and international folktales (Topelius was the first, in 1842, to call for an indigenous Finnish drama). Many generations of children have been enveloped in the magic circle of his plays, confined as they were by didacticism and black-and-white morality. However, in the course of 100 years, the performing tradition and treatment of Topelius' plays became stereotyped and flat.

The works thus became the symbol of reactionary children's theatre for the generation that created the independent theatres in the late 1960s and early 1970s and that took up the cause of theatre for young audiences with great enthusiasm. That generation believed that the fairy tale elements of Topelius' plays blurred the child's conception of reality, and threw Topelius (and with him the entire fairy tale tradition) overboard.

The lack of instructive, socially critical children's plays was overcome with patched-up texts that were tailor-made to the individual groups performing them. These works had an epic structure and dealt with mechanization, pollution, the dangers of drugs and smoking, the developing countries, and other social problems. Regardless of the scope of an issue, the pattern was to present one problem and its solution. Information and instruction were served up through fantasy elements, imaginary creatures, and magic tricks. Style was sought in the "aesthetics of scarcity" as practiced in the medieval market theatre, since on tour, performances had to be staged in a variety of spaces. The believability of the

situations depended on the actors' skill, and characters were deliciously cari-
catured types. The greatest impact of these instructive plays was to open the
doors of schools and day-care centers to the independent companies.

Children's theatre reconquered the fairy tale in the mid–1970s. The group
theatre movement had passed from simplistic social preaching to a deeper view
of the world and man. Fairy tales were now thought to express people's deepest
wishes and morality. With this shift in insights and conclusions, the current
trend is away from didacticism and instruction and toward a theatre of greater
artistic ambition.

COMPANIES

The independent companies have been pioneers in Finnish children's theatre,
although development has undoubtedly been hindered by the financial and intellectual starvation from which the groups have suffered. The continuity of
artistic development has also depended on these touring companies, even though
there has been a gradual change in the attitude of the institutional theatres, from
merely dutiful and infrequent attention to actual interest in the possibilities of
theatre for young audiences. The activity of the institutional theatres is seasonal,
however, and productions for children have still not achieved an established
position within them.

The total number of theatrical performances each year is approximately 12,000
and the number of spectators, 2,700,000 (the population of the country is fewer
than 5 million); one-quarter of these performances are for young audiences, and
the independent touring companies account for 40 percent of the performances
for children. There are fifteen independent theatre and dance companies in the
country. Companies that perform for children include the Swedish-language
Skolteatern (the oldest, founded in 1960); the puppet theatres Vihreä Omena,
Sampo, Hevosenkenkä, Mukamas, and Peukalopotti; Penniteatteri, AHAA Teatteri, and Teatteri 41, which specialize in school performances; and the modern
dance companies Raatikko and Hurjaruuth, which mount some productions for
children.

Children's theatre in Finland currently stands at a crossroads. The first national
institutional children's theatre has been founded; how the financial and artistic
resources allotted to it will affect the development of independent children's
theatre companies remains to be seen.

AMATEUR THEATRE

It has been said that every Finn has stood on the stage at some time during
his or her life; this is hardly an exaggeration! Amateur activities have recently
expanded particularly rapidly among children and young people. The Finnish
Amateur Theatre Association has been organizing a national Children's Theatre
Day for ten years. So far there have been five of these days in different parts

of the country, the idea of which is to offer people a chance to see a sampling of the kind of theatre that children and young people create when given the opportunity. The celebration gives youngsters a chance both to perform and to watch others of their age perform. Also, there are improvisations and workshops that participants can join, offering them a chance to get acquainted and work together.

Storybook classics are always part of the program but so, too, are visual performances based on improvisation, music and dance pieces, and stories that extoll heroism, adventure, danger, invention, and creativity. And most of the children's pieces seem to incorporate a happy ending and to emphasize humor. Events of this kind have shown adults what children are thinking and feeling, what it's like to live in a modern child's world. But they also tell us about dreams and longings, and about how art broadens the vision and adds color to one's life.

The birth of theatre groups made up of young amateur performers is often connected with the rise of Finnish rock music. In the late 1970s several live music associations were founded and drew attention to themselves by occupying an empty building. These bands voiced, in their lyrics, serious criticism against social evils, and more important, they sang in Finnish. Once theatre companies realized the impact that these rock groups were having on Finnish youth, they began to incorporate them into new "rock operas," thrown-together shows with sketchy plots and patronizing airs; these presentations were not successful. In contrast, young people have put together their own productions with rock music. The Desperado Group of Helsinki, of which no member is over twenty-one years old and all are amateurs, mounted an impressive production of Shakespeare's bloody classic *Macbeth*, using rock music to enhance the action.

The Finnish ASSITEJ Center organized the first Theatre Week for Young People in the autumn of 1985. The main idea was to present both professional performances of high artistic standards and the productions of young amateurs. It was hoped that this event would result in a fruitful interaction between the two groups. The week proved successful enough to be repeated; under the name Young Theatre, the festival was again held during November of 1986.

THE HELSINKI PROJECT

By the beginning of the 1980s most of the independent companies producing for young audiences had existed for more than ten years. During this time they had worked under enormous economic pressure and with no permanent playhouses. The groups had fought long and hard for the right to exist and for a measure of respectability in a society that put little or no value on things connected with children. As the years passed retaining talented and skilled professional actors became more difficult. Freedom of decision in artistic matters and a voice in choosing the repertory did not compensate for the negative aspects: the constant touring, the low pay and questionable image, the lack of publicity, and the limited audiences.

Children's theatre companies believed that they could no longer develop artistically, and they faced inevitable setbacks. They also thought that it was important to perform for both children and their parents, but they did not have access to public performance spaces (performances open to the general public could be arranged only rarely because of an acute lack of proper venues). With the exception of a few small puppet theatres, there wasn't one theatre in the country reserved for children's theatre performances.

It was in response to this desperate situation that four companies (Penniteatteri, the puppet theatres Sampo and Vihreä Omena, and Skolteatern) took action. In May 1981 they presented a joint proposal to the city of Helsinki that, in short, asked for a playhouse and sufficient financial support to form a theatre company to perform regularly for children from preschool age through teenagers. The company would perform both in the daytime and in the evening and play both puppet and live theatre, in both Swedish and Finnish. The proposal also made clear that the group not only would be prepared to perform on its own stage, but also would be expected to tour its productions throughout Helsinki and the rest of Finland.

The idea was that by combining their meager resources, the four companies would be able to offer a richer and more varied repertory. They would merge themselves into one major group with a decent stage and sufficient resources to present a viable season. This would raise the prestige and attractiveness of children's theatre not only in Helsinki, but also throughout the country. A bilingual theatre for children would prove beneficial in a country with two languages.

The city of Helsinki, however, did not show much interest in the project, claiming that no suitable buildings were available and that cooperating with the state in this kind of matter was not possible. No notice was taken of the fact that the need for a national children's theatre in the country's capital had already been recognized and commented about in several instances. The group continued its fight and bravely kept trying to find a playhouse that would be suitable.

The idea of a "national theatre" for children, in fact, did raise a great deal of curiosity and interested concern over the next several years. The question was discussed within the Central Association of the Finnish Theatre Organizations, in the Helsinki City Council, at the Ministry of Education, and even in Parliament. In the spring of 1983 a commission appointed by the Ministry of Education was given the task of investigating the possibility of founding a national theatre for children with a permanent playhouse in Helsinki. The commission, which included representatives of the state and the city, the theatre companies and theatre organizations, and Finnish ASSITEJ, came to the conclusion that both the need and the possibility existed for a national theatre for children. The Ministry of Education agreed, in principle, with the commission's findings, but the Ministry of Finance was decidedly against allocating any funds for the construction or renovation of any facilities for the use of theatre for children.

The whole project suddenly took on a new dimension when theatre authorities in the city of Tampere announced that they were planning to institute a new children's theatre in a building that had gone unused since the Worker's Theatre moved into a new space. They suggested that this new theatre become the prospective national theatre for children. Shortly thereafter another surprising suggestion was made: a private theatre company in Helsinki, Intimiteatteri, which owned a new, modern playhouse, offered to alter its current activities and become the national children's theatre. The prospect of increased subsidy from both local and state funding sources made this kind of upheaval more exciting.

There were now two proposals for a national children's theatre, in addition to the original plan, and each had its supporters. For the first time in years children's theatre was a topic of cultural and political debate. For the companies themselves, who had carried the main responsibility of professional children's theatre for the past fifteen years, the situation was, to say the least, awkward. Naturally they had hoped for a solution that would allow them to continue their work under improved conditions, that is, within the framework of the national theatre for children. Instead, it now looked as if they were to be completely disregarded.

With this in mind, Penniteatteri and Skolteatern entered into negotiations with Intimiteatteri. The three companies then presented the following proposal: Intimiteatteri and Penniteatteri would merge into a new company that would present works exclusively for children (in Finnish), while Skolteatern, which had recently been given a facility in the nearby town of Espoo, would be responsible for presenting plays in Swedish for young audiences.

Based on this proposal, the state budget of 1986 included provisions for 3 million markkas for new theatre activities aimed at children and young people. The proposed Intimiteatteri-Penniteatteri fusion became a reality at the beginning of 1987. The recently founded children's theatre in Tampere, Teatteri 2000, also got its share of funding. All of a sudden Finland had two "national" theatres for children. A third one, a regional theatre for children in northern Finland, is also planned.

This sudden and amazing development is a positive sign. But there are still many obstacles to overcome before the Finns have a properly functioning network of high-quality theatres for children and young people. Money is always a question; there is the risk that funds will be exhausted and that the work undertaken thus far will be left half complete. There is also the problem of focusing on one part of the country and forgetting the rest. Ways to promote new initiatives that do not neglect the smaller independent touring companies need to be developed. The real risk, however, is that the "solutions" may prove merely theoretical: they may look good on the surface and promote political goodwill while making no real impact in furthering children's theatre of superior artistic quality.

The Helsinki Project has already proved problematic. An independent theatre does not easily merge with a traditional company that has quite a different approach to its work. In Tampere, Teatteri 2000, in its first year of production, mounted only well-known, traditional fairy-tale plays such as *Snow White and the Seven Dwarves*. In other words, the company played it safe and stayed with surefire hits. This choice of repertory is not too encouraging to those who for years have worked for a new and creative children's theatre.

But we will wait and see what time brings. Let us hope that the story of Finland's National Theatre for Children will have a happy ending after all, that one day Finland will have a theatre that by its bright example will give all children's theatre activity the artistic inspiration that it's been waiting for so long!

Lowell Swortzell
(Prepared from materials submitted by ASSITEJ/Finland.)

France

HISTORY

Children's theatre did not become a concern in France until the 1920s. Before that time no significant theatrical activity took place that was specifically aimed at children. Charles Dullin (1885–1949), the great actor and director and an early proponent of children's theatre, warned with enormous foresight in 1928 that directors should fight against the visual elements imposed upon children by film by creating a movement to prevent audiences from leaving the theatre. He called for productions that would initiate and develop future playgoers.

Léon Chancerel (1886–1965), a pupil of Jacques Copeau, was the first to respond to Dullin's warning; in 1929 he founded the Comediens Routiers, a touring group that played to boy scout troops. In Paris in 1935 he also began Le Théâtre de l'Oncle Sébastien (The Theatre of Uncle Sebastian), which performed on Sunday afternoons. In the tradition of *commedia dell'arte*, the company of young actors trained by Chancerel improvised stock characters who directly addressed audiences at important points in the action of the plays. During the group's ten years of existence Chancerel was active on other fronts as well. He helped to establish several young actor's companies and mobilized interest and attention toward children's theatre by creating the Theatre Association for Children and Youth, the precursor to ASSITEJ. He later succeeded Louis Jouvet as president of the Societe d'Histoire du Théâtre.

These first attempts at children's theatre were interrupted by World War II, though not before Charles Vildrac and Olivier Hussenot became involved. The youth theatre movement essentially ceased during the war years, and not until the 1950s did it begin to stir once more. This revival of interest was due, in part, to new educational ideas and the role played by "sensitization," especially as exhibited in productions directed by Miguel Demuynk and his Théâtre de la

Clairière in such productions as *Les Cent Ecus D'Or (A Hundred Pieces of Gold)*, a folk comedy with music.

Even so, it was the unrest of 1968, with its violent overthrowing of traditional cultural customs, that catapulted children's theatre into real action. In fact, 1968 is considered the birth of French theatre for young audiences, which has been defined by its founders as a theatre in its own right that is not influenced by general theatrical customs or the opinions of the populace. This position, in addition to new theories about the place of children and youth in society, prompted the creation of a network of theatre companies whose works emphasized the link between the child and the artistic product. Among the most important were Catherine Dasté's Pomme Verte (Green Apple) in Sartrouville, Maurice Yendt's Théâtre des Jeunes Années (Theatre of the Young Years) in Lyons, and the Théâtre des Juenes Spectateurs (Theatre of Young Audiences), also known as Compagnie Bazilier, in Saint-Denis.

Though still small and undervalued, youth theatre was forging a position for itself based on the quality and professional character of its productions, the determination of its producers, and the growing support from its audience. In 1976 six companies were elevated to the status of National Dramatic Centers, an action that not only benefited the companies themselves, but also gave official recognition and support to children's theatre in general. Though these centers are granted subsidies, it should be noted that the amount is far less than the Cultural Ministry gives to "adult" theatres. Also, subsidy for a few children's companies does not solve the problems that affect theatre for young audiences as a whole. Nevertheless, encouraged by these few centers, theatre for young audiences has greatly burgeoned, and as it stands today, the field is widely diversified.

ARTISTIC OBJECTIVES

The one word that best defines the artistic and creative impulses of companies and individuals involved in theatre for young people is "disparity." In addition to the six National Dramatic Centers mentioned above, there are a great many professional companies, although these do not necessarily play full seasons (or even more than once or twice a week), and some simply consist of one or two actors who take shows into schools. To illustrate the situation further, of the 200 companies officially listed, only forty present regular and continuous theatrical activities.

The one common denominator shared by the majority of companies is their world view. Political objectives have been an important determinant in the works presented, and the companies are actively involved in the idea of social and political emancipation of children and youth, as well as their cultural liberation. From the beginning they have made use of artistic forms and styles, and thematic content that underscored their political beliefs. This led to trends such as those exhibited in the years 1965 through 1975 (years particularly fertile in diverse innovations), when, for example, the objective of most productions was consciousness raising. Plays were geared toward confronting the audience with the problems of society and the world around them. So young people were faced with issues of racism, poverty, women's liberation, and war, all from the dramatist's particular point of view. And although examination of these concerns was certainly valuable, the works proved to be predictably didactic.

The companies since have moved away from goals of group consciousness and now strive to affirm a unique artistic identity or a recognizable style through their literary and aesthetic choices. Within a common framework and purpose they project their individual trademarks in the competitive field of theatrical production.

RELATION WITH THE SCHOOLS

The traditional practice of teachers taking students to daytime performances specifically mounted for them has almost ended in France. Where once particular companies were associated with specific schools, the practice now is to present productions geared toward mixed or family audiences in the evening, thereby making attendance at the theatre a matter of deliberate choice instead of forced participation.

THE FUNDING SITUATION

Although one cannot deny that in fifteen years youth theatre has made visible and, in some cases, remarkable progress, it still has a long way to go. By way of example, and to expose the disparity in the system of subsidization, the most highly funded National Dramatic Center for youth receives 500,000 francs less than the least well-funded National Dramatic Center for adults. To give the complete picture, one must add that the geographical situations of the various companies play an important role in their levels of subsidy. Besides ministerial funding, the groups depend, to a large degree, on regional and local funding organizations.

In 1987 only one children's company (The Theatre of Young Years in Lyon) received additional money from a municipality. This lack of funding forces most children's groups to rent office, rehearsal, and performance space, as they cannot afford to purchase property. In addition, they are forced to tour to balance their budgets, which, ironically, makes them better known outside their home city than in it.

THE FUTURE

In the late 1970s youth theatre was concerned with the serious lack of appropriate plays available for young audiences. This problem led people who were not playwrights to write scripts, with varying degrees of success. Today we seem to have rediscovered (or perhaps only now discovered) the importance of the quality of the text for both children's and adult theatre. We have also seen a return to more formal styles of dramatic literature, in which acting, music, and rhythm are all subjugated to the primacy of the text. This movement is likely to create a totally new dramatic repertory for children.

THE COMPANIES

Théâtre des Jeunes Années

Created by Maurice Yendt, the Theatre of Young Years has been professionally active since 1968. Yendt is first an author, having written several adaptations and original plays in which he presents his humanistic concerns. *Le Rossignol et l'Oiseau Mécanique (The Nightingale and the Mechanical Bird)* denounces the tyranny and foolishness of an emperor who tries to master nature; *La Machine à Théâtre* is an exercise in playful style about truth and illusion; *Histoire aux Cheveux Rouges (The Story of the Red Head)* is about racism; and *La Marche à l'Envers (The March to Envers)* shows, in an original manner, the damage wrought by an education that is too rigorous. Though these works are undeniably stamped by a certain didacticism, they also are marked by a style of language that promotes both thought and discussion. Yendt's work has thrust him into the small group of significant dramatists for young people and enabled his theatre to create demanding productions.

Joined in 1972 by Michel Dieuaide, with whom Yendt has since directed the company, the Théâtre des Jeunes Années has vigorously promoted the idea of theatre that demands that all theatrical elements perform at their highest level. The text, the style, the scenery, the music, and the costumes must function as they do in the adult theatre, free of the childishness, mysticism, and demagoguery to which young audiences are too often innocent victims. Known in France and abroad as one of the most inventive companies, Théâtre des Jeunes Années was designated in 1979 as one of six companies titled National Dramatic Centers. In 1980 the city of Lyon assigned the theatre a home of its own from which the group can at last headquarter its activities.

Since the group was originally dedicated to the development of texts, Théâtre des Jeunes Années grants a privileged position to "their" playwright, Maurice Yendt. He is credited with the creation of a dozen plays (*The Story of the Red Head*, which has been revived ten times since its initial production, and *Etat d'urgence* [*The Urgent Condition*] are his best-known works). The group is drawn to contemporary authors, and other works in its repertory include *Kikerikiste* (first produced in 1976 and revived in 1984), by Paul Maar; *La Poupée de chiffon (The Rag Doll)*, by Jorge Gajardo, a Chilean playwright; and *Le Secret (The Secret)* and *Les Deux Bossus (The Camel Has Two Humps)*, by Richard Demancy. The company recently revealed to its young public a supposedly "difficult" playwright in Samuel Beckett when they presented *Doucement, Billy,*

Doucement, (Gently, Billy, Gently), written in 1985 and adapted from *Fragments of Theatre*.

Grenette (Lyon)

Created in 1976 by Michel Véricel and Yves Barbaut, the Grenette is organized not around a playwright, but around the desire "to make theatre very simple," with an emphasis on contemporary language. In 1979, following in the footsteps of Petit Poucet, the company produced *Des cailloux aux étoiles (The Fate of Stones)*, which toured Switzerland and Italy. Grenette also produced, in 1983, *Jeu d'écritures (The Game of Writing)*, inspired by George Perce; in 1985, returning to its sources, *Qobelett* was adapted from the *Euclestics*. Recently *Lancelot du Lac (Lancelot of the Lake)* established Grenette among the creative leaders for youth as well as a company adept at taking artistic risks. But despite the recognition it has won from the public and various amateur groups that follow its example, Grenette remains in a precarious situation, dependent on regional organizations as the major means of its existence.

Theatre for Young Spectators (Compagnie Bazilier)

From 1967 to 1971 Bazilier's Company was financially dependent on the Théâtre du Gérard Philipe (Saint-Denis), and produced spectacles in which actors shared the stage with gigantic crepe paper marionettes in works such as *En passant par la Louisiane (Passing by the Louisiane)* and *20,000 Lieues sous les mers (20,000 Leagues Under the Sea)*. In 1972 the company became autonomous and began its collaboration with dramaturg Patricia Giros. This marked the end of its work with puppets, and it moved into the sphere of more traditional presentations. By 1979 the group had achieved the status of National Dramatic Center. Its later merger with the Saint-Denis company brought about the change in name to the Theatre for Young Spectators. Each year the company presents six or seven productions of which one or two are original creations. Among them have been *Sirène d'alarme (Alarming Mermaid)*, *Le nez à la fenêtre (Nose on the Windowpane)*, *Le croquemitaine (The Bogey-man)*, and *L'exception et la règle (The Exception and the Rule)*. The group is composed of a permanent team of seven persons who are joined by about ten additional players engaged seasonally, depending on the needs of the productions. The Theatre for Young Spectators is one of the rare permanent companies for young people in the Paris area.

Marielle Creac'h
Translated by Marc Janover and Nancy Swortzell

German Democratic Republic

HISTORY

On November 7, 1946, one and a half years after the defeat of Hitlerite fascism and the end of World War II, the first professional theatre for children and young people, the Theater der Jungen Welt (Theatre of the Young World), opened its doors in Leipzig with Erich Kästner's play for children *Emil und die Detektive* (*Emil and the Detective*). Supported by progressive-minded politicians and specialists in cultural and educational matters, a completely new type of theatre started its work in the country.

Other theatres of this kind were subsequently founded in the industrial areas of Dresden (1949), Berlin (1950), Halle and Erfurt (1952). From the beginning these theatres were fully subsidized by the state and had the same legal status as the municipal or state-run professional stages for adult audiences, although workers were not paid equal wages. Initially the repertory of these new theatres was not much different from the children's programs of the municipal theatres, even though directors always made visible efforts to choose traditional plays that stood out for their marked social motivations, which promoted democratic attitudes and took children seriously.

This situation changed in 1950 after the founding of Theater der Freundschaft (Theatre of Friendship) in Berlin, which, under the provisions of the law, was to "set an example for the children's theatre throughout the GDR [German Democratic Republic]." It had a company of 180, including 34 actors and 17 musicians.

The actor and producer Hans Rodenberg, founder and first director of this theatre, brought to his new post experience gained before fascism when he worked with proletarian theatre companies and learned the prevailing theories about children's theatre as developed by Walter Benjamin and Edwin Hoernle. He had also spent fifteen years in the Soviet Union, where he saw many excellent examples of theatre for young audiences. Organizing a company of mostly young actors, he made certain that they were prepared to conquer new artistic ground and to subordinate their own ambitions to the interests of the theatre. Through its educational department the company made continuous contact with young audiences, schools, and youth organizations, which continues to this day. Co-operation with authors and the inclusion in the repertory of proven plays for young audiences from the Soviet Union finally gave rise to a program for various age groups that focused attention on contemporary plays. They dealt with current political issues and social decisions facing young people, and derived their subjects from both the present and the past.

Authors of these new plays were mostly older dramatists who belonged to the generation of early socialist writers, such as Gustav von Wangenheim *(Du bist der Richtige [You Are the Right One]* and *Wir sind schon weiter [We Have Already Made Progress]* and Hilda Zinner *(Spiel ins Leben [Play into Life]).* From the Soviet Union, plays by Lyubimova *(Schneeball [The Snowball]),* Arkadi Gaidar *(Timur und sein Trupp [Timur and his Squad]),* and Sergey Michalkov *(Das rote Halstuch [The Red Scarf])* and, from German classic literature, Schiller's *Luise Millerin (Love and Intrigue)* were included in the repertory.

At the beginning the company still had some reservations about fairy-tale plays, but after heated discussions the group recognized that a children's theatre cannot do without them. The first examples produced were *Little Red Riding Hood,* by Yevgeny Schwartz, and *The Purple Flower.* When other theatres for children and young people throughout the country adopted the principles of Hans Rodenberg they also started to develop a specific artistic policy, which found clear expression in a repertory rich in topics and genres. The fairy-tale play for the youngest audiences was firmly rooted in this repertory, despite the distortions and superficial adaptations it had experienced for decades in the commercial bourgeois theatre. The Soviet fairy-tale plays by Yevgeny Schwarz, Samuil Marshak, and Pavel Malyarevski were of special importance for their recognition of the artistic and educational values that contributed to the development of a national fairy-tale drama, still performed today as the "classics of the children's theatre."

·   Theatres for children and young people also made continuous efforts, although not with the same intensity, to perform plays of national and international classic literature: Shakespeare *(Romeo and Juliet, The Comedy of Errors),* Goldoni *(Der Lügner [The Liar], Diener zweier Herren [The Servant of Two Masters],* and *Krach in Chiozza [A Row in Chiozza]),* Molière *(L'Avare, George Dandin, Le Bourgeois gentil-homme,)* Schiller *(Love and Intrigue, Turandot),* Goethe *(Urfaust),* and Kleist *(Der zerbrochene Krug [The Broken Jug]).*

Parallel to political development (in 1952 the construction of socialism was proclaimed in the GDR; in 1955 the North Atlantic Treaty Organization was founded), new standards also emerged in theatre for young audiences in an effort to portray the revolutionary traditions of the German working-class movement.

Henceforth plays by Bertolt Brecht (*Die Gewehre der Frau Carrar [The Rifles of Mrs. Carrar], Hirse für die Achte [Millet for the Eight]*, and *Die Gesichte der Simone Machard [The Faces of Simone Machard]*) and Friedrich Wolf (*Die Matrosen von Cattaro [The Sailors of Cattaro], Professor Mamlock, Das trojanische Pferd [The Trojan Horse]*) were included in the repertory, and important new plays were written by Werner Heiduczek, Hans-Albert Pederzani, and Wera and Claus Kuchenmeister. Most of them were dramatizations of epic models in which children were the focus of attention.

Contemporary plays written in the late fifties and the early sixties were frequently derived from epic literature for children, and were mostly confined to minor conflicts between children and to their relations to parents, teachers, and educators. The consequences of this repertory to the further development of theatres for children and young people was significant because of the strong emphasis placed on educational rather than artistic functions. Even though there was open opposition to this trend, it was not until the closure of the smallest children's theatre in the city of Erfurt only a few years after its founding that its real meaning became apparent. Numerous actors and producers had lost interest in children's theatre because they could no longer fulfill their artistic aspirations.

Texts with poor dramatic subjects rendered the interpretation of child characters by adult actors even more difficult, especially since this country has no tradition for the so-called travesty performer (usually a short, diminutive actress who specializes in playing both girls and boys), who is a highly developed and common figure on Soviet stages. Also, the rapid expansion of television in the late fifties, in which children's programming occupied a large place, had a lasting impact on the theatre for children. Even if the interpretation of children by children on film and in television is normal and justified from the artistic point of view, the practice remained the exception in professional theatre. Here audiences faced the anachronism of adults portraying children in plays that more and more strived for the illusion of reality.

A new stage of development began in 1959 when Ilse Rodenberg, who up to that time had been a successful stage director at several regional theatres, was appointed director of the Theater der Freundschaft. From the outset she placed artistic objectives as the essential focus of her work. She built up a new company by engaging artistic directors and young actors from other theatres; the programs were consistently reshaped and adapted to the requirements of young audiences, so that within a short time, the theatre managed to achieve the same standards as the other stages in the capital city. Even though only a few outstanding productions were presented during the first years of her directorship (such as the musical *As You Like It*, adapted from Shakespeare by Günther Deicke with music by Klaus Fehmel), it was the sound artistic work and the courage to take risks that mattered.

In 1966, one year after the founding of the International Association of Theatre for Children and Young People (ASSITEJ), the First International Festival of Theatre for Children and Young People was held in Berlin; 300 guests from twenty-five countries attended. From this festival emanated national and international impulses for the further development of this still new type of theatre, which now began to recognize that the strength of its repertory was in the great variety of topics and genres. Whether fairy tale, classic, historic, or contemporary, these plays were all suited to acquaint young people with the world in which they lived and to arouse their interest in changing this world. The Festival pointed out once again the need to develop a dramatic art especially for children.

Fairy-tale plays, in particular, called forth the most vehement discussions. A new concept of the fairy tale emerged in the late sixties, when the Theater der Freundschaft began to cooperate with such renowned young lyricists as Heinz Kahlau, Heinz Czechowski, Elke Erb, and Adolf Endler. Instead of continuing the socially determined interpretation of characters and plots that then predominated, these authors recognized the poetic truth of the original. Nor did they attempt to destroy the epic passages of the fairy tales by severe adaptations or drastic interpolations. Their work required a new style of production and performance that repressed the former trend toward the illusionistic stage and paved the way for the adoption of acting styles of Brecht's epic theatre. It soon became evident that this was ideally suited to theatre for children because it challenged audiences to critically think over the action and to facilitate a more conscious reception and mental involvement in the play.

The active role of Horst Hawemann, a young graduate of the College of Dramatic Art in Moscow, was of special importance in the growth of this new style. His interpretation of the characters allowed performances to remain open for audience reactions and encouraged actors to give their attention to these reactions. This did not mean that he induced children to participate in the play simply by stressing outward reactions and by removing the "fourth-wall"; instead, he appealed to their intensive inner involvement in the action on the stage.

Spiel fur dem Feind (Play Face to Face with the Enemy), by Svetlov; *Die Herren des Strandes (The Masters of the Shore)*, adapted from Jorge Amado by Friedrich Gerlach with the music of Georg Katzer; *Tshintshraka*, by G. Nakhutsrishvili; and *Das bucklige Pferdchen (The Little Humpbacked Horse)*, by Erb and Endler, were only some of the productions in the repertory for many years. They demonstrated that theatre for children is capable of outstanding artistic achievements and that, like all other theatres, it will win recognition and develop its full potential.

With Hawemann, dramaturg Christel Hoffmann, and pedagogue Kristin Wardetzky, Ilse Rodenberg had found three young persons who, by utilizing their working methods, now published the first important theoretical works on specific features of dramatic art for young audiences. Their books soon had an impact on both the national and international theatre for children.

The Theater der Jungen Welt (Theatre of the Young World) in Leipzig, which had been headed from 1959 to 1977 by actor, producer, and author Hans-Dieter Schmidt, was known for its great number of premieres and first performances.

Some of them proved important for all theatres, since they tackled new subjects derived from the recent past and the present (*Tinko*, after Strittmatter by Hans-Dieter Schmidt, and *Jule findet Freunde (Jule Finds Friends)*, by Werner Heiduczek) or staged important foreign plays for children, such as *Geschichte von der verlorenen Puppe (Story About the Lost Doll)*, by Alfonso Sastre; *Ambrosio tötet die Zeit (Ambrosio Kills Time)*, by Arthur Fauquez; and *Feuervogel und Rotfuchs (Firebird and Red Fox)*, by Jan Jilek. Yet, in the course of time, some artistic problems arose; there were few changes in the company and in its style of performance, which attributed more importance to the spoken word than to the interplay between the actors. The work was further complicated by the fact that the theatre exclusively addressed children's audiences and rarely performed plays for young people.

The Theater der Jungen Generation (Theatre of the Young Generation) in Dresden was, at that time, distinguished by sound artistic achievements and remarkably continuous work. Rolf Buttner headed the theatre from 1955 to 1976. Following examples of other theatres and companies regarding a varied program for children, one of its specific features was to look at plays from the adult repertory with an eye to their suitability for young people. This not only led to an enrichment of the repertory, but also provided the actors with more possibilities for character development, which children's plays could not always offer them. In 1967 the children's theatre of Dresden was the first to open a second small stage, Theater auf der Treppe (Theatre on the Stairs), where plays for adults were staged. This stage currently is also used for performances for children because the big theatre was destroyed by fire in 1976. The company was forced to play in other theatres, and the Theater auf der Treppe was their only permanent stage.

The development of the Theater der Jungen Garde (Theatre of the Young Guard) in Hallewas was complicated. In the second half of the fifties the theatre became famous for a number of productions by stage director Siegfried Menzel, such as *The Trojan Horse*, by Friedrich Wolf, and *Romeo and Juliet*, by Shakespeare. Yet, subsequently, it faced several structural and managerial problems that halted continuous progress, so that the development of this stage was by no means dynamic and uniform.

In 1969 the Theater fur Junge Zuschauer (Theater for Young Audiences) with an independent company was founded within the municipal stages of the city of Magdeburg. Actor Klaus Urban, who had for many years been engaged at the children's theatre in Berlin, became the first director. In the first years of the theatre's existence a program for all age groups was established that included the performance of children's operas by Cesar Bregen and Benjamin Britten. Productions by guest directors soon helped to set high standards and contributed to the reputation of the group.

This was the last specialized theatre for children and young people founded in the GDR. After many discussions theatre workers arrived at the conviction that children's theatre could not be developed further by the founding of new, specialized theatres, but that the traditional national theatre network should ba-

sically be maintained (approximately sixty professional theatres and fifteen puppet theatres for a population of 17 million). This meant that the sixty professional
theatres playing for adult audiences would have to provide for the younger
audiences in their territories and adapt their repertories as necessary. As early
as 1963 all theatres were obliged to include at least two productions each season
for children and young people. Approximately ten years later, in the middle of
the seventies, the proportion of children and young people in the audiences of
all professional theatres had already increased by 40 to 50 percent and has
remained constant since then.

This remarkable rejuvenation of the audience could only have been achieved
as a result of the conditions created in three decades by specialized theatres for
children and young people. Over a longer period this process of rejuvenation
passed rather unnoticed. When the first theatres for adult audiences opened their
doors to younger audiences in the late sixties, they could rely on the experience
of the specialized theatres (repertory, age grouping) and cooperate with them in
the National Center of ASSITEJ.

When most of the other theatres followed their example in the seventies, this
cooperation no longer continued; almost all theatres tried to find their own
methods for dealing with the young audiences. The theatres for children and
young people had neither the strength nor the prestige to assert any influence on
this development, since they were themselves undergoing a process of radical
change that outwardly became evident in the management of all children's theatres.

In 1974, after fifteen years of directorship, Ilse Rodenberg, who by that time
was sixty-seven years old, handed leadership of the Theater der Freundschaft to
Klaus Urban, who had come from Magdeburg. In 1976 Rolf Büttner, who had
for twenty-one years been stage director in Dresden, also retired for reasons of
age, and Gunhild Lattmann, the former dramaturg of the theatre, became the
new director of the Theater der Jungen Generation. In 1977 management of the
Theater der Jungen Welt in Leipzig was handed over to Gunther Schwarzlose,
the former chief producer of this stage. In Madgeburg and Halle, also, there
were several changes in the management within a few years. The continuous
developments of the previous decade could no longer be maintained, especially
since other prominent theatre workers also left children's theatre in search of
new artistic experiences.

The problems that emerged from new social and artistic developments in the
GDR were even more decisive in this respect. The current stage of development
of the advanced socialist society requires constant collective communication, in
which the "discovery of art" plays an essential part. Art is also ever increasingly
acquiring a communicative function. This can apply to theatre for children and
young people when it fulfills its predominantly enlightening function: to make
the world comprehensible to the young generation.

Discussion about this issue was not confined to theory alone, but also carried out on the basis of concrete examples of stage art. In 1977, for instance, the "Workshop Days of Theatre for Children and Young People" started, which since then take place every two years for one week at Theater der Jungen Garde in Halle. With the aid of selected performances, lectures, and illustrations from other art forms, participants come to an understanding of a given theme by analyzing the achievements, failures, and objectives of the past and the next steps that should be taken to improve the future. The central issue of these talks is the belief in children's theatre as an artistic, not an educational, institution.

The basic conditions for proving this concept are as follows:

1. A constant extension of the repertory through new plays and works from national and international authors

2. A constant critical debate in public on the art of theatre for children and young people when measured by the same standards as performances in the adult theatre

3. A constantly updated knowledge of the various theatrical expectations within each age group

4. A permanent communication between the theatre, the young audiences, and pedagogues about the impact of theatre

Theatres for children and young people and the National Center of ASSITEJ are responsible for adherence to the above-mentioned principles, since they have to create the examples that will apply to other theatres, although the methods will vary from theatre to theatre.

REPRESENTATIVE COMPANIES

Theater der Freundschaft

From its home in Berlin, under stage director Dr. Siegfried Wein and with a company of 200, Theater der Freundschaft has the best opportunity for the fulfillment of the principles stated earlier. The program for the 1986/87 season envisaged seventeen productions on the main stage, ten plays on the rehearsal stage, which is frequently used, and several concerts for children. Only a few titles can be enumerated here: *Die Katze (The Cat)*, by Horst Hawemann, and *Das tapfere Schneiderlein (The Brave Little Tailor)* for the age group five to nine; *Der Vogelkopp (Bird's Head)*, by Albert Wend, and *Teufelskarl (Karl, A Devil of a Fellow)*, by Elifius Paffrath, for the age group ten to thirteen; *Icke bin doch Icke (I Am I)*, confessions of a student; *Die Insel (The Island)*, by Athol Fugard, and *Love and Intrigue* for the adolescent audiences. This theatre places special emphasis on cooperation with new authors (twelve of the titles on the repertory were premieres).

The theatre's goals include improvement of the theatrical quality of performances by the conscious use of all playing elements and the establishment of new productive relations with the audience, particularly with teachers, who are the most important allies in this respect. The theatre also succeeds by organizing workshops and courses and undertaking research into the impact of the theatre and communicative forms of acting for all age groups.

Theater der Jungen Generation

In Dresden, managed by director Gunhild Lattmann, Theater der Jungen Generation offered fifteen productions on its main stage in 1987/88 and three more in Theater aud der Treppe, including *Pinocchio*, by Lavagna/Vitalini; *Prinz Tausendfuss (Prince Centipede)*, by Schöbel (six to nine years); *Der kleine Prinz von Dänemark (The Little Prince of Denmark)*, by Letser; *Der Abendkranich (The Evening Crane)*, by Kinoshita; *Das Tagebuch der Anne Frank (The Diary of Anne Frank)*, by Frances Goodrich and Albert Hackett (ten to thirteen years); *Hamlet* and *Romeo and Juliet*, by Shakespeare; *Flügerschläge (Beats of the Wings)*, a rock drama (youth). The theatre is prepared to take risks regarding the performance of plays by younger authors and of new foreign plays; five premieres and four GDR first performances are in the repertory.

Part of the theatre's program includes tryouts of classic works (by Shakespeare and Schiller, in particular) and of plays by Brecht (*Die Ausnahme und die Regel [The Exception and the Rule]*, *Der kaukasische Kreidekreis, [The Caucasian Chalk Circle]*, *Mutter Courage und ihre Kinder [Mother Courage and her Children]*) for youthful audiences (ages thirteen to fourteen) by outstanding young directors from other theatres. The theatre makes special efforts to organize new forms of theatre-going (season tickets for families and young couples) and permanent possibilities for communication after the performances.

Theater für Junge Zuschauer

Under director Wilfred Klaus, Theater für Junge Zuschauer produces in the city of Magdeburg. It plays mostly for pupils between the ages of six and fifteen and has ten to twelve productions in its repertory. The productions of the young director Karl-Friedrich Zimmermann, who died in 1985, had a formative influence on the work of the theatre: Brecht's *Mann ist Mann*, Goethe's *Urfaust*, Kinoshito's *Der Abendkranich*, and Hacks' *Die Kinder*. A special effort is made to improve the receptiveness of the young audiences by systematic introductions to the work of the theatre before and after performances and cooperation between all institutions in the territory (professional, puppet, and amateur theatres).

Theater der Jungen Welt

Directed by Günther Schwarzlose, Theater der Jungen Welt, located in Leipzig, presented nineteen productions for children in the six-to-fourteen-year-old age group, including two operas, *Der Drache Drax (The Dragon Drax)*, by Schmidt and Reimann, and *Katz and Kätzchen (Cats and Kittens)*, by Marschak and Tiefensee. Numerous premieres by members of the company and first performances of foreign plays are scheduled: *Das Märchen vom Zaren Saltan (Fairy Tale About Tsar Saltan)*, by Alexander Pushkin; *Ein halbierter Haezschlag (A Divided Heartbeat)*, by Istvan Juhasz (Hungary); *Amely, der Biber und der Koniig auf dem Dach (Amely, the Beaver and the King on the Roof)*, by Tankred Dorst (West Germany).

Theater der Jungen Garde

In Halle, under stage director Armin Mechsner, Theater der Jungen Garde's repertory for 1986/87 included fourteen productions for all age groups, ranging from fairy tales (*Das Tierhäuschen [The Animal Cottage]*, by S. Marschak), historical plays (*Die Legende von Iskremas [The Legend of Iskremas]*, by Alexander Mitta), contemporary plays (*Die Wundernacht [The Magic Night]*, by B. Uhlar), and international dramas (Athol Fugard's *Aussagen nach einem Verhör [Statement After an Interrogation]*) to classic comedy (Molière's *La Médecin malgré lui [The Doctor in Spite of Himself]*). The theatre, which for some time has also comprised a rock group, intends to foster the development of this musical genre.

As all other professional theatres in the GDR, the professional theatres for children and young people have their own buildings. All artistic members of the companies are bound by contracts of several years' duration. Theatre-going is, above all, organized in the form of season tickets for a group or school class. In addition, encouragement is increasingly given to season tickets for families (children with their parents) and for individual theatre-going adolescents.

Friendly agreements have been concluded between the Berlin theatre and the children's theatres in Moscow and Prague, the Dresden theatre and the children's theatre in Ostrava/Czechoslovakia, and the Leipzig theatre and the theatre for young people in Kiev to give mutual guest performances. The Berlin theatre also performed in guest appearances in the Polish People's Republic, the Mongolian People's Republic, Bulgaria, Yugoslavia, Romania, Italy, France, Belgium, and West Germany. The Leipzig theatre has appeared in West Germany, Portugal, West Berlin, Angola, and Mozambique; the Halle theatre, in Syria, Jordan, and Vietnam; the Dresden theatre, in Czechoslovakia and the Democratic People's Republic of Korea.

BIBLIOGRAPHY

The scripts of almost all plays mentioned in this text and all other plays of the national children's theatre can be obtained from Henschel Schauspiel, Berlin/DDR, Oranienburger Strasse 67/68.

Hoffmann, Christel. *Theater für junge Zuschauer (Theatre for Young Audiences)*. Berlin, Akademie-Verlag, 1976.

Kinder-und Jugendtheater del Welt (Theatres for Children and Young People Throughout the World). Berlin, Henschelverlag Kunst und Gesellschaft, 1978.

Ilse Rodenberg

Federal Republic of Germany

HISTORY

The origins of children's theatre in Germany go back to the various forms of didactic theatre practiced in humanistic schools in the fifteenth and sixteenth centuries. As a learning tool, it was played at first in Latin and then, by the end of the sixteenth century, also in German. An interesting marginal manifestation is the spectacular scenery of the Jesuit school plays in the Counter-Reformation, which anticipate the beautiful *mise-en-scene* of the Christmas stories performed since the middle of the past century. During this time gorgeous settings played an important part in the presentations and presaged the decor of the later-day Christmas offerings. The eighteenth century also featured plays written especially for children as didactic vehicles that were not given public performances, but were enacted, instead, in the homes of the wealthy. Other early antecedents of theatre for young people are also found in the muscial theatre of the seventeenth and eighteenth centuries.

The actual starting point for children's theatre, which is here defined as performances especially for children acted on a stage, was the Christmas fairy tale. Private theatres, needing additional funds, tried various tactics to attract the public to attend theatrical performances more often. One activity they introduced was bringing whole families, which included children, to the theatre together. Several attempts failed before the first breakthrough came in 1854 when Carl August Göerner, actor, director, theatre manager, and dramatist, wrote a play that was a rousing success, and the presentation of the Christmas fairy tale as children's theatre was born.

Little else happened for the next several years, apart from an experiment on a year-round basis in Berlin, which foundered in 1862. During this time two distinct types of theatre emerged: (1) a theatre for children and young people that was predominantly didactic and included the production of classics in the schools, and (2) the now-traditional Christmas fairy-tale plays for children, which also began to be of interest to the rest of the family, the main purpose of which was the use of spectacle in order to attract as large an audience as possible. The first kind of theatre was educational and used the stage as a learning tool, whereas the second was strictly commercial. At the beginning of the nineteenth century, theatre for children and young people began to come under the influence of various ideologies and political movements that were partially a consequence of industrialization. These included the youth movement and various reformist pedagogies.

The quality of children's theatre declined because high artistic standards were no longer demanded. Instead, deficiencies were hidden behind theatrical magic, with as much tinsel and glitter and stage machinery as could be found. There were some countermovements, but they were too small to be consequential. The development of children's theatre then being put into practice in the Soviet Union had not yet become known in Germany; consequently Walter Benjamin intended his famous program for a proletarian children's theatre not in Germany, but for the Lett Asja Lacis in the Soviet Union. One exception to this overall lethargy was the production of *Fight About Kitch*, a play for young people written by A. Stemmle in 1931 in Berlin and performed in several cities.

After World War II a new development occurred. In 1946, in Leipzig, the government that is now the German Democratic Republic (GDR) began to organize theatres for children and young people, an activity that it continued in Berlin in 1950. The Federal Republic of Germany (FRG) followed suit in 1948, in Nuremberg, by instituting city-financed theatres with programs for children and young people. These programs spread to Dortmund and Munich in 1953. In Dortmund a specialized permanent ensemble was begun under the aegis of the city-funded theatre, and Munich's Theatre for Youth owes its existence to the private initiative and engagement of Siegfried Jobst.

The oldest theatre for children in Nuremberg closed in the 1970s but was resurrected in the 1980s as an integral children's and youth theatre of the city-financed theatre. As such, it has had to fight for its existence against the adult theatre. Dortmund's children's theatre has managed to avoid annihilation by instituting economy measures and accepting the director of the adult theatre as its head. The same situation, in terms of artistic direction, exists in Nuremberg. In Munich the private children's theatre became part of the city-financed operation in the 1960s, and is today the only children's theatre in the FRG to have its own building.

This was the extent of activity in Germany in the sixties, even though as well known an author as Erich Käestner made proposals for the establishment and financing of an independent children's theatre. This indifference was partly the fault of politicians but was also attributable to the theatre artists themselves. Most of them believed that children's theatre was second class, its audience made up of that part of the population that no one took seriously. It is, therefore, not surprising that the initial impetus for theatres for children and youth came from the GDR, and that this movement began with independent groups rather than with institutionalized theatres. The move, in the latter half of the sixties, toward an interest in youthful audiences, although a positive step for children's theatre overall, has a "realistic" explanation. Theatres were fighting a decline in attendance, and one method they used to overcome this audience apathy was "papering the house," giving away free or reduced-price tickets to young people to fill the seats.

CONTEMPORARY CHILDREN'S THEATRE

The real story of theatre for children and young people began only at the end of the sixties and was brought about not by the established theatres, but by the small independent and "free groups" that sprang up with the resistance movement in 1967 and 1968.

One of the most important of these groups was Berlin's Reichskabarett, later renamed the GRIPS Theatre, which has had a significant influence on other theatres, both in terms of repertory and philosophy. Their initial reform centered around so-called emancipatory children's theatre, a realistic, enlightened, and politically critical theatre for children with Volker Ludwig as leader. GRIPS became an outspoken enemy of the often dishonest and unworthy Christmas fairy-tale productions. Even though GRIPS, with its consciously limited concept, did not succeed on all levels, it was the innovator of a movement that created, little by little, the awareness that an independent theatre for children and young people had a right to exist. GRIPS was convinced of the necessity and soundness of this concept, not only from a theatrical point of view, but also from a societal point of view.

Around 1968 theatre for children and young people suddenly became the subject of much public discussion. Important contributions to qualitative development and crystallization of ideological and artistic criteria came from Berlin in the early 1970s. In addition to social realism from GRIPS came "message plays" from a free group called Rote Grütze. The group presented works about sex and drugs to young people, and in an exemplary manner demonstrated that theatre can often succeed where traditional methods of education fail. Another popular group of the time was Birne, a collective whose main concern was methods of participation.

The landscape of children's theatre changed noticeably during this time. In addition to the already existing children's theatres in Nuremberg, Dortmund, and Munich, a young people's branch was founded in all municipal theatres as a fourth sector of the state-financed theatre system, which also included the original three sectors of opera, ballet, and drama. Permanent, often specialized ensembles offered year-round repertories for children and young people in the Schauspielhaus in Düsseldorf, on stages in Kiel, Oberhausen, Essen, and Osnabrück, and in the Westphalian country theatre Castrop-Rauxel.

In 1979 an important step was taken in Baden-Wüertemberg in South Germany where, for the first time, the state determined the repertory to be presented on the stages of children's theatres. National theatres that performed for young audiences began to be awarded special subsidies and community theatres received 40 percent of their budgets from the county to underwrite their children's seasons. A monetary prize was yearly awarded the author of the best children's play. All this activity served to spur the movement on, and new theatres were established in Mannheim, Esslingen, Bruchsal, Tüebingen, and, later, Heidelberg. Children's theatre had become a *cause célèbre* in cultural politics.

Nevertheless, many social and artistic prejudices still had to be overcome. This was accomplished through practical work in the theatres and discussions about artistic developments in other countries. The south of Germany was influenced by children's theatre in Italy, especially by the productions of Carlo Formigoni, which featured sparse decor and emphasized the body. In the north, influences came from Sweden through the work of Per Lysander and Suzanne Osten and, later, Staffan Göethe. Other Italian and Swedish directors also had an impact on German children's theatre that can be seen in work dating from the early and middle 1980s.

CONCERNS

The many positive developments in German children's theatre are still in need of strengthening. Risks remain that theatres will be forced to close if the financial subsidies provided by the various levels of government are curtailed. This reality particularly concerns the independent groups, which receive funds mostly for special projects at irregular intervals and otherwise are without funding sources. Established authors are seldom interested in writing children's plays because royalties are percentages of the proceeds and payments for children's plays are half that of those received in adult theatres.

Unfortunately the same situation pertains to the remuneration of theatre artists. Even though some children's theatre leaders have been actively engaged in negotiations to equalize salaries between adult and youth theatres, many actors, directors, and designers are still paid less for their work in children's theatres. This creates a situation in which well-known performers and artists are not willing to ''step down'' to work in this field.

However, excellent people are employed in children's theatre, even though they are grossly underpaid and often move into the adult theatre as soon as possible. Others are attracted to children's theatre because this is where the true experimental work is mainly being done. Innovations with form, style, aesthetics, and dramatic literature have been especially successful within the confines of theatre for young audiences.

Progress has been extraordinary, given the short time period involved. In the 1970s many theatres still emphasized the emancipatory, pedagogic style. A few years later themes, concerns, and styles of performance changed while structure and organizational form stayed more or less the same. Theatre that provided explanations about the problems of the world took precedence over a theatre that emphasized artistic and aesthetic forms of expression. Improvisation often replaced literature, and the imitation of children's play was considered a substitute for the art of acting. Process was more important than product, which meant that play acting was more important than overall artistic intention. However chaotic, these changes proved positive because they allowed children's theatre to develop a style of its own. As it later turned out, the style was too narrowly limited in realism, but the field continued to be in the news all the same.

In the middle 1970s two developments came to the fore. Children's theatre now not only wanted to portray reality, but also wanted to espouse fantasy. However, it still intended to present a message and to contribute to the emancipation of children, in the social as well as in the individual and psychological spheres. By encouraging and strengthening their personalities, theatre could awaken the critical abilities of children and support their "coming of age."

THE CURRENT SITUATION

Today the child's world is still debated, especially with questions about conformity to natural laws. From the theatrical point of view, we now realize the possibility of selecting various forms of interpretation that arise from the life experience of children and young people, including fantastic fairy-tale–like situations. Fairy tales, which were banned from the stage at the end of the sixties and the beginning of the seventies, have once again become important because of the publication of *The Uses of Enchantment*, by Bruno Bettleheim. The seventies also saw the production of many plays created through improvisation. By the beginning of the eighties classics and plays by foreign authors had become popular, and the current trend is for theatres to engage authors to write commissioned plays on specific subjects.

Despite its success, theatre for young audiences does not claim the same status as theatre for adults. Its development still depends entirely on the personal involvement and initiative of committed artists and authors.

Theatre for children and young people today can be subdivided into three groups: private theatres, free groups, and companies that have been integrated into state-subsidized theatres.

An example of a private theatre, and among the most influential in the country, is GRIPS Theatre in West Berlin. Founded by Volker Ludwig in 1966 as Theatre for Children in Reichskabarett and independent since 1969, GRIPS epitomizes emancipatory theatre. Since 1969 it has premiered thirty-four new (original) plays and has toured throughout Germany and to thirteen other European countries; the company appeared in the United States for the first time in 1988 with great success. Revivals of GRIPS plays have been mounted in thirty-two foreign languages. The company has its own theatre in West Berlin and is subsidized by the senate.

One of GRIPS most topical works in *Voll auf der Rolle (Involved in the Part)*, a play about enmity toward strangers in society and among pupils during the time of the Nazis as well as today. *Linie Eins* (*Line One*), a successful musical concerning life and survival in Berlin and about hope and adaptation, is designed to make audiences laugh, cry, and reflect on their lives. Seen throughout the country, the score also became a best-selling record album.

One of the first free groups in Germany was Rote Grütze in West Berlin, which was founded in 1973. The company works as a collective and has made an international name for itself mostly with its message plays. After longstanding political and financial difficulties the group has been acknowledged with its reception of the Brother Grimm Prize in 1987 for exemplary and excellent work and receives subsidies from the senate of Berlin. To date, Rote Grütze has developed six works, two each for children, young people, and adults. As a group, these plays are the most often produced in Germany. Their most recent successful production, *Gewalt im Spiel (Force While Playing)*, looks at the everyday forces that exist between men and women, their games of power and intimidation and their quandries and frustrations.

Dortmund, one of the oldest theatres, founded in 1953 as an independent sector of the Stadttheater, was forced after ten years of autonomy to become part of the acting ensemble of the main theatre because of financial difficulties. But after protests from audiences, educators, and the press, the city decided at the end of 1986 to again make the group autonomous and give them a theatre of their own. One of their recent plays is *A Bloody English Garden*, by Nick Fisher, a work about Skinheads (a politically motivated violent youth sect that began in England and has spread throughout Europe), their wanton destruction of the environment, and a hopeful and extraordinary friendship that develops. Also in the group's repertory is *The Special Life of Hilletje Jans*, a Dutch work by Ad de Bont and Allan Zipson, which is a historical play about the life of a girl from the eighteenth century.

Another autonomous company is the theatre for children and youth in Essen. Founded in 1980 with its own ensemble and organization, it is bound only administratively to the Theatre and Philharmonic, and since 1987 has played in its own house. Led by Hildegard Bergfeld, the theatre has, since its inception, been called "a bridgehead of the Swedish theatre for children and young people, as far as the plays and the directors are concerned." In the mid-eighties the company presented the *Metamorphosen of Ovid*, for children from six years old and up; *The Cat*, adapted from Kipling, for children eight and up; and *King Ubu*, by Alfred Jarry, for young adults.

Hildegard Bergfeld
Translated by Elizabeth Gay

Ghana

HISTORY

Children's theatre in Ghana dates as far back as the introduction of religion and education into the country. During festive occasions like Easter and Christmas teachers produced plays in churches and classrooms. This was done on a small scale until the Arts Council of Ghana started to organize a children's theatre program in schools in 1966. The program was built around the concept of children playing to children, and adults were to be involved only when necessary. The aims of the program were fourfold:

1. To develop the creative faculties of children through activities, including mime, improvisation, speech, storytelling, play production, puppetry, dance, and writing.
2. To organize workshops for teachers in the fundamentals of theatre in order that they can include drama and theatre activities in their classrooms. (Teacher-training courses do not include drama or theatre.)
3. To introduce children to theatre at an early age so that a better theatre audience can be developed.
4. To produce better actors, playwrights, and technicians to ensure the future of children's theatre.

Because schoolchildren were to be used as artists, the Arts Council planned the children's theatre program in collaboration with the Ministry of Education. A pilot group of seven schools was chosen to test the program over a period of five years, during which the program operated as an extracurricular activity. Plays and dances, to which children and their parents were invited, were produced at the end of every school term. This presentation of activities generally coincided with Christmas and Easter; an additional variety program was also presented. Every year drama and dance workshops were organized for teachers. By the end of the fifth year interest in drama and dance had developed to such a degree that many schools began to ask for technical assistance. As a result of the school program, the first children's theatre festival was held in 1971, in which thirty-nine schools participated. The festival has since become an annual event.

Once the pilot program had ended, the children's theatre project was officially incorporated into the schools. At the end of each term the Arts Council goes to schools to watch their presentations. The best productions are then presented before both schoolchildren and the general public. These presentations fall into several categories: live theatre, radio programs recorded and aired on stations that have children's programming, television broadcasts, and puppet performances (this area of children's theatre is handled by adults). The children's theatre program has become an integral part of the school curriculum, and drama and dance have been taught as distinct subjects in the first-cycle schools (ages six to twelve years old in elementary school).

CURRENT TREADS AND PROBLEMS

Ghana continues to develop its children's theatre to ensure future posterity. Several problems still exist, however.

- A limited number of dramatists write for child audiences. Although there are many children's plays, most are written by foreigners and are alien to the Ghanian culture. This is one area on which energies are being focused.
- Children's theatre programs are performed in adult theatres, classrooms, and school fields. A children's theatre center where young people can come to enjoy performances as well as to develop their artistic talents needs to be built.
- Funds for the development of children's theatre are lacking; also, there are too few professionals to run school programs.
- Young people tend to focus their attention on foreign cultures and ignore their own. Programs that will entice them back to the study and appreciation of their roots need to be developed.

Children's theatre in Ghana is moving in the right direction. The promise of its future, however, will depend on adequate funding from the government.

Lowell Swortzell
(Prepared from materials submitted by ASSITEJ and Frances Sey.)

Great Britain

HISTORY

Although dramatic performances *by* children have a long and rich history, dating back at least to the late Middle Ages, the provision of theatre *for* children, at least at the professional level, did not begin until the turn of the last century, and even then only hesitantly and on a modest scale. It is really only since World War II that children's theatre in Britain has burgeoned, and the pace and variety of that growth have been remarkable.

Pre–1900

From the late medieval period onward the universities and the public and cathedral schools are all known at various times to have encouraged play readings and performances by their pupils for strictly educational purposes: teaching oral Latin, the classical authors (Plautus and Terence included), and the skills of rhetoric. By Elizabethan times a number of eminent teachers at such schools as Eton, Westminster, and Shrewsbury were writing plays in English for their pupils, arguing that drama helped to develop not only self-confidence and oratorical skills, but also the moral sense that could be derived from a study of high comedy. Nicholas Udall's *Ralph Roister Doister*, for example, was originally written (in about 1552) for performance by and for the boys of Westminster School.

Such was the popularity of these plays that they were increasingly given public as well as classroom performances. Indeed, by 1576 (the date of the building of the first professional theatre in London) certain schools had achieved considerable fame, and even some notoriety, at least in Puritan circles, as venues for dramatic entertainment. The choir boys especially, such as those at St. Paul's Cathedral and the Chapel Royal, with acting skills now formally in the school curriculum, were sought after on innumerable occasions by Queen Elizabeth and other noble families to give performances of plays that utilized their youthful charm and musical talent. Eventually the Boys' Companies, based at St. Paul's and Blackfriars, became a significant feature of the Elizabethan and early Jacobean theatre, although their performances were by now for adult audiences and placed on a decidedly commercial footing.

With the enforced closure of the theatres from 1642 to 1660, the involvement of children in theatre virtually ceased for some 250 years. Only in a handful of public schools was there any evidence of a continuing dramatic tradition, and even there it was a sporadic activity at best, often viewed with deep distrust by politicians and preachers alike. By the second half of the nineteenth century, however, the mood had changed, and the educational value of theatre within schools was being more confidently asserted, even though it was usually confined to after-hours leisure time and to the production of the classics. Bradfield School, for example, built its small open-air replica of a Greek amphitheatre for performances by boys and teachers together in 1888. This resurgence of interest coincided with the growing respectability of the professional theatre as the middle classes returned, and even Queen Victoria attended performances in the 1860s. At the palace, too, professional performances of plays were given for the royal children. For children of the lower and middle classes theatre remained, at best, an adult experience that they shared with their elders.

Even pantomime, for many in Britain virtually synonymous with theatre for children, was, for most of the nineteenth century, an adult entertainment, centering on the harlequinade with clowning and satire frequently of a sharp-edged kind. Children would more likely have been taken instead to see Astley's Circus. But by the 1860s the rival attractions of music hall, burlesque, and extravaganza had begun to exert their strong pull on adult audiences, and pantomine became associated increasingly with holiday entertainment for family audiences. By the latter decades of the century it was predominantly a Christmas holiday entertainment with children forming a large part of the audience. Its comedy became more and more geared to children's tastes, and spectacle replaced the satiric, often anarchistic plots of the old harlequinades. At the same time, a new moralistic tone crept in, clearly aimed at ensuring that children received proper edification along with the fun.[1] Thereafter, Christmas pantomines, appealing unashamedly to children and to family audiences, became a regular feature of the theatrical scene in Britain. By now their traditions have become so watered down as to be almost unrecognizable: a loose framework within which to set a variety entertainment with only the slimmest of narrative threads connecting the acts.

Another strand that emerged during the latter part of the nineteenth century was the short, fairy-tale playlets written in the hundreds for performance by children at home or in school, or even at boy scout and brownie gatherings. These were usually little more than brief entertainment pieces, wholly amateur in conception and execution, but nonetheless offering opportunity for dramatic expression within secure environments and no doubt whetting the appetite for more ambitious events at the "real" theatre.[2]

Post–1900

It was the professional theatre that provided the first play for children of any real quality: J. M. Barrie's *Peter Pan* (1904), a play that may have achieved its deservedly classic status in part because it avoided the common error of the time—that of patronizing its audience. A. A. Milne's *Toad of Toad Hall* (1929) is similarly distinguished from the general run of such plays as a drama of energy and originality and has survived many revivals. Other lesser plays for children that saw successful runs in the West End include *Katawumpus* (Calvert and Parry, 1901), *Bluebell in Fairyland* (Seymour Hicks, a "musical dream play," 1901), and *Where the Rainbow Ends* (Mills and Ramsey, a play with music, 1911). *Fifinella* (Jackson and Dean, a "fairy frolic") was given at the new Birmingham Repertory Theatre in 1912, and Laurence Housman wrote several plays for children before World War I. There was even a Children's Theatre season at the Royal Court theatre in December 1913. And during the 1920s Harcourt Williams wrote a series of plays especially for his wife's "Children's Seasons."[3] But these ventures were primarily geared to providing entertainment for children during the Christmas season. The provision of theatre for children on a more regular and sustained basis was to come from other quarters, and developed along two quite different lines: Shakespeare for older ages groups and new work for younger ages.

The touring of Shakespeare productions to schools and colleges was, not surprisingly, the first of these developments, for appreciation of Shakespeare was felt to be indisputably a justifiable and worthwhile activity for which support could be mustered from education authorities and parents. Frank Benson began touring productions of such plays as *The Merchant of Venice* to public schools in 1889, and shortly before World War I Ben Greet's company presented Shakespeare for London schoolchildren at special low rates at a variety of venues. When Greet became the Old Vic's first theatre director in 1914, he took the opportunity to extend this service and, during the 1914/15 season, instituted a series of "special matinees for schoolchildren" of Shakespeare's plays relevant to the current examination syllabus; *As You Like It*, for example, was so popular that extra matinees had to be arranged, with 4,000 children seeing the play during one week.[4] When Greet left the Old Vic in 1918 he continued to provide Shakespeare matinees for London schools, with the London County Council bearing the cost (despite a temporary withdrawal of subsidy between 1921 and 1924). In 1924 the government's Board of Education agreed that theatre visits by schools to see the works of Shakespeare were educationally justifiable and could legitimately be subsidized by local authorities nationwide, a most important precedent. Other companies took advantage of the new opportunity, notably Nancy

Hewin's Osiris Players touring "Shakespeare to Schools" nationally (1927–1968).

Two figures stand out during the interwar period as pioneers of theatre for younger children. First was Bertha Waddell, who founded the Scottish Children's Theatre (touring to schools and theatres in Glasgow and elsewhere in Scotland) in 1924. She made a serious and successful attempt to present shows that aimed less at edification than at providing genuine, wholesome, and energetic presentations of folktales and fairy tales that exploited children's love of color, pace, dance, music, and singing. Her productions avoided playing down to children and were as good of their kind as it was possible to make them. The worth of her work was finally recognized by the Glasgow education authority in 1937, which accepted that primary schoolchildren could be allowed to see the Scottish Children's Theatre during schooltime and with the costs borne by the authority. Second was Peter Slade, to become renowned after the war for his seminal book *Child Drama*, who formed the Fen Players in 1930, touring plays for children to schools and halls in East Anglia, and the Parable Players, touring theatres and halls in the southeast from 1935 to 1938. Other children's theatre ventures of note in this period are Jean Stirling McKinley's Playmates company, which toured to schools in London and the southeast (1914–1940), and Joan Luxton's Children's Theatre at Endell Street, London (1927–1931).

World War II brought with it a new attitude to the role of the arts in society, a recognition that at a time of immense strain, the country needed more than rousing speeches from politicians. Government funds for theatre were made available for the first time, and there followed a rapid expansion of national touring for adult audiences. Hard on the heels of this, though *without* the benefit of public subsidy, a flurry of new touring companies for children came into being, among which were the following: the Children's Theatre Players (Birmingham, 1943); the Motley Players, staffed by working teachers (Aberdeen, 1943); Brian Way's West of England Children's Theatre Company (1944–1951); Tom Clarke's Children's Playtime, based at the Argyle Theatre, Birkenhead (1944–1956; subsequently re-formed as the Theatre for Youth); Peter Slade's Pear Tree Players (1945–1947); John Crockett's Compass Players (1945–1952); John Allen's Glyndebourne Children's Theatre (1945–1951); George Devine's Young Vic, an offshoot of the London Old Vic Company (1946–1951); Esme Church's Northern Children's Theatre (1947–1958); Caryl Jenner's Amersham Mobile Theatre (later the Unicorn Theatre) (1948—); and John English's Arena Theatre Company (1948–1958).[5]

All these companies toured either regionally or nationally, but although the prestigious Young Vic performed in established theatres, most of the others played in schools and halls, usually deriving their small incomes from admission charges paid by the children themselves (or their parents) or occasionally from more generous-minded education authorities. They were financially hazardous operations, and many companies came and went with alarming speed. Actors were paid a pittance; not surprisingly, they tended to be young, inexperienced, mostly enthusiastic, but quick to move on to better paying, "proper" theatre jobs elsewhere.

Various organizations were established to further the cause of educational theatre and drama and to lobby for funding, notably the British Children's Theatre Association in 1959 and, shortly afterward, the Young People's Section of the Council of Regional Theatres. The Arts Council was at last persuaded to acknowledge both the importance of children's theatre (if only because it prepared future audience for mainstream theatre) and the financial crisis that all companies that catered to children faced. A committee of inquiry was set up in 1965, and its enlightened and watershed report, *The Provision of Theatre for Young People*, appeared the next year, recommending immediate life-saving grant aid for a number of touring children's theatre companies and additional subsidy for other projects and productions specifically for young people. This money, which gave recognition and a much needed boost to young people's theatre work, was channeled into three main areas: touring children's theatre companies, productions and workshops for young people (often related to plays on the examination syllabus) mounted by regional theatres, and Theatre-in-Education (TIE).

Theatre-in-Education

TIE was in its infancy when the committee of inquiry was set up but had already shown enough of its potential for the committee to highlight it in the report as a development to be encouraged. TIE had begun life in 1965 as an adventurous initiative of the Belgrade Theatre, Coventry (the first of a new generation of regional theatres to be built after the war). A unit of actors with an interest in education (called actor-teachers) was established, with financial support from both the local authority and the theatre, to tour local schools with two main objectives in mind: (1) to place the skills of actor-teachers at the service of schools that needed help in getting drama off the ground but lacked the expertise, confidence, or time to initiate their own projects, and (2) to bring the power and imaginative stimulus of theatre into the school hall or classroom.

Many influences affected the emergence of TIE. The pioneering work of Brian Way's Theatre Centre was certainly one. Another was the accelerating "drama-in-education" movement in schools, a movement that had sprung from the growing understanding in educational circles of the value of "child-centered" learning, of breaking down the traditonal rigid barriers that separated one subject from another, and of "learning by doing" (the Newsom Report of 1963 and Plowden Report of 1966 gave official recognition and encouragement to the application of these ideas in the secondary- and junior-school curricula, respectively). There had been several early pioneers of drama as an educational method, Caldwell Cook in Cambridge before World War I being one of the first. Even more influential, however, were Peter Slade (whose *Child Drama* appeared in 1954) and Brian Way (whose *Development Through Drama* appeared in 1967), both of whom advocated a central place for drama in the curriculum by rejecting the primacy of "putting on the school play" and emphasizing instead the child's own creativity and the development of personal confidence and social skills ("rehearsing for life," as Way termed it). The achievement of TIE practitioners was that they absorbed the new ideas and adapted and developed them further in the context of what theatre could offer: hence programs of work that combined play performance with educational drama techniques, actively involving pupils in the enactment of stories, solving problems and, especially at the secondary level, debating with characters on issues that arose from the play they had witnessed.

It was hoped that such programs would have spin-offs for school and theatre alike: that the impact would have long-term educational benefits, promoting curiosity and motivation for extended classroom work on the subject of the program; and that there would be greater awareness of and interest in live theatre among both teachers and pupils. Significantly, as TIE developed, it became clear just how important, in its own right, the work was (a need was identified and a unique educational resource established), and the aim of creating new audiences for the future quickly became relegated to the level of an incidental bonus, not a governing factor.

The Coventry scheme became the model for a series of similar teams established at regional theatres around the country as theatre directors began to recognize the value of this particular form of "outreach" and as education authorities became increasingly interested in the educational resource that TIE offered. Hence the setting up of teams at the Octagon Theatre, Bolton, the Leeds Playhouse, the Palace Theatre, Watford, the Lyceum Theatre, Edinburgh, and the Greenwich Theatre (all by 1970) and within a few more years at Nottingham, Peterborough, Glasgow, and Lancaster. Several education authorities even organized their own companies, most notably at the Cockpit Arts Workshop in London in 1971. By the early 1970s TIE was definably a movement and soon, aided by the formation of the Standing Conference of Young People's Theatre in 1976, which each year since then has provided an invaluable opportunity for practitioners to meet to share ideas and experiences and debate theory (often intensely!), established a reputation for challenging the accepted notions of what theatre for children was or should be.

Through the early and middle seventies companies increasingly grasped the nettle of difficult, sensitive, but undeniably crucial issues such as racism, sexism, and the power structures of the society in which the children lived. TIE had an inescapably political dimension, sprang from a largely socialist perspective (strongly influenced by the heightened political consciousness of the post–1968 era), and was, some argued, subversive. But however they were viewed, TIE programs at their best achieved a remarkable blend of passionate concern with the major contemporary issues, a belief that children should be offered alternative ways of seeing the world and encouraged to participate in the shaping of that world, *and* an ability to create dramatic structures that engaged them at their own level without being patronizing on the one hand or mystifying on the other.

Without doubt TIE has been at the forefront of developments in children's theatre in Britain and indeed in the alternative theatre movement generally. It even can be said to have had a considerable influence on educational drama. In its use especially of such techniques as "hot-seating" (an interrogation by audience members of characters in the drama) and "teacher-in-role" (when a character in the play becomes a "devil's advocate" at various points and through direct address furthers the action or challenges the children's thinking), TIE has created significant educational and theatrical styles of its own.

CHILDREN'S THEATRE IN GREAT BRITAIN TODAY

What Britain may lack by way of a strong tradition of conventional children's theatre, it makes up for in the wide range and inventiveness of theatre work it offers to young people. The following broad categories will give some idea of the diversity of work currently undertaken.

Range of Companies

The range of companies that offer theatre for children and young people is as follows:

- Young People's Theatre (YPT). As well as an umbrella term to cover *all* theatre for young people of whatever age, refers more specifically to theatre (usually self-contained play performances) for the older (fourteen and up) age range. The work at the Liverpool Everyman Theatre, Manchester's Contact Theatre, and the London Young Vic (in its current form started in 1970)—all building-based operations—is generally of this kind; so also these days is much of the work of Theatre Centre and other touring YPT companies.

- Children's Theatre. The presentation of plays for younger children (up to the age of thirteen or fourteen) by professional companies either in theatre buildings or, on tour, in theatres, school auditoriums, and community centers.

- Theatre-in-Education. Programs devised by specialist companies for much smaller groups of young people (one or two classes at most) and presented in schools or sometimes in theatre studios in close collaboration with teachers and education advisors. Active participation by pupils in the work is a recurring feature, whether through role play or "hot-seating" of characters once the play has ended. Issues of direct relevance to the pupils are addressed, although, according to the age group and the nature of the issues, these will often be distanced historically or geographically.

- "Play Days" and "Theatre Appreciation" events. Activities mainly undertaken by regional and national repertory companies (e.g., the National Theatre, many of the larger regional theatres, Contact Theatre, Manchester, and the larger YPT companies), designed to aid students in their study of examination play texts and to promote interest in and increased understanding of the professional theatre. They also may take the form of workshops, lecture/demonstrations, and performances of short plays or play extracts, given in the theatre or on tour.

• Youth Theatre. Amateur work done by young people themselves, usually organized under the auspices of the local theatre or education authority, and providing opportunities to develop theatre skills, group creativity, and collaborative working methods, culminating in annual large-cast productions. The best known and most prestigious of such groups is the National Youth Theatre, which stages a season of plays each year in London, but most cities and large towns have some such group.

Among the professional categories there is much overlapping, with TIE companies often offering children's theatre and vice versa. Puppet theatre is usually grouped with children's theatre, but many puppet companies also venture into schools to offer TIE-type programs.

Number of Companies

Currently, there are approximately:[6]

• Thirty-three children's and young people's theatre companies, mostly touring but several, such as the Unicorn and the Young Vic, based in their own theatre building. Included here, too, are such diverse companies as the Molecule Theatre: Theatre of Science for Children, Polka Children's Theatre (combining actors and puppets), and Whirligig (the commercial company directed by playwright David Wood devoted to presenting his own full-scale musical plays for children in London and on tour, *The Plotters of Cabbage Patch Corner*, 1979, and *The Gingerbread Man*, being the two best known).

• Forty TIE companies or companies whose work regularly includes TIE, as well as the major TIE and YPT companies (such as Coventry, Greenwich, Cockpit, Leeds, M6, Pit Prop, Theatre Powys/Wales). This includes the Cambridge Syllabus Players (focusing on plays being studied for examinations), Tara-in-Education (an Asian company devoted to presenting Asian perspectives in schools and other youth environments in the London area), Ludus Dance-in-Education (operating very much as a TIE company but through the medium of dance), and the Greater Manchester Archaeological Unit's TIE Team (one of a number of teams funded through the government's Manpower Services Commission, a scheme to create job opportunities for the unemployed).

• More than seventy puppet companies (ranging from the building-based Cannon Hill Puppet Theatre, Birmingham, and Little Angel Marionette Theatre, London, to such touring companies as Black Box Puppet Theatre and Northern Black Light Theatre to many one person touring operations).

• Fifteen "young people's theatre schemes" (i.e., touring and building-based organizations that employ professionals who run workshops and act as "animateurs" rather than as performing companies, such as the Royal Court YPT and some of the larger Youth Theatre organizations).

Organization and Funding

Despite the release of Arts Council money for YPT in 1966, funding has been at a very low level in relation to that enjoyed by mainstream theatre. Consequently many TIE companies have found themselves relegated to minor or subsidiary status, based at and dependent on "parent" repertory theatres. Partly because of the political dimension of their work and partly for economic reasons, many TIE companies during the late seventies and early eighties moved from being wholly TIE-oriented to being more broadly based "community and young people's theatres," serving not only young people through TIE and the occasional children's theatre piece (especially at Christmas), but also the community at large through plays geared to the interests of that community. Many companies believed that their work needed to be free not only from direct local government control, but also from the financial and philosophical constraints of their "parent" theatre. A good case in point is the Bolton Octagon TIE Team, which in 1977 separated itself from the repertory theatre and became an independent company, the M6 Theatre Company, based in Rochdale (near the M6 and M62 highways) and touring local schools and community centers and sometimes further afield.

Other companies, such as those at Coventry, Leeds, and Greenwich, have developed a more satisfactory relationship with their theatres and remain able to create an independent though complementary policy. The Arts Council has recently acknowledged that the needs of YPT are still to be met, and it is now actively encouraging its own client theatres and the Regional Arts Associations to prioritize work for young people, though as yet with little additional financing to make this possible. Indeed, recent government policy has been to increasingly push arts organizations to look for commercial sponsorship to make up for reductions in state subsidy, despite the lack of prestige that small-scale touring offers to firms and the woeful lack of reliable, sympathetic long-term sponsorship available to theatre companies in the recent past. Local authorities, too, have been and still are inconsistent in their own support for the work, some major cities being without a local TIE company, while others (such as ILEA [Inner London Education Authority], Coventry, Leeds, Rochdale, and Wigan) stand out as examples of imaginative, committed local government investment in provision for youth. At its best, YPT thrives on genuine partnership between local authority and Arts Council (or Regional Arts Association); only this type of collaborative funding seems to be able to offer the support and long-term security required for companies to develop their work and respond to local needs.

CURRENT TRENDS AND DEBATES

Content

Since the middle seventies there has been a noticeable shift in the content of plays presented to young people. Though fantasy still retains a central place in children's theatre, most characteristically in the works of the prolific David Wood, in many of the plays presented by the Unicorn, and in seemingly endless tours of *The Lion, the Witch and the Wardrobe*, an increasing number of plays, even for the youngest children, have dealt with contemporary issues. The "peace plays" of David Holman (originally a writer for TIE), presented on tour by Theatre Center in 1982, and Leeds TIE Company's *Raj* and *Flags and Bandages* in 1982 and 1984 (both of which treated aspects of Britain's imperial past and raised questions about paternalism and racism in the process) provide excellent examples of the adventurous work produced, and are further evidence of the influence of TIE on children's theatre in general.

Form

Although the major innovation in TIE has been its use of active audience participation for educational ends, actively challenging children to confront and, where appropriate, deal with problems that emerged in the course of the performance, in recent years there has been a marked shift among many companies to move away from participation programs and toward self-contained performance pieces sometimes (but only sometimes) followed by "workshops." The reasons for this are many.

1. *Economic*. When money is short it is more cost-effective to play to sixty or more children in a morning and move on to another audience in the afternoon, rather than work with a class of just twenty-five or thirty for perhaps a whole day or two half-days; also, it often looks better to funding bodies to have reached more schools in this way.

2. *Reaction*. After ten or so years of traditional participation-TIE, some disillusion inevitably set in among many practitioners. It was an exhausting method of work, was not getting the recognition it deserved, and some of the program formats were beginning to look distinctly tired or formula-bound ("always end with a trial"!) and were not having any measurable effect on a society that seemed to be, politically, shifting to the right (Mrs. Thatcher's government was first elected in 1979).

3. *The debate about theatre language*. As educators and semioticians in their very different fields were examining the ways in which meanings in the media generally were "read" and "decoded" by their recipients, so in TIE there became evident an increased concern with the ways in which theatrical meaning was constructed and with the consequent need to explore and refine the use made of theatrical imagery and the sheer theatrical power of a good performance piece. Performance standards, too, were seen in this light as greatly in need of attention.

4. *The TIE writer*. Several companies who employed writers, rather than relying solely on group-devising, began to show what could be done, notably David Holman with his *No Parasan* for M6 (1977) and David Swift with *Raj* and *Flags and Bandages* for Leeds TIE. The skill of the TIE writer was beginning to be recognized, just as was the value of performance skills. Active involvement

of the children, it was increasingly argued, did not have to be a precondition of an educational process.

A handful of companies do still regularly use and continue to develop the participation format in their work (e.g., Coventry, Pit Prop Theatre [Wigan], Theatre Powys [Wales], and Greenwich), and there are signs now that participation is coming back. Whereas many such programs of the early and middle seventies frequently relied on full-scale active involvement, uninterrupted "suspension of disbelief," and a high level of empathy from the moment a character entered the room, now the leading companies are drawing on the theory and practice of such educators as Gavin Bolton and Dorothy Heathcote (in her use of frequent "freeze-frame" techniques—stopping the action and allowing both children and at least one of the actors to come out of role to reflect on what has happened so far) and on the "forum theatre" strategies of Augusto Boal. Not full circle, but a step forward that once again demonstrates the fruitful interaction between TIE and other pioneering developments in the use of drama as an educational tool.

REPRESENTATIVE COMPANIES

Unicorn Theatre

The origins of the famous Unicorn Theatre lie far from London's West End, at the small Amersham Playhouse in rural Buckinghamshire. Conceived in 1947 by Caryl Jenner and Sally Latimer, the Amersham Schools Mobile Unit began life the next year with the aim of bringing "a true experience of theatre to young people which would last long after the performance was over."[7] The Playhouse itself closed in 1949, but Jenner was determined that the work should continue, so positive had the response been to those first, pioneering tours to village schools. Renamed the Mobile Theatre, the company began to extend its touring circuits, and as its reputation grew and its performances became increasingly sought after, its name was changed again to the English Theatre for Children. By 1957 Jenner was operating four performing companies that served some fifty education authorities, touring on occasion to northern Ireland and Malta, and in 1957, at the request of Sam Wanamaker, began two years of children's theatre provision at the New Shakespeare Theatre in Liverpool.

In 1959 the company played for the first time in London, at the Rudolf Steiner Theatre, and in 1961 started a regular season of plays for children at the Arts Theatre, first at Christmas and then at Easter. The resulting demand for a regular, year-round children's season in London proved so strong that from 1964, the company, now the Unicorn Theatre for Young People, began to present plays throughout the year, both at the Arts (performing at matinees while the adult work continued in the evenings) and at other theatres when available. But financial survival was precarious and closure looked increasingly imminent. In 1967, after the Arts Council decision to award grant aid to certain YPT companies and with the help of the London County Council, Westminster City Council, and several charitable foundations (including the Gulbenkian), the Unicorn purchased the lease on the Arts Theatre, brought to an end its national touring, and settled, at last, into a home of its own, operating now as London's only permanent theatre for children (the Young Vic mainly catering to the older age ranges and often staging shows that cater as much to adults as they do to young people). The Unicorn Theatre Club, for children between four and twelve years of age, was founded in 1962 and now numbers approximately 3,000 members.

In the early days of touring Jenner acted as both director and administrator, while the writer Wilfred Harvey provided more than fifty plays for the company, with titles such as *Pussyfoot and the Baby Train* and *St. Cadoc and the Cat*, not especially challenging as drama but at least enjoyable, and reaching audiences who would otherwise rarely, if ever, see live theatre designed for their age range. Among many memorable premieres since have been Mary Melwood's *The Tingalary Bird*, produced with rare financial support from the Arts Council, in 1964; *The Royal Pardon*, by John Arden and Margaretta D'Arcy, in 1967; and in 1968, *Parafinalia*, by Ken Campbell, once an actor with one of Unicorn's touring companies and subsequently a writer of many successful children's plays (among other accomplishments). Jenner continued to direct most of the productions herself until her death in 1973 (at the age of fifty-three). Her policy had always been to present a varied repertory ranging from ''plays especially written for Unicorn to translations from abroad, from conventional folktales to avant-garde experiments.'' Plays for children, in her view, should have ''something of value to say,'' but the Unicorn did not, she maintained, seek ''to educate or moralize or act as a political platform,'' for ''we are concerned first and foremost with the art of the theatre'' and ''if what we do also educates or moralizes or puts forward a political attitude it is the by-product of the experience of theatre but not the experience itself.''[8] This philosophy has continued to underpin the work of each of her successors, although it has, at the same time, developed in response to the changing climates and the needs of the seventies and eighties.

Unicorn's usual practice now is to play to infant and primary-school audiences during the day in term times and to offer a wide range of plays and participatory theatre workshops on weekends and during holidays. The company also recently adopted a policy of producing plays for integrated audiences of deaf and hearing children, with facilities for the hard of hearing and at least one ''signed'' performance for every production. In 1987 Unicorn celebrated forty years of continuous children's theatre and marked it by, among other things, taking one of its major triumphs, the production of *The Silver Sword* (Ian Serraillier's story of three Polish children during World War II, adapted by Rony Robinson), on a national tour, a salutary reminder of the company's peripatetic origins but with a play that itself suggests the more adventurous material with which the Unicorn now frequently deals.

Theatre Centre

Founded in 1953 by Brian Way and Margaret Faulkes to bring professional theatre into schools across Britain, Theatre Centre began touring in 1954 and is now the country's foremost and longest established such company. In the early years, Way had to rely entirely on money from commercial bookings, school by school, there being no public subsidy available until 1966. Despite the many obstacles, Way successfully pioneered forms of drama that spoke directly to his audiences and involved limited degrees of audience participation. His collection of *Three Plays for the Open Stage* (1958) and (with Warren Jenkins) *Pinocchio* (1954) demonstrate the style of play for which Theatre Centre became renowned: lively, colorful, simply but intimately staged with minimal barriers between children and performers, although steering clear of any critical view of social reality. No more than 200 children were permitted at any of the performances, which were mostly staged in the round. So popular was the operation that by the early 1970s there were seven companies on the road at any one time: five primary-school companies, four of which were performing the same repertory of plays, all rehearsed during the same period under the watchful eye of Way[9]; one secondary and one "village" company, the latter performing to mixed age groups in rural schools; and approximately thirty actors. At the London base there was also a drama center that offered practical drama workshops to local children.

In 1975, with the company well established and funded by the Arts Council on a regular basis, Brian Way handed over the directorship of Theatre Centre to David Johnston, who soon began to introduce radical changes both in the structure of the company and in the style and subject matter of its plays. An active policy of equality for black people and for women was introduced, affecting both the content of the plays and the opportunities provided for actors, and a more democratic management structure was established. The touring companies were then reorganized to reflect the new policies and the concern to improve artistic standards, which resulted in the establishment of a Women's Company, a Mixed Company, and a Workshop Unit. The first two continued to tour nationally a repertory of plays, geared as always to specific age ranges but increasingly tackling issues of direct relevance to the children's own experience, notably David Holman's Peace Plays in 1982/83 (*ABC, 1983, Susumu's Story, Peacemaker*) and, for the Women's Company, Lisa Evans' *Under Exposure* (about South Africa, for nine- to thirteen-year-olds) and Nona Shepphard's *Getting Through* (about growing up and dealing with the institution of school, for nine- to thirteen-year-olds) in 1986. From 1984 funding has been made available from the Arts Council and the London Boroughs for a Workshop Unit that offers a variety of drama skills courses, community outreach work, talks, and preparatory and follow-up advice and resources to extend the work of the two performing companies; it also offers residencies around the country, lasting from a week to a month, bringing together the performing companies and the workshop staff. Theatre Centre's recent development clearly owes much to the advances made by the TIE movement.

Currently Theatre Centre defines its aims and policy as follows:

1. To present theatre of the highest possible standard to young people

2. To use innovative forms of theatre which allow audiences to question the world in which they live and to encourage them to make positive decisions about their lives

3. To reflect, celebrate and develop the multi-cultural society of which we are a part

4. To challenge forms of oppression which are based on gender, culture, race, class or sexual orientation

5. To research and reveal the sources of these forms of oppression and

6. To give opportunity for artistic expression to those people, cultures and ideas which are and have been silenced and devalued by the prevailing values of our society.[10]

Interestingly, the very existence of a Mixed Company (from 1983), in which multiracial (as well as male-female, able-bodied–disabled, and gay-straight) casting was a priority, itself led to further developments in Theatre Centre's philosophy and style of performance. Thus the presence of, for example, Irish, Asian, and Afro-Caribbean performers drew such themes as racism and the "lost and hidden histories" of minority groups to the center of the company's work. Likewise, the Women's Company's existence led to an exploration of feminist perspectives that in turn have shaped artistic output.

The bulk of Theatre Centre's funding comes from the Arts Council, primarily for national touring, with additional money from the ILEA (for work in London schools) and the London Boroughs' Grants Unit (for "outreach" work). There is an administrative team of four, together with the artistic director, education officer, and workshop director, while each of the performing companies consists of four actors and one company manager. A measure of the esteem in which the company is now held internationally is the number of invitations it receives to perform regularly at festivals worldwide: Toronto, Vancouver, and Philadelphia in 1987, for example. In 1987 David Johnston resigned, but under the direction of his successor, Libby Mason, Theatre Centre continues to promote the artistic policy forged so successfully over the previous twelve years and to adapt and develop to meet the new educational and artistic challenges of the late 1980s.

Belgrade Theatre-in-Education Team, Coventry

The first TIE company to be formed in the United Kingdom, the Belgrade at once established itself as the model for most subsequent TIE teams and yet has been constantly in the forefront of the new developments, rarely allowing itself to settle comfortably into well-worn channels. Conceived originally as part of an ambitious plan to make the Belgrade Theatre both a cultural center and a base from which a variety of units would reach out into the community, the team was formed under the direction of Gordon Vallins in 1965. Drawing on recent developments in curriculum drama in schools, the work of the more adventurous touring children's theatre companies such as Theatre Centre, and the achievements of Joan Littlewood's Theatre Workshop company at Stratford East in London (and especially its 1963 documentary theatre success, *Oh, What a Lovely War!*), the Belgrade team devised three projects for touring to local schools: *The Balloonman and the Runaway Balloons* for infants, *The Secret of the Stone* for juniors, and *Tay Bridge Disaster* for secondary schools. At this stage the priority was to foster the imagination and creativity of the children through enacted storytelling, rather than to confront children directly with problems that they themselves had to resolve, but audience participation was central and the documentary element, so much a feature of later TIE, was very much to the fore in the latter piece.

The four-month experimental project proved successful, and in 1966 Rosemary Birbeck was appointed head of TIE together with a team of eight actor-teachers. Members of the team in those early years included Roger Chapman (who later founded TIE companies in both Bolton and Leeds), Sue Birtwhistle (later a cofounder of the TIE team in Edinburgh and then a founder of Nottingham Roundabout Company), Gordon Wiseman (later a cofounder of the Edinburgh team and later still a director of M6), Cora Williams (later director of Bolton Octagon TIE and now artistic coordinator of the Pit Prop Theatre), Paul Harman (now director of Merseyside YPT), Stuart Bennett (who succeeded Birbeck as head of department and now director of Cockpit Arms Workshop), David Pammenter (head of department, 1972–1977, and now director of the Community Theatre Arts program at Rose Bruford College), and Rory Baskerville (later director of Theatre Foundry YPT)—a group that demonstrates how influential the Coventry team has been in inspiring and nourishing TIE into a nationwide movement.[11]

As the company developed and the political and educational climates changed, so the programs themselves became increasingly engaged with the issues of contemporary society and with the need to inform young people about their world, empower them within it, and, at the same time, challenge their widely held prejudices. Subject matter dealt with during the middle seventies included, for example, pollution, law and order, and racism and gave rise to some of the classics of TIE, notably *Drink the Mercury, Example: The Case of Craig and Bentley*, and *Pow Wow*.

For more than twenty years funding from the Arts Council (by way of the Belgrade Theatre Trust) and the Coventry City Council has enabled the company to provide free services to the city's infant, junior, secondary, and special schools, and on a more regular basis than is the case with most TIE/YPT companies. Additionally, the company has, for many years, staged a children's theatre production every year in the Belgrade Theatre. Currently new directions are being explored by the team in order to reach a mass audience of young people (and adults) for its annual event, with performances and workshops in other community venues. The company currently consists of seven actor-teachers, an administrator, a stage manager, and a schools liaison officer, together with one "floating" post, usually a freelance director, actor-teacher, or designer. One of the company is designated official head of department, accountable along with the administrator to the Belgrade Theatre Trust for all aspects of the team's work. The work itself, however, is planned collectively and is usually researched and devised by the company.

Always the aim is to "present complex issues in a dramatic way which challenges the children to ask questions and often to make decisions about the world in which they live."[12] Two highly successfully programs from the company's recent repertory will indicate their continuing alertness to current issues and their commitment to participation-TIE. *Lives Worth Living* (1983) was a half-day program for fourteen- to fifteen-year-olds that tackled the question of mental handicap and our frequently thoughtless and ignorant attitudes toward it; the play was followed by a "hot-seating" of the two main characters, one of whom was handicapped, and presented audiences with a major challenge to their preconceptions. *Fire in the Mountain* (1987) was, on the other hand, a whole-day program for ten- to twelve-year-olds; it actively involved them in an investigation of the history and current political struggles of Nicaragua, seen through the lives of a particular Nicaraguan family, and touched on wider issues both personal and political. The company has recently introduced adults to TIE through special performances for parents during school tours and at least once a year through performances in the Belgrade Theatre Studio for a wider public. Unlike most YPT companies that have branched into community theatre as well, the Belgrade is wholly geared to TIE (except for the annual YPT production), and it is this orientation, and the relative security of its funding, that has allowed it the time and energy to devise all its own programs and ensure that its work is constantly at the frontier of TIE.

Greenwich Young People's Theatre

Originally known as the "Bowsprit" TIE Company, Greenwich Young People's Theatre (GYPT) has its origins in the youth theatre work of the Greenwich Theatre, initiated by the theatre's first artistic director, Ewan Hooper, in 1965 as part of his drive to establish a genuine community theatre for southeast London. The TIE company was formed in 1969 and consisted of two actor-teachers and one director (Bernard Goss), who were based at the Greenwich Theatre and worked in schools in southeast London and Kent. The next year the company moved to larger premises, an unused church in Plumstead, where the TIE and youth theatre operations could more effectively be linked and which could house performances by the professional team and the youth themselves. At this point Greenwich Young People's Theatre was adopted as the collective name for the venture. Bowsprit continued to be the name of the TIE unit until it was dropped in 1978. Still a subsidiary of the Greenwich Theatre, GYPT nonetheless has a considerable degree of autonomy, receiving financing not only from the Arts Council and the London Borough of Greenwich, but also (primarily now) from ILEA.

The policy of the company is "to provide a professional TIE service for ILEA schools in southeast London and to provide a comprehensive program of theatre arts activities for young people in their leisure time." Underscoring the actual implementation of this policy are certain principles that the company defines as follows:

1. A concern for the personal development of all individuals with whom and for whom GYPT works;

2. the selection of subject matter of immediate personal and social relevance to the audience and participants;

3. the use of methods designed to encourage analysis, increase understanding and awareness, and promote change and improvement; and

4. the extension of creative potential and enhancement of professional standards of all company members.[13]

Perhaps the most impressive feature of GYPT is the diversity of artistic and educational skills (and of opportunities offered to young people) gathered under one roof. The full-time staff of twenty-one, led by a director (currently Chris Vine, since 1985) and two team leaders, includes actor-teachers, designers, stage managers, a liaison officer, a production manager, and a musical director, all of whom contribute in some way or other to the Arts Workshops in the evenings and the projects taken into schools. Part-time specialists are also brought in from time to time for specific projects.

The variety and scope of the projects undertaken by GYPT may be gauged by noting the following examples of past work:

Race Against Time—a full-day participatory TIE program in schools that examines the causes and nature of racism, taking the form of a short play followed by interviews with the characters and discussion, together with a simulation game exploring the themes of immigration and citizenship

Time for Change—a twice-weekly full-day workshop for young unemployed people that offers the opportunity to develop drama skills, create their own theatre, and, where appropriate, apply for further education and training courses in the arts

Circles of Fire—a whole-day project at the GYPT studio theatre for groups of fourteen- to fifteen-year-olds consisting of a performance of a short play set in contemporary South Africa and a series of "forum theatre" exercises (based on the techniques of Augusto Boal), all examining the concept of social change and what makes people decide to try to change things themselves

Green Jam—a full-time three-year theatre training project for mentally disabled young adults (the first project of its kind in Britain)

In addition, there are the youth theatre workshops and productions, arts activities (drama, music, movement, photography, puppetry) for all age groups from seven to twenty-five, and presentations of performances by visiting theatre companies. This is certainly one of the most active, broadly based, and forward-looking YPT companies currently in Britain, and the hope must be that current governmental plans to abolish the ILEA will not jeopardize the survival of this important venture.

BIBLIOGRAPHY

Books

Deary, T. *Teaching Through Theatre*. London: Samuel French, 1977.
Dodd, N., and Hickson, W., eds. *Drama and Theatre in Education*. London: Heineman, 1971.
Education Survey No. 2: Drama. London, Department of Education and Science, 1968.
Education Survey No. 22: Actors in Schools. London, Department of Education and Science, 1976.
Hodgson, J., and Banham, M., eds. *Drama in Education*, vols. 1–3. London: Pitman, 1972–1975.
Jackson, T., ed. *Learning Through Theatre: Essays and Casebook on TIE*. University of Manchester, 1980; includes casebooks on *It Fits* (infants), *Poverty Knocks* (junior/secondary), and *Marches* (upper secondary).
O'Toole, J. *Theatre in Education: New Objectives for Theatre—New Techniques in Education*. London: Hodder and Stoughton, 1976.
The Provision of Theatre for Young People in Great Britain. London, Arts Council of Great Britain, 1966.
Redington, C. *Can Theatre Teach? An Historical and Evaluative Analysis of TIE*. Oxford: Pergamon Press, 1983.
Robinson, K., ed. *Exploring Theatre and Education*. London: Heineman, 1980.
SCYPT Journal (Standing Conference of Young People's Theatre), London: Cockpit TIE Team, 1977–85; after 1985 retitled *New Voices*.
Way, B. *Development Through Drama*. London: Longmans, 1967.
———. *Audience Participation*. Boston: Walter H. Baker, 1981.
Webster, C. *Working with Theatre in Schools*. London: Pitman, 1975.

Programs and Plays

Barrie, J. M. *Peter Pan*. London: Scribners, 1928.
Brand of Freedom. Pit Prop Theatre (Wigan). A three-part video recording of a TIE program in schools, with accompanying notes. Produced by Manchester University Television Service, 1984. (Available from MVTV, Manchester M13 9PL, or via Concorde Educational Films Ltd.)

Campbell, Ken. *Old King Cole*. London: Methuen, 1978.

Coffey, Denise. *The Incredible Vanishing !!!* London: Methuen, 1979.

Milne, A. A. *Toad of Toad Hall*. London: Samuel French, 1929.

Raj. Leeds Playhouse TIE Company. University of Oxford, 1984.

Rare Earth: A Programme About Pollution. Belgrade Coventry TIE Team. Edited by S. Wyatt and M. Steed. London: Methuen, 1976.

Redington, C., ed. *Six TIE Programmes (Dirty Rascals, Peacemaker, Under Exposure, The School on the Green, Questions Arising in 1985 from a Mutiny in 1789, Lives Worth Living)*. London: Methuen, 1987.

Schweitzer, P., ed. *Theatre in Education Programmes*, 3 vols. *(Five Infant Programmes [Pow Wow, Polly, the All-Action Dolly, Ifan's Valley, Hospitals, Navigators]; Four Junior Programmes [The Price of Coal, Rubbish, Travellers, Big Deal]; Four Secondary Programmes [No Parasan, Example: The Case of Craig and Bentley, Factory, Holland New Town])*. London: Methuen, 1980.

Snap Out of It: A Programme About Mental Illness. Leeds Playhouse TIE Company. Edited by R. Chapman and B. Wilks. London: Methuen, 1973.

Sweetie Pie: A Play About Women in Society. Bolton Octagon TIE Team. Edited by E. Murphy. London: Methuen, 1975.

NOTES

1. See Michael Booth, *Prefaces to English Nineteenth Century Theatre* (Manchester, 1980), pp. 194–204.

2. See Allardyce Nicoll, *English Drama 1900–1930* (Cambridge, 1973), pp. 241–242.

3. See ibid., p. 245, and J. C. Trewin, *The Edwardian Theatre* (London, 1976), pp. 163–166.

4. See Peter Roberts, *The Old Vic Story* (London, 1976), pp. 121–122.

5. See Hilary Ball, "Theatre in Education: Mapping Its Growth in Britain," in J. Hodgson and M. Banham, eds., *Drama in Education*, vol. 1 (London, 1975), p. 16; also Christine Redington, *Can Theatre Teach?* (Oxford, 1983), ch. 1, and Philip Coggin, *Drama and Education: An Historical Survey* (London, 1956), ch. 23.

6. Based on the 1987 *British Alternative Theatre Directory* (London, 1987) and on personal knowledge.

7. Caryl Jenner, "Let's Pretend," in Hodgson and Banham, *Drama in Education*, vol. 1, p. 144.

8. Ibid., pp. 148–149.

9. See Clive Webster, *Working with Theatre in Schools* (London: 1975), pp. 11–12.

10. Quoted from current Theatre Centre publicity document (1987).

11. See Redington, *Can Theatre Teach?* Appendix B.

12. Quoted from *Belgrade TIE: The First 21 years*, brochure produced by the company to celebrate its anniversary, 1986.

13. Quoted from current GYPT publicity brochure (1987).

Tony Jackson

Greece

HISTORY

In ancient Greece, theatre was family entertainment. Children and their parents attended performances that took place in broad daylight, eating and drinking and sharing the excitement of watching whole trilogies in the drama contests. Further, "orchesis," a combination of poetry, music, and movement, held an important place in a child's upbringing in the Athenian republic. Children often used orchesis to enact scenes from the *Odyssey* or the *Iliad*. Young Athenians also performed in the chorus of the tragedies, an opportunity that was considered educational as well as a great privilege and a service to the republic. If a young man was called to arms while rehearsing a play, he was exempted from conscription, even in wartime, in order to finish the production work.

In the Byzantine era the only form of theatre was the "circus" (or hippodrome), which was a popular spectacle in Constantinople but far from suitable for children. In 1453 Constantinople fell into the hands of the Turks, and most of Greece became part of the Ottoman empire and remained so for nearly 400 years. Under Turkish rule theatre was forbidden as were all public gatherings of more than three persons. The only exceptions were religious feasts, carnival, and fertility rites. All these festivities, which included folk songs and dancing, were substitutes for theatre and shared by both adults and children.

In Crete, under Venetian rule until 1669, verse plays based on chivalrous tales were written but hardly ever performed. These were so popular that grown-ups and children alike knew parts of them by heart and often recited long passages. When Crete was finally conquered by the Turks, many Cretans escaped to the Ionian Islands, taking the plays with them. On these islands during Carnival (especially in the towns and villages on Zante), groups of amateur actors, mainly comprised of young people and craftsmen, assembled and gave performances in the streets and squares; they presented the Cretan plays, popular stories, or even satires about their fellow villagers. These performances, called "omilies," achieved a degree of audience participation that many modern groups (especially those playing for children) would envy. The local teacher or a high school graduate would often help in both casting and directing. Women's roles were played by boys or young men with high-pitched voices. This kind of theatrical activity continues to the present day, although to a much lesser degree.

At the end of the eighteenth century, and especially in the years before the War of Independence (which officially started in 1821), in towns like Odessa, Bucarest, and Trieste with their flourishing Greek communities, important Greek schools were founded. In these institutions students often performed either in classical tragedies or modern plays with patriotic themes. The main purpose of these productions was to strengthen the national conscience of the young Greeks and prepare them for taking an active part in the coming revolution against the Turks. Later similar performances were organized in Greece, and after liberation the day of national independence was celebrated annually with the recitation of patriotic poems and the staging of scenes from the uprising. This tradition continues today.

All these examples have been mentioned, even though none is what one would define as "children's theatre," because they all helped to shape a tradition that has strongly influenced Greek theatre and children's theatre, in particular.

THE SHADOW-THEATRE OF KARAGHIOZIS

The Karaghiozis was initially a theatre for grown-ups[1]; soon it was producing family entertainment and now it is mainly a theatre for children. There are many theories about the origins of this theatre, the predominant one telling of the theatre's roots in the Far East. As soon as Greece was liberated many Greeks returned from Asia Minor, and they brought Karaghiozis with them. The word, Turkish in origin, means "black-eyed," and is the name of the protagonist in the plays: an ugly, cunning hunchback with one very long arm, always ready to deal blows to anyone weaker than himself.

The Turkish Karaghiozis plays were rather lewd, but their style soon changed as they were adapted to Greek tastes. Now they used stories from the recent uprising as well as folk elements, fairy tales, and songs and dances and introduced new characters from contemporary life as well as mythological heroes, like Hercules or Oedipus, or historical characters, like Alexander the Great (who was sometimes identified with St. George). Karaghiozis himself became a Greek man, usually oppressed by the rich and powerful Turks; today this character would be called an anti-hero. He had moments of spiritual elevation but would use any means such as stealing or deceiving, to ensure his survival. Although illiterate, he appears as a judge, a doctor, a vizier, a baker, a midwife, and even a ghost. He constantly looks for the one big deal that will change his life but always returns to his hut empty-handed, starving, and often beaten up in the bargain. He has a nagging wife and one to four children to feed, depending on the version of the play.

The basic implements of this shadow-theatre are a white canvas screen, flat puppets with movable parts, and some form of lighting. The figures can be either black and white or colored, cut out of cardboard or drawn on specially-prepared leather. Most important, of course, is the Karaghiozopechtes (the Karaghiozi-player), who stands behind the screen and manipulates the figures with strings or sticks. In addition, he creates the different voices for the characters, sings, renders sound effects, and generally orchestrates the entire performance. He is sometimes helped by an apprentice, often his own son. At first, the Karaghiozopechtes improvised the plays; later, they wrote them down and published them. Among the more famous of the Karaghiozopechtes are Mimaros, Mollas, Xanthos, Manolopoulos, Manos, Roulias, Memos and Spatharis.

Karaghiozis was an extremely popular theatre form. In 1920, there were approximately fifteen shadow theatres in and around Athens alone, and many others toured all over the country, adding new figures, new stories, and technical innovations as they went. This peak of activity lasted from 1920 until the late 1940s, by which time Karaghiozis was mainly a children's theatre although the entire family still enjoyed it. Very often children cut their own figures and performed for their neighbors, collecting pocket money for themselves. Postwar Karaghiozis tried to adjust to modern times by developing new plays, hence *Karaghiozis the Astronaut*.

The technical aspects were also perfected. Karaghiozopechtes used electric light and phonographs, and later tape recorders, but the spectacle lost spontaneity and simplicity. First the movies and then television proved to be too much competition for Karaghiozis and activity virtually ceased. There are always a few Karaghiozopechtes around (among them Evgenios Spatharis, Manthos, Haridimos, and Spiropoulos), and the form is now often seen on television.

PUPPET THEATRE

Puppets existed in ancient Greece and are mentioned by both Herodotus and Xenophon. Samples of them can be seen in Greek museums. In modern Greece, puppet theatre (which later became a popular entertainment for children) re-emerged around 1880. The first of the puppeteers referred to by historians were Stavros and Maridakis. The central character in the plays was Fasoulis (from the Italian Fasolino); another character, called Pericletos, (little Pericles) soon appeared. Maridakis was succeeded by Konitsiotis, who introduced yet another character, called Paschalis (from the Italian Pasquale). These were all hand puppets of the Punch-and-Judy type. During the Nazi occupation eminent personalities like painter Spiros Vassiliou, stage director Socrates Karantinos, and writer Vassilis Rotas organized puppet shows. The plays, written by Rotas, were performed for starving children who were waiting to receive their share of "free soup." Later, in areas liberated by Greek guerrillas, puppet shows also became important in the lives of children.

One of the companies that appeared during the occupation went on to become famous after the war: the Barba-Mitoussi Company (Uncle Big Nose), founded by painter Eleni Theohari-Perraki. She made the puppets, designed the scenery, and wrote the plays. Kind and wise Barba-Mitoussi and his mischievous nephew and niece, Klouvios and Souvlitsa, were popular, and entertained the children of Athens until 1984. After the war string puppets appeared with the Marionettes Theatre created by Marios Stavrolemis (later succeeded by Takis Kalajtzakis, Takis Apostolidis, and others). One can still see Apostolidis' string puppets in Athens, now under the direction of Nikos Gotsis.

In 1975 writer Evgenia Fakinou wrote a play titled *Tenekedoupoli* (*Tin Can City*), which she performed using empty cans, instead of puppets, to create amusing and interesting characters. The names and personalities of the characters were derived from the erstwhile contents of the cans, and all of them appeared in nearly every play in the series of five. In this unusual form of theatre, unique to Greece as far as it is known, each character was introduced with a "signature tune," in the tradition of Karaghiozis.

The Tenekedoupoli company ceased performing in 1981. All of the plays, which were most popular, were produced for television, and all the texts have been published and the music recorded. As it is easy to get hold of a few empty cans, the plays are still performed all over the country, by teachers and children in schools and by parents and children at home. Currently (apart from some occasional experiments like the work of Yannis Proestakis, the Gotsis Company, and the Sofianos Family, a company that mainly appears in television programs), the major company is the Greek Puppet Theatre, founded in 1977 by Takis Sarris. The group's work is addressed to older children and adults (for instance, in 1981 it produced Brecht's *The Good Woman of Szechuan*). The company espouses modern practices in which the puppeteers are not hidden, but instead work in full view of the audience; in fact, the "acting" of the puppeteers is seen as complementary to the action of the puppets. In July 1988 the company appeared at the St. Albans Festival in London in a play titled *Circus Games*.

Since 1985 an international festival of puppet theatre has taken place every summer on the island of Hydra. This is organized by the famous Swedish puppeteer Mikael Meschke, with the support of the Greek Ministry of Culture.

TOWARD A THEATRE FOR CHILDREN

According to Greek theatre historian Yannis Sideris, Konstantinos Christomanos, who founded the important New Stage Company and presented *Hedda Gabler* in Athens in 1903, produced, in the same year, a kind of pantomime for children in special matinees; these performances, unfortunately, did not continue. Grigoris Xenopoulos, perhaps the most important dramatist at the turn of the century, wrote a number of plays for children, but these were performed only in amateur productions. In 1927 a school in Piraeus asked writer Vassilis Rotas to write a play for young people; he both wrote and directed the patriotic *Long Live Messolongi*, and acted in it too. The critics were impressed with the work, which was extremely serious and dramatic, and it remained a favorite choice for school productions for many years.

In 1930 Rotas founded the Popular Theatre of Athens. During its three years of existence the company presented several plays for children, all written by Rotas. In 1932 Antigone Metaxa founded The Children's Theatre, a company in which children performed for young audiences in various venues, usually on Sunday mornings. Their first productions consisted of a combination of short plays and sketches with music, dancing, and recitations, which were adaptations of well-known children's stories, Aesop's fables, patriotic themes, and original stories conceived by Metaxa. Apart from writing some of the plays, Metaxa also directed them and designed the scenery. Called "Aunt Lena" by children who were familiar with her radio programs, Metaxa remained popular and her strong influence dominated the style of children's theatre in Greece for many years.

In the 1950s adult companies occasionally staged some children's theatre. One unusual example was a fairy-tale play in which Elli Lamberti and Dimitris Horn, two of the greatest and most popular actors of Greek theatre, appeared together. This unique presentation is reminiscent of the great British actresses who appeared in *Peter Pan* at Christmastime. Another interesting example was a production of *Snow Queen* staged by the company of Katerina Paxinou, the famous Greek actress. Both productions were mounted by stage director Takis Mouzenidis with a strong supporting cast of professional actors; in the Paxinou production the two leading roles were played by children, one of whom was Lisa Protopsalti, now one of the most distinguished actresses in the country.

In general, the children's productions of the fifties and sixties that were presented on Sunday mornings featured either actors appearing in adult evening performances or children, or both. In many cases the leading role was played by child film star Yannis Kalatzoupoulos, who later, as an adult, wrote and directed plays for children.

REPRESENTATIVE COMPANIES

The most important development in the history of Greek children's theatre started, oddly enough, in the 1970s, under dictatorship, when this kind of work was forbidden. Teachers were not allowed to take students to a theatre, nor were companies allowed to perform in schools. During this time, in 1972, well-known actress Xenia Kalogeropoulou, who had been operating an adult company since 1965, founded a children's company that remains the best-known theatre for young people in the country. In 1984 both companies moved to a new theatre with 450 seats, an Italian stage, and an ampitheatrical auditorium. The new venue was called Porta (The Gate) and the children's company was called Mikri Porta (The Little Gate).

In its first nine years the company mainly produced works from the recognized international repertory: plays from the GRIPS Theatre in Germany and the Paper Bag Players in the United States, plays by Brian Way from England and by Friedrich Karl Waechter and other German writers. In its tenth year the group produced a play of its own, *Ulyssinbad*, written by Kalogeropoulou herself. With this production the company achieved a personal style and formulated a concept of what theatre for children can and should be: a multidimensional experience for all ages, with abundant humor and imagination as well as a touch of poetry.

Ulyssinbad uses elements from the *Odyssey*, the *Arabian Nights*, and popular tales from many countries to make up the story of a brave and intelligent man who goes through a series of extraordinary adventures until he finds out "that the journey was the riddle and the riddle was the prize." The play enjoyed the astounding approval of both the public and critics, and further productions were staged in Cyprus, Tel Aviv, Liverpool, and London. Since 1982 the company has produced only one other Greek play, a script by Alki Zei. *Old King Cole*, by Ken Campbell, was presented in the summer of 1988 at the Athens Festival. After a revival of *Ulyssinbad*, a new play by Kalogeropoulou is planned; this will be a free adaptation of the *Fair Maid of the West*, by the Elizabethan Thomas Heywood.

Mikri Porta performs regularly in Athens and tours all over the country; it also has played in two international festivals (Berlin, in 1979, and Rotterdam, in 1980). Since the early seventies more than 100 professional actors have worked with the company, and a great number of them are now leading actors and actresses in Greece. The best Greek composers and designers have collaborated on productions, most of which were directed by Stamatis Fasoulis, a well-known personality in the adult theatre.

In 1973 the Children's Company of the Research Theatre appeared. This group was founded, along with an adult company, through the Research Theatre by Dimitris Potamitis. Since its inception it has presented a play every year with regular week-end performances for general audiences, extra performances for schools, and tours throughout the country. In addition to being its founder, Potamitis is also the permanent director of the group. The repertory, dealing with either modern issues or adaptations of classic texts, almost always tries to elicit active participation from young audiences. This practice is facilitated by the ampitheatre structure, which includes a stage surrounded by seats on three sides.

Apart from English plays by James Bridie, Ken Campbell, and David Wood, most of the works produced by the company are original Greek plays by Yannis Xanthoulis, Vassilis Mitsakis, Phemi Kanellou, Irene Maradei, and Potamitis himself. Attendance has been overwhelming, and many of the plays have been revived after a few years. One of the highlights of the group's work was *Grandfather's Aristophanes Stories*, by Potamitis, which is a free adaptation of five Aristophanes plays, *Birds, Lysistrata, Plutus, The Acharnians*, and *Peace*, and has been translated into English and Japanese.

In 1974, when democracy was restored in Greece, there arose great enthusiasm for all kinds of cultural activities and many new professional companies appeared. Among them, in chronological order, are the following.

The Theatre of the Sun, founded in the mid–1970s by a group of actors under the direction of Andreas Papaspyrou, has mostly produced plays from the GRIPS Theatre or by Lev Ustinov. It prefers to perform in its own theatre but also plays in schools and open-air theatres in the summer. Most of the repertory is amusing and lively with an emphasis on social messages.

The Cafe Theatre Hamletino, founded in 1979 by Ghiorgos Nikolaidis, has four permanent members. The group's goals include (a) encouraging dramatists to write plays for children (its repertory consists solely of works by Greek writers), (b) experimenting with ways to elicit maximum participation from the children, and (c) using modern technology to turn the stage into a place of "expectation and surprise."

Company 81 was founded in 1981 on a cooperative basis by four actors: Nana Nikolaou, Nikos Daphnis, Christos Kelandonis, and Ghiorgos Michalakis. A variety of established directors, composers, choreographers, and actors have collaborated on productions, in which music, dance, and audience participation are important. The group believes strongly in the creative potential of communal work and in a popular entertainment that uses everyday language to say "something important." Nearly all of their plays are Greek, among them works by Evgenios Trivizas. The best work to date was a production of *The Dream of the Scarecrow*, a play about a scarecrow who makes peace with birds and dreams of being able to fly; basically, it is about freedom. Company 81 performs in various theatres and is always ready to travel.

In 1985 the Aeroplion Theatre opened. It is managed by a board chaired by actor Nikos Kamtsis and has presented three plays, one by Kamtsis himself (*Good Morning Don Quixote, Welcome, Gulliver*). The company's work is oriented toward an aesthetic style that will "stimulate the innate capacity of the children for dreaming."

The six companies mentioned above all receive regular subsidies from the Ministry of Culture that cover 15 to 25 percent of their annual expenses. To complete the picture of children's theatre in Athens, some of the important productions offered by other companies in recent years should be mentioned.

The Stoa Theatre, which usually performs for adults and is one of the most important theatres in the country for fostering new playwrights, has produced four children's productions. The most notable was *Gaitanaki*, by George Sarris, the story of old Nicholas, who regains his youth in order to travel around the earth and teach the whole world the song of peace. This play has been produced by seventeen professional companies in Greece, Cyprus, and the Soviet Union. The internationally famous Arts Theatre of Karolos Koun has produced one children's play, *The Adventures of Tzitziri*, by Ghiorgos Armenis.

The company Alphavitari has produced two plays for children by Yannis Xanthoulis. *Climb on the Roof, Let's Eat the Cloud* is the story of a little girl who feels stifled by everyday family life and decides to live on the roof of her apartment building, where she meets her long lost grandmother and has many extraordinary adventures. This is considered the best play by one of the most outstanding of Greek children's playwrights. The Alexandrakis-Galinea company staged a professional production of *Tom Saywer*; the Aloni company presented an adaptation of Mozart's *The Magic Flute*; the Palkoscenico company (which plays for both children and adults) has performed for the Greek communities in Canada; the Center for Classical Ballet has produced three works combining ballet and theatre (*Don Quixote* among them); and a version of *The Emperor's New Clothes* by Yannis Kalantzopoulos was presented by a company/cooperative that included among its actors Emilia Ipsilandi, president of the Greek performer's union.

The National Theatre in Athens has produced two children's productions, Maeterlinck's classic *The Blue Bird* and a play by Greek writer Ghiorgos Ioannou, but has not persevered in these attempts. On the contrary, the National Theatre of Northern Greece in Salonica has been producing plays for children since 1977. Since 1984 the productions have incorporated puppets as well as live actors, an initiative of Kiriakos Argyropoulos. Other companies in this city include the New Theatre of Salonika, founded in 1983, and the Children's Company of the Theatre Workshop, which is no longer in operation. Since 1983 many of the larger cities have founded municipal theatres that have, in addition to their work for adults, presented credible children's productions.

Not many professional companies work in the provinces, but there are some. One important group is the Theatre Workshop of Chania, founded by Elpida Braoudaki. Also significant is the Desmi company and its production several years ago of *Our Friend Aesop*, a verse play by Yannis Negrepontis. This work has since been revived many times.

CHILDREN'S THEATRE TODAY

To summarize the situation, in Greece many companies perform for children (the exact number is difficult to ascertain but it is certainly more than fifty). A committee of the Ministry of Culture selects the companies to be subsidized; this selection is based on judgments about a group's work in the past. Another committee, this one from the Ministry of Education, selects productions to be presented for schoolchildren. It is significant that both committees usually choose the same companies and productions.

Although there is a great deal of children's theatre in Greece, the general standards are not yet satisfactory. Many companies are ruled strictly by box office considerations and have not attained professional-level skills. It is encouraging, however, that more productions of a higher quality are appearing each year and that standards, in general, do appear to be rising. The most difficult goal is the creation of more original plays of real artistic value; this will not happen until children's theatre stops being a "poor relation" of adult theatre.

Apart from the need for good texts and the financial difficulties involved, a practical problem is space. Even a company with a theatre of its own must perform, when invited, in unsuitable movie houses and school halls. Most productions are staged to be presented in "real" theatres; they are not pieces staged in the "theatre-in-education style" of children's theatre in other countries. These productions lose much when they are presented in schools with less than adequate theatre facilities. Also, transportation is expensive, and because companies have a responsibility to perform for the children of the less privileged cities and suburbs, this becomes a difficult problem to solve; it is one of the reasons that theatrical performances are not yet part of the school curriculum. Only two or three of the more successful companies perform up to eight times a week; others perform as little as three times a week, which is not enough to cover expenses even with subsidies.

Still, there are many new initiatives each year and the situation is changing. Sometimes the Ministry of Youth purchases and distributes free tickets to young people. Unfortunately this is not a regular practice. Free tickets are given to workers and seamen, in particular, so that they can take their children to the theatre. Two organizations that are especially active in this respect are The Workers Home and the Seaman's Home. A recent practice that is becoming widespread is for factories, banks, and other businesses to "buy" whole performances and offer tickets to workers and their families. This is also done on a regular basis by municipal councils. Greek ASSITEJ and the Actor's Union are trying to persuade the state to organize festivals and seminars, and to give annual prizes to raise the level of theatre for children. The country's goals are far from being reached, but the important thing now is that the mentality is changing; once beliefs change, action is not far behind.

BIBLIOGRAPHY

There are no Greek books about children's theatre. The ASSITEJ Center is now preparing a volume that will be published in the near future.

Plays

Armenis, Ghiorgos. *The Adventures of Tzitziri*. Niki.
Fakinou, Evgenia. *Tenekedoupoli*. Kedros, 1977.
———. *Awake Tenekedoupolis*. Kastaniotis, 1979.
———. *The Great Journey of Melenios*. Kastaniotis, 1979.
———. *Mr. Ultramer*. Kastaniotis, 1980.
———. *Kourdistan*. Kedros, 1987.
Ioannou, Ghiorgos. *The Hen's Egg*. Kedros, 1981.
Kalantzopoulos, Yannis. *The Emperor's Clothes*. Kastaniotis, 1988.
Kalogeropoulou, Xenia. *Ulyssinbad*. Ithaki, 1982.
Metaxa, Antigone. *The Children's Theatre*. Dorikos, 1982.
Negrepontis, Yannis. *Our Friend Aesop*. Kedros, 1979.

Potamitis, Dimitri. *Tales in Reverse*. Gnossi, 1982.

————. *Tales of Grandfather Aristophanes*. Diachroniki and Doudoumis, 1985.

Rotas, Vassilis. *Plays for Children*. Har i Boura.

Sakellariou, Haris. *Spinthovolakis*. Kastaniotis, 1986.

Sarris, George. *Gaitanaki*. Kedros, 1979.

Trivizas, Evgenios. *The Dream of the Scarecrow*. Hestia, 1985.

Valavani, Eleni. *Aristophanes' Peace*. Dodoni, 1979.

————. *Menander's Shield*. Dodoni, 1984.

Xanthoulis, Yannis. *The Colored Magician*. Cactus, 1978.

————. *Drums, Trumpets and Red Sweets*. Cactus, 1979.

————. *Climb on the Roof, Let's Eat the Cloud*. Astarti, 1980.

The Tenekedoupoli company, the Children's Company of the Research Theatre, Mikri Porta, and Company 81 have all recorded songs and fragments of plays from their productions on tapes or records.

Karaghiozis Theatre

There is a large bibliography about Karaghiozis theatre, and a great many of the plays have been published. Among them are the following.

In English (as well as Greek)

Ghiaganos, Ap., Ar. Dinglis, and I. Dinglis. *The World of Karagiozi Figures*. Hermes, 1976.

In French

Caimi, Giulio. *Karaghiozi ou La comedie greque dans l'ame du theatre d'ombres*. Athens: Hellinikes Technes, 1935.

Roussel, Louis. *Karagheuz ou un theatre d'ombres a Athenes*. Athens, 1921.

In Greek

Karaghiozis. Three volumes of plays by Mollas, Xanthos, and Manos with a long introduction by Ghiorgos Ioannou and bibliography. Hermes, 1971–1972.

Mistakidou, Ekaterini. *Shadow Theatre in Greece and Turkey*. Hermes, 1982.

NOTE

1. Information in this section was based on Aliki Bacopoulou-Halls, *Modern Greek Theatre: Roots and Blossoms* (Athens: Diogenis Athens, 1982).

Lowell Swortzell
(Prepared from materials submitted by ASSITEJ/Greece, Daisy Kanghellari, and Xenia Kalogeropoulou.)

Hong Kong

HISTORY

Hong Kong is a young city, not yet 100 years old, with a population of 6 million. It is also an international center of cultural exchange with a long history of Western influence. In 1980 it had its first professional production for children, *Shtokkerlocker and Millipilli*, a German play translated into Cantonese.

In the area of children's theatre, English and German influences have been particularly strong. Two years ago, as a result of a contest, Hong Kong had its first original children's theatre script. Theatre for young people is now well established, with a repertory that includes fairy tales, Chinese legends and myths, adaptations from novels, and translations of international classics, as well as original scripts. One professional theatre group, Chung Ying, specializes in children's theatre and school tours. The Hong Kong Repertory Theatre also devotes about 20 percent of its work to younger audiences.

A festival is held every year around Christmastime; it is organized by the Hong Kong Arts Center, a nongovernmental body, with funding from commercial sponsors. Groups from all over the world have been invited to perform at the festival, including Japan's Kaze-No-Ko and the United States' Paper Bag Players.

Children's theatre is now developing in four main directions:

1. It is keen to find new themes and new ways of creating children's theatre, which includes experimenting with improvisation, creative dramatics, and audience participation.

2. It is striving to develop the tremendous potential of youth theatre, although it is difficult to key into the rhythms of young people, who predominantly respond to Checkers, Kenji Sawada, Matsuda Seiji, and Michael Jackson.

3. It is also developing theatre-in-education (TIE), applying theatre techniques to the teaching of language, counseling, and moral education. The aim is to convince ed-

ucators of the value of drama, which they could use as a means of communicating with and influencing young people.

4. It is strengthening contact and exchange with other countries in order to get new ideas and inspiration and to spread the message of peace and goodwill between Hong Kong and the world.

THE CHUNG YING THEATRE COMPANY

History

The Chung Ying Theatre Company was formed in 1979, and since the early 1980s it has performed twenty-nine plays of which twelve were in Cantonese and seventeen in English. It has played to a total audience of 200,000. At first the group was entirely British and, consequently, all productions were spoken in English. Today Chung Ying employs a full-time staff of thirteen local Hong Kong Chinese and a British artistic director. Seventy percent of the productions are now performed in Cantonese. Some British actors are occasionally hired when the company produces an English work, but the artistic director is currently developing the English skills of the resident Chinese actors, so this is no longer necessary.

Over the years the group has intensified its work in schools and community halls, and it is the only professional company in Hong Kong practicing TIE. Chung Ying offers a wide range of productions for both Cantonese and English-speaking members of the community. Classics, musicals, children's plays, family entertainment, and thought-provoking new scripts all have a place in its repertory.

Financing

The company was established under the auspices of the British Council in 1979. In 1982 it became independent and was incorporated as a nonprofit organization under the Companies Ordinance. A government grant was received for the first time in 1982. The group now receives funding from the government through the recently established Council for the Performing Arts of Hong Kong. Private and commercial sponsorship have always been sought to supplement the grants from the government, in order to improve and develop the company's work more effectively.

Aims

Chung Ying seeks to accomplish the following:

1. To develop an audience for live theatre through a program of performances in schools, theatres, and community halls

2. To promote the use of TIE and encourage the growth of drama teaching within the school curriculum

3. To exploit the potential that comes from being a multi-cultural, bilingual company by transmitting the skills and experiences of both Eastern and Western drama.

4. To give work opportunities to young Hong Kong writers, designers, composers, and directors that allow them to explore and develop their talents

Representative Plays

Chung Ying has an extensive repertory that extends from Shakespeare's *Twelfth Night*, Georges Feydeau and Maurice Desvallieres' *L'Hotel du Libre Exchange*, both performed in Cantonese, and Shaw's *Pygmalion* in English to *The Dragon's Disciples*, based in Chinese mythology, and *The Fantastic Fairground*, a theatrical version of a children's comic strip intended for family audiences.

I Am Hong Kong, by Raymond To and Hardy Tsoi, is a bilingual presentation for audiences that speak either Cantonese or English; it is aimed at adolescents fourteen and above. The play explores the challenges that Hong Kong now poses to a group of young people, six Chinese and one British. Commencing with a "cartoon" view of the past century and a half, this series of sketches and songs becomes involved with present-day Hong Kong—its accomplishments, its resentments, and its hopes. Finally, through the developing relations between individuals within the group, the seven actors energetically explore different attitudes about the future of the city, a future that is in the minds not only of those who live there, but also of people around the world.

To Whom It May Concern, devised by company members, concerns a handicapped youth brought up in Hong Kong without love or care who faces frustration and emotional suffocation. She longs for independence and hopes that through her own struggle she can acquire sympathetic consideration from society and help bridge the gap between the handicapped and able-bodied.

The Insect World, an adaptation by Rupert Chan of the famous Czech play *The Insect Comedy* by Karel and Joseph Capek, is a satire about modern man that reminds us that whatever happens, man's intense enthusiasm for life will triumph. A tramp wandering through the countryside falls exhausted on the ground and dreams that he shrinks to the size of the insects that inhabit the grass around him. He observes and comments on the eccentricities and obsessions of the various species. The beetles and their greed fascinate him, the ants and their lust for power disgust him, but he entirely sympathizes with the young chrysalis waiting to be "born" into an idealistic modern world. The play was performed in secondary schools for audiences between fourteen and sixteen years of age.

The Chinese Legend: The Dragon's Disciples, dramatized from mythology by Rupert Chan and members of the company, was performed for children between the ages of five and eight. After a war of the gods the earth is in chaos. Fifteen giant turtles are sent by the Emperor of Heaven to support the earth on their backs. However, Uncle Dragon, chief of the giants, steals them away. The Emperor of Heaven is shocked and sends the gods of laziness to persuade the disciples of the dragon to return. This fanciful adventure also includes audience participation.

Lowell Swortzell
(Prepared from materials submitted by ASSITEJ/Hong Kong.)

Hungary

HISTORY

In Hungary the development of art, and particularly the art of theatre, cannot be separated from historical trends. For long decades in the nineteenth century, theatre was one of the arenas of the national struggle for the general use of Hungarian, the language of the people. Since then theatre companies have remained champions of national independence and the demand for progress. In the first half of the twentieth century, however, theatre was largely turned into an entertainment business, with the genuinely social and cultural roles of the institution relegated to the background.

Theatre for children, one of the Hungarian theatre's newest offshoots, has existed for about thirty-five years. Its slow and sometimes conflict-ridden development can be properly understood only if it is traced as a reflection of the historical events of the period and of changes in universal theatrical culture.

The year 1949 is regarded as the Year of the Change in Hungarian history. Because of the cold war, the division of Europe became an inevitable reality, bringing with it the historical and practical experiences of the Soviet Union, which resulted in Hungary in the nationalization of small companies, the beginning of collectivization in agriculture, and acceptance of the one-party system. After the development of a unified state-controlled national educational system, the cultural institutions (theatres included) were also taken under state ownership. At that time, in autumn 1949, the Young Pioneers' Theatre and the Youth Theatre started in Budapest. In addition, virtually every provincial theatre in the country addressed a production to children—Harriet Beecher Stowe's *Uncle Tom's Cabin* during that first season.

This is not to say that earlier there were no productions intended for children in the capital city or in the provinces. During the few months of the Hungarian

Council Republic in 1919 several measures were taken to give every citizen genuine access to the treasures of culture and the arts. One of them was to set up the Workers' Theatre for Children. Between the two world wars the National Theatre and the Municipal Theatre offered performances for youth, and several children's theatres operated in Budapest more or less regularly, although at a low artistic level. Uncle Lakner's Children's Theatre was the best known and longest-running institution of this type. Artur Lakner was a cinema director who wrote and directed plays for children under twelve from 1926 until his deportation in 1944. Performances were staged in the City Park or in a rented theatre on Sunday mornings. Most of the plays had been authored by Uncle Lakner himself, who cast the children's roles with children (a number of whom later became well-known actors). The productions were rather sentimental in taste and the standards were of the professional entertainment business. The management knew that child performers were sure to make a hit.

Most of the legitimate theatres made a practice of holding occasional performances for charity, or for the children of the staff and employees and their friends at Christmas or other holidays. These were, however, not bona fide children's productions. The *Lattie-Mattie* plays, written for the highly popular comic actor Kálmán Latabár and shown as a series before 1945 and afterward again at the Budapest Operetta Theatre, were, on the other hand, the real thing. With their simple plots and their stumbling and sometimes stuttering hero, who is always ready to champion truth against difficult odds and who always comes out the winner, they brought the world of folktales to the Hungarian stage.

The Young Pioneers' Theatre and the Youth Theatre

The work of the Young Pioneers' Theatre, catering to children under ten years of age, and the efforts of the Youth Theatre, presenting plays designed for adolescents, were radically different from these earlier essays of dubious taste. Half of the repertory of these two companies consisted of Hungarian plays, and 40 percent were made up of works by Soviet authors.

The first half of the 1950s was dominated by the personality cult both in the Soviet Union and in the people's democratic countries, among them Hungary. Although there were some undeniably significant social and economic achievements, political anomalies and exaggerated economic development activity strained the ideology of the period, and artistic trends bore the marks of dogmatism. The growth of literature, the arts, and the theatre suffered from a narrow interpretation of socialist realism, from opportunism, from the need to give priority to agitative aspects and a didactic message, and from the fashionable neglect of artistic form. The contradictions inherent in the general ideological and political conditions of the times affected the stage productions for children too.

On the one hand, classic Hungarian novels for young people by standard authors were adapted to the stage, such as Mór Jókai's *The Iron Man's Sons*, Géza Gárdonyi's *The Stars of Eger*, Zsigmond Móricz's *Be Good Unto Death*, and Ferenc Molnár's *The Boys of Pal Street*, as well as tales like *Mattie the Gooseboy*, *King Matthias in Debrecen Town*, and *The King Who Sneezed Away His Kingdom* and outstanding Soviet works like Ostrosky's *The Steel Is Tempered*, Makarenko's *Forging the New Man*, Gaidar's *Timur and His Team*, and Algier's *Zoya*. On the other hand, "educational" plays were staged that were written according to the topical political themes of the day; consequently they proved shallow even in their didactic effects.

The outspoken aim of the theatre was, on the whole, correct and honorable: an effort was made to acquaint children and young people with the glorious traditions of history, to set the examples of boys and girls who worked or sacrificed their lives for the defense of the homeland or of other people in scenes of everyday life. However, the way this was done, not divorced from the general tendencies of the times, led to doubtful results. The valuable works achieved the aims for which they were designed, but the political plays, in which actors and directors were forced to drive home the views of the period, did not.

The two theatres, which survived several reorganizations, fusions and separations, and renamings, were in a somewhat different situation. They had collected excellent companies and their productions were staged by outstanding directors, such as Imre Apáthi, Béla Both, István Egri, Ferenc Hont, Lázló Vámos, and Zoltán Várkonyi, men who are regarded as definitive personalities of the Hungarian theatre. They generally gave voice and form to the written plays, so that both the virtues and the faults became clear and were in fact magnified. In this way they involuntarily depicted the negative figures, who were almost invariably better characterized in writing than the heroes, who always seemed rather shadowy and stereotyped.

From 1954 on changes took place in the program policy and acting style of the two theatres. Valuable works now tipped the balance and, at the same time, the performances were no longer specifically addressed to children or adolescents. In 1956 the two theatres lost their identity of playing for youth, and consequently the Hungarian capital was left for four years without productions designed for children.

Children's Opera in the Provinces

The Young Pioneers' Theatre and the Youth Theatre were typical products of the time, but an entirely different taste marked the special performances for children in the provincial theatres. Although in the year of nationalization several provincial theatres featured *Uncle Tom's Cabin*, there were only a few performances for children in the provinces. Then, in 1953/54, the theatres came out with a series of fairy-tale operas. The regular resident authors of the theatres in Szolnok, Miskolc, Győr, and Kecskemét chose *Little Red Riding Hood*, *Snow White and the Seven Dwarves*, *Hansel and Gretel*, and *Cinderella* to be set to music. There were some years in which three towns witnessed Cinderella operas by three different composers at the same time. To be sure, in stage scenery and the taste it reflected, these operas resembled the rather sentimental performances of the children's theatres that functioned between the two world wars. It was a long process before such classic plays and adaptations of novels as *The Iron Man's Sons*, *Be Good Unto Death*, and *Three Poor Tailor Lads* could be turned into melodramatic musicals.

There was no real change in repertory until about 1960, when the domestic situation had become sufficiently consolidated after the crisis of 1956 to permit theatre for children to receive more attention and start on the way to sound development. Clearly, it is not enough to pay attention to current problems; it is also necessary to think in terms of the future. Careful thought, broad vision, and deep concern are needed for the proper treatment and education of children and young people. With this philosophy, children's theatre entered a new phase of development in Hungary.

Theatre Without a Company

In 1960 a children's theatre again opened in Budapest. Called the Bartók Theatre for Children, it was directed by Margit Duka, but it had no company and no playhouse. The new institution offered performances first in a small hall and later at the Budapest Operetta Theatre, one of the largest in the country, and at culture houses. Adolescents came in groups led by teachers on weekday afternoons, while young children, accompanied by their parents, saw performances on Sunday mornings.

Despite the rather difficult circumstances under which it had to operate, the Bartok Theatre made an important contribution during the first ten years of its existence. The leaders and directors of the theatre strove to bring high-standard literary material to the stage, to replace overly elaborate scenery with symbolic sets that appealed to the imagination of the child. They wanted a program that would strike the proper balance between the finest fairy tales, historical plays, and plays about today. Out of the three or four premieres scheduled each year at least one was by a contemporary Hungarian writer or playwright, a practice that made Hungarian authors more interested in writing plays for children. Some of the new pieces in fact were written by great poets, and these works have firmly held their place in the repertory: Zoltán Jékely's *King Matthias' Shepherd*, Géza Képes' *The Tale of the Fisherman's Daughter*, Zoltán Zelk's *The Girl with the Thousand Names*, and Emil Kolozsvári-Grandpierre's *Star-Eyes*. Other plays treat timely problems that face children and young people, for example, Mária Halasi's *In the Last Row*, which is about the adjustment problems of a Gypsy girl in school, the prejudice of some of her classmates, and how she overcomes it. The performance of the play was followed by the first Hungarian experiment to test the effect of a play on children who saw it. Indirect methods were used to find out whether seeing the play had altered the views and increased the tolerance of children.

The Formation of the Hungarian ASSITEJ Center

It was becoming increasingly obvious that the cause and development of children's theatre in Hungary had fallen behind when compared with the neighboring countries, in which extensive networks of children's theatres were known to operate (for instance, in the Soviet Union, Bulgaria, and East Germany, a considerably larger number of performances were offered for children than in Hungary).

This recognition also increased the wish that Hungary should join in the work of the International Association of Children's and Youth Theatres (ASSITEJ), which had been in operation since 1964. The Hungarian Center of the organization was set up in 1971 and given the following mandate:

- To join educators in affirming the role of the theatre in the aesthetic education of young people
- To help raise a generation of theatre-goers who are interested in culture and the continuation of theatrical life
- To guarantee that every Hungarian theatre hold performances for children and young people that have genuine appeal, strengthen their love for theatre, and encourage cultural self-improvement
- To organize cooperation between theatres for children and youth in the provinces and those working in Budapest
- To arrange end-of-the-season festivals at the Bartok Theatre that acquaint Budapest audiences with the most successful productions of the provincial theatres and of the best amateur companies
- To build international contacts in order to promote the regular publication and popularization of plays for children from abroad and to foster the promotion of Hungarian plays outside the country

Even from the distance of more than fifteen years, it seems that these objectives have set a comprehensive but still realistic program for the managers and promoters of the theatre for children in Hungary. The fact remains, however, that only a few of these tasks have gained a satisfactory solution so far.

A REAL HOME FOR THE CHILDREN'S THEATRE IN BUDAPEST

While children's theatre was improving its position nationwide, the sharing of the Bartók Theatre with other, usually better established companies proved a drawback in Budapest. Moreover, as the films, radio, television, and film dubbing were employing more and more actors and actresses, the Theatre for Children found it increasingly difficult to engage the players it needed. The decision that was finally made provided only a partial solution: the Budapest Theatre for Children was given a permanent home in the somewhat dilapidated building of the one-time Young Pioneers' Theatre, but it was denied a company of its own. Later, after Margit Duka's retirement, a new director was appointed to head the theatre in the person of István Kazán, the stage director.

The new director, attempting to give the theatre a new image, wanted to modify the name by leaving out "for Children." The new Bartók Theatre intended to be a theatre for all children and young people, for the age range from six to eighteen. Along with this change came the aim that every child in the four upper grades of primary school in Hungary should be taken or sent to the theatre at least twice a year. Even if the Bartók Theatre had been able to double the number of its performances through a miracle, it could not have lived up to this goal!

The program structure was substantially altered; in addition to children's tales and adventurous historical and modern plays addressed to adolescents, a significant place was given to what were called youth musicals. Because teenagers were interested above all in contemporary music, it was thought that they could be reached if pop music was married to plays that featured modern conflicts and problems. In order to meet the challenge of this new task, István Kazán created an actor-training studio and in 1973 was finally able to organize the Bartók's own company, which consisted largely of young people starting their acting careers. This new policy denied the presence of significant stage personalities who had contributed memorable performances in the earlier period.

THE CURRENT STATE OF CHILDREN'S THEATRE

In 1977 Judit Nyilassy took over the guidance of Budapest Children's Theatre. By dropping plays addressed to teenagers, she altered the artistic focus and set a ceiling on the number of premieres permitted in a year (four first nights and an occasional studio performance), but it was too much to expect that she should find instant solutions to all the basic problems. She hired new actors for the company, engaged a young director, a stage designer, and a dramaturg, and tried to introduce new genres (showing, for instance, the Mozart opera *Bastien and Bastienne* with inserts of scenes from a modern short story), staged science fiction stories, and every season gave a new play by a young writer (Béla Horgas' *Tsiki You Witch*, István Csukás' *The Little Circus*, István Juhász' *Half a Heartbeat*, László Marsall's *Sparklette and the Dragon*, Péter Szentmihályi-Szabó's *Visitor from the Infinite*, István Juhász' *Francis Runs Away*, and Anna Kiss' *Silly Mill*). But the overall artistic level of the theatre was slow to change, and it proved impossible to maintain a stable company. Consequently there was no marked change in public prestige and professional recognition.

Children's Theatre Comes into Its Own in the Provinces

Although there was only one theatre in Budapest for all the children in this capital city of 2 million persons, in the provinces each of the ten theatres scheduled performances on a regular basis. The southwestern university city of Pécs, one of the oldest and culturally richest in the country, was the first to include two plays for children or young people annually and then gradually the other provincial theatres followed.

By now every provincial theatre offers at least one play for children, most of them mounting two productions for children or teenagers. Of course, the standards of performance vary. In the theatres that are known for their high level the children's productions are also ambitious and successful. But where the performances for adults are of an uneven standard, or the art direction of the theatre weak, the children's performances suffer even more.

Although most of the theatres that offer productions for children in the provinces select plays that have already run at the Budapest Children's Theatre, there are also works commissioned by provincial companies. Of the 100 plays submitted for the drama contest of 1979, the best were soon staged.

New Initiatives in Budapest

Since the early 1980s the situation has changed radically in regard to children's theatres in Budapest. The growing demand for productions suitable for children faced by a single theatre unable to meet that demand prompted other companies into action. The József Attila Theatre, in a big Budapest working-class district, and the Thália Theatre, known for its penchant for experimentation, offered performances. The Thália in fact introduced some new playwrights, among them Ervin Lázár, who wrote *The Fairy with the Seven Heads*, and Pál Békés, who authored *Concert on the Square*.

Péter Levente created a highly original kind of children's theatre at the Microscope Stage, the name of a well-known political cabaret in Budapest. This actor-director creates theatre for children in the four-to-seven-year-old age group or, more precisely, uses a theatrical approach in his cathartic play groups. Levente has been acclaimed for his work by parents, psychologists, sociologists, and educators alike. Whenever possible, he uses their assistance. His production titled *The Stray Space-Ship* is professionally and artistically well structured and playful, and leads children to absorb the new information it presents. Collective physical participation is encouraged; at the same time, the theatrical environment stimulates a high level of psychological activity and cathartic insight. A similar approach is used with children of the same age group by a team in the Budapest Children's Theatre (e.g., in its staging of Márta Tömöry's fable *Master Meow*).

Some important independent theatrical ventures have emerged in recent years, particularly the theatre of the Budapest Eötvös Lóránd University of Arts and Sciences and a tiny theatre in the Big Boulevard of Budapest calling itself The Playhouse. The University Theatre staged *Mrs. Borsh's Birthday*, based on a cycle of poems by Ágnes Nemes-Nagy, a great poet who is also noted for her excellent children's verse. As Mrs. Borsh, Margit Dayka, the marvelous old actress, easily brought the children under her spell and won their natural cooperation. *Crafty Peter*, a folklore-inspired comedy by Sándor Weöres, perhaps the greatest living Hungarian poet, whose verse for children and poems for adults are hard to separate, was impersonated by actors from the National Theatre company on the University Theatre's stage. The high-spirited, absurd performance by the actors, the musical effects, which were an integral part of the play, and the skillfully stylized scenery all prankishly underscored the atmosphere.

Twiggillee, by István Csukás, one of the most successful children's story writers, offered a delightful theatrical experience for adults as well as children at The Playhouse. This happy though thoughtful story about children searching for their identity was made unforgettable by the performance of five excellent actors whose comic fervor charmed the audience. The production demonstrated once again that children's theatre needs strong and fascinating artistic personalities even more than adult theatre. The successful *Twiggillee* cast staged *The Blue Bay*, which provides insight into the often controversial relation between man and nature.

Mrs. Borsh's Birthday, *Crafty Peter*, *Twiggillee*, and *The Blue Bay* (and other memorable productions offered since the 1950s) make it clear that the really successful performances for children are also enjoyed by parents and other adults. In other words, in artistic approach there is really no sharp line between adult and children's plays, although the different age groups respond on different levels and at different depths.

AMATEUR GROUPS

The existing theatres cannot offer a sufficient number of acceptable performances even in their own areas, and so they certainly cannot meet the national demand. The best amateur ensembles, therefore, assist the legitimate theatre in its mission to improve the artistic taste through productions that will be remembered as genuine theatrical experiences. Children's theatre in Hungarian amateur dramatics always has existed on two levels: adult amateur actors playing for children and children playing for their classmates and peers. The activities of adult amateurs achieved significance, particularly in the middle eighties, when most of the groups came to realize the new possibilities inherent in playing for children. Some ensembles, for instance, the Budapest Playhouse for Children, led by Éva Mezei, perform only for and with children. Other groups always keep adaptations or compilations of children's music and verse in their repertories. Productions in which children themselves play the roles are the most extensive and most important area of amateur activity. For long years schools and dramatic clubs gave performances that emphasized production values rather than the child performers. The effort to put on a "good performance" made the style generally redolent of the "cute" and saccharine plays for children between the two world wars. The teachers acted as directors and gave instructions to the child actors, most of whom did not have the experience, even if they happened to have the imitative talent, for character portrayal.

Drama Groups and Play-Acting Methods

About 1973–1974, however, there was a general change in approach. People interested in the theatre, along with those interested in psychology and education, began to learn new methods and techniques that had been in use for some time outside the country. In the course of creative games and dramatic exercises (such as rhythmic practice, improvisations, fantasy games, charade-like exercises, modern dance etudes, group drama, and collective dramatization exercises) the leader plays with the children, always considering the ages of the players, their sensitivity, and their emotional and intellectual aptitudes and range. Such activity is primarily directed at the personality development and self-liberating relaxation of the players. These exercises can grow into formal performances expected to draw others, too, but only if the participants become individually and collectively mature enough for their age group.

Luckily, a number of professional actresses apply the methods of creative games when they compile and present programs for children, among them Kati Sólyom and Jutka Halász, who have developed the genre. Whether she bases a program on the finest ballads and folk poems or tells tales and sings, Kati Sólyom always plays with the children, affectionately, directly, and informally. Jutka Halász almost exclusively sings poems set to music, and her method is similar to Sólyom's.

József Ruszt, who introduced "initiating" theatre performances, was soon followed by others in this effort in which adaptations are presented of standard works of Hungarian and world literature included in the school syllabus, or of interesting writings connected in some way with nonliterary aspects of the curriculum. Sometimes comments are interjected; the play or adaptation is presented in a cross section or in rehearsal, where various interpretations can be discerned and stops can be made. These performances not only make students acquainted with the work itself, but also give them a chance to understand some phases of the creative process in the theatre.

THE FUTURE

Hungary has shown that today theatre for children and young people no longer means the tale- or adventure-story–type productions of professional theatres. The concept has grown more complex. Nevertheless, if we look at the recent history of theatre for children in Hungary, we find that contributions from professional theatre have been most significant, with the presentation of some 300 plays during the period under review. Of the works performed, 65 percent were by Hungarian writers, 7 percent were classic foreign works, 14 percent were by Soviet authors, and 14 percent were by authors of other nationalities. More than half of the plays were adaptations of narrative literature. The breakdown of Hungarian works alone shows that 61 percent were by contemporary Hungarian authors, 15 percent were folktale adaptations, 12 percent dramatizations of tales in opera form, and 12 percent rearrangements for the stage of works by non-contemporary Hungarian writers.

The historical survey and the figures presented must make it clear that children's theatre has given important opportunities for Hungarian dramatists to make their debuts. However, not even these impressive numbers can make one forget what has been a frequent complaint of both critics and the theatres themselves: that only a few of the plays written and produced were truly significant and really suitable for the purpose of making good theatre for children.

Since the early 1970s there has been an increased development of productions for children. Various concepts championed by different children's theatres have become more sharply polarized than in the past and sound artistic competition is now a reality. To be sure, children's theatre can truly fulfill its mission of helping personality development only if its existence, position, and growth are no longer considered merely the internal affair of the profession (and of the by now allied professions of education, and social and child psychology), but a public cause. Society cannot be indifferent to what will be the emotional and aesthetic education and culture of the people who will greet the third millennium.

The primary question is not whether the theatres then will have audiences, but what kind of audiences they will have. That question also asks what sort of people our children will become. As the most complex artistic experience is provided by the living theatre, children's theatre bears a tremendous responsibility, a much greater responsibility than the current entertainment industry for adults. Consequently it does matter how children's theatres relate to their audiences and whether they regard them as partners. It is important that theatre people be willing to learn from the creativity of children and offer them only the best works in the best possible productions.

Those who want to train and educate people certainly have plenty of work before them for the next thirty-five years, but what should not be forgotten for a single moment is that a children's production is theatre and not a schoolroom!

Lowell Swortzell
(Prepared from materials submitted by ASSITEJ/Hungary.)

India

In India, *on paper*, theatre for young people is considered very important. However, in a country of 781.37 million persons, with an illiteracy rate of 63.8 percent, a child labor force of 17 million, and unemployment figures totaling approximately 26 million,[1] theatre of any kind is not high on the priority list. This is not to say that theatre does not exist in India. It does and has for centuries, but it no longer receives the kind of patronage it previously enjoyed.

HISTORY

The roots of children's theatre can be found in the nineteenth-century epic poem *Balacharitam*, which depicts the boyhood of the god Krishna. Both Krishna and Rama were heroes in the fourteenth-century folkplay *Ramlila and Raslila*. Other epic works were also dramatized, which children saw and sometimes performed in school presentations. And so, through literature and national dances, a drama emerged that from the beginning included young people.

In modern times children's theatre began in the 1950s when Samar Chatterjee opened the Calcutta Children's Little Theatre (CLT), where he trained children in theatre arts. When Chatterjee moved to New Delhi in 1954, he took his theatre with him, once more providing young people with an "artistic outlook" and an outlet for developing their talents in singing, dancing, speech, and acting. Chatterjee's idea spread to Bombay, where a branch of CLT had a short life. His original company became known as the Delhi Children's Theatre (DCT) and still operates today, working with young people between the ages of five and fifteen at four school centers. DCT provides a platform for other schools in Delhi through its workshops and annual productions.

Rekha Jain started UMANG in 1979 to provide a haven for the underprivileged children of her locality. It is basically a neighborhood theatre "of the children, by the children and for the children'' that organizes play festivals and holiday programs. Emphasis is on dance-drama, culminating in an annual performance. The National School of Drama in New Delhi does arbitrary and sporadic work by organizing holiday workshops that are production-oriented. There are, however, no full-time professional companies in India except puppet companies.

Music Theatre Workshop, started in 1979 and now run by Faisal Alkazi, meets on Sundays and caters to children from different schools. The accent is on creative drama; all plays are evolved out of workshops through study, research, discussion, and improvisation. As the company's name implies, each production is a musical. The thrust is not on production, but on integrating theatre and music into the education of young people. The group mounts one major production each year, and *Kidstuff*, directed by Barry John, is their best known work.

Theatre Action Group (TAG) (directed by John), which began in 1973, aims to provide "fun plays for children that are light, flexible and mobile, that provoke children and stimulate involvement and sometimes participation." TAG's first productions were performed at schools outside Delhi before being performed in the city itself. The company presents one major production each year, although they try to do more, and all their work is geared toward children. Presentations are largely in English because most of the private schools in Delhi instruct in English; these schools are both willing and able to pay for the company's performances. Government schools do not have provisions for such programs because the education department lacks the authority to allocate funds for theatrical activities.

Awishkar in Bombay, whose president is Vijay Tendulkar, started in 1971, and its children's theatre unit, Chandrashala, began in 1979 with Sulbha Deshpande as its director. So far, ten dance-drama productions for children have been produced. The group also undertakes such projects as dance-puppetry and painting. Their most popular presentation was *Durga Zali Gauri*, directed and choreographed by Guru Parvatikumar.

The Madras Players in Madras consists of a group of theatre enthusiasts who attempt to produce at least two productions each year. Khilona, based in New Delhi, comprises three trained professionals: V. K. Sharma, Subhash Udgata, and Amita Udgata. This group joined with Barry John's TAG, as their goals were similar, and both groups hope to bring more awareness to schools and teachers through drama.

The collaboration between TAG and Khilona marks the first instance of a full-time professional theatre-in-education company dedicated to the following goals:

1. To foster drama as a subject in schools and, more generally, to foster the use of theatre as a medium of instruction for all teachers

2. To create plays especially for and in collaboration with schools on themes relevant to children's needs

3. To organize long-term workshops on a regular basis in which theatre is used to teach a specific area of study

4. To function as a resource center to assist teachers

5. To provide ideas and personnel to institutions that want to become involved in drama and theatre for young people

6. To serve as a remedial drama unit by applying theatre as an educational and therapeutic activity in the service of children with special needs.

Khilona became professional in October 1987, after four years of attempting to produce just one play in the schools and make a living from it.

In Baroda there is The Playhouse and the Bal Bhavan Society. Both were started in 1980–1981 and have since acquired reputations for high-quality productions and for initiating and spreading the children's theatre movement into various parts of the country.

The problems faced by professionals and others involved in children's theatre seem to be common. No one is really concerned that there are few artistic goals to speak of, since theatre is an extracurricular activity and not considered a serious endeavor. Generally, schools demand a comedy as the class play production. There is no school in India in which theatre is an established area of study, research, or experimentation.

THEATRE-IN-EDUCATION

In India, because the term "theatre" is directly related to performance and entertainment, there is no distinction between theatre by children and theatre for children. Given this condition, theatre-in-education (TIE) or youth theatre has not caught on there. In fact, TIE is a concept that even educators still do not grasp. The realization that TIE can be a useful instrument to disseminate information and education by way of entertainment has not set in. TIE can broaden children's perspectives about the world in which they live, about its complexities and difficulties; according to a rare and recent newspaper report discussing TIE, "schools in India have neglected the educational aspects of this activity. Very few schools give emphasis to adopting this technique to help children deal with causes that touch them, situations that confront them, emotions that burden them, problems that puzzle them."

No one wants to suggest that through theatre, children will be able to deal with all their concerns and solve all their problems. But if teachers researched and provided students with the requisite information, presented different points of view and facts on a given topic, and then prepared a script in conjunction with the pupils, this would provide an outlet for the young people to express their views freely and without fear. Teacher training in this direction is wholly lacking. Courses that train teachers should at least make them aware of TIE.

Educational planners have discussed TIE at numerous national, state, and regional level meetings, presenting plans, projecting ideas, and submitting notes and reports. They also have tried to promote TIE and youth theatre by talking to heads of institutes, but little attention has been paid. The belief that theatre can help in the intellectual and emotional development of children is not widely held throughout the education system in India.

Drama and theatre are often described as new subjects and regarded as frills. In a country the size and diversity of India it is foolish for a program to try to have uniform guidelines; each state has its own ministry, under the central government, with discrete powers. To discover the policies of the different states and territories with regard to youth theatre and its implementation is a Herculean task that cannot be accomplished without a national input and a dissemination center. Notwithstanding, one can make some generalizations.

Rural Performances

Theatre in rural areas is usually performed by companies comprised of families who are traditional artists. The groups are close-knit, and only members of the same family are initiated into the art, which involves song, dance, music, and drama. Such traditional artist-families are found in each state in India, but their presentational styles differ. The common factor among the groups is that they all perform mainly for religious festivals, with productions related to myths and epics. Sometimes the performances go on for days; for example, the presentation of the *Ramayan* begins at dusk, stops at dawn, and continues again the next day from the point at which it stopped. This can continue for up to ten days. The Rural Development Programs begun by the government have formulated plans to support these artist-families, whose plights are terrible. Attempts also have been made to involve rural and urban youth in the promotion and maintenance of this type of folk theatre.

Urban Performances

Most cities have amateur theatre groups that are founded and disbanded at regular intervals. Some groups have survived and are doing good work, but they are entirely dependent on sponsorship and donations for their existence. The few companies doing well are professionals in cities like Delhi, Bombay, Calcutta, Madras, and Bangalore.

Theatre is not a well-paid profession in India, and the general public is not well disposed toward the field. There is only one government-supported training school, the National School of Drama in New Delhi, which has its own repertory company but does not guarantee jobs to its graduates. The school is currently undergoing a crisis; the popularity and financial rewards of films and television have lured potential students away from live theatre.

The lack of status of youth theatre, severe academic pressures, and absence of job security also contribute to the lack of involvement of people who might otherwise assist in the advancement of the children's theatre movement. However, a few associations are trying to help: the government-sponsored Yuvak Mahotsav (Youth Festival) and the Bal-Natya Mahotsav (Children's Drama Festival), organized at the local, state, and federal levels. There is also the Sangeet Natak Academy (Music and Drama), which operates at various state levels.

Baroda, a city with an estimated population of 1 million, was at one time a great cultural center where youth theatre received suitable patronage, support, and recognition. At that time many youth theatre groups performed in various regional languages, including Gujarati, Marathi, Hindi, and English. Today there are only two of these companies left because most people, including youth, would rather watch television. Also, there isn't adequate audience preparation. The University of Baroda has a Faculty of Performing Arts, but the curriculum for the lower grades does not include drama. At the primary schools there are performances on a nonformal basis, and the secondary schools include mandatory study of music and art, but not drama. In fact, even the study of literature is not offered at any school in Baroda.

Still, there is some activity in the city with respect to theatre for young people. The Gujarat Music, Dance and Drama Academy, a government-sponsored organization, gives awards for the most talented students in each of the arts. There is a committee that organizes camps and writing competitions in children's drama. And one community center of the Jeevan Sadhana Trust is experimenting with mime in the performing arts.

CURRENT PROBLEMS

The problems today include the following:

1. Lack of financing and rehearsal space are endemic, faced by most theatre personnel, and hamper any regular activities for the creative development of children and for operating a professional company mounting continuous productions. Problems abound relating to the financial aspects of producing and paying workers.

2. The education system, which itself is "Victorian" and maligned by teachers and bureaucrats alike, gives low priority to the arts in this technological age. Many children go through school without any introduction to or meaningful experiences with painting, writing, poetry, singing, drama, theatre, or dance.

3. There is a lack of awareness among teachers and parents about the importance of drama and theatre.

4. There is a lack of trained and committed personnel.

5. Academic pressures are tremendous because the schools emphasize the quantity of the information passed on to students rather than its quality. As children get older, their school load gets heavier, and many who want to participate in extracurricular drama activities cannot because there is not enough time after homework and studying are completed.

6. The theatre, in general, is in poor condition:
   a. Meager patronage
   b. Few playhouses
   c. Small minority audience, as theatre is not a regular or traditional activity
   d. Lack of training facilities

e. View of theatre as a not respectable or financially rewarding profession

f. Lack of appreciation of the validity of creative activity for children among parents and school authorities

g. Growing competition from movies and television, even though the condition of children's films and television programs is as poor as that of children's theatre.

In general, children receive too little attention in India. It is not surprising that young people seem to have little inner bent toward originality or creativity. Theatre for the young is currently in limbo, fighting for survival and recognition. Although many talented people have left the field and there are what look to be insurmountable obstacles, and the road ahead seems long and lonely, the future is not without hope. If serious-minded theatre people continue to come together and form groups that give free expression to ideas that underscore the importance of theatre for young audiences, India will one day have to heed them.

BIBLIOGRAPHY

Books

Dosa, Pragji. *Bal Rangbhoomi.*
Swaminathan, Mina. *Drama in Education.* 1968.

Recommended Plays

Jain, Rekha. *Aanokha Vardan.*
Lal, Laxmi Narayan. *Billee Ka Khel.*
Paranjpay, Sai. *Jadoo Ka Shankh.*
Sakhardande, Madhav. *Durga Zali Gauri.*
Srikrishan. *Pariksha.*
Tendulkar, Vijay. *Kho Gaye Baba.*

NOTE

1. *The Illustrated Weekly of India*, 1981 Census.

Arun Agnihotri

Iran

HISTORY

1829. In this year the play *Story of Molla Ebrahim Khalil, the Alchemist,* written by Mirza Fathali Akhondzadeh (1812–1870), pioneer in playwriting and theatre criticism in Iran, was translated from Turkish to Persian by Mirza Jaafar Gharachedaghi. Akhondzadeh was attracted to theatre, and specifically to playwrighting, as an educational tool that could provide guidance and insight for youth. In the Persian translation of the play is the following statement: "Play translated by Gharachedaghi in Alchemy traditions, useful for all, especially children." Although *Story* is not a children's play, as such, it is generally considered the beginning of children's theatre in Iran.

1859. Abdorrahim Najarzadeh, known as Talbov, took advantage of the play form (question/answer/discussion) in writing *Safineh Talebi.* (In this case, *safineh* means a sailing ship that passes to show the ways of the world.) Talbov is considered a pioneer Iranian children's playwright, and although he did not initially intend to write plays, his success with the genre is recognized as a significant step forward for children's drama and theatre in Iran.

1924. Jabar Baghcheban, another pioneer of children's drama in Iran, cooperated with and supported theatre groups in Tabriz (capital of East Azarbayejan Province). He was also an actor who started a kindergarten in Tabriz with various educational programs, which included drama and theatre.

1929. Baghcheban established the first kindergarten in Shiraz (capital of Fars Province). Here he applied his innovative style of theatre in modern education. In his autobiography he writes on the subject:

At the time, there were no educational materials in Iran for children, such as handworks, games, plays, musical lyrics, or poems. I prepared these materials with my own innovations and hands and thoughts and pen, in a form even richer than is customary today.

With the use of folk stories which I remembered from childhood, I wrote plays, poems, musical lyrics, and puzzles for children. In the play's performance, I prepared various animal and insect masks.

Baghcheban also wrote a book titled *Children's Life, for Kindergartens and Elementary Schools*, which, in addition to poetry, music, and puzzles, included three plays: *The Old Man and the Radish*, *The World and the Shepherd*, and *Khanom Khazouk (Lady Khazouk)*. He wrote a total of six plays for children, three of which are unpublished: *Lion the Gardner*, *Shangoul-o-Mangoul* (the story of a mother and three goats), and *Arguments of Two Fairies*. All of the plays had several performances at Baghcheban Kindergarten in Shiraz. In his autobiography he refers to the mounting of the works and explains how he personally made the masks and costumes, and how he prepared decorations suitable for the plays. Baghcheban is considered the best of the early Iranian children's playwrights and the first children's theatre director in Iran.

1931. The first kindergarten was established in Tehran by Ms. Bersabeh, and it closely followed the educational programs established by Baghcheban. Various dramatic plays were included in the curriculum, among which were *The Mouse and the Cat* and *The Old Man and the Radish*.

1938. In this year the first acting school was established in Iran through the influence of some intellectuals and artists affiliated with the Pahlevi court. In their opinion, theatre should play as effective a role in the advancement of social goals as radio, the press, textbooks, lectures and assemblies, and cultural foundations. The school trained actors and also produced several plays, written especially for the students. The pieces generally had simple structures, superficial dialogue with patriotic implications and royal slogans, and the intent of the writers was limited to the promotion of the new social culture by introducing audiences to the advantages of modern life, the necessity of literacy, and avoidance of drug addiction. A distinct style of drama emerged from the acting schools (light but educational) that ultimately developed into programs titled "literary societies" in elementary and secondary schools all over Iran.

The annual reports of the Organization for Thought Development confirms this:

The play presented to the audience at the end of the ceremonies was very interesting. In particular, the actors, who were mostly graduates of acting and were masters in this technique, performed their parts and duties with utmost capability. The writer of the play had included several different and basic topics in this play which are essential for society. Knowledge of these topics is necessary in order to awaken the people regarding their special duties towards loving the country and the shah: encouragement of marriage, protection of the country's interests, faith in increasing the fundamental progress of recent years, creating a spirit of heroism, and the greatest duty of citizens which is having pure love for the country and shahanshah.

1940. The trend in kindergarten dramatic plays continued. According to *Iran Embrouz* magazine (*Iran Today*), a play was performed by children in the annual ceremonies of a kindergarten named Shokoufeh. Pictures were taken of parts of the performance and these were the first published photographs of children's theatre in Iran. The play dealt mostly with the good and evil natures of people and their destiny.

1941–1957. Activities were limited to kindergarten plays and works performed in elementary and secondary schools. These consisted of funny but superficial dramas performed by professional groups in theatres in Tehran and some other cities. In essence, there was no real children's theatre activity in these years. One interesting note is the establishment, in 1956, of the College of Dramatic Arts, which was affiliated with the Ministry of Culture and Arts, out of which emerged a new trend—puppet theatre for children.

1957. Amin Ghezanlor and his mother instructed a group interested in puppet theatre at the office of dramatic arts and, with the same group, produced puppet plays for children. Titles of some of the plays performed by Ghezanlor's group proves that they were interested in issues relevant to children's theatre; they also preferred old stories with moral implications. This group is credited with introducing Western-style puppet theatre to Iran. The group started training elementary- and secondary-school teachers, who were invited to attend performances and seminars through ads published in *Namayesh*, a magazine published by the Ministry of Culture and Arts. The puppet troupe traveled around the country, touring its plays and training teachers.

1964. Ghezanlor's group was active until this year, after which children's theatre activities in Iran were again forgotten.

1971. The Institute for Development of Children and Young Adults, established to produce children's works and bring activities for children and young adults under one roof, after a period of sporadic activity in theatre, set up its dramatic branch by performing *The Radish*, which was enacted by the first professional children's theatre company in Iran. The group was formed by American director Don Lafon, and the members of the technical staff were all involved in the activities of the Iran-America Society. After several presentations the group ceased performing because of cultural conflicts. A few years later the same people formed the Child Theatre branch of Iranian National Television.

The Radish, written by Bijan Mofid and directed by Don Lafon, was performed as a side program at the Shiraz Art Festival. There are some interesting points to note about the plays performed by the children's theatre group of the Institute for Development of Children and Young Adults (IDCYA).

1. Performances were presented on a "round stage" that consisted of a piece of colored carpet around which the audience sat. This "stage" facilitated both touring and nontraditional performance spaces, such as libraries.

2. This kind of informal staging led to enhanced communication with the audience and greater cooperation between the actors and audience.

3. These performances marked the first use of simple language and straightforward, realistic acting.

4. The success of the performances gave credence and credibility to children's theatre and, because most of the group were graduates of theatre from the College of Fine Arts of the University of Tehran, to the university theatre program.

1972. The Center for Theatre Education of IDCYA, taking advantage of the theatre students at the University of Tehran, selected the first class of theatre education students and taught their method of working with children in a short course. This is considered the first step in the development and promotion of children's theatre (in its many definitions) in Iran as a whole. In addition, the first professional puppet theatre company of IDCYA was formed under the supervision and direction of Oscar Batek, a Czech puppeteer, who had been invited to Iran to set up a puppetry course at the College of Fine Arts.

1974. A child T.V.-theatre group was formed. The list of professionals in children's theatre continued to grow, as the field began to incorporate playwrights, directors, actors, and designers.

1975. The professional theatre company of IDCYA was replaced by an amateur group that went to Germany to participate in a children's theatre festival. This was the first foreign tour of an Iranian children's theatre company. It should be noted that the main activities of the Institute are related to production; there is seldom any diversification into publishing, holding seminars, or compilation of statistics related to the performances. For instance, there is no record of the names of actors, number of performances, number of audience members, or similar data available for any of the activities of professional or amateur theatre groups.

1976. The first puppet theatre festival was organized by the Institute's production center. This positive step attracted the attention of many people who were interested in puppet theatre and its influence on young audiences.

1977. Theatre was included as one of the major courses at the first Iranian school for gifted students. The dreams of people such as Seyed Ali Nasr (one of the founders of today's theatre in Iran) and Mehdi Namdar (founder of the field of Theatre at the College of Fine Arts, University of Tehran) were then realized. Students in the school are introduced to acting, directing, playwrighting, and criticism during two academic terms through the methods of "real-life simulation." Creative drama is used as a tool in utilizing the creative abilities of these students. Behrouz Gharibpour, who had gained some experience as an actor in children's puppet theatre and as a theatre instructor, playwright, and director of children's theatre, was in charge of this class. In his work he benefited from the cooperation of Hunter Wolf, a professor at the University of Southern California.

1979. The theory of "real-life simulation" was applied at the theatre education and puppet theatre center of the Institute on a large scale by Gharibpour and eighty graduates in more than 150 libraries throughout Iran. The outcome of this experience was intercity festivals among members of theatre and puppet-theatre classes. Many plays were written based on real-life situations, and topics dealt with the lives of children and young adults. Also, because the children's first theatrical experiences, both in writing and performing, were positive ones, many of them became interested in further immersion in professional and amateur theatre. (The festivals, for various reasons, were short-lived and not followed up as they should have been.)

THEATRE TODAY

After the fall of the imperial regime and the establishment of the Islamic Republic, children's theatre enjoyed a noticeable revival. The first theatre especially for children was established at the site of the library of the Institute; in a short time the whole building was allocated for use as a children's theatre. As a result, children's theatre, after half a century, finally had a place of its own. The building houses two theatres, each of which holds 150 to 200 persons. It is run by the actors and technical staff of the Institute and is active in live and puppet theatre. Once children's theatre had a place of its own, it began to attract parents, who attended performances together with their children.

Some of the group's activities since its inception include the following:

1. Performance of twenty-nine plays and puppet plays for a total audience of 152,016.
2. Publication of the following books:
    - *Introduction to the Realm of Semi-Dolls and Puppet Shows*, by Behrouz Gharibpour.
    - *Ostad (The Master) Learns Puppet Theatre*, by Gharibpour. An introduction for young adults to traditional puppet theatre and its wide acceptance in Iran.
    - *What Is Theatre? How Is It Born? And How Is It Performed?* written and translated by Gharibpour. Introduces children and young adults to theatre and teaches different methods used in performing a theatrical work.
    - *Complete Book of Puppet Theatre*, by Gharibpour. Includes an introduction of puppet theatre, methods of making and using various dolls and puppet stages for young adults and instructors.
    - *Art of Puppet*, by Bil Baird, translated by Javad Zolfaghari.
3. Taping the plays performed at the center, which were then broadcast on Iranian television.
4. Training cultural instructors at the Institute in the use of theatre and puppet theatre for storytelling classes.

The center is engaged in few international activities. After the Islamic Revolution the main energies of the theatre center were directed inward, toward playwrighting, directing, and educating the child and adult audience. Since 1983 puppet theatre productions have been the primary concern of the center, and efforts have been made to educate audiences as to the capabilities of puppet theatre.

Main centers that are currently active in children's theatre include The Institute for Development of Children and Young Adults (as a teaching, training, and educational organization as well as a producing group); the Ministry of Education (administers at the school level through a division called educational affairs), which organized their first children's theatre festival in 1987; Health Organization (in relation to kindergartens and their affiliated educational units); Islamic Republic Radio and Television; and mosques (as cultural and side activities).

Dramatists who write (or wrote) plays for children include Jabar Bagcheban, Bijan Mofid, Reza Babak, Behrouz Gharibpour, Davoud Kianian, Reza Fayazi, and Jannati Atai.

Directors in children's theatre include Behrouz Gharibpour, Marzieh Boroumand, Kambiz Samimi Mofakhan, Hassan Dadshekar, Hamid Abdolmaleki, Reza Fayazi, Reza Babak, Bahram Shah-Mohammadlou, and Ardeshir Keshavarzi.

Behrouz Gharibpour

Iraq

HISTORY

Theatre fulfills the important function of being the most immediate link between art and society. Children's theatre is one of the most effective mediums because it develops a cultural and intellectual consciousness in children and creates an increasing aesthetic awareness. It also helps them to understand human relationships. The term "children's theatre" applies to performances by adults (professional or amateur actors or groups) for an audience of children, in either a public theatre or a school hall. The term does not apply to plays in which children perform.

As such, children's theatre is relatively new in Iraq. An overall view embracing the numerous elements that have contributed to the establishment of the Iraqi theatre, in general, and to children's theatre, in particular, from the point of view of dramatic art and entertainment, must have as its starting point the immediate aftermath of the July 17, 1968, revolution. These were years in which there was an intense and ardent enthusiasm such as seldom has been experienced before that marked the birth of a new concept: theatre as part of the revolution's ambitions and aims for education, culture, and the arts. What these years achieved is in fact the realization of the dreams and ambitions of many teachers, performers, producers, writers, and individuals interested in the development of the visual arts.

It is not possible to look at children's theatre in isolation from its relation to children's culture as a whole. The educational impact of children's theatre is, without doubt, equal to the impact of the mass media (radio, television, cinema, and the press). Children's theatre is actually a much more exciting medium that helps to create a critical mind in the child through use of action, character conflict, contradiction of emotions, reality and fantasy, and the theme of the play. To be effective, children's theatre should come as a direct response to the child's intellectual and aesthetic needs, exciting his curiosity and imagination.

A brief look at the beginnings that preceded the establishment of children's theatre follows, as does a detailed look at the achievements since the revolution. The drawbacks in the development of a national theatre, in general, and a children's theatre, in particular, are partly caused by a lack of experience and familiarity with theatre as a whole. Arabs have been late in acquiring the performing arts; moreover, circumstances have not been favorable in the development of a children's theatre that in turn would create a generation of experts in this field.

BEGINNINGS: THE SCHOOL STAGE

The real interest in children's theatre began in schools with the activities of elocution societies. These groups were largely responsible for early "theatre" because they began to include acting in their activities in the 1930s. Each society had an advisor or instructor, usually a teacher of Arabic chosen by the school committee. His duty was to guide his students in giving speeches and recitals and in performing short scenes.

The instructors used to stage brief scenes acted by a small number of students. Themes revolved around current topical, social and national issues. Raoof Al-Khatib, teacher at the Ma'moonia, Baroodia, and Al Fadel primary schools during the thirties, was one of the most famous instructors in this field. Because he was aware of the impact of drama and its effectiveness in broadening the mind and encouraging the emotions, he started publishing a series of pamphlets for primary-school students in 1938. The first in the series was "Modern School-Play Scenes, with Some Scientific and Literary Poems for Primary Schools."

In his study "Children's Literature in Iraq—1939" the researcher Fuad Abbas refers to a series of stories for children aged nine through twelve written by a group of young authors. The first in the series was *The Red Girl*, a poetic narrative in seven pages.

Generally speaking, the primary schools were largely responsible for the establishment of the roots of children's theatre in the thirties. This primarily resulted from the fact that all children from ages six through twelve attended these schools. Historical documents also reveal that all schools had an "arts season," in which social and historical plays were performed (usually in school yards) in addition to other activities, such as displays of arts and crafts.

By the early fifties these school productions came out in public, in theatres such as The Sha'ab Hall (or King Faisal Hall as it was then called). The initiative of Abdul Kadir Rahim was tremendous in this field. As a result of the growth and expansion of these activities, the Ministry of Education founded special offices to supervise and assist these productions in the capital and around the country. Graduates of the Institute of Fine Arts were sent to assist in creating plays and to hold annual festivals and competitions.

LATER DEVELOPMENTS

Children's Culture House

One of the organizations of the Ministry of Culture and Information, the Children's Culture House was established in 1977 and specializes in all aspects of children's culture. It is also a publishing house for children's books, magazines, and other publications.

Two magazines, *Majalatti* and *El Mizmar*, begun in the middle seventies, were the roots of the Children's Culture House. Editors of these magazines formed an acting group that gave several performances seen by hundreds of children. In 1972 the group presented *The Flower and the Butterfly* and *The Flying Circle*, both adapted and directed by Izzi Al-Wahab, and both acted by children themselves. *The Flower and the Butterfly* starts in a fantasy world and gradually moves into reality—a world of birds, trees, and children united together against the invader. *The Flying Circle* is about the daily life of children in the streets and in school: truant schoolgirls fly in "circles" from town to town, see strange things, and then return home, where they become studious and hard-working. The general outline of the play is educational. The production used colored slides to represent the different places visited by the girls, such as the oil fields in Kirkuk and Al Zawra Park in Baghdad. The two plays were performed at the National Theatre (part of the State Organization of Theatre and Cinema).

The National Troupe of Acting

The National Troupe of Acting was founded in April 1968 within the State Organization for Theatre and Cinema. Currently its members are mostly graduates of the Academy of Fine Arts and the Institute of Fine Arts. The company has the National Theatre as its base (550 seats) and also uses the Revolution Mobile Theatre (524 seats). (The new premises of the National Theatre will seat 900.) The National Troupe of Acting became interested in children's theatre in its second season (1969). Despite prevailing difficulties, the troupe has done its best in performing plays for children. Its first experiment was *On the Tabrizi Wing*, by Alfred Fen, adapted and directed by Fawzi Mehdi.

The effective initiative, however, was with the productions of *The Bird of Happiness* (1970) and *The Wooden Boy* (1972), both adapted and directed by Qasim Mohamed. *The Bird of Happiness* is about a boy in conflict with disease. He dreams of resting in the lap of nature, where he encounters a conflict between an imaginary animal, Aldio (who represents Evil), and the Bird of Happiness (who represents Good). The conflict ends with the victory of Good, and the boy wakes up having learned that he should fight evil and not give up to disease. *The Wooden Boy*, an adaptation of the famous Italian fairy tale *Pinocchio*, is about a poor woodcarver who cannot sell his work. When he decides to make a leg for his table to replace a broken one, it becomes clear that there is a spirit imprisoned inside, the spirit of a wooden boy. The woodcarver releases the spirit and adopts the puppet. But evil powers start working that make him disobey his "father." Ultimately the powers of good redeem him and direct him back to an honest life.

The Daisy (1975), written and directed by Sadoon Al Obaidi, is considered the first original children's play in Iraq. The play is about the conflict between Good and Evil. Discipline, order, hard work, and happiness are represented by flowers, butterflies, and man, whereas Evil, which tries to destroy the good work of the others, is represented by dangerous insects, scorpions, and snakes. But it is the unity of the good powers that ultimately triumphs. *Spring's Army* (1976), adapted and directed by Salim Mohamed Jawad Al Jezairi, was performed together with James Noren's *Aladdin and the Magic Lamp* (1976), directed by Obaidi. The 1977/78 season included *The Weaver's Daughter*, adapted by Jezairi and Kamil Al Sharqi and directed by Bahnam Michael, and *The Barrack*, written by Taha Salim and directed by Ismail Khalil.

The Orange Star (1978), by Ghazi Mehdi and directed by Muhsin Al Azzawi, was performed for student cadets. The orange star symbolizes the search for the unknown. The action takes place in a village whose inhabitants are used to sleeping and waking by the nightingale's songs. The bird is a symbol of the Party, as he engineers their lives in order, belief, and truth; its songs represent the seven pillars of modern society and a sincere belief in the principle of the revolution. When one looks at the National Troupe's efforts, one can clearly see the troupe has been able to bridge the gap between children and the stage. It has been careful to consider all the critical and press reviews, and it has given great consideration to comments from children.

The State Organization for Theatre and Cinema, Research and Studies Statistics unit, made a survey of the audience of *The Barrack*. Of a total of 240 questionnaires, 180 were distributed to young people and children (the target audience) and 56 to adults, mostly teachers and parents. The questionnaires were not well suited to the children, but two of the questions were relevant, as far as the children were concerned: (1) Do you prefer the play to be spoken in (colloquial) Arabic or classic Arabic? (2) How do you rate the play you have just seen? The results were divided into two categories by age group, starting with children who were eight years old (no children younger than eight were given questionnaires). The opinions about the play's language depended on the age group: the younger children preferred spoken, colloquial Arabic, whereas the older children preferred classic Arabic. In answer to question 2, the ratings were as follows: very good, 59.24 percent; good, 13.59 percent; fair, .54 percent; poor, 0 percent; and no comment, 26.63 percent. In general, most of the audience enjoyed the performance.

The National Troupe's role in the promotion of children's theatre in Iraq is evident. Most of their productions take into consideration the aesthetic and educational aspects of theatre for young people and also adhere to a general political revolutionary trend that balances with the children's intellectual abilities.

Radio and Television

The State Organization for Radio and Television has several departments concerned with children's programs, both on radio and as television plays. Iraq T.V., Radio Baghdad, and Sawt Al Jamahir all present plays for children. The Organization formed an acting group that specialized in children's theatre in 1975. This company was well received and garnered enthusiastic reviews in the media around the country. The principal initiators of the group were Izzi Al Wahab, Mohamed Abdul Azziz, and Hussein Kadoori.

Wahab presented his *The Clever Chicken* using actors from the new company. The piece is a confirmation of the revolution's motto: "He who does not produce, does not eat." The play was performed at the National Theatre. *Good Morning, Happiness*, by Farouk Salloum and Sami Abbas Al Zubaidi, and directed by Azziz, concentrates on a contemporary hero with all of nature's powers on his side. The group also performed *The Lion and the Rabbit*, written and directed by Azziz, and *The Friends of the Farm*, adapted and directed by Wahab. These plays confirm the facts that survival is for the fittest and that strength comes from unity and work.

Zita, a Duck and a Mule was coproduced with the local Committee of the Union of Iraqi Students, Hay Al Salam. A folktale about three animals who agree to farm the land together, it focuses on a mule who betrays his colleagues and eventually drowns in the river as just punishment for his transgression.

The Academy of Fine Arts

The Academy of Fine Arts was established in the early 1960s. Its Drama Department has grown considerably, especially since the Academy became part of the University of Baghdad. In 1978 the Academy invited Dr. Hans Dieter Schmidt, an expert on children's theatre in East Germany, to come to Iraq as a visiting scholar. During his stay in Baghdad, which lasted for several weeks, he gave lectures on children's theatre and directed Samuel Marshak's *The Animals' House* (with music arranged by Hussein Kadoori). He also supervised the mounting of his own play, *The Old Bus Antar*, which was directed by Sami Abdul Hamid. Both plays were translated by Dr. Faik Al Hakim.

Other Acting Groups

The Karbala Acting Group has also been active in children's theatre. This group performed two plays in 1977: *Sab'Al-Sabamba (The Chief Lion of the Lions)*, and *The Uncertain Hunter*, directed by Ala' Al Obaidi, a 1971 graduate of the Academy.

Unions and Clubs

The unions, such as the Union of Iraqi Students and Youth, popular social committees, and other social clubs, such as Ur Club, have encouraged performances and have themselves produced several presentations.

Foreign Troupes

There have been several foreign acting companies in Iraq that have come at the invitation of the Ministry of Culture and Information. They have been responsible for the productions of mimes and puppet theatre, as well as for lectures and seminars on children's theatre.

THE REPERTORY

There were few actual children's plays before the revolution, with the exception of Abdul Sattar Al Qaragoli's *Stories from the History of the Arabs* (Vol. 1, 1948, and Vol. 2, 1950). These two volumes plus Qaragoli's *Little Abdulla's Father* (1958) were the only substantial plays written for children and young people. After the revolution, however, there has been an intense and enthusiastic movement toward all aspects of children's culture. The establishment of several organizations in this field encouraged dramatists to write children's plays in a modern context. The most promising of the playwrights for children are Qasim Mohamed, Sadoon Al Obaidi, Abdul Razzak, Abdul Wahid, Khalil Shawqi, Farouk Salloum, Sami Abbas Al Zubaidi, Jabbar Sabri Al Attiyah, Farouk Ohan, and Issa Jaffar Majid.

The following table lists the local plays performed for children. From this list it becomes obvious that children's theatre really began to take effect during the mid–1970s.

Title of Play	Group	Year
On the Tabrizi Wing	National Troupe of Acting (NTA)	1968
The Bird of Happiness	NTA	1970
The Flower and the Butterfly	*Mizmar* and *Majalatti* editors	1972
The Flying Circle	*Mizmar* and *Majalatti* editors	1972
The Wooden Boy	NTA	1972
The Daisy	NTA	1975

The Rock	Union of Iraqi Youth	1975
The Flying Draper	Group 76 of Dramatic Arts	1976
Aladdin and the Magic Lamp	NTA	1976
Good Morning, Happiness	Radio Baghdad Children's World	1976
The Rabbits' School	Bulgarian Zagwar Puppet Theatre	1976
Spring's Army	NTA	1976
Sab'Al-Sabamba	Karbala Acting Group	1977
The Lion and the Rabbit	Radio Baghdad Children's World	1977
The Uncertain Hunter	Karbala Acting Group	1977
The Weaver's Daughter	NTA	1977/78
The Clever Chicken	The Radio and TV Acting Group	1977
Martyrdom	—	1977
The Old Bus Antar	Students—Academy of Fine Arts	1977
The Shepherd and the Mermaid	—	1977
The Animals' House	Academy of Fine Arts/ Drama Dept.	1978
The Three Cats	Al Mohag School	1978
Zita, a Duck and a Mule	Union of Iraqi Youth	1978
The Barracks	NTA	1978
The Orange Star	NTA	1978

BIBLIOGRAPHY

Children's Theatre. Baghdad, Children's Culture House/Ministry of Culture and Information Studies and Research Dept., 1979.
A View of Children's Theatre in Iraq. Edited by Ahmad Fayadah Al Mafraji. Baghdad, State Organization for Theatre and Cinema, 1978.

Farouk Salloum
Translated and edited by Lubna Alaman

The most popular play in the English language for young audiences, James Barrie's *Peter Pan*, has been seen in frequent productions since it was first produced in 1906. In this famous scene Peter instructs Wendy and her brothers how to fly to Never Land. Karen Cole played Peter in this Broadway musical version, which toured throughout the United States in the mid-eighties (Courtesy of Karen Cole).

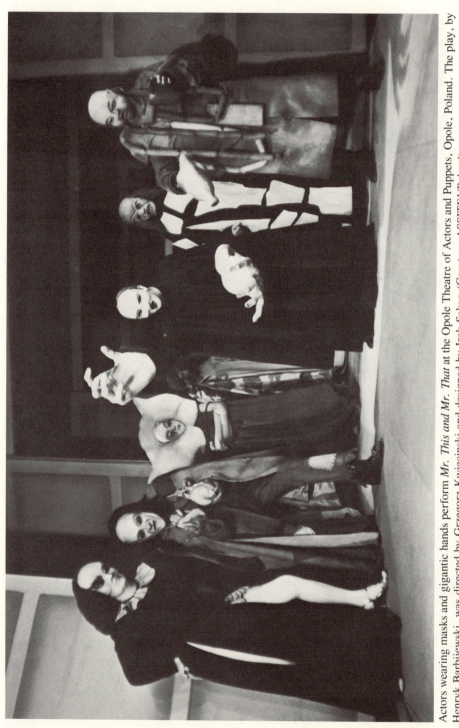

Actors wearing masks and gigantic hands perform *Mr. This and Mr. That* at the Opole Theatre of Actors and Puppets, Opole, Poland. The play, by Henryk Barbijewski, was directed by Grzegorz Kwięcinski and designed by Irek Sołwa (Courtesy ASSITEJ/Poland).

Bright costumes and high spirits characterize *Three Fat Men*, a popular comedy by Yuri Olesha, at the Moscow Central Children's Theatre, performed since the early eighties (Courtesy ASSITEJ/USSR).

A map becomes the entire set for *A Humanoid Is Crossing the Sky*, a Russian science-fiction play by A. Khmelik and produced by the Theatre for Young Spectators in Riga (Courtesy ASSITEJ/USSR).

Young and old gather in a Lesotho park to see performers from the Marotholi Travelling Theatre present a play dealing with contemporary problems such as immunization and migrant labor. No scripts exist because each performance is improvised and guided by the response of audiences, who are urged to participate in the action (Courtesy of Zakes Mda).

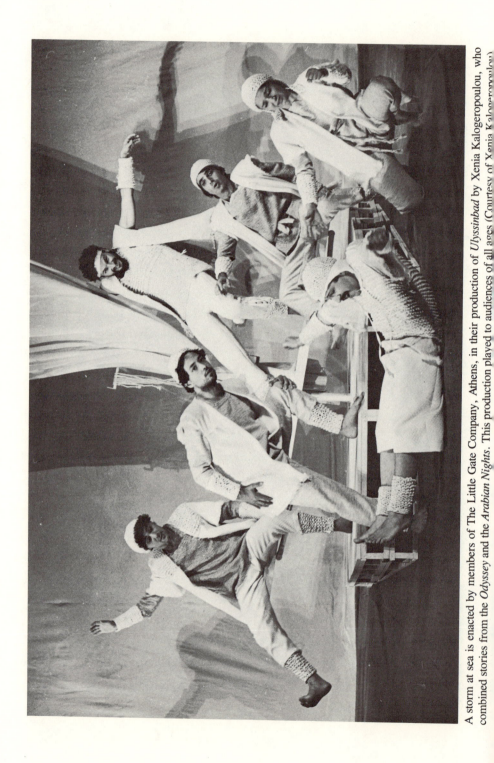

A storm at sea is enacted by members of The Little Gate Company, Athens, in their production of *Ulyssinbad* by Xenia Kalogeropoulou, who combined stories from the *Odyssey* and the *Arabian Nights*. This production played to audiences of all ages (Courtesy of Xenia Kalogeropoulou)

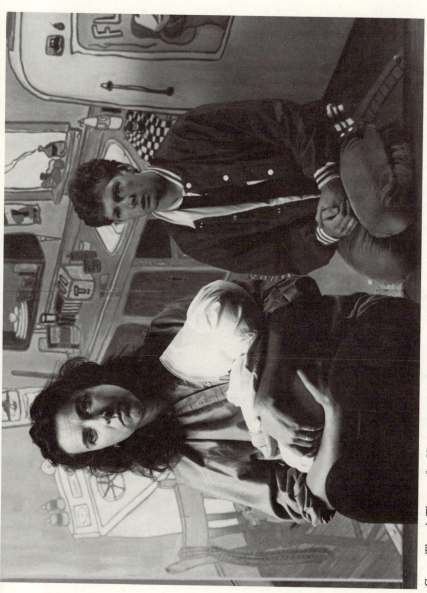

Green Thumb Theatre for Young People of Vancouver, British Columbia, Canada, in a tense moment from *One in a Million*, a play by David Holman. Shown are Sam and his mother, who cradles a new baby. Holman's plays are widely produced in Great Britain, Canada and Australia (Courtesy ASSITEJ/Canada).

Jacob Two Two Meets the Hooded Fang, adapted from Mordecai Richler's story, has been one of the most popular productions given by the Young People's Theatre of Toronto. A play intended for audiences aged six years and up, it has been revived several times throughout the 1980s (Courtesy ASSITEJ/Canada).

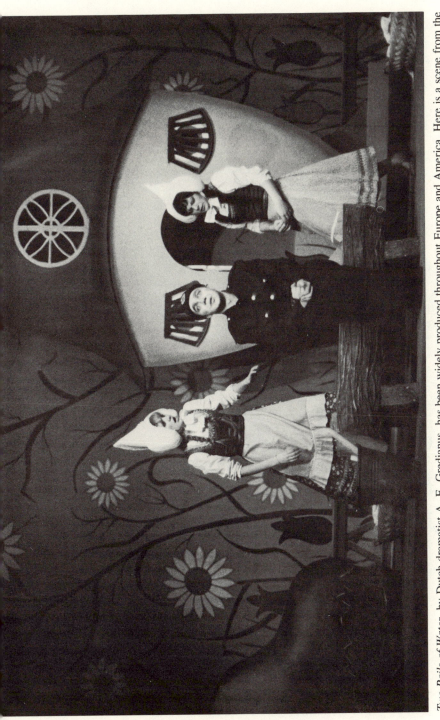

Two Pails of Water, by Dutch dramatist A. E. Gredianus, has been widely produced throughout Europe and America. Here is a scene from the Turkish production, directed by Nurtekin Odalous, at the State Theatre (Courtesy ASSITEJ/Turkey).

A realistic moment from *Honeyspot*, by aboriginal dramatist Jack Davis whose plays deal with multicultural issues. The play was commissioned by the Elizabethan Theatre Trust of New South Wales and widely toured Australia in 1986. The production was directed by Richard Tulloch (Courtesy ASSITEJ/Australia).

Israel

HISTORY

The history of Israeli children's theatre is related to the development of Hebrew drama and theatre, and is based on the ideological and social goals that the Hebrew theatre set for itself and practiced from its earliest days. Hebrew theatre first emerged as part of the national and cultural revolution at the end of the nineteenth century. Because of the absence of theatre in Jewish tradition, the Hebrew theatre was, from the start, a secular institution as well as a vital part of the cultural revolution of the Zionist movement. It aimed to revive ancient Hebrew and turn it into a living language—the language of those who wanted to establish new life for an ancient nation—in the land of Israel. In fact, Hebrew theatre was a bone of contention in "the war of tongues." This term refers to the conflicts between Jews who were Zionists and who left Europe for Palestine and the Jews who stayed in Russia or who emigrated to the United States. Those who stayed in Russia or emigrated to the United States promoted a popular Yiddish theatre (which was also a new phenomenon at that time), while the Zionist movement gave birth to the Hebrew theatre—a theatre that could celebrate the Hebrew language and that would voice the Jewish people's aspirations for national rebirth.

Origins

The first Hebrew theatre, Habima (The Stage), was founded in Moscow under the patronage of Constantin Stanislavsky and the Moscow Art Theatre. Habima's actors, most of whom were amateurs, went through professional training at Stanislavsky's studio. In 1926 these actors brought with them to Palestine Stanislavsky's acting methods, directing techniques, and high artistic standards. Most of the theatrical activity in Palestine at this time, however, was carried out by nonprofessional actors, and it almost always was connected with social and educational institutions. In fact, the first Hebrew productions in Palestine premiered in a high school.[1]

The Beginning

Back to Zion, by Moshe Lilenblum, presented in 1891 by the students of a high school in Jerusalem, contained characteristics of Israeli children's theatre that were to become evident in later years: it was performed by nonprofessional actors, it addressed a national problem, it aimed to deliver an ideological message, and it was performed during the holiday season (as most productions were until the 1970s).

The Holiday's Pageants

In the early years of the Jewish settlement in Palestine, three professional theatres were based in Tel-Aviv, but intensive amateur theatrical activity took place all over the country, in schools, in community centers, and in kibbutzim (collective farms). This activity focused on creating unified cultural traditions by transferring religious rituals of the Jewish holidays into public secular ceremonies. Schools, communities, and kibbutzim eagerly presented festive pageants in an attempt to reconstruct the rituals held in the ancient kingdom of Judea and Israel during the period of the first and second temples. These pageants aimed to bridge the gap between ancient traditions and the rebirth by providing modern national meanings for traditional ancient Jewish religious rituals. Colorful productions were mounted in which both children and adults performed in school yards and public places during the various holidays.

The tradition of the holiday pageant is still practiced in the Israeli school system. In fact, major effort and artistic energy can be observed in the public schools as they continue to present pageants to celebrate the holidays or the end of the academic year.

State Support

Funding began as early as 1926, and today the Israeli theatre as a whole is supported by the state. This is done to fulfill the cultural needs of the individual, to use theatre as an aid to further the spread of the new language, to disseminate national ideas or values, and to create a unified culture for immigrants from all over the world as they rapidly coalesce into a single society.

The Center for Dramatic Materials

In the early 1940s the Histadrut (the central organization of trade unions) supported the work of amateur groups and of directors who presented productions for young audiences in the schools and community centers. The Histadrut's Division of Culture established an office to collect and distribute dramatic materials for children and youth. Moshe Zeiri (who has directed the center for more than thirty years) collected scripts from all over the country of holiday pageants and children's plays written to be performed by various amateur groups.

The Center for Dramatic Materials served for many years as a mediating agency by providing schools, kibbutzim, and communities with both professional directors and dramatic scripts. Some were written by teachers or directors, many were composed by groups who had worked together to form festive pageants, others were translated from various foreign languages (mainly German, Polish, and Russian), and still others were stage adaptations of classic children's literature. In the late 1930s the Hebrew Teacher's Union initiated support for a children's theatre troupe that was composed of and directed by union members. The activity of this group, The Teacher's and Pre-School Teachers' Theatre, was short-lived and has not yet been documented.[2] This was, however, the first attempt at public children's theatre aimed at answering the growing demand for children's theatre production.

Cultural Interest

Since the early days of the Jewish settlement in the land of Israel, the Israeli public practiced the Jewish tradition of "normative" free-time activity. Katz and Gurevitch, who studied Israeli culture, pointed to the Israeli sociocultural norm that influences the cultural behavior of the individual and forms his self-image.[3] According to this norm, theatre attendance is a "proper respectable manner of time spending." The cultural norm is one of the reasons for the great popularity of theatre in Israel. It may also be one of the reasons for the growing demand for children's theatre production that mainly arises during the holiday seasons and summer vacations, when parents want to provide their children with proper educational activities. The desire for children's theatre productions gave birth to a commercial theatre that dominated from the early 1940s until 1970 and is still quite successful today.

The Commercial Theatre

The Israeli commercial children's theatre comprises various troupes that are created as needed and, therefore, come to life largely during holidays and vacations. Some of the commercial productions are given by professional actors of the public theatres who seek extra income. Some productions are performed by semiprofessional actors (often family members of the producers) and designers. The dramatic scripts presented by the commercial troupes are based on well-known fairy tales such as *Little Red Cap* and *Cinderella*. Some of the producers have recently staged short versions of television programs or series that are successful with young audiences. One of the more popular titles is *Little House on the Prairie*, based on the American novels of Laura Ingles Wilder.

At first the artistic standards of most commercial productions for children were low. Scripts drawn from literature often were adapted by nonprofessionals (producers or directors) rather than by experienced playwrights. The staging and acting were poor and sometimes overdone to the degree of vulgarity; in many cases sets and costumes were executed without care. Producers used materials left over from previous productions, assuming that young audiences would accept them. Some managements seemed to believe that being young meant being ignorant, undeveloped, and unable to appreciate aesthetic values.

First Attempts at Professional Children's Theatre

During its short history, Israeli drama and theatre underwent major developments, resulting in significant achievements at home and an international reputation abroad for high artistic standards. However, these achievements did not extend to children's theatre. From 1926 to 1964 the public repertory theatres presented only six children's plays and there was no professional theatre or drama for children. Furthermore, no public support had been given to children's theatre or educational theatre and no scholarly work had been undertaken in this area. Israeli theatre criticism, which was always professional and well heard, paid no attention to commercial children's theatre; consequently young audiences were left in the hands of the commercial producers described above.

In 1964 the Cameri Theatre of Tel-Aviv decided to present the child audience with good professional theatre. Thanks to the endless efforts of Orna Porat, a distinguished actress and a member of the Cameri Theatre Board of Directors, the company determined to present at least one production every year. Between 1965 and 1968 the Cameri presented five plays, all of which were successful, and one, *Uz Li Gutz Li (The Midget and the Riddle)*, became one of the theatre's greatest hits and is still presented every year.

Uz Li Gutz Li, a children's theatre masterpiece, is a musical fairy tale written by Abraham Shlonski, one of Israel's greatest poets, and directed by Yossi Izraeli. The verse play, with its unique mixture of sophisticated language and a simple story line, can be easily followed. The music and setting were provided by the Cameri Theatre's best professionals, and the acting was superb. As any good children's theatre production should, *Uz Li Gutz Li* attracted both children and adults, and the company was rewarded artistically and economically for their efforts in presenting quality theatre for young audiences.

Uz Li Gutz Li was followed by productions of *Adventure in the Circus, The Princess and the Shepherd,* and *Treasure Island*. Even though none of these possessed the poetic qualities that Shlonski's language contributed to *Uz Li Gutz Li*, they were good productions and attracted young audiences from all over the country. The Ministry of Education, encouraged by their success, decided to establish a national children's theatre that would bring artistic production to every corner of the country.

CHILDREN'S THEATRE TODAY

The National Theatre for Children and Youth

The National Theatre for Children and Youth (NTCY) was established in 1970 under the direction of Orna Porat, who acts as the general director of the company until this day. To meet the ideological goals and cope with the circumstances described above, NTCY set up a working plan that is still in use today.

The theatre offers ten productions annually. Performances are directed for three age groups: children five to ten years old, or preschool to fourth grade; children eleven to thirteen years old, or fifth to seventh grade; and young people fourteen to eighteen years old, or middle- and high-school students. In its first year the theatre tried to produce plays that would serve the needs of youth ages sixteen through eighteen. Since the 1970s, however, NTCY decided to concentrate on performing for younger audiences and allow the needs of older children to be met by the regular professional theatre companies, in some cases cooperating with them. NTCY also co-produces plays with other theatres, as in the case of Sophocles' *Antigone*, which was presented in 1984 in association with the Haifa Municipal Theatre. In other cases NTCY supports public theatres when they present plays suitable for youth by funding, providing transportation, or booking companies through its own distribution system.

The productions are divided into two groups: four to five of the annual list are full-scale mountings intended for conventional theatres, and they demand elaborate settings and sophisticated equipment and machinery. The other productions are on a smaller scale, designed to fit into classrooms or school dining halls. These utilize simple mobile sets and perform with a small ensemble of actors. When the large-scale productions tour, children are driven to the theatre accompanied by their teachers. The smaller productions travel to nearly every school in Israel. Israeli children are regularly driven to see one to three large productions and attend another two at school during each academic year. Because NTCY repeats its best productions every three to four years, it provides new generations with the best of Israeli theatre, some of which have become ''classic pieces'' and constitute a common cultural background for all Israeli youth.

In order to present young spectators with a variety of performing arts, the company ranges from realism to *commedia dell'arte* and story theatre. In addition, the theatre cooperates with the Yuval puppet theatre, the Israeli Pantomime troupe, and the Israeli ballet, each of which performs each season. The repertory is designed to respond to the developmental and emotional needs of different age groups. It intends to present the best classic drama along with the best of Jewish and Israeli literature that deals with Israel's history and current social problems and issues.

In its early years (1972–1975) the repertory of NTCY was mainly composed of classic dramas, such as Shakespeare's *Twelfth Night* and Molière's *The Miser*, as well as plays that dealt with Jewish history, such as *The Diary of Anne Frank*. During the same period Orna Porat directed *The King's Daughter*, which became one of the theatre's major successes and was presented many times at international children's theatre festivals. *The King's Daughter* contains stylistic features that are characteristic of NTCY during its formative period. The performance is based on a dramatized poem by national poet Hayim Nachman Bialik. Porat took the events in the poem and located them within a legendary Oriental surrounding, which was created by the use of Yemenite musical motifs, dances, and costumes.

In the mid-seventies NTCY continued this Oriental style in full-scale productions using colorful costumes, elaborate sets, and other nonverbal elements. Most of these, such as *The Garden of Freedom*, are intended for younger children who are particularly susceptible to the wonders and magic of fairy tales and fantasy as well as to the magic and splendor of the theatre.

Along with the Oriental fairy tales, the theatre adapted several classics, such as *Winnie the Pooh* and *The Wizard of Oz*. Priority was also given to staging Israeli poetry; the works of Alterman, Goldberg, and Molodovska were brought to the stage in the form of poetic revues composed of poems, songs, and short sketches. They became the main repertory of small-scale productions presented to elementary-school children nine to twelve years old, who are familiar with the works of these poets in their classroom curriculum.

Whereas the larger productions were directed by well-known professionals, such as Edna Shavit and Leonard Shach, the smaller productions were given to unknowns, many of whom later became the leading directors of NTCY. In the late seventies NTCY opened its doors to a young generation of Israeli playwrights who concentrated their efforts on dramatizing specific areas of Jewish history. Ephraim Sidon wrote three comedies that were well liked by the middle age group of children and were appreciated by theatre critics, who began to review productions for young audiences. Tzipi Pines, one of the best young directors of the theatre (who later became the director of the Beer Sheva Municipal Theatre), directed a stage adaptation of Devora Omer's *Sara: The Heroine of Nili*. The play deals with a young woman who, at the beginning of the century, risked her life to help the British army wage war against the Turkish empire, which at that time occupied Palestine and oppressed the Jewish population. *Sara: The Heroine of Nili*, staged in the realistic style and geared toward middle-school students, was a powerful production and the first attempt to deal with Israeli history and political issues.

Israeli history and social drama are the main subjects of the documentary drama for children that has formed a major part of the repertory since the late 1970s. Hagit Rechavi, a playwright and director who has worked with the company since the early 1980s, has presented eight plays that deal with activities of young people during the Israeli War of Independence, the immigration to Palestine in the 1920s, and conflicts between high-school students and the establishment. Rechavi has been followed by a third generation of young playwrights and directors, who came to the theatre in the early 1980s and focused on the current issues of Israeli society, such as the problems of deprived children and the Arab-Israeli conflict.

In 1986 the theatre mounted thirteen productions composed of a mixture of genres, styles, and topics from those mentioned above. Twelve of the thirteen productions were written by Israeli writers, most of whom started their careers working with this company, which today has become a "drama laboratory." Young artists are consistently bringing new ideas and new forms to provide young generations with up-to-date materials and to contribute to the overall development of Israeli drama for children.

One of the concerns of NTCY is to develop the area of theatre education by fostering high aesthetic values and appreciation of theatre among young audience members. Since its establishment in 1972, the educational unit has provided a variety of activities for students, teachers, and parents. It has introduced them to Israeli drama, as well as to the language of the stage and the world of the theatre. The company conducts lectures for teachers and parents in relation either to specific productions or to dramatic genres and theatrical styles of performance.

In the early 1980s the theatre developed a form called "A Day of Theatre," during which students experience day-long theatre-related activities such as theatre games, creative drama, and meetings with the artists. They attend a performance that is followed by a discussion. The company also conducts workshops for teachers who want to incorporate drama techniques in their classroom, providing them with practical activities as well as written materials.

Since 1980 the educational unit has published prompt books that offer the script and pertinent information about each production. The book published for Peretz's *Miracles on the Sea* was written by Dr. Shosh Avigal and presents the historical background of Peretz's work. It introduces techniques of story theatre, the style in which this production is performed, and devotes a chapter to the masks and music that are essential to its success.

Since 1986 NTCY has been the largest repertory company in Israel, and the only public theatre for the young. Several units travel the country each day presenting sixteen productions in 260 cities, villages, and kibbutzim, totaling more than 1,500 performances. The theatre offices are located in Tel-Aviv, but the company has no home-based theatre facility. It is a mobile theatre that has made the schoolrooms across the country its home. The group employs about fifty professionals, and audience attendance is approximately 200,000 young people annually. It is now a major theatrical company of Israel.

The artistic activity of NTCY has had a major influence on Israeli children's theatre. The professional standards set by this company challenged commercial producers, and many of them have improved their productions to meet the demands of a more sophisticated audience.

NTCY is the only professional company that works the year round. In 1985 the Theatre Group of Neve Zedek, a new socially and politically oriented troupe, presented a social comedy for children called *The King Wants to Sleep*, which deals with the virtues of democracy. This entertaining and educational production ran for 300 performances and was seen throughout the country. In 1986 the national theatre, Habima, produced an adaptation of Korczak's *King Matia* in a colorful musical performance that became Habima's greatest hit of the season. In 1987 the Haifa Municipal Theatre offered an Italian comedy for children in the style of the *commedia dell'arte*, and the fringe troupe of Eli Don Cohen presented an avant-garde adaptation of *Alice in Wonderland*.

Today children's theatre is equally as popular as general theatre in Israel, which is the most popular art form in the country.[4] Since the late 1970s NTCY has sponsored an Arab children's theatre troupe that is active in Haifa, and there is growing interest in theatre among young Arab audiences. The growing success of Israeli children's theatre is now well covered and reviewed by the Israeli press and the electronic media. During the holiday season most major newspapers publish a special guide for young theatre audiences. In 1985 the Israeli Ministry of Education nominated a committee of theatre artists and educators to study the state of art and performing arts education within the school system. The committee suggested incorporating theatre education into the schools' curriculum and recommended that every student attend at least three theatrical performances annually. This is another demonstration of the growing awareness of the importance of children's theatre and its contribution to the development of young people.

NOTES

1. See M. Kohansky, *The Hebrew Theatre* (Jerusalem: Weidenfeld & Nickolson, 1974), 9.

2. Razi Amity authored a dissertation about the history of Hebrew/Israeli children's theatre. This work is the only scholarly work in this field. CUNY Graduate Center, New York, N.Y., 1989.

3. E. Katz and M. Gurevitch, *The Secularization of Culture: Culture and Communication in Israel* (London: Farber & Farber), 92–93.

4. See S. Weitz and G. Rahav, "Developing New Theatre Audience: The Case of Israel," *Assaph: Studies in the Arts*, no. 1: 137–146.

Shoshana Weitz

Italy

HISTORY

During the seventeenth century the Italian actors of the *commedia dell'arte* became famous all over Europe (including Russia) for their particular style of improvised performing. Traveling troupes who endured long and dangerous journeys continued over the next centuries, sometimes offering puppet plays and comedies concerning the *commedia dell'arte* character Pantaloon in special performances for children. A revival of this type of professional theatre came in the 1920s, but still there was no organized theatre expressly for young people until the young actor Sergio Tofano founded his Teatro di Bonaventura, for which he wrote numerous plays. Published in 1951, these comedies are still read, adapted for film and television, and performed today. The twenties also saw the first appearance of Giovanni Manco's theatre, which, like that of Tofano, was linked to traditions of the *commedia*, in that comic characters emerged who became popular with audiences and, consequently, reappeared frequently in new plays.

A professional theatre established by Giusseppe Luongo toured the country for the next twenty-two years. It was joined in 1953 by the Angelicum Company in Milan, which offered a repertory of plays drawn from the *commedia* as well as from traditional stories and fairy tales. In the 1960s a new leader developed in the person of Don Raffaello Lavagna, who wrote plays and urged the creation of an international organization that could sponsor regular meetings that included performances of plays from various nations. Thus Italy became a founding member of ASSITEJ, and in 1970 hosted the Third Congress in Venice.

Plays that dealt with actual experiences and problems of children and young people grew in number in the 1970s and became the particular trademark of Teatro del Sole in Milan. Here Carlo Formigoni, drawing from his experiences at the Berliner Ensemble, developed plays on current issues and advocated Brecht's works as part of his repertory.

When the Ministry of Tourism and Theatre gave official recognition to children's theatre during the 1971/72 season, initiatives began to define a national theory and system of production. In this structure, companies are urged to organize and develop from an artistic base, each finding its own process but together sharing in exhibits, seminars, and workshops in which exchange, feedback, and stimulus take place regarding production choices and procedural questions. These activities aim at creating stability and become a point of reference from which new methods can be developed. As a result, a network of sixteen centers now regulate bookings and relate companies to schools and community life through a series of demonstrations, performances, film programs, exhibitions, debates, educational courses, and specialist seminars. The centers encourage experimental projects in cooperation with schools as well as between different art forms; they foster children's theatre by publicizing its goals and activities among public administrators and the press. In this way the centers form a relationship between schools and theatres, keeping a constant eye on the instructive and formative development and providing teachers with tools for relevant discussions after performances.

Children's theatre in Italy, however, does not address itself exclusively to schools, but also aims productions at audiences of mixed ages and at the family unit, taking in grandparents and grandchildren at the same time. Sunday performances are directed toward families with the specific hope of winning a larger public to the theatre.

Since the middle eighties the centers have brought about an important collaboration between the private and public sectors. They work through local government organizations within each large city to generate cultural creativity that stimulates and highlights policies of public administration. The government, through the Ministry of Theatre, supports companies, cooperatives, societies, and associations and assists in planning and organizing their work. The Italian Theatre Council (ETI) handles national distribution by establishing territories and arranging for theatres and spaces in which companies perform. The Council is also responsible for the promotion, publicity, and development within each region, as well as for initiating activity in areas where there may be none. The Council assists centers with research projects and long-range planning. It is through the efforts of the centers and the Council that Italian theatre for children and young people has been officially recognized by the government in the bulletin of the Ministry of Tourism and Theatre.

The Ministry has published the figures for the 1985/86 season, which show that seventy-seven companies gave 8,021 performances. Tickets were sold to 1,373,845 children and young people, and the number of days worked by all participants totaled 99,032. The Ministry of Tourism and Theatre, in recognition of the evolution of children's theatre, has steadily increased its economic assistance from 80 million lira in the 1974/75 season to approximately 6 billion lira in the 1985/86 season. The expansion of productions and research centers is also the result of increased investments made by local councils that see this art as an effective instrument for the cultural development of their regions.

Children's theatre in Italy once chose to concentrate its activities largely in the school environment by staging plays in classrooms or outdoors before teachers and their pupils. But over the years productions gradually moved into theatres, and attendance became more regular than it had been with sporadic school appearances. Today more productions than ever are seen on well-equipped stages that offer the best theatrical aesthetics. Audiences include children aged six to fourteen years who represent the primary-school age (although occasionally one finds children of kindergarten age, from three to five). A second group is made up of the general public who attend matinees, often including parents and children, and other adults who come out of their own interest. Children aged eleven to fourteen seldom are seen at public performances, but rather attend with their school groups.

The problem of a general absence of the fourteen-to-eighteen-year-old age group is confronted by attempting to create an interest in theatre through workshops during regular school activities, by organizing theatrical exhibitions in the afternoons and evenings and by creating theatrical spaces dedicated to the very young and adolescents. Certainly professional children's theatre has won the school audience, but a lot more work must be done in consolidating public theatre attendance during leisure time. It is only in this way that a continuous regeneration of new audiences can be achieved.

REPRESENTATIVE COMPANIES

The following survey of companies demonstrates the wide geographical distribution of children's theatre throughout Italy and shows the affinity of each group to its own region, the major dramatic concepts and artistic trends of the theatres, as well as their structural organization.

By traveling the length of the country from south to north, one can draw up an exploratory itinerary, starting at Bari. There the young Compania Teatro Kismet, which is enriched by the work of director Carlo Formigoni, has already made a name for itself in the international field. In the central south, at Aquila, the Uovo company, which produces its own shows, also organizes interesting demonstrations of its work. Among the various activities happening in Rome in children's theatre (the Theatre of the Marionette degli Accettella, the Teatrino in Blue Jeans, and the Grande Opera), the Ruota Libera stands out for its stylistic coherence and for the quality of the dramatic energy it injects into its own productions, directed by Marco Baliani. One of the best offerings by this company is *Oz*, which tackles the theme of rejection and violence through a unique reworking of *The Wizard of Oz*. The Teatro Stabile in Rome has a section for young people, performing workshops and productions.

In Perugia the Gruppo Fontemaggiore pursues a dramatic concept dealing with themes of space. The Teatro del Canguro from Ancona, which coordinates the local Centro Teatro Ragazzi, has distinguished itself since the end of the seventies with the quality of its puppet shows, based on the use of puppets worked from below and moved against a black backdrop. The view of cultural activities in Tuscany is portrayed by the development of children's theatre in the late seventies and the eighties through profitable organization of productive works. The leading light in this operation is Sipario Stregato, who has promoted a movement of companies and cultural activities in Cascina by collaborating with the Teatro delle Pulci from Pisa, and has been able to go beyond the local scene to develop interests that have found a place in the national sector.

In the vicinity of Lucca the Teatro del Carretto puts on a particularly visually attractive and colorful production by manipulating scenery and scenic objects to the accompaniment of tasteful, eloquent sounds. At Prato the Teatro di Piazza o d'Occasione has been in existence since 1971. By starting out with experiments in dramatics for children and adults, it has developed its own kind of theatrical methodology based on the teaching of theatrical art and the processes of visual communication. The Teatro dei Piccoli Principi from Sesto Fiorentino offers spellbinding shows created by Alessandro Libertini, whose style recalls the modern figurative arts. Florence is the base for many companies that operate in the field of puppet theatre (for example, Teatro in Tasca and Gran Teatro Mascara).

Emilia-Romagna provides a broad and interesting look at the children's theatre and companies working in that region. The circuit, Un posto per i ragazzi, has undertaken significant projects and gained an ability to negotiate with public administrations. The activity in the region has its roots in traditional participation theatre, represented by exponents of family art: Maletti in Modena, Ferrari in Parma, and Sarzi in Reggio Emilia. At Parma the Teatro delle Briciole has put life into a Center for Children's Theatre with its productions based on the poetry of objects that recite, recount, and create an atmosphere, objects that are present in our everyday lives but that take on a new and profound meaning on stage, especially when seen in relation to the story and authors represented, who range from Kipling to Ibsen and Agatha Christie.

The Baracca of Bologna produces situation and narrative shows, based mainly on the contributions of the actors. The same company manages the Sanleonardo Centro Teatro Ragazzi, overseeing its organization and programming. The Teatro Evento, which is also based in Bologna, is renowned for its workshop activity in youth detention centers and also for the work it does in organizing a "young people's" theatre. Reggio Emilia is the stage for the Teatranti Company, which develops its work as an actors' theatre.

In Romagna the lively activity of the Teatro dell'Arca is well worth noting; it creates productions that blend the importance of the text with a study of interpretive movements and the actor's role. Another important company is the Accademia Perduta, which puts on a revue at the theatre called Il Piccolo. The Compagnia Drammatico Vegetale has its base in Mezzano in the province of

Ravenna and takes its inspiration for creative work from a wide variety of literary sources. The indisputable center of theatre is in Piacenza, thanks to the presence of the Gruppo Teatro Gioco Vita, which, since 1978, has put its efforts into production after having been one of the main protagonists of the phenomena of audience participation and free expression.

The region around Venice also offers a host of companies and enterprising activity with varying themes. In Venice itself the Regional Cultural Association Arteven acts in an organizational role for the regional circuit of children's theatre. In Verona Centro Teatro Ragazzi is the permanent site, providing a center for teachers to carry out and document complex studies and for the planning of regional programs, as well as for organizing the annual Giornate Internazionali di Teatro Ragazzi (International Days for the Children's Theatre). Vicenza is the home of the Cooperativa Teatro Piccionaia, run by the Carrara company, a family of artists who put on shows that recreate the phases of a child's development in a fantastic setting, emphasizing the scope of the symbolic value of sound and color.

The Tam Teatro—Musica Aquilone works out of Padua; it is made up of three musicians/artists/performers whose theatrical activity is based on the interpretive study of how the actor blends expression of movement with his musical identity. The company La Contrada in Trieste has for many years carried out production work with its emphasis on the actor, which gave rise to the Children's Theatre Festival at Muggia.

The Sala Fontana in Milan represents a Center for the Children's Theatre, managing an impressive circuit of companies in this sector along with the Children's ETI. It also organizes workshops for the schools. The Center has a special relationship with several production companies: the Teatro dei Burattini from Varese and the Teatro dell'Arcobaleno. The city also claims a wealth of other activities and companies. The Teatro del Sole has been in existence since the early part of the seventies and has always firmly held to its precepts of poetic and creative modes: an interest in fables, the practice of improvisation, the study of themes of myths, exercises in a series of work methodologies, and the characteristics of a poetic approach to the product of theatre. The Teatro del Buratto, a solid, private company, manages the Rassegna Primotempo in conjunction with the ETI, and promotes seminars and courses to bring those in theatrical and educational circles up to date. The protagonists in their theatre productions have always been animated puppets against a black background, huge costumed figures that the operators wear or that are placed on the top of tall poles and moved by various people.

Gianni and Cosetta Colla are descended from an artistic family that for centuries has designed and animated puppets. Quellidigrock, for many years involved in teaching mime, combines this work with creative courses for young children, often using silent language. The Teatro Laboratorio Mangiafuoco mixes traditional puppets and original dramatic activities. The Strumento Concerto puts on didactic musicals, using instruments that come from all over the world.

Claudio Cavalli combines his own sense of humor as an entertainer with aesthetic scenic creations that he manipulates with great skill.

The Lombardy is represented by the Centro Teatrale Bresciano from Brescia, one of three public theatres for a particular area of activity aimed at young people, schools, and teachers. The Teatro Viaggio in Bergamo is involved in a series of programs with the cooperation of the local Public Administration, directed toward the schools through its own Center for Children's Theatre. The actors in these productions, who are particularly interested in direction and scenography, are greatly influenced by classic children's literature.

The Teatro all'Improviso in Mantova is a puppet theatre that also organizes a convention. La Spezia in Liguria is the home ground of Maria Baronti, an actress who has specialized in the role of narrator. The Teatro della Tosse in Genoa, which started in 1975 around the dual-named Tonino Conte—Lele Luzzati, combines its work for adults with the creation of shows for children, using the most varied languages of the theatre. The Teatro dell'Archivolto is formed by actors who have graduated from the theatre school based in Genoa and who provide a constant source of amusement and innovation with their comic theatre.

The city of Alessandria is the first step en route to the Piedmont, where the local Teatro Comunale is assigned the task of coordinating the Center of the Children's Theatre. An institution aimed at the schools in the city and the region, this Center works with a historic company called the Assemblea Teatro. Alba, in the province of Cuneo, has also made room for a Center for the Children's Theatre, run by the actors of the Teatro dell'Angolo, who organize the programming and the educational activities of the theatre for the schools in the area.

Turin is the setting for the first important formation of the children's theatre. The Teatro dell'Angolo manages a theatre company called the Teatro Araldo as a center for the children's and youth theatre that is open for evening programs. The style of work of this company, which enjoys international renown, gained its start from its direct relationship with children and the knowledge of their world. The Assemblea Teatro also has a long history, having been involved in children's theatre since 1976, enriching the school environment and giving seminars and workshops along with productions. The Compagnia del Bagatto, which has made the transition from traveling theatre to children's theatre, is involved in many methods of communication and runs a study workshop. The Granbado, which started out from an interest in clowning, has moved to a type of theatre of the absurd, staged in surreal surroundings and set within situations that have no narrative, but are full of pure entertainment formed by gesture and language.

The Doctor Bostik, which concentrates its work in the area of the marionette and puppet theatre, is the creator of scenery achieved through a blend of craftsmanship, a sense of fun, and the implementation of various materials. The Lupi, a historic company with origins dating back to 1787, stages traditional shows for children and young people. The Teatro Laboratorio from Settimo, a lively company even in its methods of organization, puts on evocative shows and uses fascinating audiovisual structures and objects from everyday life, evoking an intense psychological atmosphere.

The Settore Ragazzi e Giovani of the Teatro Stabile in Turin began at the end of 1978 as the initial undertaking of the public theatre, specializing in production and organizational activities for schools. The International Festival for Children and Young People constitutes a highly prestigious, artistic, and organizational undertaking, serving as a meeting place, a debating circle, and a theatre for comparison between national and foreign work methods, and creating critical interest among the specialists, experts, and representatives of local administrations.

The islands around Italy have strong traditions in theatre with the Pupi della Sicilia (in Sicily) and in the study of puppets (for example, Otello Sarzi's Teatro delle Mani), and as such represent the focal points of children's theatre there. The companies mentioned here are a cross section of the modes and various styles to be found throughout the country.

CHILDREN'S THEATRE TODAY

Styles of performance have undergone several major changes in recent years. In the 1970s the vogue for "participation" began, which strove to involve playgoers in the action rather than have them remain passive onlookers. This style emphasized audience participation not only to assist in the development of the plot, but also to participate in the performance itself. The hope was that theatre would become an event shared equally by performers and audience in a space that had no fourth wall separating them. Later experiments were undertaken to perform in places that would bring actor and child still closer together, in workshops and laboratories where questions could be asked and suggestions made by audiences as to how they wanted the plot to develop. More and more, children contributed and collaborated in the creative process.

Today even more emphasis is placed on research and workshop experiences that involve children and their teachers in the construction of a play. This process relies heavily on improvisation and the development of new work methods. Ironically, these new methods often are based substantially in the tradition of *commedia dell'arte*, which requires careful and sensitive involvement that is always ready to exploit every reaction for the good of the characters and the style of performance.

Consequently a new style of acting has emerged that, although still in an embryonic stage, can be defined as decisively anti-academic in its emphasis on body language, spontaniety, and open-endedness. Sometimes the style or form seems to be more important to the performers than the contents of the play itself. Normal scripts do not exist; themes are mere "pretexts" for invention and exceptional creativity, often arrived at through chaotic, though exhilarating experimentation. Yet in each case these attempts are made at the child's level as the actors put themselves in the child's place with all possible sincerity. To do this they study pedagogy, child psychology, and anthropology as well as seek advice from experts.

Themes that serve as the basis of inspiration are drawn from the world of fables and heritage of oral story-telling. The fable, revisited with the help of Vladimir Propp and Bruno Bettelheim, seems to be a perfect structure for this type of theatre, with its direct plot that invites the invention of stage techniques in unusual lighting, settings, and costumes.

These innovations brought about the need for new definitions of words, such as drama, recital, direction, script, and scenography, each having been rediscovered to have substantially different meanings and values now than in the past. One aspect that has become clear is that this new type of creativity is fundamentally collective in its need for actors and directors to "live the scene" in all its aspects. One group, together directing, writing, and acting over a period of three or four months, can claim the collective ownership of a production method that they have developed for themselves.

The 1980s have witnessed a reexamination of fiction and literary heritage ranging from classic children's literature to adult literature in hopes of uncovering new meanings and significance in style and content that can be explored in performance. In this way each company determines its cultural preferences and explores its own methodologies to create a distinctive style. As a result, some theatres have given back to children the pleasure and importance of listening, the use of grand themes, and previously forbidden existential subjects spoken in modern language. Today we notice a maturation of theatrical linguistics in a children's theatre that is able to create a high-quality product that maintains its own historical roots and guarantees continuity and development.

Lowell Swortzell
(Prepared from materials submitted by ASSITEJ/Italy.)

Japan

HISTORY

Kabuki, the famous traditional drama of Japan, is said to have been started by a group led by a girl named Izumo-no-Okuni at the end of the sixteenth century. As was the case in Western countries, in Japan, too, young boys and girls played an important role in the early days of theatre. Plays were not performed expressly for children, but the children became part of the adult audience. It was not until around the turn of the nineteenth century that the belief arose that children should be given a drama adequate to their own needs, just as they were provided books suitable for their own age.

Sazanami Iwaya, a famous pioneer of Japanese juvenile literature, introduced German plays for children that he had seen during his stay as a lecturer at the Oriental Linguistic School attached to Berlin University. When he advocated the performance of these plays, great interest arose from, among others, Otojiro Kawakami and his wife, the actress Sadayakko Kawakami. In October 1903, with the help of Takehiko Kurushima, who was one of Iwaya's followers, they performed the first children's plays in Japan. Under the title *Otogishibai* or fairy play, these consisted of two dramas: *The Gay Fiddle*, which was a stage version of an old European tale, and *The Judgment of the Fox*, drawn from an epic poem by Goethe.

Kurushima established the first drama company for children, consisting of young amateur members. He dramatized and produced typical Japanese folktales, such as *Momotaro*, and also works by Iwaya. The company was soon disbanded because of financial failure, but its members continued playing matinees of "Children's Day Show" on Saturdays and Sundays on the stage of the Yarakuza Theatre, the first Western-style theatre in the country. Their shows lasted for twelve years, from 1909 through 1920.

In the 1910s Japan experienced a new drama movement influenced by modern Western theatre. Using this impetus, theatre workers attempted innovative drama based on modern views of children. Among these efforts was the Minshuza Company's performance of Maurice Maeterlinck's *The Blue Bird*, directed by Ryoha Hatanaka, who had studied theatre in the United States. The production was a great success, and the play became one of the most popular in the repertory of children's theatres. Kaoru Osanai, one of the leaders of the new Western theatre movement, also showed much interest in children's theatre. He translated and produced a number of good foreign dramas for children, such as Stuart Walker's *Six Who Pass While the Lentils Boil*, an American play. In his later days Osanai eagerly introduced the works of Natalia Sats of the Moscow Children's Theatre.

During the 1930s Japan entered the "dark winter" under militarism and fascism. When the new theatre movement was suppressed by the government, children's drama also was placed under strict control. Instead of a rich drama, only certain approved plays were allowed to be performed by a few theatres with their much depleted companies.

After World War II, children's theatre again began to flourish because some theatre workers believed that it was indispensable. As a result, several adult companies gradually began to present children's plays. Among the most memorable was Samuel Marshak's *The Twelve Months*, performed in 1954 by Haiyuza Theatre, one of the best of the new-drama companies. The production created such excitement that many young people were influenced to enter the field of children's theatre after seeing it.

After U.S. occupation ended Japan experienced a period of great economic growth; mass media rapidly developed into the flourishing days of television and technology. At this time children's drama met with new problems. Mass media attracted many of those who once had been engaged in children's theatre, some of whom gave up low-profit theatre work in favor of television. In the meantime commercial dramatic companies emerged that produced children's drama simply as showy extravaganzas, with the result that some theatres trying to present quality drama for children were financially ruined.

Also at this time a fresh energetic generation of theatre practitioners started to enter the field. They had lived through the war and its aftermath and had a burning desire for peace. Moreover, they believed in good drama for children. Supporting organizations were founded to cooperate in the development of children's theatre and to overcome financial difficulties. The spectators' movement, called either Oyako-gekijo or Kodomo-gekijo, a kind of drama league, was one of the results of this organizational drive. It spread across the country through the efforts of mothers and young people who wanted children to enjoy good dramas, not commercially motivated ones. In 1979 Japan became affiliated with ASSITEJ and established its Japanese Center in the hope of promoting fruitful international cooperation in the dramatic movement for children and young people.

CURRENT CONDITIONS

Almost all professional theatrical companies in Japan are affiliated to JIENKYO (Japan Union of Theatrical Companies for Children and Young People), which had a membership of sixty-seven in 1982. Following are statistics concerning the activities of these companies that provide basic information about the current situation:

A. Repertory

Type of Audience

Theatres only for children and youth	55
Theatres for adults and children	12

Type of Plays

Living drama theatres	48
Puppet theatres	14
Silhouette theatres	5

B. Place of Performance

Theatres mainly visiting kindergartens and primary schools	49
Theatres mainly visiting high schools	18
Theatres mainly performing at community centers or halls	1

C. Location

Theatres in Tokyo district	45
Theatres in Osaka district	8
Theatres in other districts	14

D. Performance Numbers

There are 2,473 theatre members in these sixty-seven companies, and their activities in 1981 were as follows:

- Living drama: 8,415 places, 12,465 stages, 8,538 days, 7,163,816 audience members
- Puppet/silhouette: 8,244 places, 10,955 stages, 6,182 days, 3,768,584 audience members

Almost all the performances are sponsored by the theatres themselves, although there is limited government subsidy for performances on tour in local cities and remote rural areas. A few tour performances are funded by the business sector. Of all the performances:

- Played in schools: 63 percent
- Played at children's drama leagues: 13 percent
- Spontaneous stages: 6 percent
- Others: 18 percent

E. The Making of a Theatre

Three illustrations follow:

1. A big theatre:
   - Staff: thirty-seven men, thirty-eight women
   - Six separate performance groups that appear throughout the country
   - Total working days: 1,003 days on 1,396 stages
   - Average working days per person each year: 180

2. A medium-sized puppet theatre:
   - Staff: seventeen men, ten women
   - Three separate performance groups
   - Total working days: 700 days on 929 stages
   - Average working days per person each year: 200

3. A small live-drama theatre in a local city:
   - Staff: five men, seven women
   - One performance group
   - Total working days: 92 days on 142 stages
   - Average working days per person each year: 92

Trends

One of the common features among Japan's children's companies is that, with few exceptions, they have school visits as their main activity. They have accepted the challenge of performing in school gymnasiums without any effective theatrical equipment, or even a stage, and, as a result, have produced various innovative styles of presentation. At schools, lighting and setting must be much simpler and more functional than in traditional theatres, so overdecoration and spectacular tricks naturally have been excluded. The performers benefit by this simplification, for without lighting or settings to rely on, their basic skills inevitably must improve before the frank eyes of the children. Because of the economic need to keep budgets low for travel and accommodation, touring theatre has to limit the number of staff to as few as possible; therefore, each performer must be able to act in several styles.

The realities of touring also demanded new styles of drama and production. Plays now tend to break through the proscenium arch and are most comfortably played on the same level as the audience. Representative plays in this style include *Gaily Hans*, by Tohru Tada, and *Near by Mt. Kachi-kachi*, by Keisuke Tsutsui, both produced by Theatre Kaze-No-Ko; *Fatty Lion*, by Shin Shikata, produced by Theatre Nigatsu; and *Robot Kamii*, by Taruhi Furuta, produced by Theatre Urinko. Of other examples, Theatre Kaze-No-Ko's *Trunk Theatre* and

Two Plus Three are unique because they do not place emphasis on the story, but on the ingenuity and originality of the performers themselves.

At the same time, changes also took place in the field of puppet theatre, so that now there is little distinction between the puppet show and the living theatre. For example, the Puppet Theatre Musubiza's *Songokuu, the Magic Monkey* (produced by Yukio Sekiya) drastically changed the image of puppetry by placing the performers, who use basic techniques, out among the audience.

The companies have also actively tried to adopt various traditional techniques of Kabuki, Noh, and Kyogen into children's theatre. Zenshinza Theatre, whose performers are well trained in the Kabuki tradition, produced *Sanaho-daiu* (written by Asaya Fujita), into which were interlaced typical Kabuki techniques and the traditional reciting style of Sekkyo-bushi. Another example is Kansai-Geijutsuza Theatre's *Tsuchigumo* (written by Akio Araki), which also successfully adopted the Kabuki style. These plays leave a deep impression on the high-school students who have seen them.

In puppetry, similar approaches have been made by combining folktales with traditional techniques. Among them was The Puppet Theatre Hitomiza's *The Flag of the Boy Kintaro*, by Rintaro Suda. Traditional puppetry, called Bunraku, which is accompanied by the chant of Joururi, formed the basis of The Puppet Theatre Kurarute's production of *Onna-goroshi Abura-jigoku*, directed by Seiji Yoshida. This drama, originally written by Monzaemon Chikamatsu in the 1700s, still possesses the power to deeply move audiences when seen in its modern adaptation.

THE PLAYS

After World War II, theatre for children and young people was reconstructed; theatre practitioners, teachers, and dramatists wanted to tell audiences about the misery and inhuman aspects of war and to cultivate in them a keen sense of humanity so as to make the next generation grow into a peace-loving people. It is no wonder, therefore, that many anti-war plays are presented. Some tell directly of wars, such as Shin Shikata's *A Rose of Shalon and Mozel*, Taku Shibazaki's *Mother Told Me the Story of War*, Akira Saneto's *Two Umekos*, and Akio Araki's *Alive Are the Cats Alone*. Others, taking the form of folktales or changing situations of time and place, present struggles of young people who try to find humanity against fascism or conservative and suppressive ways of living, such as Akira Saneto's *Don't Look Back, Pedro*, Tohru Tada's *The Caledonia Sets Sail*, Ado Murayama's *The King of Cooks*, and Sirou Yataoka's *The Tiger of the Osaka Castle*.

As the only country damaged by atom bombs, Japan also offers many works telling children of the dangers to the existence of the earth itself by nuclear weapons. Among them are Akio Araki's *The White Ship on Dream Land* and Ryozo Yagi's *The Blue Sea of Ototo and Pippi*.

With the great influence of modern Western drama, companies often offer

European and American works, such as *The Ugly Duckling, Hansel and Gretel, The Blue Bird, The Merchant of Venice, Alice in Wonderland, Poil de Carotte, The Twelve Months*, and *Six Who Pass While the Lentils Boil*. They also present nonsense tales, science fiction, and farces, which contain positive themes of guiding children and young people into healthy ways to live. Examples include *Come Down from the Tree, Bunna*, by Mikio Komatsu; *Hidden Fort*, by Takaaki Odera; and *Bekkanko-Oni*, by Asaya Fujita.

SCHOOL-VISIT THEATRE

In 1981 JIENKYO-affiliated theatres played to audiences totaling almost 11 million persons. Of this number, about 6.6 million pupils enjoyed performances at their schools. That is to say, almost 60 percent of all showings of JIENKYO theatres played in school auditoriums or gymnasiums. This type of touring is called "school-visit theatre."

About 20 million pupils are currently enrolled in kindergartens, elementary schools, and lower secondary schools. Roughly speaking, one-third of all Japanese pupils saw school-visit theatre in 1981, giving this form a prominent place in the field of children's theatre. In the nearly thirty years of operation some lessons have been learned: School-visit theatre seems to be a uniquely Japanese style pioneered by children's drama practitioners, who have contributed much to the field.

Before the war there were no theatre buildings for children in Japan. In 1959 the Tokyo metropolitan government constructed the Tokyo Metropolitan Hall for Children, with 800 seats, but since then only ten more children's theatres have been built in the country. It was this situation that prompted performers to visit children at their schools. Carrying rucksacks filled with stage costumes and settings, performers toured from school to school so pupils might see their plays. Here and there they found teachers who were ready to receive them because the teachers knew how effective drama is for a child's growth. In cooperation with teachers, school-visit theatre has successfully developed throughout the country.

Such a visit usually begins with transforming the auditorium or gymnasium into a theatre. Every window must be blacked out with curtains, lighting apparatus set up, and chairs put in rows. The theatre staff, usually ten to twenty members, does all the work, whether as stagehands or as truck drivers, and then, when all is ready, acts as performers. It takes approximately two hours to set up the theatre and one and one-half hours to dismantle it—all this for a ninety-minute play. Physical exhaustion finally led the performers to ask, "Do we have to change a gymnasium into a fully furnished theatre, or is there some innovative way to create a dramatic and exciting space without all this work?" Different companies found varied solutions to the problem: some by using few set pieces or no settings at all; some by discarding stage costumes in favor of playing in street clothes or casual rehearsal wear; some by performing not on a stage, but on the floor, with children surrounding the action.

School-visit theatre can take advantage of closeness to the audience in ways that ordinary theatre cannot. By breaking the proscenium arch, performers can directly sense what the children are feeling and can keep in close touch with their responses so that a lively level of communication develops between performers and audience. This proximity also encourages children to participate more actively in the performance.

When brought to the school, productions give students the opportunity to discover the wonder of living theatre, especially those who would never willingly go to a theatre on their own. If the first play that one sees is tiresome, one will probably avoid the theatre in the future. Therefore, every school visit must be a decisively positive encounter for each child. The current condition of children in Japan is quite critical: there are many cases of delinquency, violence, and emotional disorder among children and youths, inflicted, in part, by the frustrating test systems in schools and a flood of unhealthy influences by television programs. Some people believe that Japan's children no longer hold any interest in living theatre. And in fact because a great many children have never been to a theatre, the performers often encounter bad manners during school-visit tours.

However, the performers never find such children annoying because they believe that the children simply want to attract the performers' attention and to communicate with the performers in their own way. To the performers' pleasure, during performances the children become quieter and quieter, until there is utter silence. At this moment the performers are most proud of their work, for then an exquisite mutual sympathy flows between stage and audience, and the performers know that their productions are contributing to the development of deep emotions and keen sensitivities in the children.

School-visits put a tremendous burden on the theatre staff. On a typical day a company member gets up at 6:30 A.M., arrives at an elementary school at 7:00, and at once unloads the truck and sets the stage by 10:00. The first performance runs from 10:30 to 12:30, followed by lunch and recess for one hour; the second performance goes from 1:30 to 3:30. Immediately after the performance the staff member helps to clear the stage, loads the truck by 5:30, and returns to the theatre office. After supper the actor takes a lesson from 7:30 to 9:00, goes home at 10:00, and falls into bed at midnight. Little time exists even for meals: usually ten minutes for breakfast, twenty minutes for lunch, and thirty minutes for supper.

Performers often want to diminish their workloads by not serving as stage-hands, but critical economic conditions prohibit engaging additional crew members. This level of effort quickly exhausts company members, both physically and spiritually. Furthermore, theatre workers receive neither a pension nor an old-age security system, and the government takes little interest in the poor conditions of stage artists.

In Japan both music and art are among the regular subjects in the school curriculum, but drama is not. When compulsory education was introduced in the 1880s, drama was considered frivolous, "a vagabond's pasttime." The situation has not yet improved, although drama is now offered as a club among many after-school activities. But because so few teachers are trained to help students, the level of the drama clubs remains low. The problem is exacerbated by the flood of commercially based television programs, which students eagerly mimic. Although children as well as the educational authorities still fail to realize drama's rich cultural value, the subject is gradually being introduced into educational activities by those teachers who know how it can liberate children's hearts and minds and who realize its effectiveness in education.

The performers think that a "spirit of play" is essential, and therefore emphasize the necessity of dramatic activity, because playing in an imaginary world can help children to develop their abilities to survive. Some schools successfully overcome such problems as delinquency and excessive test pressure through dramatic activities. Some mothers also testify to the marvelous results they experience in the parent-child drama league. One of them says:

Our children enjoy six plays a year at least and it seems to me they are able to recognize various values. For example, when they saw the puppet show *Alive Are the Cats Alone*, which depicts the violent air-raid on Tokyo in 1945, they recognized the horrors of war and the dreadful waste of lives. Then one month later when the television news reported that a baby had been found dead in a coin-operated locker at a local station, my child murmured to me, 'Mother, how dare anyone throw away such a precious life?' I am certain she kept that puppet show alive in her heart.

That children can learn the preciousness of life through plays brings great happiness to all those who work in theatre.

THE SPECTATOR'S MOVEMENT FOR CHILDREN'S THEATRE

The spectator's movement started at Fukuoka City in 1966 and spread throughout the country during the 1970s with the name of either Children's Drama League or Parent-Child Drama League. In 1981 there were 302 leagues operating with more than 330,000 members in all. Each league has developed its own activities according to the needs of the community, but the common aim of each is the healthy growth of children through cultural activities.

Each year leagues offer between four and six performances, including live theatre, puppet shows, variety shows, music, ballet, opera, and Kabuki plays. As the number of leagues increases, performances are arranged to accommodate individual theatres and audiences. In 1980 there were 1,847 regular meetings with 2,552 performances (an average of five meetings a day across the country); members themselves select performances for their regular meetings. Even though the quality of work improved as the movement grew, there were problems between drama leagues and performers; eventually these were solved through written agreements after prolonged consultations with representatives of the league, the actors, and the musicians. These terms bring spectators and performers together as fellow workers in the quest of culture for the nation's children. With such favorable cooperation the movement is sure to develop in the future.

Another important aim is to offer free dramatic activities. After enjoying performances at the regular meetings, children naturally want to perform themselves. As they began to attend more and more meetings, members became involved in such group activities as playing dramas, reading books, singing, hiking, camping, practicing sports, flying kites, and sponsoring festivals. In 1980 a total of 367,711 members participated in the free activities conducted by drama leagues.

These activities restore warm, lively human relations in the communities and encourage children to become more active. Moreover, child members of drama leagues have more friends to play with than do nonmembers. Two major objectives were corroborated in 1981 at the national assembly of the All Japan Association of Children's Theatre Spectators: one is to provide all children with opportunities to enjoy the performing arts and the other is to play a role in creating a cultural movement for children that is open and sound in responding to their needs.

Today it is essential to keep energies focused on these objectives in order to allow Japanese children to grow strong at a time when they are manipulated by television and when new administrative pressures from the severe "rat race" of the school system are being faced. Rapid growth in the membership of the drama leagues proves the need for such a movement, which is leading children's theatre in Japan to a new stage of development.

Lowell Swortzell
(Prepared from materials submitted by ASSITEJ/Japan.)

Korea

HISTORY

Foreigners who have visited this country in the past century have written that Koreans love singing and dancing. Although history shows that children's theatre started during the Kokuryu dynasty in the fifth century, there is a question as to whether the traditional Korean children's play, which consists of much staging and movement, can be considered a "play" in the Western connotation of that word. In any case, traditional theatre for young people is still performed out of doors, which affects its style.

The First Period (1920–1945)

Historically, the first period of modern children's theatre started when Korea was ruled by Japan; this abnormal political situation had a great influence on theatre for young people. The first playwrights for children (in the 1920s) were not dramatists, but nationalists or authors of literature who were unable to work from the viewpoint of the theatre. But in 1923 Jung Hwan Bang, a specialist in children's fairy tales, wrote a play, *Bagful of Song*, which was published in a children's magazine. Soon thereafter Ko Sung Shin's *Magic Hat*, Hae Song Ma's *The Blindman and an Elephant*, and In Sup Jung's *The Fool* were published.

In 1925 Suk Jung Yun wrote *An Owl's Eye*, which won a prize for the best children's drama from *Dong Ah*, a Korean newspaper. That one of the largest newspapers in the country would hold a playwriting contest shows that children's theatre was indeed important to the populace. *An Owl's Eye* was produced in 1925 by a group of college students. The same year Dahlia, a children's drama club, was organized and gave its opening performance, a dramatization of *Looking for a Summer Bird*.

In 1927 many foreign dramas were translated into Korean, such as Bocasha's *Until the Bean Is Cooked*, which was also performed by college students at the Chosun Theatre, and *A Scarecrow*, performed by the same group. Baik Yang, a children's play group organized in 1930 by Yun Pyo Hong, presented many of his works, including *The Lost Doll, Double Rainbow, The Stone Bridge*, and *Sun Ja and a Doll*. In addition, plays written by Ki Yoon Mo, Jin Soo Kim, and Song Kim were all published at this time. The year 1940 saw a decline in new works written for young audiences. The Japanese colonial government became more repressive in its rule, and this affected children's theatre, forcing it to become restrained. The only play published that year was Joo Hoon Lee's *The New Road*.

Because the people who were writing plays for young audiences during this period were not primarily interested in the theatre, but in the political situation, the works themselves are not of high quality. Also, there was no real emphasis on improving the plays or developing the art of children's playwriting, since the plays had a limited political purpose and existed only to serve that purpose.

The Second Period (1945–1970)

After liberation from Japan in 1945 Yong Il Kim, Byung Hwa Choi, and Sung Hwan Yun organized the Institute of Children's Art and formed a children's play group, Ho-Dong. This group became popular, and soon broadened their activities from stage drama to radio drama. In 1946 Ho Yo's play, *An Adventure*, was aired, and the first collection of plays for children, *Hand in Hand*, was published by Ki Hwan Bang. Drama entered the elementary-school curriculum in 1950 with the inclusion of Tae Ho Choi's *A Duster*, for fourth graders; So Chung Kang's *Flowers and a Butterfly*, for fifth graders; and Ki Hwan Bang's *When Spring Comes*, for sixth graders.

Nondramatists were still busy in this period writing plays for young audiences. Sookil Ahn, a prominent critic who wrote about the history of Korean literature, published two children's dramas in 1951: *Flowers and a Butterfly* and *An Honor Student Who Shines Shoes*. A significant event in the fifties was the founding of the Children's Drama Festival in 1956 by *Junnam*, a newspaper published in the southern part of the country. More than thirty groups participated in this festival, which played an important role in fostering young dramatists.

In 1961 the Korean Children's Drama Association was organized; it published a gazette called *Children's Plays*. The Institute of Korean Children's Play also began operations at this time, and *Drama for School Kids* was published by Pyung Joo, Hyo Sun Eh, and Moon Hyung Hong. Joo, the most important figure in Korean children's theatre in the late fifties and early sixties, wrote plays for young people and organized a production of his *Birds* in 1961. The production was revived in 1963 and 1964 and performed for Korean children living in Japan.

The years 1964 and 1965 saw the creation of several children's theatre groups, which performed such dramatizations as *The Death of the Magpie* and *Why a*

Frog Cries When It Rains. Since then ten more theatre groups have been established, and each performs a repertory of traditional Korean folktales and foreign works. The 1960s also introduced performances of children's plays in churches and cathedrals. Suk Hyun Lee produced works in Catholic churches and published *Collected Dramas for Catholics*; Ban Lee did likewise in Protestant churches and published the play *Flecked Little Angel* in 1969.

Although this was a period of much growth in children's theatre, both in quality and in quantity, it still had not found a regular place in the school curriculum, alongside the arts of dance, music, and painting.

Third Period (1970–1985)

In 1970 children's theatre in Korea entered a new phase, which was signaled by full-scale productions by professional adult actors. Several companies, including Hyun Dai and Min Jung, began to perform works for teenagers. In conjunction with the government and private enterprise, the companies contributed greatly to improving the quality of theatre for young people. A characteristic of this third period was Korea's entry into ASSITEJ; Korea also participates in congresses and invites foreign companies to visit and perform. Korean ASSITEJ has a membership of more than 150 persons. There are ten professional children's companies in Korea, not counting puppet theatre groups and troupes made up of children.

One of the major issues today is developing children's plays that meet both educational and entertainment criteria. In order to do this Korea needs to explore techniques of educational drama and theatre and to develop ways to measure the effectiveness of drama in the curriculum.

REPRESENTATIVE PRODUCTIONS

The 1987 repertory included a wide variety of offerings, such as The Minjung Theatre Company's *Heidi*, a musical play in seven scenes; The Third Stage's production of *Children of a Lesser God*, Mark Medoff's Broadway success; The Myungjak Theatre Company's *The Prince and the Pauper*; and The Hyundai Theatre Company's *The Magic Flute*, set in modern times.

Song of Filial Piety, adapted from a legend by Paek Yeo and performed by the large Drama Troupe Family based in Seoul, tells the story of the twenty-first king of the Chosun dynasty, Yungio. When Yungio moves among his people to see how they live, he is impressed by Mr. and Mrs. Hong's filial piety. They are poor but devoted to their parents, and Mrs. Hong cuts and sells her hair for money to celebrate her mother-in-law's sixtieth birthday. The king, very moved by this, helps Mr. Hong to win first place in the state examination. After he is given the job as the king's messenger, Mr. Hong inspects the local government and saves people from distress.

Dreaming Stars, by Dai Sung Youn, performed by the Dong-Rang Theatre for Young People of Seoul, is a play-within-a-play about a group of youngsters who imagine the arrival of three men from outer space in Korea. The aliens come to understand and help the people they meet by using their magical powers to make children feel their parents' love. In return, they are loved, which enables them to repair their damaged spaceship and return to their home star, happy for the first time in their lives.

Wandering Star, again by Youn, is a musical that was produced by the Dong-Rang Theatre for Young People. Between its premiere, in May 1985, and August 1986 it was seen by more than 100,000 teenagers in 161 performances. It was also performed in Adelaide, Australia, in April 1987 as part of the Ninth ASSITEJ Congress. An old man searching for his runaway grandson goes to the detention room of a police station where seven boys and girls are under arrest. They are charged with watching illegal videotapes, dancing at a discotheque, sleeping together in a cheap hotel, and drinking and roaming the streets at a late hour. In song and dance they vent their indignation against their parents and the society they hold responsible for leading them to commit these crimes. They complain about the educational system, which fosters severely competitive college entrance examinations; about television, which poisons and numbs their minds; and about unsympathetic parents.

The next morning when the parents arrive to take their children home, reconciliations are made and they leave happy; the detention room is empty except for the old man, who must continue to look for his grandson. During the curtain call he joins the company in ''The Song of Youth,'' which the audience is also invited to sing in a rousing finale.

Ban Lee

Lesotho

HISTORY

The Theatre-for-Development Project was started in 1982 by a joint working party of the National University of Lesotho's Institute of Extra Mural Studies (IEMS) and the Department of English. Its goal was to initiate and support community development and self-help programs through the use of drama. The target areas were rural communities in the Roma Valley and the Lesotho Institute of Correction.

In 1984 the project was funded by the Ford Foundation through the World University Service. Funding enabled the project to improve program flexibility and increase community impact. Before funding, the project was limited because it operated without a budget and within the confines of a semester course on Practical Theatre offered by the English Department.

Between 1982 and 1985 the project produced a number of plays dealing with such themes as reforestation, cooperative societies, and rehabilitation of prisoners. These plays were successfully performed in the target areas, and most of them were broadcast over Radio Lesotho for a wider audience.

MAROTHOLI TRAVELLING THEATRE

In January 1986 the performing group of the Theatre-for-Development Project decided to adopt the name Marotholi (from Marotholi-a-Pula, which means raindrops) Travelling Theatre (MTT). It is hoped that this will be a permanent company based at the university. It continues to be run jointly by IEMS and the English Department. Although it gets its personnel of trained performers from those who have successfully completed a one-semester Practical Theatre course, MTT operates throughout the year outside the confines of the course. Its most active period is the winter break (June through August), when the students work full-time for the project.

Until recently the Theatre-for-Development Project has been using a method of theatre known as agitprop (agitation propaganda), the form used most in didactic theatre, since it has been found to have a strong rallying potential for people to organize themselves into action groups. Although its creators may be outsiders, as is the case in this project, where students go out to the communities with prepackaged productions that they have created themselves, the theatre is oriented toward the people. The actors are able to respond to local situations because they have gone through a five-step process, including information gathering, information analysis, story improvisation, rehearsal, and community performance.

It has been discovered that in agitprop, the level of critical awareness about specific themes such as family planning, nutrition, human rights, and sanitation may not be very high, since these themes are raised from outside the community. Another weakness of this method is that there is no community participation, and the spectators become mere consumers of a finished product. Post-performance discussions may lead to individual action on a short-term basis. MTT continues to use the agitprop method when necessary, but now its dominant methods are those known as "participatory theatre" and "theatre for conscientization."

In participatory theatre, participation is both goal and methodology. Theatre is produced by and for the people with the help of catalysts ("catalyst" refers to outsiders with specialist skills in theatre and community development). In participatory theatre there is also improvisation within the specific parameters of the themes. The main difference between this method and agitprop is that members of the communities themselves are the performers rather than a group from outside. In essence, the members of the Marotholi troupe become catalysts.

Participatory theatre is able to raise community issues, involve people in discussing these issues, and mobilize people to take action on the issues. Because the catalysts must get the community members involved in presenting the dramatic program, it becomes necessary for them to stay for some days in the community and to improvise, rehearse, and perform the plays with community members as both actors and spectators. This has proved impossible, since MTT works throughout the whole of Lesotho and can spend only a few hours in each village. However, the company will continue to use participatory theatre in villages that are in the Roma Valley and close to the university.

The method MTT has found most effective is a modification of theatre for conscientization. As a methodology, this is really a higher level of participatory theatre. The main difference between the two is that in the former, the spectacle is produced by and for the people without spectators, since those who may initially be spectators later become actors. Improvisation happens throughout the life of the production, and the direction that the play takes is never preplanned. However, here, too, catalysts are necessary because the performers must acquire the essential skills to mount an effective production.

The Latin American theatre practitioner Augusto Boal has developed a methodology in which two main phases transform spectators into actors: "simultaneous dramaturgy" and "forum theatre." In simultaneous dramaturgy professional actors perform a short scene suggested by a local person, halt the action at the crisis point, and ask the audience to offer solutions. The actors become like puppets and perform the actions strictly on the spectators' orders. The "best" solution is arrived at by trial, error, discussion, and then audience consensus. Thus the action ceases to be deterministic; everything is subject to criticism and rectification. Anything can be changed by any spectator at a moment's notice without censorship. The actor does not cease his role as interpreter.

Forum theatre as a methodology refers to a case in which actors and spectators converge. The participants tell a story with some social problem and then improvise, rehearse, and present it to the rest of the group as a skit. The audience is asked if it agrees with the solution. Any spectator is invited to replace any actor and lead the action in the direction that seems most appropriate to him or her. He or she must not make speeches, but must act to evoke responses from the others on the "stage." This method goes much further than simultaneous dramaturgy, as the spectator loses his or her safe seat once the line of demarcation between actor and audience is destroyed.

Such theatre offers the means whereby all possible paths may be examined. Through these methods theatre becomes not only a medium of communication, but also a vehicle for social analysis. The emphasis is on self-education. Consciousness is raised from inside, a result of group analysis of social reality and power relations. When the spectators become actors the catalyst group is no longer necessary. It is at this stage that participation and control increase. The spectator has become a dramatic actor and then a social actor.[1]

MTT has modified this method. Because the company operates under the auspices of government and nongovernment agencies such as UNICEF (United Nations Children's Fund), Rural Sanitation Project of the Ministry of Health, and Expanded Program of Immunization, the themes with which it deals are those that promote the services of these agencies, and it becomes necessary for the company, as catalysts, to select the content of the play. Therefore, in this case the play does not begin with a short scene suggested by a local person; the company itself improvises and rehearses the scene.

Right from the beginning the audience is invited to participate, and Boal's two main stages are combined. The spectators are free to comment or come onto the stage and act. Throughout the play there is discussion and debate on the issues raised. In most cases audience discussion and the action of the play flow into each other, as the members of the audience tend to easily shuttle back and forth between the world of the play and the world of the community. In this way theatrical performance becomes a vehicle for discussion and social analysis. Post-performance discussion, as in the case of agitprop, becomes unnecessary; the spectators have reached a consensus on the various issues during the play.

REPRESENTATIVE PLAYS

All plays are improvised by the troupe; none is scripted. The plays are different at every performance, since audience participation plays a large role in determining not only the direction of the play, but also the dialogue. The following summaries will give an idea of what the plays are about.

Immunization

The play centers around Thabang, his wife, 'Mathato, and Thabang's mother, 'Mathabang. Thabang works in the mines in South Africa, and his wife and mother stay together in a village in Lesotho. The young couple had two children who died in infancy. The play is about the importance of immunization as protection against the illnesses that often cause infant mortality. The play starts when 'Mathabang and 'Mathato are in a court case. 'Mathabang is accusing 'Mathato of disrespect toward her. 'Mathato has been spreading gossip that 'Mathabang is a witch and is the cause of her grandchildren's deaths. During the court proceedings it is learned that the children were never taken to the clinic; traditional herbs were used whenever they were ill. 'Mathato is reprimanded by the village elders.

'Mathato becomes pregnant again. Friends advise her to make it a point to take the child to the clinic this time. In fact, she should start visiting the clinic during the pregnancy. She stubbornly rejects the advice, saying that she believes in the herbs her mother taught her to use. When the child is born she is again advised to go to the clinic. A physically handicapped man who contracted polio while an infant tries to persuade her to take the baby to the clinic so it will not suffer the same fate. A nurse from the clinic begs her to come, but in a haughty manner 'Mathato refuses.

After several more failed attempts to get 'Mathato to the clinic, during which the child becomes sick, the father takes the child himself. Injections are given and explained to the audience, and eventually the child recovers. Seeing this, the mother is convinced of the necessity for regular clinic visits and immunizations, and the family is reconciled.

Migrant Labor

The play revolves around the lives of two Basotho migrant laborers, Lebona and Motale, who work in the mines in South Africa. They are from the same village in a rural area of Lesotho and both are married and have children. Because their employer will not allow them to bring their families to the mine town, their wives and children must stay in the village. The husbands are allowed to visit their homes some weekends. Basically, the play is about the tribulations that migrant workers go through because of this situation. It attempts to encourage the men to get involved in integrated rural development programs when they return to their home villages.

Rural Sanitation

The play is centered around Sek'hoek'hoe, his wife, Manchoati, and their daughter, Nchoati. This family lives in a remote village in the mountains of Lesotho. The principal issue that the play addresses is sanitation: it encourages people who live in rural areas to construct toilets and develop hygienic habits so as to minimize the spread of germs and illness.

Using Folk Media

MTT has incorporated modes of folk media into some of its plays. The dominant form used is *lifela*, especially at the beginnings of plays. *Lifela* are folk poems recited in a half-singing, half-talking manner, almost like a Gregorian chant. They are popular in the rural areas, whose men and women are known throughout the country as champions of *lifela*. These people are able to create poems on the spur of the moment that comment on current events. Sometimes there is an impromptu dialogue between two *lifela* singers, both composing lines as they go along. Often *lifela* are satirical, and plays that have incorporated them have proved to be popular, since they are a recognizable medium. Spectators are able to join in, and because the *lifela* are recited at the beginnings of plays, they put the audience at ease immediately.

Folk songs are used in all plays, and audiences always join in with the singing. Another mode of folk media that is used effectively is *liphotha*, a dance form that is performed to the rhythm of singing and hand-clapping. The company has discovered that although folk songs and other modes of folk media such as *lifela* and *liphotha* are usually regarded as entertainment, they can also be effective as a communication medium in a country such as Lesotho, which has a strong oral tradition.

NOTE

1. See Pru Lambert, "Popular Theatre: One Road to Self-determined Action," *Community Development Journal* 17, no. 3 (1982): 244.

Zakes Mda

Malaysia

HISTORY

Theatre forms in Malaysia can be catetgorized as belonging to one of three main periods: traditional, transitional, or modern.[1] These periods are each distinct in their roots, content, styles, and purposes.[2] The oldest forms (traditional theatre) date from the nineteenth century or before, and although many are heavily indebted to Chinese and Indian traditional genres, they have been transformed into distinct Malaysian forms, which do not distinguish between children's theatre and adult theatre. Dance, drama, music, song, and design, presented as an integrated whole ("total theatre"[3]), usually comprise a sufficiently exciting medium for adults as well as for children.

The plays depict legends imbued with moral tones, and as the audiences are all familiar with the characters and basic story lines, written scripts and scenic exposition are not needed. Actors improvise from standard materials, using open-air performing spaces with minimal or no stage sets. The acting is highly stylized and presentational, usually requiring great skill because the major emphasis in traditional theatre is on the perfection of performance technique. Training, therefore, is rigid and disciplined, and begins when a child actor is very young. Skills are transmitted through a master-apprentice relationship from generation to generation, and the child is constantly involved in acquiring and refining these skills. Children are not given much opportunity to perform until they are older and closer to mastery of their art. However, in some forms the more promising younger artists are permitted to play in introductory scenes before the entrance of the experienced players, or to play secondary or background roles.

Adolescents, often the children of troupe members, were also taken on as performer-apprentices of *bangsawan*, the principal transitional theatre form. *Bangsawan* emerged and flourished in the 1930s during the period of British colonial rule, when increased urbanization and Westernization created a mass audience for professional commercial theatre. It is an outgrowth of *tiruian wayang parsi* (Imitation Parsee Theatre), itself a Malay adaptation of a semi-operatic genre, *wayang parsi*, introduced from India in the late 1800s. Like traditional plays, those of the transitional forms were improvised from a plot line or scenario, incorporating legends and popular tales from classic Indian, Arabic, and Malay literature. Later Chinese and even Western materials were incorporated, extending the repertory and increasing the form's appeal to Malaysia's multiethnic population.

Besides borrowing Western content and thematic elements, "it was the first type of Malay theatre to be closed and to have a proscenium stage" (modeled after the British-style "picture frame" theatre[4]) and to make use of scenic illusion. It has been called a transitional form because it bridges the gap between traditional and modern theatre and contains elements from both.[5] Child audiences were particularly attracted to *bangsawan* performances. They had spectacular scenic designs, glamorous costumes that were colorful and ornately sequined, special effects and a strong fantasy element, famous stock characters, comedy song, and dance routines between scenes, and stylized speech and movement that bordered on the melodramatic—all of which are irresistible to children.

Modern theatre can be said to have begun in the 1930s. With British colonization came the British educational system, with its practice of establishing dramatic associations in the schools. The plays performed were generally English, especially Shakespeare, in imitation of the approved repertory of such associations in England. This practice left little room for the manifestation of indigenous creativity. Even today many English-language school productions are of English plays, the only change being that from attempts at Shakespeare to attempts at Western musicals and Western fairy tales or legends. In the late 1930s the Malay Teachers Training College, which had theatre as part of its training syllabus, experimented with the injection of local images into school performances. Between 1929 and 1930 a Malay scholar named Za'aba had Charles and Mary Lamb's *Tales from Shakespeare* translated and published, making Shakespeare's characters and stories accessible to the teacher trainees, and permitted their adaptation into *bangsawan* performance, which, with its declamatory, presentational style, lent itself well to this process.

The stirring of Malay nationalism in the 1940s inspired a burgeoning of a nationalistic drama with a distinctly local content, including the first original children's play, *Macam Mana Kassim Di Ubatkan (How Kassim Was Cured)*, a didactic piece that teaches the effectiveness of modern medicine.[6] When several such plays were successfully produced in local high schools, activist playwrights saw an opportunity to parallel and counteract the influence of the British plays performed in the British-style schools. To this end, some of the new plays written for local schools featured general themes from the Shakespearean canon, with Shakespeare's heroes replaced by local heroes from the *Malay Annals*.

The first truly modern theatre form, *sandiwara*, achieved its popularity in the 1950s, with the high tide of Malay nationalism. In many ways it was a reaction against *bangsawan*, although it adapted some of the conventions of *bangsawan* and traditional theatre. Like the earlier forms, *sandiwara* was didactic, used symbolic characters or stereotypes, and dramatized Malay history and legend. However, it was much more realistic in style, and its plays also drew material from contemporary society. After independence in 1956 a group of writers emerged who chose to write in Malay. These playwrights wrote for both adult and child audiences, and some of their plays could be categorized as children's versions of *drama moden* (modern drama), a highly realistic genre greatly influenced by Western and Indonesian playwrights who became active in the 1960s.

The plays were compiled into two volumes for staging by secondary schools. One was an anthology written by Mustapha Kamil Yassin titled *Lakuan Ria* (*Happy Performance*) and the other, a collection by various playwrights titled *Mari Berlakun (Come and Perform)*. These dramas "exposed a dynamic interplay of traditional and modern values. The ritualistic plots and characters envisioned children playing roles and espousing values they would soon adopt as adults."[7] It is very likely that the *bangsawan* style of performance dominated these plays.

Through the 1960s this local modern theatre was confined to teacher-training colleges and Malay-language schools. The colonial educational policy continued: theatre was only an extracurricular activity, and an unimportant one at that. Despite independence, the potential for theatre to promote social change and the continued growth of a vital, indigenous culture remained largely unexplored and unexploited throughout the decade. Soon after the traumatic racial riots in May 1969 that gripped much of urban peninsular Malaysia, a number of Malaysian poets, artists, playwrights, and theatre people began to review their past in an attempt to comprehend their confusing present. This investigation, they hoped, would help them discover how they might infuse a local and directly communicable identity into their work.[8]

Noordin Hassan, a playwright and director, has often been viewed as one of the pioneers in this search for a new direction. He brought elements of traditional theatre's performance style (e.g., call-response poetry, chorus, music, *bangsawan*-type comedy, and mime) into modern plays and thus developed a "new aesthetic": a theatre with a Malaysian identity that was to affect the whole theatre scene, including children's theatre.

A number of committed educator-practitioners contributed to the 1970s revolt against the paternalistic, British-influenced theatre in the schools. They thought that the content of foreign plays was too alien, and the style too formal. This creative leadership also turned away from realistic theatre and from the concept of children as "mini-adults," a development that finally allowed children to be themselves and to play themselves. The door was thus opened to a more imaginative and relevant theatre for children. All these creative rebels had had some exposure to children's theatre in the United States, experience in adult theatre, and institutional backing, and they had shared a goal: the forging of a theatre with a Malaysian identity.

Mustapha Kamil Yassin, formerly a lecturer at a teacher-training college, expanded his interest in children's theatre while earning a master's degree at Indiana State University. He wrote his thesis on "A Proposal for the Future of Children's Theatre in Malaysia" and put his theories to work when teaching a children's theatre course at a local university. His student production toured the northern states and was well received.

Vijaya Samarawickrama, a university lecturer who also took a master's in children's theatre (at the University of Hawaii), was inspired to infuse children's plays with markedly local imagery. His students were encouraged to research local legends, myths, tales, songs, verse, and fantasy and to write original scripts based on these materials. Three published works resulted from these efforts. One, titled *Dewi Bunga* (*Flower Goddess*), was produced and televised nationally in 1974. Another, *Azad Dan Gergasi* (*Azad and the Giant*), was given an extremely successful production by university students in the mid–1970s, in the "participation-play" style.

In 1974 Patrick Yeoh, a teacher now turned journalist, published *Plays for Malaysian Schools* in both English and Malay. He advocated the use of characters and situations from the immediate environment. The same year a visiting lecturer from America, Lois Long, wrote the first participation play to be produced in Malaysia, also with localized references, music, and verse. This play, *The Magic Bag*, was originally played in English by university students. In 1978 it was restaged in Malay by Elizabeth Cardosa, and toured to selected rural schools as the first of a number of productions by the Children's Theatre Program of the Komplex Budaya Negara (National Cultural Complex), hereafter referred to as KBN.

Cardosa, who held a performing arts degree from a local university, was well acquainted with Malaysian as well as Western theatre. In the KBN program, which involved volunteer schoolchildren aged seven to fifteen, she introduced creative dramatics approaches, extending the children's training into areas of design, puppetry, music, and related arts. She was also responsible for the design and implementation of an outline of program objectives.

Zainal Latif, formerly lecturer in children's theatre at the University Sains Penang, helped to revive *silat* (Malay martial arts) in the theatre. *Silat* had characteristically been featured in *bangsawan* but had disappeared in the *drama moden* period. Latif adapted it for use in story theatre in the local *Cerita Cerita Sang Kancil* (*Mousedeer Tales*), which toured the rural areas in the northern states.

Most of these contemporary children's theatre performances returned to traditional staging methods—in the round, often in open spaces and at ground level, permitting physical proximity between audience and actors. The participation element was reminiscent of traditional comic characters, who disregarded stage boundaries and often intruded into the spectator space. This return to traditional methods was reinforced by the abandoning of sets, with actors resorting to mime to set the scene. Traditional forms such as *wayang kulit* (shadow puppet theatre) and *silat*, and various conventions from other traditional genres, found their way back onto the contemporary stage in these experimental children's shows.

In 1979 Janet Pillai filled the position of children's theatre instructor at KBN after Cardosa left the program to pursue a master's in the field. There was no established structure or formal curriculum, and the program's stability depended on the determination, stamina, and experience of the leaders and participants. The program was located at KBN, which houses performers and instructors in traditional dance, music, and song, as well as contemporary visual artists. This factor, together with the varied theatre backgrounds of the leaders, inspired a multimedia approach to teaching and performance. Sharing a space with traditional artists, constantly being exposed to their activities, and interacting with them had a definite influence on the creative directions taken by the children.

The main emphases of the classes were creative dramatics and the skills of acting, dance, music, and martial arts. Aspects of production were woven in with the other studies. The children were expected to research the areas they chose as their specialties. They were also given the opportunity to switch character roles in response to newly gathered materials or newly acquired skills. Often whole scenes were reevaluated and revised between performances in response to audience reactions. Spontaneity was cherished and encouraged at all times.

The success of the KBN Children's Theatre Program motivated the Ministry of Culture to set up two workshops in 1981 and 1982 that acquainted participants with the methodologies used by the KBN program and by the University Sains Penang children's theatre group. As an offshoot of these workshops two Councils for Schools' Theatre were established outside the school system, involving teachers and children's theatre workers. But before these developments, theatre-oriented schoolteachers had already begun agitating for more effective children's theatre in their communities. In 1980 the northern state of Kedah organized a children's theatre workshop, and an adult theatre group on the east coast organized a 1981 seminar on the "Role of Drama in School Curriculum." The organizers of these efforts also produced children's plays. The national museum in Kuala Lumpur sponsored a program led by artist Elsa Noor and others that combined visual art, puppetry, and creative dramatics. Meanwhile Noor worked with other adults to create a private puppet theatre for children.

Subsequently two free-lance artists, Thangarajoo and Yusof, specialists in puppetry and mask-making, set up similar classes in children's public libraries and privately built a joint puppet theatre troupe under the sponsorship of Dewan Bahasa dan Pustaka (Language and Literary Agency). Clearly the dissent against the state of theatre in the schools was led by people in theatre and other institutions who were free of the pressures of bureaucratic tradition. These individuals fostered new ideas and provided the grounds for experiment, while educational planners continued to show little concern. Although some of these experiments have been short-lived, "the best of them have measured their successes and failures against their self-imposed yardstick of constant regeneration in the context of making a communicable Malaysian theatre."[9]

Perhaps the most significant outcome of the KBN experimental program was not specifically intended: the synthesis in performance of traditional theatre techniques and concepts—and a communicable, local content—with the creative processes of contemporary Malaysian children's theatre, borrowed and adapted from its Western counterpart. As mentioned above, traditional theatre has always been highly popular with child audiences, and the enthusiastic reception given to the KBN productions results largely from the inclusion of traditional performance elements. The mixture of dance, song, story, music, and colorful design elements; the discursive, episodic dramatic structure; the alternation of comic, farcical, melodramatic, and genuinely serious elements; the recurrence of plots with which the children are already familiar, and of strongly stereotyped characters who are used in predictable patterns; stylized speech and gestures; improvisation and consequent spontaneity; simplicity of staging and the use of mime instead of elaborate sets[10]: taken together, these characteristics of traditional theatre create a total theatre that proves to be an exciting and appealing medium for children. The characteristics at once allow for simplicity in characterization and in the unfolding of plot, suitable for younger children, and for a depth and complexity of ideas or themes that can be portrayed symbolically, giving performances relevance for older children.

However, the adaptation of these characteristics was modified by modern practices as well. The traditional transmission of performance patterns from master to apprentice was retained in the children's active interaction with KBN's performing artists, but the students were amateur theatre practitioners, not apprentice professionals (the children being part-time volunteers). An improvisational process was extensively used, as in traditional theatre, but guided by quite a different set of rules derived from Western creative dramatics. Many children's theatre leaders perceived in creative drama a valid substitute for the holistic socialization role that traditional theatre had provided children before modernization, with its resulting emphasis on specialization. Some aspects of the program, however, were strictly modern. For instance, the instructor would often assume the role of a modern-style director who oversees all aspects of production, a practice alien to the performer-centered, improvisatory traditional forms.

THE CURRENT SITUATION

Theatre in Malaysia is fast losing ground to electronic media and film. It is not change itself that is to be feared, but the creation of a cultural vacuum; the technology and content of these imported "alternatives" have little association to existing indigenous values, concepts, or folkways. Yet the urban populations bend over backwards to transform themselves in accordance with the new patterns. The chasm between traditional and contemporary fashions thereby becomes so great as to render traditional practices and art forms untenable, to be discarded as "ancient," "uncivilized," and "slow." This situation is viewed with great anxiety by Malaysian theatre people, who envision a cultural catastrophe.

Of course, a dynamic culture cannot do without departure and change, and culture must inevitably adapt to a changing human environment. What is urgent and crucial is to disallow a further widening of the gap between old and new while accepting the transition. The use of traditional theatre forms and elements, and the acquisition of traditional theatre skills, provides participants and spectators with a critical connection to what is fundamental in the indigenous philosophies and cultural values that are their birthright and perhaps their only true "treasure." Contemporary children's theatre in Malaysia, then, helps to maintain as living entities "the foundations and familiar forms which provide an association to existing symbols and actions."[11] It has made considerable strides toward the creation of a more meaningful and communicable theatre, one that helps to ground Malaysians more firmly in their unique and irreplaceable world.

BIBLIOGRAPHY

Brandon, James R. *Theatre in Southeast Asia*. Cambridge, Mass.: Harvard University Press, 1967.

Camoens, Cantius Leo. "History and Development of Malay Theatre." Thesis. University of Malaya, 1981.

Jit, Krishen. "Contemporary Children's Theatre in Malaysia." Theatre Studies, 1983.

Langner, Susanne K. *Philosophical Sketches*. Princeton, N.J.: Princeton University Press, 1948.

Nanney, Nancy K. "An Analysis of Modern Malaysian Drama." Ph.D. diss. University of Hawaii, 1983.

Pronko, Leonard C. *Theatre East and West: Perspectives Toward a Total Theatre*. Berkeley: University of California Press, 1974.

Yassin, Mustapha Kamil. "The Malay Bangsawan." In *Traditional Drama and Music of Southeast Asia*. Papers presented at the International Conference on Traditional Drama and Music of Southeast Asia, Kuala Lumpur, August 27–30, 1969. Edited by Mohd. Taib Osman. Kuala Lumpur: Dewan Bahasa dan Pustaka, 1974, 143–153.

NOTES

1. Factual information in this entry has been drawn from an article by Krishen Jit titled "Contemporary Children's Theatre in Malaysia," 1983. This article has been reproduced from an article published in the *Children's Theatre Review*, 1984, titled "Children's Theatre in Malaysia."

2. Nancy K. Nanney, "An Analysis of Modern Malaysian Drama." Ph.D. diss., University of Hawaii, 1983, 8.

3. Leonard C. Pronko, *Theatre East and West: Perspectives Toward a Total Theatre* (Berkeley: University of California Press, 1967), 182.

4. Mustapha Kamil Yassin, "The Malay Bangsawan," in *Traditional Drama and*

Music of Southeast Asia, ed. Mohd. Taib Osman (Kuala Lumpur: Dewan Bahasa dan Pustaka, 1974), 143–153.

5. Cantius Leo Camoens, "History and Development of Malay Theatre." Thesis, University of Malaya, 1981, 147.

6. Krishen Jit, "Contemporary Children's Theatre in Malaysia," p. 5.

7. Ibid., 6.

8. Ibid., 13.

9. Ibid., 28.

10. James R. Brandon, *Theatre in Southeast Asia* (Cambridge, Mass.: Harvard University Press, 1967), 115; also, Yassin, "Malay Bangsawan," 146.

11. Susanne K. Langner, *Philosophical Sketches* (Princeton, N.J.: Princeton University Press, 1948), 4.

Janet Pillai

Mexico

HISTORY

Theatre for children and young people in Mexico today is not what it was at the beginning of the century, when there were only popular puppet shows in which children took part as members of the audience. The most important puppet group, which dates back to 1835, was Rosete Aranda Brother's Company, composed of puppets, an orchestra, and choreographers.

The Twenties and Thirties

The major theatrical activities of the twenties and thirties were simple entertainments with puppets and patriotic and religious festivals. The Guiñol Theatre was created during the cultural movement of the thirties called "Cultural Missions," a popular educational campaign for health and literacy. Later on the Department of Extracurricular and Aesthetic Education increased the activity of the Guiñol Theatre by fostering the employment of dramaturgs, painters, and puppet players. Among the first artists were German Lizt Arzubide, Ramón and Lolo Alva de la Canal, Lola and Mireya Cueto, Roberto Lago, José M. Díaz, and Lucrecia González Valiente. These artists brought the Guiñol Theatre to various schools and districts in Mexico City as well as throughout the entire country. Rosario Castellanos and Marco Antonio Montero, participating in the educational campaigns, brought shows to remote native areas.

The Forties and Fifties

In the forties and fifties the National Institute of Fine Arts and the department that preceded it organized a theatrical movement directed toward children that was staged at the Palace of Fine Arts. The plays were adapted from classic

European literature and stories of Mexican authors. The artists involved in these presentations were Clementine Otero, Fernando Wagner, and Concepción Sada. The authors and adapters were Otero, Ermilo Abreu Gómez, Emilio Carballido, Sergio Magaña, Magda Donato, Salvador Bartolozzi, Salvador Novo, Wagner, and Sada. Choreographers included Julio Castellanos, Julio Prieto, and Antonio López Mancera, and the actors were students from the School of Theatrical Arts. The plays included *La Reina de las Nieves* (*The Snow Queen*), *Pinocchio y el Dragón* (*Pinocchio and the Dragon*), *Pinocchio en el País de los Cuentos* (*Pinocchio in the Land of Stories*), *Cucuruchito y sus aventuras Fantásticas* (*Cucuruchito and His Fantastic Adventures*), *El Pajaro Azul* (*The Blue Bird*), *Sueño de una Noche de Verano* (*A Midsummer Night's Dream*), *Don Pirrimplin en la Luna* (*Don Pirrimplin on the Moon*), *El Coronel Astucia* (*The Cunning Colonel*), *El Viaje de Nocresida* (*Nocresida's Trip*), *Marujilla*, and *Don Quijote*.

The Sixties

In the sixties there was a change in the management and organization of theatres. The population throughout the country had multiplied, but especially in the capital city, where scientific and technological advances had changed lifestyles to a greater degree than witnessed before. Mass communication was in evidence everywhere. Other factors also affected the theatre: the political movement of 1968, the rise in the cost of gasoline, and the immigration from other cities to Mexico City.

The Mexican theatre, in general, and children's theatre, in particular, are stimulated by new ideas and the need to bring theatre to children, young people, and all those who almost never have the opportunity to go to the theatre. During this same decade the National Institute of Fine Arts and its Department of Theatre, under Héctor Azar's direction, created the Center of Children's Theatre, where lectures, courses, expositions, and workshops are given. The Department of Popular Theatre works with "street theatre," which is performed in plazas, squares, gardens, churches, courtyards, and esplanades. The Department of Theatre in Schools organizes theatrical shows at the National Fine Arts Institute theatres and at the Palace of Fine Arts for different age groups: nursery, primary, and high school. The Institute of Social Security, on the other hand, supports theatrical activities for children in its Social Security Centers in Mexico City and in some states of the Mexican republic. Independent groups are also beginning to emerge.

The Seventies

A rise in theatre activities was seen in the seventies. During this decade the independent groups increased their work for children and young people and the marginal public. They founded a movement called CLETA, which originated from the university protests and continues today through organizations such as

Zumbón, Matlatzincas, Zopilote, and Cero. These are collective groups that live and work for the theatre. Their lifestyles and creations are independent, and they present stage plays of Mexican authors and original collective pieces. Their productions are simple and easily adapted to every kind of space that can be put to theatrical use.

Some new playwrights have emerged who write exclusively for children, and known authors, like Emilio Carballido, occasionally write for children. The National Institute of Fine Arts increased its theatrical activity directed toward schools. Theatre not only was presented in playhouses, but also went into schools in a program called "Theatre Goes to the Schools," inspired by José Solé and directed by Xochital Medina. The actors play in patios, corridors, or classrooms, and extracurricular activities were promoted with seminars for teachers and students. Independent groups such as Matlatzincas and Circo, Maroma y Teatro (Circus, Tightrope and Theatre) engaged in similar programs.

During the seventies the Mexican government disseminated, through various institutions, cultural activities, especially those in theatre. The Secretary of Public Education, the Secretary of Communication and Transportation, the National Commission of Public Supplies, the Electricians' Union, the National Institute for Child Protection, the National Institute of Native People, and the Office of Popular Culture all promoted and subsidized popular theatres, which served audiences ranging from young children to senior citizens. They formed brigades and groups that appeared in all types of spaces, including the streets where lines of people wait to buy food, auditoriums, union theatres, and schools. On a somewhat smaller scale these programs were presented in other cities of the republic, such as Monterrey, Jalapa, Guadalajara, and Puebla.

The Eighties

The eighties brought economic crisis. Today it is difficult for established theatres to produce shows because of high costs: rent for the theatre, payment of taxes, and salaries, among other expenses. This condition is felt everywhere but especially in children's theatre, which has always been ignored by the adult theatre and is considered by others to be a minor art. Nevertheless, the independent groups fight for survival, and the specialists who have been organized through the years still safeguard and publicize their aims. Despite the difficulties during this decade, the public demands high artistic quality from a theatre that cannot provide the expensive productions of the past.

Even though the current age has been called the "austerity decade," some benefits can be recognized that bring improvements through the interest of young playwrights who write for young audiences, such as Alejandro Licona, Jesus Gonzalez Davila, Wilebaldo Lopez, Leticia Tellez, Reynaldo Carballido, Jose Lopez Arellano, Sabina Berman, Teresa Valenzuela, Miguel Angel Tenorio, Martha Sastria de Porcel, Claudio Patricio, and Guillermo Hagg. Their plays are published in specialized magazines such as *Escenica* and *Repertoir* or by

Mexican United Publishers, which has made an important contribution by specializing in children's and young people's theatre.

Assistance for publicizing productions and for conducting research comes through a variety of official institutions, such as the National Institute of Fine Arts, the Secretary of Public Education, the Institute of Security and Social Services to Workers in the Service of the State, and the National Institute of Social Security. Without their assistance, companies could no longer exist. The touring theatres now reach more people in rural communities and cities who have never seen theatre. One such program, directed by Socorro Merlin, is geared toward handicapped children with learning disabilities who require special attention; this group also travels to the farthest parts of the country and plays before farmers and native citizens.

Theatrical programs are reinforced with other activities, such as courses, workshops, and conferences, and with national and international exchanges and competitions like those promoted by the National Fine Arts Institute with young people from high schools and political delegations. In the last competition more than seventy groups were enrolled as a consequence of this theatre program. Theatre people are not alone: they have projects and plans of action; they meet and support one another through nongovernmental associations such as ITI, ASSITEJ, UNIMA, and AITA to form long-term objectives that could not be established without a community spirit among theatre enthusiasts. These associations face difficulties, since they receive little economic support, but they are important for the consolidation and dissemination of theatrical ideas and methods of exchange and are of great help to Mexican theatre artists.

The sociopolitical and economic conditions in the recent years, contrary to what might be expected, have contributed to a better theatre for children and young people in a way that responds to the country's current needs. It confronts mass communication yet maintains its position as an inherent expression of humanity, as a means of communication and catharsis, in order to continue giving children and youth pleasure within a sound pedagogical context and preparing them to be conscious of their role in society.

Socorro Merlin
Translated by Elisa de la Roche

The Netherlands

HISTORY

Children's theatre is a paradox; although created for children, it is produced and played by adults. It becomes, therefore, a reflection of the elements that move and influence those adults. This dichotomy is clearly visible in the history of children's theatre in Holland.

1920–1945

If we consider children's theatre to be created by professional producers for an audience of four-to-eighteen-year-olds, then its history starts between World Wars I and II. Before this, children's theatre was performed *by children* in many ways but especially by political and religious organizations. The Catholic mystery plays also offer a prime example: large productions given in stadiums in which thousands of girls took part in mass spectacles written around religious subjects.

Ida Last, a woman from Amsterdam, produced plays in the 1930s inspired by Communist ideology with casts consisting of children; one such piece was *De Vrolijke Brigade (The Merry Brigade)*. She considered theatre a means of education, and the youngsters not only acted, but also participated in the management of her organization. Because Last met a great deal of trouble from the authorities, her new plays were read by officials before she was allowed to produce them. The increasing threat of war finally forced her to stop her activities, although comparable organizations with conservative or nationalist-socialist perspectives continued to operate without problems.

During this period professional adult companies also included children's plays in their repertories. Although they were interested in young audiences, they were more motivated by the income brought into their box offices. By performing for children, companies were able to fill houses, especially during the traditionally slow summer months. Their repertories were based on fairy tales, adaptations of popular children's literature, and comics from the children's pages of the newspapers.

Het Vereenigd Toneel (The United Stage) staged *Joop Terheul* in 1924/25, a play adapted from a popular girls' book. Het Hofstadensemble performed *Boefje* in 1923 and *Bruintje de Beer en Wim de Das* in the early thirties, both drawn from children's literature. These companies also perform for adult audiences. The company called Jeugdamusement (Children's Entertainment) was the first to specialize in theatre for young people with their 1928 production of *Pietje Bell*. General opinion held that although acting skills were not of high quality, this really didn't matter in children's theatre. For this reason, many second- and third-rate performers were contracted to play for younger audiences. It wasn't until 1936 that a top-level professional company was formed, Het Nederlands Theatre voor kinderen (The Dutch Theatre Company for Children). Their first play was *Fatsrevot*, and in 1937 they staged *Mijnheer Prikkebeen*. This period of development came to an end with the start of World War II; the entire field was at a virtual standstill until 1945.

1945–1968

Dancer Hans Snoek was requested, by the authorities, to "do something with children" for the liberation celebrations. As a result of this request, she started the dance company Scapinoballet. Scapino, the rogue of *commedia dell'arte*, acts as an intermediary between the young audience and the performing dancers. The mime company Carrousel also was founded at this time. Both companies are still in existence today, even though in the early days the actors and dancers had to moonlight as teachers and in the adult theatre in order to make enough money to continue performing for younger audiences.

In 1946 Het Limburgs Jeugdtoneel was founded and continued the prewar repertory of fairy tales, which they still perform. Ida Last also started a new company with children, Circus Elleboog, a children's circus, which still exists. In 1950 De Raad voor de Kunst (The Arts Council) made the first official statement about the field: "Children's theatre is there to familiarize young people with the classic and modern repertory, without lapsing into duplication of the repertory theatres." Puck was the first subsidized children's theatre company because it met the stringent demands of the Arts Council. The group's priority in its productions was the aesthetic education of its audience; after that it strove to achieve high quality. Most of the plays performed were written by Cas Baas and Mies Bouhuys. Even though Puck played as many as four performances a day, it still had to perform adult theatre in the evening to make ends meet. This schedule proved too taxing, and in 1957 the company ceased its children's performances.

In 1954 Stichting Nieuw Jeugdtoneel (New Children's Theatre) began operations. Their first director, Cruys Voorbergh (who was succeeded by Erik Vos), is now a successful director in adult theatre. In 1957 the group changed its name to Arena and jumped into the void left by Puck. Performances were based not only on scripts, but also on improvisation. Important writers for the group included Aad Greidanus, Jan Staal, and Mies Bouhuys. Like Puck, Arena ultimately had to cease its children's programs, which it did in 1970, and now performs exclusively for adult audiences.

In addition to serious financial difficulties, the children's companies of this period faced another significant problem: lack of facilities. All existing groups had to deal with a dearth of adequate accommodations, and it seemed that children's theatre was destined to be played in small, badly equipped theatres.

1968–1981

The basis for today's children's theatre was actually formed in this period. Many social and political changes took place, which included the student revolts in Paris, Amsterdam, and Berkeley. For theatre, too, this was a turbulent time. Nineteen hundred sixty-nine was the year of the so-called Aktie Tomaat (Action-tomato), wherein young directors, actors, and playwrights literally chased the establishment theatre out of the playhouses by heaving loads of tomatoes at the stage during performances. Their complaints included charges that traditional theatre was old-fashioned, turgid, and rigid, that acting was generally atrocious, and that no one had made provisions to "build a young and new audience."

In theatre schools and on stages the position of theatre in society was discussed. The activists wanted the producers to be aware of the potential of the stage as a forum, not simply a place for entertainment. They wanted theatre to be given room and an opportunity to develop along progressive lines, since they believed no public institution could be totally disconnected from the social and political ideas that supported it. They wanted to see plays that spoke to such issues as people's changing roles, emancipation for both men and women, and equal rights. Out of such discussions, consciousness-raising theatre was created. Before 1969 many companies' performances revolved around the idea of creative education for children. One example was Proloog, which always invited audience members to participate. This style of performance sounds more liberal than it actually was, for often the children, forced to go in a certain direction, did not like these productions.

As a consequence of the social and political changes in the country, the views and objectives of children's theatre changed. Creativity for its own sake was abandoned, and theatre now had to provide children with a perception of the fighting spirit necessary to withstand a society that was becoming hardened and highly computerized. GRIPS, a company from Berlin, was the seminal influence in this movement and an excellent example for Dutch producers. Proloog adapted GRIPS plays; Wederzijds followed their methods of production; and STAUT, a company that originated from the University Theatre in Amsterdam, took up the practice of traveling into the children's neighborhoods to present their works.

These companies all worked directly with children, creating theatre in a new, anti-authoritarian manner. They then took the subtle step of becoming social-critical theatres, with the actors functioning more as instructors. STAUT was one of the few companies that carefully and extensively documented its methods and reported them at large.

Other groups operating during this period were Het Vestzaktheater (1963–1987), Pssstt (1965), and Theater Wim Zomer (1968). Because they mainly performed in schools, they reduced costumes, stage sets, and props to a bare minimum. The child actor remained an important part of children's theatre at this time. This form of theatre continued until 1976, when it was abandoned because it didn't adhere to prevailing notions of the purpose of theatre for children and young people; too often children were manipulated, a practice that now ran counter to the stated ideological objectives. Moreover, many believed that it was easier to present the youngsters with sociopolitical messages when they were sitting quietly in the audience. Companies such as Proloog, Genesius, Stiktog, and Maccus worked in this manner, while Tejater Teneeter operated according to the "Boal method" (as developed by Augusto Boal and expressed in his *Theatre of the Oppressed*), in which the actors presented a play first and then the work was redone with children in some of the roles. In this way the audience could still directly affect the outcome of the play.

The themes of these works had no special appeal or relevance for the young audiences, and the political message, like as not, was well over their heads. What can children do with or about the struggle of the working class or the concept of social equality? It was not until the end of the seventies that producers and directors began to gear the subject matter of the plays toward the audience. Even then, the topics were still socially determined: divorce, role patterns, paternalism, and aggression.

Another hallmark of the period from 1968 to 1981 was the collective method of working. The whole process of mounting a production was a group effort in which every member had to be active. So, actors worked in public relations and accounting; administrators took part in training programs and in discussions about artistic concerns and policies; and performances were based on the personal experiences of the members of the group. Not surprisingly, the period did not produce any noted playwrights or directors. It was not until later, when the need for specialization was felt, that the most talented (or most ambitious) actors directed performances. Because this group method of creating theatre is an exhausting procedure, it soon began to affect the working relationship in the companies and the health of individual members. By the beginning of the eighties most companies had to employ outside professionals to perform certain jobs.

Another characteristic of the period was that theatre was used as a method to reach a social or political objective; it was not an objective in itself. This caused much controversy and conflict, and in many cases led companies to disband. Inferior artistic quality also remained rampant. Most actors had little professional training; they were drama teachers or students from teacher-training colleges.

As a general rule, the quality of the performances was inversely proportional to the enthusiasm and idealism of the company members. Within all this chaos there were still companies that worked according to traditional ideas: they simply staged entertainment. In 1978, at the Children's Theatre Festival, the various factions were all represented, but they would not listen to one another's ideas or attend one another's performances.

1981 to Present

The eighties have seen tremendous growth in the number of children's companies, from about 50 at the end of the seventies to 225 in 1987, an enormous achievement, given that Holland has a population of approximately 14 million persons and a surface area of only 41,000 square kilometers. The groups all consider themselves professional, although there is great variation in style, discipline, and quality. All genres of theatre are represented: standard drama, puppet theatre, mime, dance, and music.

Puppet theatre, which boasts a long history in Holland, has undergone some fascinating developments since the early eighties and is now moving steadily away from the traditional puppet stage and toward a style in which both the puppets and the puppeteers are visible performers. Poppentheater de Poppenkeet, Het Speeltheater, and, until recently, Jozef van de Berg are striking examples of this shift. Dance, mime, and music still follow traditional paths, and have undergone less upheaval than either the puppet or the dramatic companies. In dance and movement, especially, there is a strict separation between educational and theatrical performances, the former geared toward demonstrating characterization and fostering an understanding of the discipline. These presentations are often related to school activities.

TRENDS

In the "standard drama" companies the sharp contrasts between social/political and entertainment-oriented groups have largely disappeared. Producers finally discovered that no matter how socially relevant a topic was, it still had to be presented by a company of talented artists who adhered to a minimum level of quality in order to capture and keep the attention of a child audience. The distinctions between companies now are based on the kind of repertory they tend to produce. The major trends are as follows:

• *Working on the basis of a script, either specially written or translated for the production.* During the first years after the demise of the "collective method" of production few scripts were available. Even scripts from abroad were not collected or kept in an archive. This need led to the founding of the Children's Theatre Library in 1983, in which scripts from all over the world, especially from Germany and Scandinavia, are housed and made available to companies.

- *Working on the basis of classic (world) repertory.* Theatre Pssstt has presented this kind of play selection since its founding in 1965. Director and writer Herman Frank chose fairy tales and plays from Shakespeare *(King Lear)* and Beckett *(Waiting for Godot)* as the company's first productions. Studio Peer, directed by Fred Delfgaauw, produces works such as *Peer Gynt, The Tempest*, and *Macbeth.* In addition to being a good adaptor, Delfgaauw is a gifted puppeteer, which greatly adds to the visual elements of his productions.

- *Working on the basis of existing children's literature.* Adaptation of popular literature was especially prevalent directly after the collectivist period. It was soon discovered that a good book does not always make a good play! Some successful adaptations included those based on *Karel en de kindermoordenaars* (Peter Pan Produkties, 1987), *Kleine Sophie en de lange Wapper* (Stix, 1985), and *Het bange dierenbos* (Het Amstel Toneel, 1985).

- *Working on the basis of improvisations drawn from experiences of the actors or children.* Productions include *Onder de voeten kietelen*, by the group Spektakel, which explores the surroundings of young children, and Peter Pan Produkties' *Witland* (1986) and Burrp!'s *Da tafel van vier*, both about children's playing.

- *Experimental productions.* These search for new forms and new directions. Companies working in this manner include Weedrzijds, directed by Ad de Bont and Alan Zipson, with designers Cees Landsaat and Rene de Sonneville and composer Guus Ponsioen. This same production team formerly worked with Het Vervolg, creating striking productions that caused some controversy. Sometimes their works are shocking, but they are also praised for their artistic vision and the example they set for other children's theatres both in Holland and abroad.

- *Productions based on design.* Visual aspects are the hallmarks of these presentations. An example is Frans Malschaert's Theatre Sirkel. He was originally a painter and a sculptor, which clearly shows in his work, especially *Vuurrood* and *Blok.* Both plays incorporate sets in which structures are built onstage during the performance. In 1985 *Vuurroos* won the Hans Snoek award, given yearly for the best children's theatre production.

Based on the above categories, it should be obvious that a play's theme or central topic is no longer the most significant factor: design, quality of acting, and a good script have all become essential. Although these changes have resulted in better theatre for young audiences, they have also had one negative effect. Groups now tend to handle subjects in too mature a manner or work them out in ways that do not match the children's perceptions. Sometimes the companies forget that productions should appeal to the youngsters in language, visual style, and subject matter, and that all three are important. This problem notwithstanding, the people working in the field of children's theatre today are daring in their willingness to tackle new forms and to experiment, qualities that are not present in the adult theatre.

THE CURRENT SITUATION

In contrast with other countries, theatre companies in Holland are not connected with particular theatre buildings. Even in adult theatre only four or five companies have their own playhouses. Most groups do have some kind of combination rehearsal/office space, but the economies of others do not allow even this level of expenditure, and they must rent rehearsal space and do their administrative work out of a member's home. Only two theatres present plays exclusively for children: De Krakeling (1978) in Amsterdam and Jeugdtheater Hofplein (1985) in Rotterdam. Both contract with professional companies that perform for the general public on Wednesday, Saturday, and Sunday afternoons: during the week they sell out to school audiences. In addition, both theatres work directly with children by offering drama courses and productions put together by young people under professional supervision. Depending on their financial means, companies either employ an independent manager or are administered by a management agency. In the case of very small or destitute groups business affairs are handled by the actors; this causes problems, in that it is hard for performers to be on stage and arrange bookings at the same time.

There are three levels in the Dutch subsidy system:

1. *The state.* The Ministry of Culture grants two kinds of financial help. The first is a subsidy that covers all operating costs for three years. At the end of this time the group is evaluated and compared with other groups of its kind by the Arts Council. Only one company has this subsidy at any given time (it is currently held by Het Amstel Toneel, which receives 1.2 million guilders, or $800,000, annually). The second subsidy is granted for three months and covers the costs connected with mounting a new production. The total amount of money available for these grants is also 1.2 million guilders, and there are thirty to forty applications yearly, of which fifteen to twenty are granted. Companies and groups involved in special projects from all over the country are eligible to apply for these grants.

2. *The provinces.* There are twelve provinces that each grant two kinds of subsidies to companies from the province. Approximately seven groups receive grants that cover the major part of their operating costs, while twenty-five companies receive enough money to enable them to mount new productions.

3. *The cities.* Cities are responsible for the purchase of performances; they provide money to organizations that are involved in children's theatre programming.

The Dutch subsidy system engenders a great deal of confusion. Companies have trouble understanding whether they are considered provincial or national and even for which grants to apply. Applications are due one and one half years in advance. This kind of long-term planning is difficult for companies that perform an average of 150 times a year and also mount new productions, all from September to May (little happens in the summer months). Also, sponsorship of the performing arts is a relatively new concept, although it occurs regularly in the visual arts and some concert series. To date, little underwriting of children's theatre has been given, and most companies derive the vast majority of their income from the box office. As the country's economic recession worsens, less money is available for the arts, even though interest in children's theatre is widespread. In addition, even in areas in which money is less of a problem, the theatres in which children's companies perform are so small (120 to 400 seats) that it is impossible to make a substantial profit. All of this contributes to a situation in which people in the field are underpaid and often switch to more lucrative jobs in adult theatre as soon as an opportunity presents itself.

Artistic, Social, and Educational Objectives

These artistic objectives are generally held by most theatre companies: to achieve the highest quality possible and a discrete identity in both style and design. To meet these objectives, groups hire the best personnel they can within their financial means. Many companies also try to develop their own acting styles; the urge to innovate is strong.

Social objectives, which were so important in the sixties and seventies, are no longer paramount. Social questions now have to do with where performances take place—in schools, community centers, or theatres. Performing in schools and community centers hinders artistic aspects of the productions, such as sets, lighting, and props, but brings theatre to where the audience lives, as opposed to bringing the audience to the theatre. Wederzijds has chosen to perform in schools with productions designed to be presented without any traditional theatrical support. Scapinoballet, like Werkcentrum Dans, solves the problems inherent in performing in schools in a different way. They stage simple, educational pieces accompanied by classroom lessons. The children later take a trip to the theatre to see more elaborate performances.

Like social objectives, educational objectives have largely been relegated to the background of children's theatre. Although teaching of one kind or another is implicit in any kind of performance, productions are no longer used to explain social and political problems. Most companies have also stopped giving drama lessons in schools, leaving this to drama teachers. The era of children's theatre providing complete drama-in-education projects is definitely over.

Many obstacles stand in the way of realizing these objectives. The biggest, of course, is money. Companies cannot improve their artistic level if they do not have budgets sufficient to hire talented actors, designers, playwrights, and directors. In addition, the Academies of Theatrical Arts pay no attention to children's theatre; there are few trained actors with specializations in children's theatre. The proliferation of companies is also a problem; in this small country 225 groups performing for children is too great a number. In many cases companies survive only because audiences do not recognize quality (or lack thereof) and because many of the people who organize programs for children don't know which companies are available, since there is no central booking system for children's theatre.

The late 1980s could prove to be a turning point for children's theatre in Holland. For much of the decade the country has been exhausted from the need for constant experimentation. Like the pendulum of a clock, children's theatre moved from the extreme left of the sixties and seventies to the extreme right of the eighties. It is now time to find a state of balance. Holland needs to seek a form of theatre in which all the knowledge gained from years of experimentation is utilized, a form that makes children's theatre understandable and appealing to children. Some groups, like De Blauwe Zebra, Tejater Teneeter, and Speelteter Gent (from Dutch-speaking Belgium), seem to have found the beginnings of this form. Many other companies have yet to reflect on what it is they want, while others are wrestling with the question of whether to continue performing for children or move solely into adult theatre. This uncertainty has recently resulted in the presentation of many family-oriented productions (for both children and their parents). Unfortunately it has also resulted in a dearth of productions aimed at four-to-eight-year-olds.

These problems notwithstanding, Holland can be proud of its contributions to children's theatre, which are respected throughout Europe. Dutch scripts are being translated and performed abroad, and Dutch companies are invited to perform at international festivals. Until recently Sweden and Germany were considered leaders in the development of children's theatre in Europe, but Holland has taken over that distinction. There is much admiration for the vision and courage Dutch producers have shown in their willingness to experiment and innovate to advance the field of theatre for children and young people.

REPRESENTATIVE COMPANIES

De Blauwe Zebra (The Blue Zebra)

This group was started in 1985 from the remains of a previous company, Lijn Negen (Line Nine), which went bankrupt in 1984. The group is supported by the province of Overijssel ($173,000), the city of Kampen ($12,000), and the Ministry of Culture ($96,500). Their first performance, *Een loket (An Office Window*, 1985), was recorded for television; in 1986 *De blauwe zebra* was first performed and proved a tremendous success. Like *Een loket*, it is a mixture of associations, longings, fantasy, humor, and music, skillfully performed by the group. Members include Hans van den Boom (director and writer), Cees Debets, Willeke Hieminga, Jur van der Lecq, and Wim Selles (actors and musicians).

In 1987 their production of *De stenen van Moutsouna (Stones of Moutsouna)* received the Hans Snoek award for the best children's theatre performance. The jury described the presentation as follows: ''This performance is rich in contrasts, in which characters, music and facial expression show more than words can tell. Recognizable family situations are cast in unexpected forms.'' The production was geared toward children six years old and older. The company's next production will be *Een 1/2 tuinhuis (Half a Garden House)*.

In the words of director Boom:

I don't invent anything special for anybody. First, I think of characters without thinking of any actor in particular. Later, the actors can add a lot to their characters. I work with music, stage sets and costumes which inspire each other. I also figure out a philosophical discourse that provides the play with a basis. Finally there is the script, which I use to explain to the actors how I see the characters. A production is the sum of twelve people and many other things. Even the fact that the office is painted red one morning can influence the process. Basically, productions are made upon improvisations and a script that's fixed in an early stage of the production period. Our working process is supported by an intensive training program in certain disciplines like flamenco dancing and music lessons.

De Blauwe Zebra has a board of directors that is responsible for all financial matters and for setting general policy. Daily management is handled by the manager, the director, and one representative member of the group. This triumvirate is responsible for implementing board policies, annually planning the repertory, handling publicity, and preparing materials for and reporting to the board. There are also regular company meetings about which both the management team and the board are kept informed. The current repertory includes *De blauwe zebra*, script and direction by Hans van den Boom, age nine and older; *De stenen van Moutsouna*, script and direction by Boom, age six and older; *Een 1/2 tuinhuis*, script and direction by Boom, age nine and older.

Netherlands Children's Theatre

The Netherlands Children's Theatre (NJT) was founded in 1976 as an amateur, collective operation performing a traditional repertory. The company worked this way until 1984, occasionally receiving modest subsidy from The Hague. In 1984 Jeroen Rooijackers was appointed director, and was charged with professionalizing the group, creating an artistic identity, and raising the quality of the productions. The company now receives substantial funding of $180,000 from The Hague and added amounts from the Ministry of Culture, as needed.

Jeroen Rooijackers describes his production process as follows:

Most NJT productions are based on improvisations, partly because so few scripts are available that fit into our artistic style and partly because improvisation enables us to get as close as possible to our audience. Children have unbridled imaginations. They can change all the objects in their surroundings according to their fantasies. This capacity for transformation is the starting point for every NJT production. The actors put themselves in the place of the children; they give props and set an associative value. In this way, the subject of a performance is researched in an improvisational way. The material is not fixed into standard scenes until very late in the process, at which time costumes, lighting, a full set and props are added.

NJT is administered by a board, and daily management is handled by a manager and the director. The group works according to a strict division of tasks. There is a solid core of five actors; guest directors, designers, musicians, and technicians are contracted on a per-production basis. The current repertory includes *Sne-*

euwwitje (Snow White), 1987, directed by Rooijackers, for age six and older (this piece was co-produced with the Percussionists Ensemble of the Hague Residential Orchestra); *Molleman*, 1988, script and direction by Ingrid van Leeuwen, for four-to-eight-year-olds; *Het woekerende woud (The Rampant Forest*, based on *Sleeping Beauty)*, 1988, directed by Rooijackers.

Tejater Teneeter

Founded in 1976, Tejater Teneeter has its roots in Studenttheatre, whose first members were young Dutch students and dramatists. Since its inception the group has aimed its work toward children and young people, using the examples provided by Jorg Richard and Augusto Boal. Their audience ranges from four to fifteen years old. Since 1980 the company has been subsidized by the city of Nijmegen and the province of Gelderland ($350,000) with additional funding from the Ministry of Culture, as needed. In 1988 Tejater Teneeter consisted of nine persons and presented two productions. Directors, playwrights, and designers are contracted on an ad hoc basis. Before 1983 company members developed the scripts, which were based on socially determined issues; after that year the repertory was chosen by the relevance of a play's topic to the child audience.

Rinus Knobel discusses the working process:

In the early stages, everybody searches for potential plays. The twice-weekly concerts (evenings filled with theatrical experiments and exercises) turn this research into a constant activity. When a choice is finally made, based on improvisation and discussion, the script has to be revised or totally rewritten, a process in which the company is minutely involved, as they are in the designs for the costumes and sets. The director is responsible for all activity during the rehearsal period, usually eight to ten weeks. This work process is also supported by training workshops given by the director for that specific production.

The company has a board that advises on artistic matters and is responsible for all finances. Daily management is handled by the manager and artistic director. Important decisions are made by the entire company. The group is considered a cooperative in which solidarity is much valued and is considered the basis for the high quality of the work produced. The current repertory includes *Zomer (Summer)*, 1986, written by Romain Weingarten, revised by Pauline Mol, directed by Andy Daal, for age ten and older; *Yvonne*, 1987, written by Witold Gombrowicz, revised by Daal and Rinus Knobel, directed by Daal, for age eight and older; and *Driekoningenavond (Twelfth Night)*, 1988, revised by Daal and Knobel, directed by Daal, for age eight and older.

BIBLIOGRAPHY

Plays

Broekman, Flip. *Valse wimpers (Fake Eyelashes)*. 1981.

de Bont, Ad. *Het bijzondere leven van Hilletje Jans (The Particular Life of Hilletje Jans)* 1984.

———. *Geheime vrienden (Friends in Secret)*. 1983.

Eykman, Karel. *Liefde en van dattum (Love and You Know What)*. 1983.

Mol, Pauline. *Dag Monster (Bye, Bye Monster)*. 1986.

Snoep, Ella. *Groeistuipen (Growing Pains)*. 1984.

Books and Dissertation

Derriks, Mechtild, and Peter Godefrooij. *S.C.O.-Rapport*. Amsterdam: University of Amsterdam, 1984.

Ehrenstein, Rob, ed. *Jeugdtheater geen Kinderspel*. Amsterdam: International Theatre Bookshop, 1983.

Olink, Hans, ed. *Jeugdtheater in Nederland. Een reus op lemen voeten*. Amsterdam: C. J. Aarts/Stichting Wederzijds, 1986.

Van Otterloo, A., and N. van Rossen. *Bestuurlijke verantwoordelijkheid in beeld*. Arnhem: Nederlands Theater Instituut, Federatie Kunstenaarsverenigingen, 1986.

"Van theorie naar praktijk." Ph.D. diss. Instituut van Theatersetenschappen, University of Amsterdam, 1984.

Verschuren, Herman, ed. "En nu over jeugdliteratuur." Librarian's magazine, special issue on children's theatre. Den Haag: NBLC, 1986.

Marla Kleine

New Zealand

HISTORY

Theatre for young people in Aotearoa (native name for New Zealand, population 3,303,000) encompasses several fields: children's theatre, concerned with classes and performances for and by children; theatre-in-education (TIE), concerned with performances and workshops by professional actors in schools and communities; youth theatre, concerned with performances by young people themselves; puppet theatre; and a variety of transient groups and individuals. Development of these areas of theatre for young people has been sporadic and piecemeal with occasional bursts of excellence. Since the 1960s a number of professional theatres have been established, together with significant improvement in New Zealand playwriting. The time is right to look again at what is offered to the children of New Zealand.

The appropriateness of much of the existing dramatic material is in question. Because work has largely been based on a European tradition, there is a pressing need to relate to New Zealand's identity as a South Pacific nation so that young people have an understanding of today's society in a global context. In the late 1980s a number of issues were addressed through a collaboration among artists, educators, and arts-policymakers who were concerned with the needs of young people and recognized that young people should have a stake in decision making about the programs they would see and in which they would take part. A concept of performing arts residencies in schools is being developed to improve the quality and status of all work for and with young people. Short-term pilot schemes are being jointly funded by the Arts Council and the Department of Education. These programs will be supported, carefully monitored, and recorded. Given this new development, here is the past and current history.

THEATRE-IN-EDUCATION

In New Zealand TIE has made the largest and most consistent continuing contribution to theatre for children, although currently, owing mainly to economic factors, few groups remain in operation.

A number of professional adult companies have supported TIE teams of professional actors performing plays for children in schools as well as the plays offered in the home-base theatre at holiday times. There have also been a number of autonomous groups. Some of these companies have performed similar shows in people's homes, factories, hospitals, and other institutions. Despite the input of dedicated practitioners, few groups have been sustained for prolonged periods of time because of a lack of financial viability and because of burnout among company members. Auckland's Theatre Corporate, which recently ceased operations, was such a company. It began in 1975, performing Story Theatre, and continued for ten years, touring primary and secondary schools and community venues. In addition to plays, the group offered workshops in theatre skills.

The New Zealand's Players Quartet was one of the earliest groups to tour schools. Established in the middle fifties after the demise of the New Zealand Players (New Zealand's first full-time professional company), this constantly changing quartet performed four programs during the school year for nearly twenty years. Programs often consisted of excerpts from plays or literature-based projects. Other theatres, such as Court Theatre Christchurch and Mercury Theatre Auckland, made similar performance-based offerings in their early years. The Dunedin-based Southern Comedy Players provided a similar service in the South Island in the sixties.

The Children's Art Theatre toured for many years from its base at the Four Seasons Theatre in Wanganui; but here again, this company is no longer in existence. The work was performance-based and uneven in quality, but it was offered at a time when there was little else available to young people. Many groups have recently tried to tie their programs to curriculum needs and relate to social change, performing works devised around issues of concern to young people or presenting plays written and based on discussions with youth.

An autonomous group, outstanding in its intentions, was the Wellington-based Town and Country Players. Founded in 1980 and evolving from a Pre-Employment Program scheme, it toured towns and rural areas for several years, aiming to provide a service to New Zealanders neglected by mainstream art and culture; the group recently folded. Troupers Theatre Christchurch is another autonomous group that has persevered since 1980 with its work in schools. Programs designed to remind audiences of their heritage were primarily based on the work of established writers but occasionally were devised from original sources. An example of the latter (using Court Theatre as its base) was a play about life during the East Coast gold field days, a part of which depended on the reaction and suggestion of the children who participated in the action.

Te Ohu Whakaari, an independent Maori group working for young people in theatres as well as in schools, was created in 1983 and closed late in 1986. The group incorporated traditional Maori and Polynesian culture, myths, and legends and contemporary work of Maori writers and poets, creating innovative performances through storytelling and movement. The Maori actors dealt with their culture and assisted with bilingual programs in the primary schools. This work was part of the renaissance of Maori artists who address issues of cultural diversity in Aotearoa. Te Ohu Whakaari's very existence was a political statement.

In the early eighties the Manukau Theatre worked in the predominantly Polynesian area of South Auckland. Out of this short-lived company rose the historically significant, small Statement Theatre Company of three: a Maori, a Samoan, and a pakeha. They presented only New Zealand material and in particular six short stories, *Stones from the Spring*, interchangeable and adaptable according to age level and the needs of the audience.

Today issues such as unemployment, equal opportunity, gender, racism, nuclear tensions, conservation, and world hunger and law-related and other problems are considered by TIE companies. Most community theatres from time to time have supported such groups, in particular Downstage Theatre Wellington with Stage Truck. Other children's theatre companies have included alternative groups such as Amamus, Red Mole, Theatre Action Living Theatre Troupe, and Beggar's Bag, which offered issue-based, heritage, and visionary work. Community-based groups such as Playback Theatre, Action Education, and Dramadillo are still in existence, as they offer other activities besides performance. There are a number of small-group and individual performers for children: clowns, jugglers, mimes, and storytellers (both Maori and pakeha). Puppet groups include the New Zealand Puppet Theatre, which has just established a delightful museum of puppets from many countries.

YOUTH THEATRE

Youth Theatre is a significant and rapidly developing movement in theatre for young people. The issues mentioned above are the concerns of adolescents, and a number of plays have been written or devised after discussion with them. Young playwrights are also developing. After Interplay (the first International Young Playwrights Conference held in Australia) it was observed that what the young New Zealanders lacked in theatre arts experience they made up for in tone and quality of writing. The plays are quite political in their perspective. The Young Playwright's Festival "No Kidding," recently held in Wellington, reinforced this observation. There have been Youth Theatre groups supported by most theatres, in particular the Fortune Downstage and the Depot (the latter run as a collective). Downstage has a full-time education officer for youth and community work. The Auckland Youth Theatre was originally founded as part of the Youth Theatre activity of Central Theatre. It is now autonomous and offers professional actor–drama tutors for classes that involve 200 young people weekly. Students perform plays regularly.

The Northland Youth Theatre at the Civic Center, Forum North Whangarei, is now in its fourth year and prospering. In a five- to six-week summer residency eighty or so young people from ages fifteen to twenty-one gather with professional directors, musicians, and theatre personnel. They predominantly work on original material and usually present three full-length pieces to peers and public.

The Young Stagers group has been in existence for many years. Originally formed from junior members of the Manurewa Theatre, the group caters to children and teenagers who are interested in all aspects of theatre. Regular classes are held, and the students (Maori, Pacific Island, and pakeha) perform in productions throughout the year.

Youth theatre work, which is based on the needs and aspirations of young people, is likely to have an increasingly higher profile in the future.

CHILDREN'S THEATRE

In the main, quality performances of plays for children have been the responsibility of the professional theatres, which largely offer plays during school holidays. In recent years the theatres have performed a number of plays by New Zealand writers. From time to time a number of other children's theatre groups have existed in the main cities of New Zealand; these have not involved full-time professional actors, although they have received professional assistance from directors, teachers, and administrators.

The Canterbury Children's Theatre, Inc., is unique in that it has survived for twenty-five years. Twice a year the group presents adult actors in plays for children, except when a child role is essential. A variety of classes in creative drama and movement are held for children age eight and older. In 1965 the Malthouse, a picturesque Victorian landmark now well over a century old, was converted into the home of the Children's Theatre. It was an impressive achievement.

Since 1965 Dunedin Teachers' College has sustained a children's theatre program with workshops for children, who may also perform plays for their peers. Other teachers' colleges have presented occasional high-quality performances for children both in halls and in schools.

OTHER ASPECTS OF CHILDREN'S THEATRE

From time to time festivals of children's theatre take place, encompassing productions from local schools (youth theatre at the secondary level) and educational organizations and work from the local community theatre classes for children. With the growth of sixth-form certificate courses in drama, a number of secondary-school groups share performances with primary schools as part of their course. This work is usually devised by the students according to perceived needs. Many schools have a history of excellent productions that involve many students. Some have published work based on local history, such as mining disasters and the depression, and popular causes, such as the peace movement.

THE FUTURE

With insights developed from the performers in school residencies and the increasing energy from youth theatre groups based on students' needs, Aotearoa is now ready to consider fresh approaches to theatre for young people. Companies that have foundered in the past have not had the advantage of true partnership with others. There is a need for collective energy, group decision making, and a breaking down of territory. Cognizance of and consideration for cultural diversity will be a main preoccupation.

Sunny Amey and Nonnita Rees

Norway

Norway is a small country with approximately 4 million inhabitants. Half of it is above the arctic circle and mostly mountainous. The country is famous for its fjords, coastline inlets that, if stretched out, would encircle the equator twice. The winters are long and dark, but in recompense the light is plentiful the rest of the year. Much money is spent on outdoor sports, even though many Norwegians think the money would be more wisely used for the arts and theatre, especially since a recent poll showed that more people went to art exhibitions and theatre performances than to sports events. Technologically, Norway is well developed, and the oil fields in the North Sea have made a great impact on the economy. One of the aims of the Norwegian Forum for Children's and Young People's Theatre is to channel more of this money toward theatre for younger audiences.

THEATRE

In 1987 ten institutional and regional theatres were supported by the state (which amounted to grants totaling 321.5 million kroner). Riksteateret, the National Touring Theatre, which travels to small towns throughout the country, and the Norwegian Opera in Oslo received the large majority of the subsidies for operating expenses underwritten by the government. The National Theatre and the Norwegian Theatre in Oslo, the National Scene in Bergen, the Rogaland Theatre in Stavanger, and the Trøndelag Theatre in Trondheim, as well as the five regional theatres created since the sixties, also receive substantial state subsidies and smaller grants from municipality or county funds. Even so, the need to earn more money from the box office is steadily becoming a reality. There are no large theatre companies that perform exclusively for children and young people, although Oslo boasts a municipal puppet theatre, Oslo Nye, and some of the independent companies in Bergen, Oslo, and elsewhere offer children's theatre as a standard part of their seasons.

CHILDREN'S THEATRE

Of the ten institutional and regional theatres, only a few regularly play for children. The National Scene in Bergen usually stages two productions a year for children. Also, the Bergen International Arts Festival, which takes place in May and June, regularly features children's theatre productions as part of its program. Trøndelag Theatre works with independent groups so that if they do not have a production of their own to offer young audiences, the partner company is invited to stage one. Rogaland Theatre has a children's theatre department that oversees productions in which adult actors perform for children or children (with professional direction) play for other children. And Hålogaland Theatre normally offers a production for children or youth that they tour through a large area of northern Norway. The remainder of the institutional theatres produce either no children's theatre or only one or two small productions each year. Few offer anything for youth.

It is obvious that little of the government's subsidy funds are spent on theatre for children and young people. This, however, is changing. Because the institutional companies are being challenged to cater more to new audiences, there has been a steady increase in the number of performances geared toward younger audiences.

The Oslo municipality recently created the Black Box Theatre with two stages (or rather two black rooms with lighting equipment and seats) so that independent groups will have a place to perform in Oslo. One of these "stages" was supposed to be for performances for young audiences. So far this has not happened, since the stage is expensive to rent, especially for independent groups with little subsidy. In Trondheim, on the other hand, three groups obtained a house from the municipality where they created the Theatre Avantgarden. They give regular Sunday performances as well as those on weekdays. They also travel to and perform in schools in the surrounding districts and throughout the country.

Studio Teatret, one of the independent groups that belongs to the Theatre Avantgarden, arranged an exciting and novel theatre experience in *The Ice Theatre*. Collaborating with German ice sculptor and architect Jürgen Spelda, they invited families, during two of the coldest weeks of the year (minus 20 C.), to take part in a special event. In the dark winter night they produced a theatrical "happening" based on improvisation and acrobatics, and incorporating color, music, fire, ice sculptures, and other materials. Although the entire audience loved the presentation, the children, especially, were entranced.

The independent companies were the innovators in children's theatre throughout the 1970s. An example of the impact of the independent groups is the following statistic: in 1977 sixteen companies played 793 performances for child audiences out of a combined total of 1,050 performances for the year. Teatersentrum, the organization that represents the independent companies, was established in 1977 and publishes a journal titled *Spillerom*. Not restricted to children's theatre, the journal has published articles that detail the amateur theatre movement and community theatres, genres that encompass the younger population as well, both as performers and audience members.

Whereas the institutionalized theatres grudgingly present a few children's productions each year, the independent theatre groups travel extensively throughout the country to reach their young audiences. Only a small percentage of their work is underwritten by the government, which is regrettable, given the important work they do in introducing young people to theatre. In 1987 the state gave only 6 million kroner to thirty-eight independent theatre companies; of that amount, 4 million to 5 million kroner was spent on theatre for young audiences. (In comparison, in 1987 the Danish government allocated 55 million kroner to support theatre for children and youth.)

THE REPERTORY

The large institutional theatres used to give one performance a year for young audiences, around Christmastime. The first recorded professional performance for a child audience dates back to the 1870s. Playwright and director Bjørnstjerne Bjørnson offered Molière's *Bourgeois Gentilhomme* for the children of factory workers at the Christiana Theatre (which later became the National Theatre in Oslo) in 1866. After the turn of the century there was a growing tradition at the major repertory companies (in Oslo and Bergen) to stage Christmas performances for children based on folktales, and by the 1920s this tradition had become established. Adaptations of fairy tales written by the Brothers Grimm and Hans Christian Andersen also became part of the repertory. At this point new plays were also being written for child audiences, although they were mostly within the framework of the fairy tale. A good example of this is Sverre Brandt's *A Journey to the Christmas Star*, which was performed in Oslo in 1924 and in Bergen in 1925; the play was later made into a film, and is still popular fare during the Christmas season.

In the 1950s playwright Thorbjørn Egner's fantasy plays (*People and Robbers of Cardemon Town* and *The Animals in the Hakkebakke Forest*) initiated a move away from the traditional fairy-tale structure. In these works the audience meets good and bad characters, but when the good prevail there is room for and acceptance of everyone. Egner's work has been translated into many languages, and a film is now being made of *People and Robbers*.

As an alternative to Egner's fantasy world, Anne Cath Vestly's books and plays about family life in modern apartments, about rural and city conflicts, and about growing up gave a more realistic and socially relevant form to children's theatre in the early sixties. Sociopolitical themes and issues became more dominant as the independent companies of the seventies were formed. Although not predominantly children's theatres, these groups often performed for young audiences. Most of the plays presented were written by the companies themselves, based on research about an issue that was then collaboratively developed into a production through improvisation and group writing. An example of one such company is Musidra in Oslo. It is still in operation and has transformed several of its productions into television-theatre for children and youth audiences.

From the late seventies and into the eighties there has been a return to fairy-tale motifs and fantasy plays, but with an awareness and consciousness of the events of the sixties and seventies. In other words, issues are still being explored, but within a growing search for new theatrical forms and styles to overcome the restraints imposed by social realism. Most plays are currently script-based, either as dramatizations of children's literature or as original manuscripts. One writer is Rune Belsvik, a young dramatist from western Norway. Plays from other countries are also being mounted, as with the works of Swede Astrid Lindgren and the German GRIPS Theatre. Also, well-known dramatists for the adult theatre are starting to become interested in writing for young audiences, and new writers are assisted by two new institutions:

1. The Open Theatre in Olso, to which both new and experienced writers can send manuscripts. The works are either presented at an open reading by professional actors for an interested audience with a discussion afterward or given twelve rehearsals with a director and actors and a public performance.

2. The Academy for the Art of Writing, in Bergen, subsidized by the Kulturfondet (State Endowment for Cultural Activities). The Academy offers a four-month course for dramatists who write especially for younger audiences.

RADIO AND TELEVISION

Although many Norwegian children, especially in the more sparsely populated regions of the country, seldom get to see live theatre, they do have access to regular radio drama. Every Saturday evening since World War II the Norwegian Broadcasting Corporation (NRK) has aired a play for children. According to audience researchers, 15 percent of Norwegian children listen to the plays; additionally, an impressive 7 percent of adults prefer to listen to the children's plays rather than to plays broadcast for them. The Children's Section of NRK schedules its programming so that no two children's programs are aired simultaneously on radio and television. In this way there is never a conflict in children's programming, and the young audience can get the full benefit of these works.

The staff of the Children's Section, which includes two dramaturgs, are responsible for the repertory, and they have been able to simulate the theatre of fantasy, the social realistic theatre, and the theatre of humor and excitement. Television offers special, and separate, programs for children and youth. Children's programming often includes puppet performances, but traditional theatrical plays do not appear regularly. The puppet artist Ivo Caprino, over the years, has delighted children through his folktale productions on television. So, too, have members of the Mykle family, who pioneered puppet theatre for children on stage and for television.

AMATEUR THEATRE

The oldest amateur theatre tradition in Norway (and of theatre as such in the country) is the School Play of the Humanists. In 1562 Absalon Pedersøn Beyer staged *The Fall of Adam* with his pupils from the Latin School outside the cathedral in Bergen. This is believed to have been the first public theatre performance in Norway. There are scattered records of the humanistic school play tradition throughout the next century, and it is known that the great Norwegian-Danish dramatist Ludvig Holberg (who wrote comedies influenced by Molière) has seen and participated in such plays when he was a student at the Bergen Cathedral School. Few records have been found that document drama or theatre in schools during the eighteenth century. The reason for this is probably that Lutheran pietists regarded theatre as sinful and effectively stopped the productions. Norwegians are still suffering from this attitude today, which may partly explain the relatively weak position that dramatics holds in their school curriculums.

In modern times the school play has been a feature in many of the high schools as the culmination of the school year, but in most cases it is considered an extracurricular activity. A few high schools (notably in Oslo and the Bergen area) have offered theatre as a class; this is the exception rather than the rule. A recent development is the effort of Sogn and Fjordane Regional Theatre (in western Norway) to establish an acting course with Førde Gymnas. The most gifted pupils will be offered internships after finishing the high school course, either with the regional company or with its mother company, The Norwegian Theatre in Oslo.

Actor training for children and teenagers also has taken place through private establishments. In 1920 Inga Bjørnson (a niece of the dramatist) ran an acting school for children for more than thirty years. It was named The Children's Theatre, but colloquially, it was called The Children's National because she modeled its operation on that of the professional theatres in Oslo, notably the National Theatre. Many well-known Oslo-area actors, before and after the war, were members of Bjørnson's school. In 1957 Elisabeth Gording's Children and Youth Theatre became an alternative for young people from Oslo who wanted to learn to act. Although Gording's venture was essentially an acting school, it was built on an approach that combined traditional theatre arts and the principles of creative dramatics imported from the United States. Her aim has been to arouse aesthetic interest, to work creatively together, and to offer an alternative to the growing commercialization of children's culture.

An interesting effort that involves mixing professional adult actors with child amateurs is being practiced at the Rogaland Theatre in Stavanger. The director and playwright Bjorn Endreson pioneered this concept in the 1950s, and it is still a popular children's activity in Stavanger. The children become members of a dramatic club run by the Rogaland Theatre. Here they work with creative dramatics, improvisation, and scripted scenes. The most gifted ones are then singled out and offered parts in the children's play(s) for that season. The repertory ranges from musicals like *Annie Get Your Gun* to adaptations of fairy tales, such as *Cinderella* and *Little Mouse Mei*.

Apart from these examples of specific child-oriented theatrical operations, the Amateur Theatre Movement has a long tradition in rural areas as well as in cities. Large groups like The Young Farmer's Association, alcohol-abstinence organizations, and the Labor party's youth divisions have offered stages to young people to explore theatre and to present plays. Often this platform has been used for didactic purposes, but it also has resulted in entertainment and fun.

Today amateur theatre is flourishing and the movement encompasses many young people as both cast and audience members. The Norwegian Amateur Theatre Council, founded in 1980 through the initiative of the Department of Culture and Science, is incorporated in the National Budget (2,920,000 kroner in 1987). More than 1 million spectators see the 18,870 performances given by 1,872 companies. Some of the amateur theatres try to combine education and production, for instance, Vestlandske Teaterlag (a West Coast amateur theatre venture), which offers three-year courses for people who want to work with children performing for children. They have both drama teachers and young directors on their staff.

THE CHILDREN'S THEATRE PROJECT IN HORDALAND COUNTY

Initiated by the Norwegian Council of Culture through its Committee for Children's Theatre, the Children's Theatre Project is subsidized by a grant of 2.2 million kroner, of which one-third was given by the Hordaland Municipality and two-thirds by the Council. This three-year pilot project is administered by the Kulturhuset in Bergen, and its goal is to test different models in order to discover a system that will develop and support dramatic activities for children and young people.

The project is divided into four main areas: (1) what professional theatres have to offer children and young people; (2) the activities of the amateur theatres and of the children themselves, in and out of school; (3) the use of theatre and drama in schools and kindergarten; and (4) theatre by and for the mentally handicapped. The many results of this fruitful project, thus far, include the founding of the Hordaland Theatre for children and youth (the Hordeland area is on the west coast of Norway) in May 1988 and the initiation of an annual children's theatre festival for local amateur companies.

The new theatre will be exclusively professional, and with state funding and close connections with Sogn and Fjordane Regional Theatre it aims at becoming a West Coast regional theatre whose trademark will be the use of neo-Norwegian dialect. The Hordaland Theatre is also affiliated with the "Innvik," a ferry-turned-theatre-boat that will present performances in the Norwegian fjords.

THE NORWEGIAN ASSITEJ CENTER

The Norwegian Forum for Children and Young People's Theatre/ASSITEJ was begun in March 1982. ASSITEJ's concern has been centered around such questions as, What kind of theatrical experience do we offer children? Do we know enough about the needs of children? Is it necessary to provide specific training for actors who perform for children? What roles should authors and critics play in children's theatre? Since 1982 ASSITEJ has been busy arranging seminars, workshops, and festivals, which have been enthusiastically attended by people from across the country. Some of the events include the following:

* Seminar on TIE with the Cockpit Theatre, London
* Workshops on folktale analysis and dramaturgy
* The first Nordic Children and Youth Theatre Festival, with a seminar on the theme "Quality: What Is It?"
* Summer course with a study of the structural analysis of folktales, and using movement as a conveyer of inner meanings
* A visit to Moscow by one board member
* A course in Keith Johnstone's improvisation techniques
* The Norwegian Festival of Theatre for Young People
* Publication of the *ASSITEJ Journal*
* Meetings with politicians
* Seminar on children's and youth theatre critics
* Several seminars for dramatists
* Professional storytelling evenings
* Seminar on how to tell stories with the French storyteller Abbi Patrix
* Seminar with Froschteater from Switzerland
* Seminar with Nellie McCaslin of the United States about drama and theatre in schools
* Three Norwegian groups chosen and sent to the Second Nordic Festival in Helsinki
* International Storytelling Festival

MOVING INTO THEATRE-IN-EDUCATION

Conferences, lectures, and practical work groups have been arranged in which teachers, drama teachers, and actors have participated. These have resulted in exciting TIE programs for elementary- and secondary-school students that have received due recognition in drama, theatre, and educational journals. There is definitely a growing interest in TIE both in the schools and from educational authorities.

DRAMA-IN-EDUCATION

Although drama has been part of the school curriculum since the 1930s as a result of progressive educational influences on curriculum, the dramatic activities have been scattered and mostly contained within the language arts and social sciences. During the 1960s Norwegian drama pioneers introduced influences from American creative dramatics and British drama-in-education into the country. Norwegians have become familiar with Winifred Ward, Geraldine Brain Siks, Isabel Burger, and Nellie McCaslin, as well as with Peter Slade, Brian Way, and Rose Bruford. The American child drama tradition was pioneered by the Swedes Elsa Olenius and Dan Lipschutz and the Norwegian Ingrid Boman. (The latter is now a producer of children's programs for the Norwegian Broadcasting Corporation.) British child-drama influences came to Norway mostly through literature, visits, and people going to England to learn the techniques. A notable effort in the areas of mime and dramatization was carried out by Grethe Nissen, who, through several books, introduced Rose Bruford's speech and drama methods.

In the seventies and eighties the National Association for Drama in Schools (Landslaget Drama i Skolen, or LDS) has been, through its courses and publications, the most instrumental agent for disseminating theory and methods of drama-in-education. In addition, this organization has worked politically with the education authorities to foster this area of schooling.

Today it is fair to say that Norwegian drama-in-education is based mostly on theories and methods similar to those of Dorothy Heathcote and Gavin Bolton of England. However, the Norwegians' interest in exploring contemporary issues and sociopolitical themes has made the field more politically committed, a trend that has been enhanced by the influences of the Latin American Augusto Boal, the Swede Bjørn Magner, and the Dane Janek Szatkowski. Also, there is a definite attempt to view and practice process and product as parts of a whole; in other words, that both aesthetic theory and practical methods have become areas that the drama teacher must master.

Drama is not yet a discrete subject in Norwegian schools, but the new National Core Curriculum (1987) strongly advocates drama as a teaching method and cross-curricular activity. In addition, drama has been indirectly mandated in the curriculum by being mentioned as a specific activity within such subjects as Norwegian, social sciences, music, and physical education (kindergarten through grade 9). It is offered as an option in junior high and high schools (grades 7 through 12) if there are drama teachers on a school's staff. Norway is one of the Scandinavian countries that has been most successful in integrating drama into the national curriculum. During the academic year 1987/88 the National Schools Council, in cooperation with Bergen College of Education, funded an in-service project to educate drama specialists in different regions as resource personnel for instructors who want to teach through drama and theatre. The National Association for Drama in Schools publishes the journal *Drama* quarterly. This is the only drama-in-education journal in Scandinavia, and has sub-scribers in all the Nordic countries.

RECENT DEVELOPMENTS

In January 1988 a new government report on "The Art of the Stage" was issued. This greatly awaited document that delineated official future policies pertaining to theatrical art made no significant contributions, however, to the field of theatre for young audiences. Basically, it repeated recommendations made in the 1976 Cultural Councils Report: (a) to strengthen the education of actors working in theatre for young audiences; (b) to stimulate actors in insti-tutionalized theatres toward experimental work in the field of children's theatre, and (c) to support the development of new plays for children and young people.

The report does underscore a concern about the growing competition from new technical media and asserts the importance of giving children the opportunity of experiencing a live art form. Therefore, it also made recommendations of a quantitative nature: to increase the number of performances for children by (a) establishing theatre advisors in each county whose major task would be to provide performances for that county, (b) increasing the number of touring productions that go into schools, and (c) strengthening the subjects of dance and drama in schools.

The report had few recommendations about how to qualitatively improve professional theatre for young people.

BIBLIOGRAPHY

In addition to ASSITEJ and LDS in Oslo, the major research sources for information on drama and theatre for children and youth are the University of Trondheim (Department of Drama, Film, and Theatre), the University of Oslo (Theatre Department), and Bergen College of Education (Drama Department). Trondheim has produced research on the history of drama-in-education and on children's theatre; Oslo, on amateur theatre; and Bergen, on the history of drama in education and curriculum development.

Two important books (both written by faculty members of the University of Trondheim) are Nils Braanaas, *Dramapedagogisk historie og teori* (Trondheim: Tapir, 1985) and Viveka Hagnell, *Barnteater—myte och meningar* (Malmo: Liber Forlag, 1983).

In 1976 the Norwegian Council of Culture printed an overview and evaluation of the status of children's theatre in the country at that time, together with constructive recommendations about how this field should be developed in the future. The government, through its funding, and the institutional theatres, through their repertories, have not, however, given enough priority to following up the recommendations outlined in the report.

The journal *Drama* (published by the National Association for Drama in

Schools, Oslo) has been in print since 1961 and is a good source for researching the developments in the fields of educational drama and theatre as well as in children's theatre.

Education for and of drama teachers is not as readily available or as good as it should be—the result, no doubt, of drama not being mandated in the kindergarten through grade 12 curriculum. However, full-time courses (for periods of one to one and one half years) are offered at Bergen College of Education, the University of Trondheim, and the State College of Arts and Crafts in Oslo.

As of 1988, a curriculum guideline in drama (grades 1 through 9) will be available for teachers throughout the country, printed by the National Schools Council as a supplement to the National Core Curriculum of 1987.

Stig Eriksson
(Prepared from materials submitted by ASSITEJ/Norway.)

Poland

HISTORY

The history of children's theatre in Poland has precursors that reach back to the Middle Ages, when young people participated in liturgical performances both inside and outside church walls. The old Polish "szopka," a kind of puppet nativity play performed in villages up until modern times, probably had its origin sometime in the Renaissance, as did performances in Jesuit schools that were associated with religious holidays. In the eighteenth and early nineteenth centuries on the great estates of the Polish aristocracy there were court theatres composed of child actors (much the same as the earlier Elizabethan "boy theatres" in England) whom the nobles hired ballet masters to train. Also, throughout the period of the partitions of Poland (1795–1918), school theatres continued to exist and were important in preserving the Polish language and its literature. Nevertheless, the history of theatre for children in Poland does not begin in earnest until the twentieth century.

In 1900 Maria Weryho-Radziłłowicz, an educator and author of stories for children and theoretical works about child psychology, opened a marionette theatre for children in Warsaw with a play by Andrzej Niemojewski titled *About the Prince Enchanted into a Bear*. This theatre existed from 1900 to 1904, at first performing only on Sundays and holidays and later twice a week. It charged a small admission price and seems to have been popular with both children and critics. In the repertory were such plays as *Hansel and Gretel, Christmas*, and *Little Red Riding Hood*, by Or-Ota; *The Queen of the Hummingbirds and the Seven Dwarves*, by Zapolska; *The Magic Flute*, by Gębarski; *Wars and Saws*, by Młodowska; *Lazy Johnny*, by Hoffman; and many others. Maria Weryho also organized playwrighting competitions and exhibitions of French and Italian marionette art. Hers was the forerunner of many professional puppet theatres for children in the interwar years.

After World War I Poland was reunited after about a century and a half of partition and occupation, and many cultural organizations, including theatres by and for children, were able to become more active. In 1919 Jędrzej Cerniak created the Union of Folk Theatres, which published its own periodical, *Folk Theatre*, and printed many articles about the role of theatre in the education of children and youth. Of these, two by Lucjusz Komarnicki, written in 1926, were especially important: "The Enchantment of the Theatre" and "School Theatre." Komarnicki believed that school theatre should not imitate professional theatre. Instead, he proposed the inclusion of drama in the educational program of the schools in skillfully planned, improvisational sessions that included activities that were an extension and transformation of children's games. He rejected the usual school repertory as useless, and instead proposed dramatizations of short literary pieces by the children themselves. The purpose was not to produce a new generation of budding actors and actresses, but to develop the latent creativity in every pupil, and in this regard Komarnicki's work paralleled that of Winifred Ward in the United States at roughly the same time.

Another important theoretician and practitioner of the interwar years was Zdzisław Kwieciński, who promoted what he called "Self-generated Theatre in the School," which meant letting groups freely create drama using ideas from their own lives. He intended this method to be a theatre of self-expression that could also serve a therapeutic social function. Therefore, a great deal of thought was put into picking subjects for the drama work that were relevant for all members of the group. In Kwieciński's theatre the group worked on an outline based on real-life events and then improvised dialogues in rehearsals and performances. He worked from 1933 to 1939 in the Lublin schools.

In the professional theatre Juliusz Osterwa, a well-known actor and director, initiated a "school stage" in 1932 in the Słowacki Theatre in Kraków by presenting a repertory of interest to young people between the ages of eleven and fifteen. So successful was the experiment that school stages were also established in Bydgoszcz, Wilno, and Katowice. In 1934 Osterwa organized, as part of the Reduta Theatre in Kraków, a theatre for children under the artistic direction of Maria Dulęba with the motto "To teach, not bore; to entertain by teaching."

In the meantime the tradition of Maria Weryho's pre–World War I marionette theatre was carried on by the Warsaw puppet theatre Baj (Storyteller). This theatre, founded by the Workers Society of the Friends of the Children of Żoliborz (a district in Warsaw), was the most famous puppet theatre of the interwar years, and today's lively activity in puppet theatre in Poland can trace its roots back to the Baj and the work of playwrights Maria Kownacka and Lucyna Krzemienicka. Kownacka wrote ennobled fables in which people are rewarded for working hard and being good; she also pioneered the use of folklore in children's theatre. Krzemienicka's plays adhered to the formula of "a golden heart conquers all." It was Kownacka and Krzemienicka who created the style characteristic of the Baj, and one can still see their plays on puppet stages today. The Baj inspired the founding of several other puppet theatres in Opole and Zakopane.

Successful puppet theatres also prospered in Poznań, Kościerzyna, Silesia, and Wilno in the interwar years.

The period just after World War II, from 1945 to 1956, saw the development of the nationalized puppet theatres, and the establishment of the dramatic Young Spectator's Theatres in three cities: Kraków, Łódź and Warsaw. Puppet theatres were established in almost all cities of any size in Poland, and the Polish branch of UNIMA (Union Internationale des Marionettes) opened at this time. The Groteska Theatre in Kraków and the Marcinek Theatre in Poznań were especially well known and developed a consistent, highly professional way of working. However, the Young Spectator's Theatres were a rather dismal failure. Characterized by neither interesting repertories nor performances, they had reached, by the 1950s, a state of ideological and artistic crisis. Essentially, they were dumping grounds for actors and directors who were unsuccessful in the adult theatre.

In 1956, amid the wave of slogans of renewal that accompanied the post-Stalinist "thaw," the Ministry of Culture and Art decided to close the Young Spectator's Theatres. The period from 1956 to 1970 was a time of complete stagnation as far as live theatre for children and youth was concerned. The regular dramatic theatres that normally performed for adults produced a few plays a year for children, mostly adaptations of either children's classics like *Anne of Green Gables*, by L. M. Montgomery, or selections from school required reading lists. The main artistic achievement of the dramatic theatres in those years, as far as productions for children went, was the performance of *The Unusual Adventures of Mr. Kleks*, by Jan Brzechwa, under the direction of Kazimierz Dejmek (one of the best-known directors of the period) in the National Theatre in Warsaw in 1965.

The puppet theatres, however, were able to sustain their development during this period and continued to build their own distinctive style. Plays based on folklore became popular, especially in the 1960s, as exemplified by the work of Natalia Gołębska and Ali Bunsch in the Miniatura Theatre in Gdańsk. Many plays based on the ethnographic research of anthropologist Oskar Kolberg were performed in the puppet theatres. This emphasis on folklore had stylistic consequences for stage design and directing and determined the artistic "coloring" of puppet theatre. It also held negative consequences when, by the end of the 1960s, nearly everyone in the puppet theatre was performing folk theatre.

One of the most important authors of the period was Krystyna Miłobędzka, whose plays are described by Henryk Jurkowski, president of UNIMA, as not really plays, but "scenic poems."[1] She builds a broadly associative imagery and infuses it with her own worldview. Two of her most important plays for children, still played in the puppet theatre today, are *Siała Baba Mak*, based on children's games, and *My Home Country*. *Siała Baba Mak* is about the power of reason over words, while *My Home Country* uses the principle of children's mythic thinking. Out of the simplest building blocks and sounds the children build their own world of simple things and emotions, a world of habits and attachments.

Two other important artistic innovators who began working at this time were the designer and director Leokadia Serafinowicz, for many years artistic director of the Marcinek Theatre in Poznań, and Jan Dorman, director of the Theatre of the Children of Lower Silesia. Serafinowicz' artistic vision was the perfect compliment to Miłobędzka's poetic texts. She brought an artistic style to the puppet theatre that was in a direct line from the theatre of Gordon Craig and the Polish director Leon Schiller. Jan Dorman also was a tireless experimenter who tried to establish genuine links between the child audience and what they saw onstage. His productions were marked by a special artistic ability and research into how children perceive the world.

In 1971 a group of artists and scholars gathered around the Marcinek Theatre in Poznań to organize the first Biennale of Art for the Child. So began an effort to gather the best in art for children in one place and to scientifically study all types of children's art, not just theatre, and relate them to developments in child psychology. In this same year Theatre Ochoty, founded in Warsaw, began to build its program of activities for children. In 1972 the Ministry of Art and Culture conducted a festival of performances for children that now is held every two years, alternating with the Biennale. Earlier an annual festival of puppet plays and an international biennial of puppet plays had been established. In 1981 the Polish branch of ASSITEJ was founded.

Since 1981 various institutions engaged in theatrical activities for children and youth have been organized. The All-Polish Center of Art for Children and Youth in Poznań now hosts the Biennale of Art for the Child. In addition, the Center is supposed to examine all innovations in art for children and art education in Poland and from abroad. It is a repository of information on art for children and can also give financial support to the most ambitious plays. The activities of the Center for Theatrical Education of Children and Youth in Gdańsk will be described in more detail later.

In this most recent period live theatre for children is coming back to life. Traveling theatre troupes perform their own plays with portable props and simple scenery that they can use in nontraditional spaces. One of these groups, the Wierzbak Theatre in Poznań, has presented a repertory based on the fairy tales of the Grimm brothers and Hans Christian Andersen and also an original play, *Convex*. They have specific educational and artistic goals that are realized through performances and correspondence with children after the engagement, making them widely recognized as one of the most interesting new children's theatres of recent years.

CHILDREN'S THEATRE TODAY

Two types of professional children's theatre are found in Poland: dramatic or "live actor's" theatres and puppet theatres. The more than twenty professional state-financed puppet theatres devote most of their repertory to performances for children. However, although the state dramatic theatres produce some children's theatre, performances for the young remain, for the most part, a marginal activity. Although live theatre for children and youth is reviving itself after a long period of dormancy, the puppet theatres still constitute the principal source of professional children's theatre in Poland.

Puppet theatres do not necessarily present puppet plays exclusively. Many of them mix human and visual media: puppets, live actors, props, and masks may all be used in various combinations. Nevertheless, the repertory of the puppet theatre generally caters to the needs of the very young, that is three- to nine-year-olds, even though companies certainly are capable of providing a repertory rich enough to satisfy viewers in the ten-to-sixteen-year-old age bracket. But as yet most have failed to do so.

The most ambitious puppet directors create a theatrical medium that is primarily visual. Their companies often have large technical staffs that are capable of producing sophisticated puppets, scenery, props, animated objects, and other kinds of special effects. Graduates of the two state schools that specialize in training actors and directors for the puppet theatre have been especially interested in visual experimentation in plays for adolescent and adult audiences. For example, the Opole Puppet and Actor's Theatre, under the direction of Grzegorz Kwieciński, recently presented a play called *Panto i Pantamto* (*Mr. This and Mr. That*), and the Wrocław Puppet Theatre, under the direction of Wiesław Hejno, offered a puppet production for adults based on Kafka's *The Trial*.

The puppet theatre medium in some ways dictates the repertory of fairy tales or folktales, often with a similar structure: a journey by the protagonist in order to solve a problem. For example, in *Damroka and the Griffen*, by Natalia Gołębska, a medieval Polish princess decides to make a dangerous pilgrimage to appeal to a magic griffin for help in the Poles' fight against the Teutonic knights. In *Mr. Quill the Tailor*, by Kornel Makusyński, the hero journeys to a distant city where it rains all the time. Finally, near the end of the play, the protagonist always reaches his or her destination and solves the problem, and everyone lives happily ever after. By presenting mostly fairy tales and folktales, the puppet theatre acts as a preserver of traditional Polish culture, which appears to be one of its major social goals.

Of course, some puppet plays deal with contemporary issues, but they are rare and almost always use animated objects. For example, in *What Time Is It?* by Zbigniew Wojciechowski, clocks participate in the fate of the characters, and in *Night of Miracles*, by Józef Ratajczak, toys from the nursery come to life through the imagination of the child. Puppet theatre practitioners generally believe that even if they are to be modern, they must avoid copying the world of men, or they will lose their specific style and artistic vision.

In recent years a number of initiatives have been taken to fill the gap between the traditional puppet theatre repertory and the adult repertory. It was felt that although ten-to-sixteen-year-olds had "grown out of" fairy tales, they were not quite old enough for adult theatre. Two of these initiatives, implemented by the Theatre Ochoty Center of Theatrical Culture in Warsaw and the Center for

Theatrical Education of Children and Youth in Gdańsk, are described in the "Profiles" section that follows. In addition to these, the National Festival of Plays for Children and Young People, first created in 1979 and held every two years since then, is becoming increasingly more successful in reactivating interest in dramatic theatre for children. The festival is subsidized by the Ministry of Art and Culture, the Voivodship (provincial) office, the municipal office in Wałbrzych (the city where it is held), and ASSITEJ. The festival works on the basis of a competition: the six best performances by dramatic theatres are selected by a qualifying commission and, along with one performance by the host theatre in Wałbrzych, are judged by a jury at the festival. Other events accompany the festival in which puppet theatres, nonprofessional school groups, and foreign companies also present their work. In addition, seminars on theatre for children are held.

The Biennale of Art for the Child, already mentioned, is organized by the All-Polish Center of Art for Children and Youth in Poznań. The Center also sponsors seminars on the state of dramaturgy for children and invites guest artists such as Peter Schumann of the Bread and Puppet Theatre of the United States to come to Poznań to conduct theatre workshops. In 1985 the Ministry of Culture and Art established a Central Repertory Library of Dramatic Works for Children and Young People in Warsaw that accumulates and preserves plays for children. The library plans to publish a bulletin devoted to modern world plays for young people and is in contact with similar institutions worldwide. Additionally, there is a competition for new plays for children and young people organized by two dramatic theatres in Silesia to seek out new works. In 1985 seventy plays were sent to the organizing committee of this competition. Since 1981 the area of live theatre for children has progressed enormously, although it has yet to become as well established as the professional puppet theatre.

Besides professional theatre, Polish children have the opportunity to take part in numerous amateur theatre groups that exist throughout the country. These groups are sponsored by various organizations such as local houses of culture. A national forum of children's and young people's theatres, sponsored by the Education Authority, is held annually in Poznań where approximately forty of the best amateur groups present performances and winners are selected. Leaders of these groups decided to create a Pedagogue-Drama Instructor Club under the auspices of ASSITEJ. A stage for presentations of children's and young people's amateur companies is available at the national headquarters of the Polish Path-finders' Union in Warsaw, where once a month the best groups from all over the country perform. Thus the amateur theatre scene in Poland is lively and active.

According to Halina Machulska, president of ASSITEJ/Poland, the artistic goals of each children's theatre, whether professional or amateur, are to create an integrated theatrical work in which all elements are harmonious and in which modern trends in educational thinking meet with a concern for the universal problems of man.[2] This theatrical work, however, must view life from a vantage point near that of children and youth. When one looks at "children's theatre" this way, *all* plays are potentially plays for children or youth. For example, *Hamlet* might be played as the fight of a young man who wants to be noble against the brutal world that surrounds him. Machulska believes that if we could only understand the term "children's theatre" in this way, then the repertory in theatres for youth and children would be much broader-based.

The educational and social goals, to Machulska's mind, are similar to the modern understanding of education through art. Theatre must wake up the child's ability to creatively relate to the world, inspire the child to self-realization, educate, and stimulate sensitivity and imagination through play. Finally, according to Machulska, art must help children to recognize and overcome the dangers of modern life. These goals can be realized not only through children watching plays, but also through different forms of participation in theatre. She advocates the child's taking part in improvisational drama activities, which constitutes a growing trend in Poland. Machulska thinks that participation enables theatre people to understand the needs and interests of youth and helps the theatre to find a proper repertory and form to interest young audiences.

Perhaps the foremost problem facing children's theatre is the lack of interesting modern scripts, a situation that plagues both puppet and dramatic theatres that perform for children. Some practitioners, especially in the puppet theatre, believe that restaging classic fairy and folk puppet plays is good enough, and that children's theatre actually should shield children from adult problems of contemporary life as long as possible. Others simply are more interested in visually interesting production styles, and so questions of content are irrelevant for them. However, many children's theatre practitioners express the view that few plays are being written for children because the pay for such writing is minimal. One young directing graduate of the state puppet theatre school in Białystok declared, "I'd like to direct a new play, and I tried to find one, but there simply aren't any." Perhaps the existence of the new children's play competition will spur the creation of interesting texts, which eventually may find their way into the puppet theatre repertory despite the fact that the award is intended for "live" plays.

Children's theatre in Poland is plagued by other problems as well; theatre critics show little interest in performances for young people, and a great deal of parental conservatism prevails. Unfortunately parents tend to disapprove both of new texts and new production styles in an attitude that often seems to exclaim, "If it was good enough for me, it's good enough for my child." Dramatic theatres are plagued by two additional problems: sometimes the attitude of actors toward productions is not serious enough and professional theatre managements often underestimate the importance of good performances for shaping the needs and preferences of future adult spectators. And, with the exception of the specialized puppet-theatre schools, the regular drama schools do not offer special training for children's theatre. Yet a tendency exists not to allow talented performers to work in professional theatres (including children's theatres) if they lack drama school certificates.

REPRESENTATIVE COMPANIES

The State Puppet and Actor's Theatre Miniatura in Gdańsk

The Miniatura Theatre, originally called the Łątek Theatre, was opened in 1947 by the Totwen family. Their repertory largely consisted of their own adaptations of Polish children's stories. From 1947 to 1950 the Łątek was a private theatre in which the Totwens did everything themselves.

In 1950, when the theatre was nationalized, the repertory was changed to include adaptations of Russian folktales, and in 1951, with the firm establishment of socialist realism in the theatre, the Totwens departed. Replacing them was Ali Bunsch, soon to become one of the most famous designers in puppet theatre. In 1952 Natalia Gołębska, a director and playwright for the puppet stage, also joined the theatre, and together Bunsch and Gołębska changed the artistic direction of the theatre, including its name to Miniatura. During the next fifteen years they created the special style for which the Miniatura became known: huge productions that filled the whole area of the stage with fantastic scenery and special magical effects. They experimented with different materials (for example, Plexiglas) for creating puppets and used every kind of puppet—marionettes, hand puppets, rod puppets, and mechanized puppets. Complicated puppets had to be operated by more than one person (sometimes up to eight), and occasionally there were complex animated objects (like a castle or the aurora borealis). The whole performance gained stylistic unity not by using the same type of puppets, but by mixing a variety of puppets with live actors.

Gołębska gave the productions their content, often adapting folktales herself, while Bunsch was responsible for the theatre's visual aspects. Michał Zarzecki, who had worked with the Totwens as a young man and then studied in Czechoslovakia, returned and rejoined the Miniatura as actor and director in 1960; he was a perfectionist who was able to consolidate the vision of Gołębska and Bunsch. Edward Dobraczyński, a choreographer who joined in 1961, trained the operators to make puppets move and dance like human beings. For more than fifteen years the core group at the Miniatura remained the same, and even throughout the 1970s Bunsch and Gołębska would return to guest-direct revivals of their productions.

The theatre is currently organized according to the basic pattern of state theatres in Poland, with a managing director, an artistic director, and two literary directors. More than 100 persons are employed in the theatre, a large number of whom are technicians in the workshops. All productions are built by the theatre itself, including such special effects as a working miniature automobile. At the moment the theatre building is under renovation (and has been so since 1983) but is scheduled to reopen in the near future.

The 1986–1987 repertory of the Miniatura was *Królowa Śniegu (The Snow Queen)*, adapted from Andersen, a rock musical directed by Zbigniew Wilkoński; *Szarate*, a compilation of the juvenalia of Stanisław Ignacy Witkiewicz, directed by Zbigniew Wilkoński; *Nim Zakwitnie Margierytka (Before the Daisy Blooms)*, by Małgorzata Włodowska, directed by Hubert Bierawski; *Słoneczna Zajączek (Sunny Bunny)*, directed by Hubert; and *Baśń o Pięknej Parysadzie (The Fable of Beautiful Parysada)*, adapted from Bolesław Leśmian by Natalia Gołębska and directed by Vojo Stankovski.

Theatre Ochoty Center of Theatrical Culture, Warsaw

The Theatre Center, established in 1971 on the initiative of actors, directors, and playgoers, is under the direction of the husband-and-wife team of Jan Machulski and Halina Machulska. From the beginning the Center was intended to be a family theatre that would offer more than productions; all presentations have two parts, the play itself and discussions with the spectators before, during, or after the performances. The repertory consists of such classic plays as *Hamlet* and *A Doll's House* and adaptations of modern works for children. Some plays are directed for children, others for teens, while still more are aimed at the entire family.

All plays are staged in such a way as to emphasize intimate contact between players and audience in a small auditorium with flexible seating. Discussions are conducted by the actors, the director, and, depending on the type of performance, by lawyers, physicians, or psychologists. The length and form of the discussion varies from play to play. For example, in *Measure for Measure* the main character stops the performance to ask the spectators for help in making a decision. Before the performance of *John and Mary* an actress in the role of a TV reporter greets playgoers in the hall and asks their opinions about love at first sight. Responses are videotaped and shown on a screen after the performance.

The company also engages in many "paratheatrical" activities. It operates a drama center at which 120 young persons, ages twelve to eighteen, meet after school twice a week to learn about theatre. Workshops are given in drama, poetry, music, dancing, pantomime, stage design, and directing. Each member of the group is obliged to participate in three short dramatic projects. After three years graduates receive diplomas and are eligible to become drama instructors for amateur groups. The best students and instructors spend two weeks during the summer at drama camps, taking part in workshops. At the end of the session there is a ceremony of being admitted to "the drama fans' club."

The Center has also been instrumental in introducing drama-in-education to the Polish schools through its workshops for teachers and an exchange with the Greenwich Youth Program Theatre in England, which regularly sends a group of actor-teachers to conduct training sessions with Polish teachers. Teenagers aged fifteen to eighteen have the opportunity to present their own creative work on the Center's "debut stage." On the second Tuesday of every month when the professional actors have their day off, a presentation of poems, paintings, monologues, and songs is held. A commission selects the best pieces, and among the spectators are always distinguished professional artists who analyze the work and write reviews.

Another type of activity is the performance of plays for parents who have young children. While the parents see a play in the main auditorium, their children are taken care of upstairs by one of the actors, who entertains the youngsters with a puppet show. Performances by children for children also are prepared and then shown at an open-air spring festival, in hospitals, and in centers for handicapped children.

The 1986–1987 repertory of Theatre Ochoty includes *John and Mary*, by Merwyn Jones, adapted and directed by Bożena Strykowna and Tomasz Mędrzak (family); *Pilot*, by Roger P. Davis, directed by Jan Machulski (family); *Crime and Punishment*, by Dostoevsky, adapted and directed by Machulski (family); *Porywacze Marzeń (Daydream Hijackers)*, by Robert Alexander, translated and directed by Halina Machulska (young people); *Ten Trzeci (This Third One)*, by Edward Hoornik, directed by Machulska (parents with young children); *Hamlet*, by Shakespeare, directed by Machulski (family); *Stachura—Szedłem Prosto Dalej (Stachura—I Went Farther Straight Ahead)*, adapted from the poetry of Stachura by Barbara Czołkowska, directed by Machulska (young people); *Lęk (Fear)*, by Machulski, directed by Zdzisław Tobiasz (young people); and *Adam i Ewa (Adam and Eve)*, adapted from Mark Twain, directed by Ryszard Zatorski (young people).

Center for the Theatrical Education of Children and Youth, Gdańsk

The Center had its beginnings in 1977 when Józefa Sławucka organized a series of lecture-demonstrations on theatre for pupils in the sixth form at four Polish primary schools. This experiment was so successful that after three years, it spread beyond Gdańsk and in 1982 became a national institution, the Center for the Theatrical Education of Children and Youth with Sławucka as its director. The Center is financed from the National Fund for the Development of Culture, but the costs of the implementation of its educational series are covered by different institutions: housing cooperatives, district councils, town councils, and rural councils. Activities are now carried out in seventeen of the forty-nine administrative districts in Poland and with the cooperation of fourteen professional theatres. More than 60,000 pupils saw the educational series in 1986, which consists of two lecture-demonstrations: "We Get to Know the Theatre" for primary-school pupils aged twelve to fourteen years and "Talks About the Theatre" for secondary-school pupils aged fifteen to seventeen years. Although written to be delivered by professional actors, sometimes the lectures now are performed by the pupils themselves. Although the Center cooperates with some secondary schools for academically gifted children, the main thrust of its work in secondary schools is with vocational students, who have little exposure to culture or even to traditional classroom instruction.

The Center's main goal is to work out a methodology of theatrical education for children and young people; but by "theatrical education" not only do they mean education *for* the theatre, but *through* the theatre as well. The Center acknowledges three elements to the successful "propagation of culture": the home, the house of culture, and the school. Various materials are published by the Center for teachers, culture house instructors, and drama group leaders. The Center also sponsors seminars and workshops in theatre history and drama-in-education for these groups.

In addition to the lecture-demonstration series, publications, and workshops, the Center is involved in preparing performances on its own stage (Scena Centrum) for young audiences. It has permanent places for the presentation of these performances in all the districts with which it cooperates. After performances, discussions with the audience are held by various experts such as philosophers, psychologists, and professors of literature from the university. The Center is also involved in taping a series of radio dramas made by young people themselves, and it sponsors conferences on educational theatre for participants (theatre people, social scientists, and educators) from all over the country.

The repertory of the Scena Centrum (1986/87) was *Sami o Sobie (About Ourselves)*, a play compiled from literary works sent by young people in response to a nationwide literary competition sponsored by the Center, by Tadeusz Pilszkiewicz and Krzysztof Wojcicki, directed by Tadeusz Pilszkiewicz; *???*, a play made by condensing *Party*, by Mrożek, and *Waiting for Godot*, by Beckett, and playing them as if they are one play, directed by Jerzy Nowicki; and *Prometeusz (Prometheus)*, by Aeschylus, directed by Florian Staniewski.

BIBLIOGRAPHY

Books

Awgulowa, Janina, and Wacława Świetęk. *Małe Formy Sceniczne w Pracy Przedszkoła (Small Scenic Forms in Pre-School Work)*. Warsaw: Wydawnictwo Szkolne i Pedagogiczne, 1982.

Domańska, Wiesława. *Przedwodnik Repertuarowy Teatru Lalek (A Guide to the Puppet Theatre Repertory)*. Warsaw: Centralny Ośrodek Metodyki Upowszechniania Kultury, 1976.

Dorman, Jan. *Zabawa Dzieci w Teatr (Children's Entertainment in the Theatre)*. Warsaw: Centralny Ośrodek Metodyki Upowszechniania Kultury, 1981.

Estreicher, Stanisław [Jan Krupski,] pseud. *Szopka Krakowska (The Cracow Nativity Play)*. Krakow: Tow. Miłosnikow Historyi i Zabyrkow Krakowa, 1904.

Górny, Andrzej. *Teatr Lalki i Aktora w Poznaniu, 1945–70 (The Puppet and Actor Theatre in Poznań, 1945–70)*. Poznań: Wydawnictwo Poznańskie, 1971.

Iłowski, Stanisław. *Teatr Lalek Teatrem dla Wszystkich (The Puppet Theatre Is a Theatre for Everybody)*. Warsaw: Wydawnictwo Związkowe, 1963.

Kostaszuk, Krystyna. *Polskie Sztuki dla Dzieci, 1945–1979 (Polish Plays for Children, 1945–1979)*. Warsaw: Agencja Autorska, 1979.

Jurkowski, Henryk. *Z Dziejow Poglądow na Teatr Lalek (From the History of Opinions on Puppet Theatre)*. Warsaw: Instytut Sztuki PAN, 1968.

————. *Teatr Dzieci Zaglebia 1945–1974 (The Theatre of the Children of Lower Silesia 1945–1974)*. Warsaw: Instytut Sztuki PAN, 1976.

————. *Teatr Lalek: Zagadniena Metodyczne (Puppet Theatre: Method Problems)*. Warsaw: Centralny Ośrodek Metodyki Upowszechniania Kultury, 1979.

————, ed. *W Kregu Warszawskiego "Baja" (In the Circle of the Warsaw "Storyteller")*. Warsaw: Panstwowy Instytut Teatralny, 1980.

Michalska, Monika, ed. *Informator Repertuarowy dla Teatru Amatorskiego (Repertory Information for the Amateur Theatre)*. Warsaw: Centr. Poradnia Amatorskiego Ruchu Artystycznego, 1968.

Rybotycka, Lidia. *Gry Dramatyczne. Teatr Młodziezy (Drama Games. Theatre for Young People)*. Warsaw: Wydawnictwo Szkolne i Pedagogiczne, 1976.

Ryl, Henryk. *Dziewanna i Lalki (Shepherd's Club and Puppets)*. Łódź: Wydawnictwo Łódzkie, 1967.

Słońska, Irena, ed. *Teatr Młodzieży (Youth Theatre)*. Warsaw: "Nasza Księgarnia," 1970.

Strzelecki, Zenobiusz. *Scenografia (Stage Design)*. Poznań: Teatr Lalki i Aktora "Marcinek," 1970.

Sztaudynger, Jan, *Od Szopki do Teatru Lalek (From Nativity Play to Puppet Theatre)*. Łódź: Wydawnictwo Łódzkie, 1961.

Plays

Januszewska, Hanna. *Tigger*. Warsaw: Agencja Autorska, 1963.

Miłobędzka, Krystyna. *My Home Country*. Warsaw: Agencja Autorska, 1969.

Maleszka, Andrzej. *Giants*. Warsaw: Agencja Autorska, 1986.

NOTES

1. Henryk Jurkowski, "Aktualne Problemy Teatru dla Dzieci i Młodziezy" ("Current Problems of the Theatre for Children and Youth"), *Sztuka i Dziecko: Materiały I Biennale Sztuki dla Dziecka* (Poznań: Wydział Kultury PRN, 1973), 194.

2. Interview with Halina Machulska, April 3, 1987.

Kathleen Cioffi

South Africa

HISTORY

The Republic of South Africa covers 1,124,000 square kilometers and is divided into four provinces; Cape, Transvaal, Orange Free State, and Natal. There are also several so-called independent homelands. Each area has a major urban center, four of which have theatre complexes with resident theatre companies: Cape Town in Cape; Pretoria, Johannesburg, and Vereeniging in the Transvaal; Bloemfontein in the Orange Free State; and Durban and Pietermaritzburg in Natal. In addition, there are eleven universities with specialized departments of drama and theatre studies and, in most instances, their own theatre buildings. Nine of these are situated in the four urban centers listed above; the only exceptions are the University of Zululand and Rhodes University. The University of Zululand is beyond the Durban-Pietermaritzburg area and does not, as yet, have its own theatre building. It has a fledgling department of theatre studies and to date has not produced children's theatre. Rhodes University, in the Eastern Cape, offers children's theatre for the local community, but only rarely. The other universities are discussed herein.

Given the vast geographical area involved, it is impossible to give a detailed record of all the children's theatre activities in the country. There may be numerous small companies or individuals doing worthwhile work in different communities that is not documented and, consequently, impossible to track down.

This entry, therefore, gives a brief history of and commentary on the following:

- The efforts of individuals who attempted to establish a South African children's theatre in the 1940s

- The state-subsidized theatre established in 1947 and split into four provincial arts boards in 1961

- The work of several drama and theatre studies departments at universities

• The work of independent companies not subsidized by the state

• Some important current playwrights

Some conclusions also are drawn concerning the following:

• The two approaches to children's theatre: the spectacle approach, designed for entertainment, and the educational approach, which is sometimes related to sociopolitical issues

• The effect of apartheid on children's theatre in South Africa

• The future of children's theatre in South Africa

EARLY HISTORY

Children's theatre productions, when they are defined as performances of scripted or unscripted material specifically aimed at the entertainment and/or education of young people, is a First World concept. South Africa, as a direct result of its colonial past, is a mixture of First World and Third World elements. No record in tribal writings can be found of any type of performance specifically designed for children. There are vivid descriptions of various storytellers who performed the folklore and collected the wisdom of a tribe for members of all ages. One can conjecture that this was both entertaining and educational for the audience, but strictly speaking, tribal traditions fall beyond the accepted definition of children's theatre and the scope of this entry.

First World colonists arrived in what is now called South Africa in 1652. They were Dutch Calvinists, who governed the colony until it was taken over by the British in 1806. It remained a British colony, with increasing measures of self-determination, until it attained full independence from Great Britain in 1961. The first record of children's theatre in South Africa can be traced to 1857, when special matinee performances of pantomimes were presented in Cape Town by Sefton Parry, an actor-manager from Britain. With his company of approximately seven players, Parry continued to present pantomime and other forms of theatre to Cape Town audiences until 1863.

From the 1870s British and American theatrical companies brought not only pantomimes, but also dramatized adaptations of *Uncle Tom's Cabin, The Prisoner of Zenda, The Three Musketeers*, and *Robin Hood* and of Dickens' novels *Bleak House, David Copperfield*, and *A Christmas Carol*. At first these productions, which toured to Durban, Kimberley, Johannesburg, Pretoria, Bloemfontein, and the eastern Cape towns, were intended for combined audiences of adults and children, but by the turn of the century overseas companies were bringing plays specifically for children. These included *Bluebell in Fairyland* and *Alice in Wonderland*. Leonard's Rayne's company, the most famous of the British companies, presented *Peter Pan* in 1919.

Sometimes actresses in the British companies stayed in South Africa and built careers for themselves in theatre, including children's theatre. Several British teachers also became involved in the establishment of children's theatre. Therefore, South African children's theatre was, and sometimes still is, largely based on British models.

TOWARD AN INDIGENOUS CHILDREN'S THEATRE

During the 1940s a turning point was reached when a teacher exchange program was launched between Britain and South Africa, bringing a number of innovative teachers to the country. Celia Evans from Wales, an active member of children's theatre organizations in Britain, started a campaign in the Transvaal in 1942 for the establishment of children's theatre in South Africa. A year later she formed an organization called Children's Theatre Incorporated in Johannesburg. From the outset she hoped that this group would become a parent body and that other branches would be formed in centers like Cape Town, Pretoria, Durban, and East London. In her publication *Beginners Please: A History of Children's Theatre in South Africa* Patricia Storrar states that Celia Evans believed "that nothing but the best was good enough for young unspoiled minds. To offer anything second rate would have been beneath her contempt; or rather beyond her understanding."[1]

The stated aim of Children's Theatre Incorporated was to "foster the things of the mind among young people, to bring them the whole glowing, fermenting world of drama and its allied arts." This was to be achieved, according to the Articles of Association, by establishing children's theatre centers and providing them with the "very best available entertainment, instruction, tuition and guidance in music and the arts." Productions were to be given in English and Afrikaans and were to be performed for all children in South Africa at the lowest possible admission prices. The company hoped that exposure to the arts would develop in children a "sense of appreciation" and "sound artistic standards," so that they would be able "to employ their leisure in future years in a worthy fashion."[2]

Children's Theatre Incorporated was to employ only professional actors of the highest caliber and to mount productions that were both lavish and elaborate. These lofty ideals, ironically, resulted in the demise of the organization when escalating costs, particularly actors' demands for higher salaries, could not be met. Still, under the energetic leadership of Celia Evans, the Johannesburg branch of Children's Theatre Incorporated had presented seventy-four productions of fairy tales and adventure stories over a period of twenty-two years. Some of the most spectacular offerings included *The Snow Queen*, directed by Isobel McLaren with costumes and sets designed by Myrrha Bantock; *The Wizard of Oz* and *Peter Pan*, directed by Taubie Kushlick; and open-air performances in Rhodes Park of *The Taming of the Shrew*, directed by Mary Holder. In addition to drama productions, and in keeping with their stated aims, the company also presented ballets, symphony concerts, marionette shows, readings, and recitals, all specifically intended for audiences of young people.

Another influential British teacher, Rosalie van der Gucht, arrived from England in 1940. After two years at a teacher's training college in Grahamstown she joined the staff of the drama department of the University of Cape Town. She became the most significant driving force behind the establishment of children's theatre in Cape Town. In 1950 she was approached by the Children's Theatre Incorporated of Johannesburg with a view toward establishing a branch in Cape Town.

Despite good intentions, the idea, once put into practice, did not work well. The reasons were partly practical and partly aesthetic. The two centers were far apart, making communication difficult; moreover, complications arose in the financing of the Cape Town branch. The Johannesburg branch insisted on keeping an extremely tight rein, financially and aesthetically, on Cape Town productions, and van der Gucht's ideas about the nature and practice of theatre for children differed radically from those of Evans and the other members of the parent organization. After five years and several attempts at compromise the Cape Town branch split away from Children's Theatre Incorporated and formed, in January 1956, an independent organization called Theatre for Youth under the leadership of van der Gucht.

The fundamentally different approaches of Evans and van der Gucht represent the same dichotomy still to be found as a central problem in the recently established South African Association for Drama and Youth Theatre. Evans believed firmly in the "magic" of the theatre, and to this end her productions made use of elaborate settings and sophisticated stage machinery that the audience could watch with wonder. Van der Gucht's approach, on the other hand, was one of simplicity, and it encouraged participation rather than observation; she wanted to harness not only the entertainment possibilities, but also the educational ones. She used simple sets and costumes and concentrated on the inner meaning of events and what the play had to offer in its educational objectives. Brian Way's innovative *Pinocchio*, adapted by Gretel Mills and directed by van der Gucht, and *Kalulu the Cunning Hare*, directed by Gretel Mills herself, were performed in theatres, school halls, and classrooms in Cape Town and surrounding areas, using an informal arena-style stage with the children sitting on the floor close to the actors. In addition, both directors attempted to involve the audience in participation that, to some degree, actually influenced the action of the play. Other examples of this approach include van der Gucht's productions of *Arena Entertainment* in 1952 and *Let's Make an Opera* in 1954.

The Theatre for Youth organization believed, as did Children's Theatre Incorporated, that standards of performance in children's theatre productions had to be the finest available. However, instead of employing only professional actors—an expensive business, as Children's Theatre Incorporated was to learn—Theatre for Youth used the students of the University of Cape Town's drama department as a nucleus of performers. The students were trained by van der

Gucht and others not merely as actors, but also as performers well versed in the educational implications of children's theatre. Infrequently professional actors were invited to take leading roles in productions, so that students could also learn the techniques of acting from experienced artists. This type of training proved invaluable to the young actors, many of whom subsequently continued to work successfully in adult theatre as well as in children's theatre. Moreover, some of van der Gucht's students went on to do pioneering work toward the establishment of professional children's theatre groups in other areas of the country. Most notable among these were Robin Malan, who became the leader of Pact Playwork in the Transvaal in the 1970s, and Janice Honeyman, who has written and directed plays for children all over South Africa.

In 1962 Children's Theatre Incorporated abandoned its policy of employing professional actors for productions because it could no longer afford to do so. As a result, standards fell, which, coupled with the organization's difficulty in obtaining plays suited to the idea of spectacle, brought about the company's demise in 1965. Theatre for Youth, however, continued to function until 1986, still using students from the University of Cape Town. In addition to its productions of plays for young audiences, the organization instituted annual winter schools for children in the early 1970s in which young people explored and experimented with theatre forms, including movement, mime, improvisation, communication excerises, directing, acting, and stage management. In his doctoral thesis, "The History and Development of Children's Theatre in English in South Africa," Walter Greyvenstein discusses the far-reaching influence of van der Gucht on children's theatre in South Africa:

It was Theatre for Youth and its Winter School that produced the Cape Town personalities who have subsequently appeared in the forefront of children's theatre. These include Phyllis Klotz, who has tended to specialize in Theatre-in-Education programs; Gay Morris and Esther van Ryswyk, both lecturers at the university with a special interest in theatre for children; and Lieske Bester and Graham Boxall, who, together with Glenn Day, established the Imps Drama Workshop in 1974.

Janice Honeyman, Robin Malan, and Annie Barnes can be added to the list.

THE NATIONAL THEATRE ORGANIZATION

In 1947 the National Theatre Organization (NTO) was founded as a result of the indefatigable work of Mr. (later Dr.) P.P.B. Breytenbach. The organization was to be run on funds provided by the state. Although their headquarters were in Pretoria in the Transvaal, the NTO was commissioned to bring theatrical productions to all the major urban centers of the country as well as to as many of the rural towns as possible.

Initially, the NTO catered specifically to adults, although for certain productions special matinee performances were arranged for young people, usually at the secondary-school level. After ten years as a state-subsidized professional theatre company, the NTO began to realize the importance of theatre for children and young people. In 1959 it appointed three young actors, Jannie Gildenhuys, Leonora Nel, and Cobus Roussouw, who, after visiting Europe to observe the latest practices in theatre for young people, toured the country offering dramatized versions of literary texts to high school pupils, as well as theatre for young people of all ages. The size of the company was gradually increased, and it subsequently performed an average of 115 school literature programs and sixty-five performances of children's theatre each year.

This group worked in close ensemble, sharing the acting, directing, designing, administration, and backstage duties in rotation. In addition, they performed in both English and Afrikaans. It is significant that members of this company are today among the foremost actors and directors in adult theatre, proving that their earlier experience in the youth company was instrumental in the development of fundamental theatre skills and sound professional attitudes. Yet, unfortunately, not one of them continued to lobby for or be involved in children's theatre.

THE PERFORMING ARTS BOARD

The Youth Group of the NTO continued to function in schools around the country until the NTO was disbanded in 1963 in order to form four separate state-subsidized theatre companies, one for each province: PACT in the Transvaal, Cape Performing Arts Board (CAPAB) in the Cape, NAPAC in Netal, and PACOFS in the Orange Free State. Initially, only CAPAB and PACT formed special companies for children's theatre and school programs, and for the purposes of this article, commentary is confined to these two groups. Although NAPAC and PACOFS did similar work, their productions were sporadic and, when they occurred, documentation was not always sent to the Center for South African Theatre Research. Consequently information is not readily available.

The PACT youth company came into being under the direction of Leonora Nel, one of the founders of the NTO's youth group, who continued the practice of presenting both children's theatre productions and programs based on the literary texts required for study in the Transvaal senior secondary schools. A radical change in the company occurred in 1974 when Robin Malan became the director of the youth group, which he renamed PACT Playwork. His influence represents a milestone in the history of youth theatre in the country. Trained as both an actor and a teacher, he created a symbiotic unity of theatre and education that resulted in an integrated cultural enrichment for audiences and Playwork actors alike. Malan had recently visited Britain when he took up his post at PACT, and there he had encountered a new form of youth theatre called theatre-in-education (TIE). He decided to make TIE the basis of PACT Playwork's work.

Under his influence the company moved away from the practice of simply presenting abbreviated, dramatized versions of literary texts in their school programs and toward TIE programs that, although based on specific texts, had definite educational objectives beyond the retelling of the story. A particularly remarkable example was Peter Terry's TIE program on *Romeo and Juliet*. Using the participant's knowledge of Shakespeare's text as a springboard, Terry explored the notion of prejudice in South Africa by including easily identifiable scenes, scripted by the actor-teachers, that ostensibly centered on the friction in Northern Ireland. The parallels (and differences) with the South African situation and the situation in Northern Ireland were apparent, resulting in lively debate that continued in the schools long after the company had left.

During Malan's period as leader of the Playwork company thought-provoking productions included the company-devised *All in a Tangle*, about factory workers who agree to become puppets for the boss and then have to untangle themselves when their strings become snarled; Peter Terry's *The Lamont Case*, about the tarring and feathering of an Afrikaner dissident; and an innovative play created by the actors called *Goings on at Dingemalerie-Donag-Dell*. It introduced pleasant, fun-loving characters in an unspecified community in which, as a result of the appearance of certain purple flowers, the people became less pleasant and started quarreling. The audience was asked to help solve this problem, and in the second half of the production the children's suggestions were explored. In spontaneous improvisations the company acted out the children's ideas in order to find the most viable solution for the community. The "play" thus changed from one performance to the next, depending on how the children developed the plot.

By 1978 PACT Playwork was giving, according to Greyvenstein, an average of 450 performances per year in schools, with a total attendance of more than 85,000 young persons. This included both the literary-based programs for the senior secondary schools and an average of four different primary-school TIE programs on subjects as diverse as mathematics, grammar, history, geography, pollution, health, road safety, tribal life, war, and cruelty to animals.

In addition to its TIE work in schools, the PACT Playwork company also presented at least one children's theatre production each year. These were invariably innovative, the most memorable of which were *Starbright*, scripted and directed by Janice Honeyman; *Old King Cole*, written by Ken Campbell and directed by Robin Malan; *A Christmas Carol* and *Brer Rabbit*, directed by John Rogers; *Winnie the Pooh*, directed by Malan; and *Die Hertekoning*, directed by Alwyn Swart. (*Starbright* is discussed in more detail in the section on current playwrights).

Under Malan's leadership the Transvaal became a center of excellence for children's theatre and TIE. Playwork's TIE programs, particularly, reflected relevant sociopolitical issues and thus, given the needs of the country, served as fine examples to be followed by other TIE practitioners in South Africa. Malan, however, found it increasingly difficult to work within the confines of PACT's management policy and the rules laid down by education departments, and left the country in 1978 to teach in Swaziland.

His assistant director, Alwyn Swart, took over the running of Playwork, and under his direction the company continued to present exciting work. Swart was particularly keen to use the inherent sociopolitical nature of the TIE process to stimulate young people in South Africa to think analytically about the society in which they were living. Under his leadership the Playwork TIE programs became more radical. He encouraged Peter Terry and other directors to explore and extend the parameters of the medium. It was during this time that Terry devised and directed the program on *Romeo and Juliet* and several other provocative pieces of work. Swart himself devised and directed challenging and socially pertinent programs based on Afrikaans literature and, for the first time, extended TIE to nursery schools.

Predictably, given the conservative nature of education in South Africa, the increasing radicalization of the Playwork company's work led to its demise in 1984. The Transvaal Education Department, which subsidized the school programs, found TIE, and in particular Peter Terry's programs, "dangerous." They demanded that PACT return to the safe dramatic presentations of condensed books. Swart protested vehemently on behalf of the company, but he was not sustained by PACT's own administrators, who supported the education authorities, declaring that TIE was not the sort of work that PACT ought to be doing and expressing the curious notion that it inhibited the growth of the actors!

Swart attempted to keep TIE and Playwork alive, despite the restrictions imposed by both PACT and the education authorities, but the frustrations made his work impossible and in 1984 he left the company. Several of the actor-teachers resigned, and Playwork, as such, was dissolved. PACT continues to present school programs, based on condensed versions of literary texts, that incorporate no active pupil participation or textual commentary, using ad hoc actors and directors. So ended what was the brightest chapter in the history of children's theatre in South Africa.

The work of the CAPAB was aimed at pure entertainment until Eileen Thorns became head of its youth drama group in 1974: "I chose and looked for scripts which examined socially relevant issues and where possible, applied them to the South African environment and conditions" she wrote in a questionnaire sent out by Walter Greyvenstein for his doctoral thesis: "I would like to see my own work developing in writing scripts that reflect the changing South African environment and somehow make children aware of this through drama and theatre."

Under Thorns' leadership the CAPAB group produced TIE work similar to that done in the Transvaal, as well as some exciting children's theatre productions. Unfortunately, however, Thorns, too, felt the pressures of state disapproval and administrative policy, and in 1981 left the CAPAB youth group. She is now involved in educational television.

The current position of children's theatre by the state-subsidized organizations in South Africa is bleak. Despite the fact that children form a sizable proportion of the population and their parents, as taxpayers, are contributing to the running of these organizations, the performing arts boards seem disinterested in children's theatre. Since the late 1970s PACT has produced five plays for children, CAPAB five, NAPAC three, and PACOFS approximately five (the precise number is difficult to determine because PACOFS' documentation is incomplete). It is little wonder that audience figures in these organizations are declining for, although there are obviously other reasons, one cause must be that fewer and fewer adults have been exposed to theatre in their childhood.

THE ROLE OF DRAMA DEPARTMENTS AT UNIVERSITIES

The drama (theatre studies) departments, while training their students in theatre, are often responsible for keeping children's theatre alive in their communities. Professor Robert Mohr, who succeeded Professor van der Gucht at the University of Cape Town when she retired in 1971, continued to labor in children's theatre and in TIE. Among other productions he presented were Aubrey Berg's *Story Theatre* and *The Tale of the Red Dragon* and Susan Broer's adaptation of Edward Lear's *The Owl and the Pussycat*.

During the seventies Esther van Ryswyk, a lecturer at the university, did pioneering work in Cape Town and its environs by introducing TIE into Cape schools. At the time CAPAB did not become actively involved in TIE and was not to do so until the appointment of Eileen Thorns in 1976. In the intervening period the only TIE programs for children in the Cape were those done by van Ryswyk and the University of Cape Town students. Together they devised and performed a wide variety of school programs that sought not only to explore certain curriculum areas in dramatic form, but also to attempt to make young people aware of some sociopolitical issues confronting their parents and the government.

Van Ryswyk explored and extended the parameters of TIE in schools and set a high standard of TIE in the Cape province. Both TIE and children's theatre continue to be part of the curriculum for theatre studies at the University of Cape Town, but since van Ryswyk's resignation from the university the amount of work done has depended on the presence on the staff or among the students of directors who are sufficiently interested in the medium to devise programs.

In Natal, according to Greyvenstein, as in Cape Town, it was the university drama department in Durban that initiated interest in children's theatre after the early days of pantomime and the visits by the Leonard Rayne company. In the 1950s, under Professor Elizabeth Sneddon, people like Joan Little began to direct plays specifically for children. It was not until 1964, however, when one of the students at the university, Jane Osborne, directed *Alice in Wonderland* as part of her directing course, that a sustained interest in children's theatre developed. This continued and was considerably extended when Professor Pieter Scholtz took over from Sneddon in 1967. Scholtz, one of Sneddon's students, not only directed children's theatre productions with the students in the department, but also, from 1970 onward, began writing plays especially for children. *Thurkaari:*

Demon of the Curry Powers was written and produced in 1970 and *Miranda and the Magic Sponge*, in 1975.

Scholtz has become an important exponent of children's theatre. In addition to the two plays mentioned above, he has written and directed *The Amazing Adventures of Tambootie the Puppet* (1979), *Mr. Big Strikes Again* (1980), *Pappa Mario and the Grande Circus Adventure* (1982), *Tambootie's London Adventure* (1986), *The Astounding Antics of Anthony Ant* (1987), and *Samantha Seal* (1987). Although sociopolitical issues are not overt in Scholtz's work, there is a moral background to the plays. For example, Samantha Seal, Wally Walrus (who has a proverb for every occasion), and the nosey, chattering Scrounger the Seagull fight for the right of *all* seagulls to live in peace and safety.

As a result of Scholtz's work at the speech and drama department, Durban University's influence has spread to other institutions in Natal, such as the University of Durban-Westville and Edgewood College of Education in Durban, and to the University of Pietermaritzburg and the teacher's training college there. There is no doubt that tertiary-education institutions form the bedrock of children's theatre in Natal.

In the Transvaal the students of the drama department at the University of Pretoria present at least one season of children's theatre per year. The School of Dramatic Art at the University of the Witwatersrand in Johannesburg also produces plays specifically for children, but it does so infrequently. The same can be said of the drama departments at the universities of Potchefstroomin in the Transvaal, Stellenbosch in the Cape, and Bloemfontein in the Orange Free State.

INDEPENDENT THEATRE COMPANIES

In South Africa professional theatre companies that are not subsidized by the state are known as independent theatre companies or managements. Several of these operate in major urban centers, but few do work especially for children.

The Space Theatre (later renamed the People's Space Theatre) in Cape Town existed from 1972 to 1983. During that time the company became renowned for opening its doors to people of all races at a time when most theatres, including state-subsidized theatres, only admitted whites. (All theatres in the country subsequently have been opened to all who want to attend performances.) The People's Space Theatre presented challenging sociopolitical plays to adults and children alike. The children's theatre productions, although not obviously political, nevertheless attempted to present audiences with the kinds of ideas and information unavailable in the state-run schools.

One of their first productions for children, directed by the well-known actress Yvonne Bryceland, was *The Thirteen Clocks*, by James Thurber. This was followed by, among others, *Workplay*, devised and directed by Robin Malan; *Gameplay*, devised and directed by Henry Goodman; and *The Crafty Tortoise*, based on an African folktale written by Fatima Dike and directed by Pippa Duffy.

Under the auspices of the People's Space Theatre several TIE programs were compiled and presented to schoolchildren of all ages. Some of these were based directly on literary texts required for study in secondary schools, whereas others dealt with more general areas of interest that held social relevance. Sometimes these TIE programs and some of the plays for children, like *Theatre Roundabout*, were taken to areas outside Cape Town so that they could be seen by children who, for financial or other reasons, were not able to travel to the city center.

When the People's Space Theatre closed, the Baxter Theatre Management became a base for children's theatre in Cape Town. Thus an independent theatre company, The Glynn Day Children's Theatre Company, was established in June 1986 with the aim of introducing children to theatre with all the conventions of lights, sound effects, costumes, and sets. Here the children are encouraged to participate in the action but only within the limits of the script. In a sense, this is much the same aim that was envisaged by Celia Evans and Children's Theatre Incorporated (1943–1965).

The success of the company is a clear indication of interest in and need for entertainment for children in the Cape Peninsula area. Eight productions were mounted in the first eighteen months of the company's existence—three in 1986 and five in 1987. With the exception of *Three Cheers for President Charlie*, by South African playwright James Ambrose Brown, the productions have all been based on classic novels like *Alice in Wonderland*, fairy tales like *Goldilocks and the Three Bears*, and nursery rhymes like *Mother Goose* and *The Old Woman Who Lived in a Shoe*. Nearly every performance has played to a full house, and in one year more than 2,000 individuals and schools or other organizations have asked to be put on the company's mailing list.

The leaders of the company are Glynn Day, who worked extensively with Robin Malan in the early 1970s, acted for Theatre for Youth under Rosalie van der Gucht, and established three Drama Workshop Companies for children, where he taught and directed young people for twelve years; Pippa Duffy, who has established herself as a talented actress, singer, and composer and who writes the music and lyrics for productions and also acts in them; and John Dennison, who has worked with Glynn Day over a number of years and is an accomplished actor and singer, and who has a special talent for communicating with young people.

Although the Glynn Day company works in a traditional fairy-tale/nursery-rhyme medium, its productions attempt to give new life to the original texts with the addition of lyrics and music. The company concentrates on teaching the young the conventions of theatre and provides a common meeting place for children in Cape Town. This notwithstanding, their work represents mere entertainment at a time when there is an urgent need for children (and adults) to become aware of sociopolitical issues that could contribute toward a changing South Africa. If numerous other theatre companies also presented work for children, the lack of socially relevant material by Glynn Day might not be felt so keenly. As it is, however, this is one of but a handful of companies that are active today in South Africa, and its sole use of fairy-tale and fantasy material is therefore questionable.

The Market Theatre Company, an independent theatre company in Johannesburg in the Transvaal, which has the same commitment to presenting socially relevant theatre to the public, has been in existence for thirteen years. Between 1976 and 1979 the company presented four children's theatre productions, all directed by Janice Honeyman. Unfortunately, since then, their management does not appear to consider children's theatre a priority. Since the early 1980s they have presented only three children's theatre productions.

PUPPET THEATRE

Currently there are several puppet theatre companies operating in the children's theatre medium, of which the Handspring Puppet Company, directed by Adrian Kohler and Basil Jones, is the most renowned. The company tours the country with its productions and, in addition to puppet theatre performances for children, they conduct workshops in puppetry for teachers and students at teacher-training colleges. Its work is largely based on indigenous scripts written by members of the company or other South African writers. Productions have included *Mbira for Passela* and other plays based on African folktales, and animal stories such as *Gertie's Feathers*, about an ostrich whose feathers have been plucked for a smart boutique in Cape Town. Gertie daringly retrieves her feathers, which have meanwhile been dyed a bright pink, and, in wearing them again, becomes the "smartest" ostrich on the farm.

The company has recently been commissioned by health associations to create puppet productions to increase children's awareness of health hazards. In this line they have produced *The Mouth Trap*, written by Jones and Kohler, about oral hygiene, and *The Girl with the Flower in Her Mouth*, written by John Caviggia and Esther van Ryswyk, which deals with the health problems of two families. One family's problems are related to stress and the other's, to overeating. Trix and David, one child from each family, meet a tramp who, after listening to their problems, gently guides them with his questions to an understanding of the reasons for their unhappiness. They realize that their families need to adopt healthier lifestyles, and the members of the audience are asked to give them advice on how to achieve these.

The directors of the company, Kohler and Jones, are innovative, creative artists who are constantly searching for new material, ideas, and techniques. Lately they have stripped away the conventional masking curtains of the puppet theatre stage so that the puppeteers are visible to the audience. This has allowed for the exploration of special relationships between the puppets and their manipulators: in one instance the relationship was seen by the audience as one in which the manipulators represented the alter egos of the puppets.

CURRENT PLAYWRIGHTS—A SELECTION

Up to 1954 the playscripts presented for children were almost exclusively imported from Britain and the United States. In this year, however, James Ambrose Brown wrote his first indigenous script for children, *The Three Wishes*. He followed it with several others, such as *The Circus Adventure, Three Cheers for President Charlie*, and *Amelia's African Adventure*. Amelia, a china doll whose home is a Victorian dollhouse, is sent to Africa as a gift to the daughter of a Scottish missionary and explorer, Dr. Livingstone. She is accompanied by other dolls, Mrs. Noah, James the Butler, and Major Chutney. In Africa they meet the Cloth Lion and Sambo, the wicked crocodile, and their subsequent adventures are essentially African.

A growing body of indigenous plays for children includes, besides the plays of Pieter Scholtz, the work of three playwrights. Janice Honeyman belongs to a new generation of playwrights for young audiences. Schooled in the van der Gucht approach, she writes and directs plays for different companies, and her name has become synonymous with children's theatre, although she has been equally productive in adult theatre. Her first play, *Cape Parade Adventure* (late 1960s), introduced a new style that combined entertainment with educational material that touched on social issues.

In a later play, *WAM* (Wolfgang Amadeus Mozart), she introduced children to the young Mozart, his sister Nan, his two bird-like friends Pappageno and Pappagena, and the two rogues Humperdinck and Pumpernickel. She made use of some of Mozart's music, such as the Horn Concerto and the duets from *The Magic Flute*, and, together with a script written in rhyming couplets and some prose, sought to combine musical education and understanding with musical and theatrical experience. The result was a joyful, meaningful celebration of Mozart and his music.

Starbright, a nativity play, is an unusual adaptation of medieval mystery plays set in a modern South African context. The action takes place in a children's playground with the jungle gym representing heaven. Joseph's donkey is a soapbox cart, and the shepherds use the dialect of Cape farm laborers. In her production of the play Honeyman created powerful symbols in the way she suspended the disbelief of the audience. For example, the baby Jesus was represented by a pillow with the face of a baby embroidered on it. The pillow was brought to Mary concealed in an apron that the angel Gabriel fastened around her. The "baby" was "born" by pulling the pillow out of its pocket in the apron. This done, Mary kissed the embroidered face, stroked the woolen hair, and wrapped the "baby" in her shawl.

Since the beginning of the 1980s Annie Barnes has been writing and directing plays especially for children. She started the Two Hoots Company in Cape Town and later moved to Johannesburg, where she created the Out of the Box Company, one of the country's few professional groups that exists solely to perform educational theatre for children. Despite its small size, it does powerful work, such as Barnes' plays *The Jubba Jugga Junkyard Jollies* and *Rainbow Land*, a script about conservation.

Staged by PACT in 1987, *Danny and the Desert Girl* was written by Peter Terry, who, since leaving Playwork, has become known as an actor and, lately, as a playwright. Danny is a boy of Western culture and experience, while the Desert Girl, Oxana, represents the tribal experience. They meet while Danny is trying to free his father, who has been jailed unjustly by the government. As Oxana helps Danny a special friendship develops. At first the youngsters tend to ridicule the differences they perceive in each other, but gradually they come to realize that their backgrounds, although different, are of equal importance and that only through a synthesis of their cultures is the rescue possible. They also become aware of the abuse of power in both Western and tribal communities; the sociopolitical undertones are apparent to young audiences, and comparison with their own situation is inevitable.

A PERSONAL PERSPECTIVE

In 1979 the first national association, the South African Association for Drama and Youth Theatre (SAADYT), was formed. The aims of SAADYT are to bring together people involved in youth drama and theatre; to improve and extend current practices; and, in a resolution adopted in 1987, to work through educational drama and theatre toward a just and democratic society. Since its inception SAADYT has tended to concentrate, in workshops and conferences, on classroom drama (creative dramatics) and TIE, at the expense perhaps of children's theatre. There does not seem to be a direct link between SAADYT's interests and the practice of children's theatre by professional theatre companies. However, given the alarming decline in the number of children's theatre productions presented by these companies, it appears that SAADYT could play a vital role in encouraging children, their parents, and drama practitioners to examine the state of children's theatre in South Africa and, ultimately, in making representation to the theatre companies to look to the needs of children as well as to those of adults. It appears now that if SAADYT does not become involved in this way, children's theatre will either continue to be only a "poor relation" to the arts or, more seriously, be ignored altogether. The picture is dismal but not without hope.

Less hopeful, however, is the situation with respect to TIE. Having realized the subtlety of the TIE form and its inherently social content, the education authorities in South Africa appear to have taken fright. Some have banned any form of pupil participation in programs, and all have demanded a return to the simple dramatic presentation of abbreviated literary texts. It would be unwise to underestimate the power of the authorities, for in the past, and up to the present, they have provided the funds for school theatre programs. Moreover, only programs that have been approved may be presented in the schools under their jurisdiction. Considering the fact that there are but a handful of private schools, this would make the financial survival of independent TIE companies difficult, if not impossible.

One possible way out of this invidious situation would be to find funding for TIE in the private sector and to establish independent companies to function not in schools, which is the natural place for them, but in outside venues and at times other than normal school hours. In the current economic climate the chances of finding necessary funding and of creating the necessary infrastructures are slim. Nevertheless, there is a glimmer of hope.

Finally, one cannot leave the arena of children's theatre in South Africa without considering the effects of apartheid, for, inevitably, they have left and still do leave their mark. For years only white children were allowed to attend performances. Now that theatres are open to all, there is an understandable reluctance on the part of black parents to send their children to the theatre and, moreover, no tradition for doing so. Admission prices, when added to the cost of transportion, make theatregoing a luxury beyond the economy of most black parents.

Apartheid policies also dictate strict adherence to racially separate schools. The only exceptions are the few private schools that are not funded, or are only partially funded, by the state. This condition makes it impossible to present schools' programs with racially mixed casts, which would at least give children the opportunity of seeing people who are defined as "different" working together. It also makes impossible the fruitful exchange of ideas and experiences across racial barriers. TIE *could* function as an important medium for exploring racial and other social issues and for promoting tolerance and understanding within this fractured society, if the system of apartheid education did not halt progress in this direction.

One cannot imagine a more suitable and fruitful common meeting place for children than the theatre, for there they would be able to share the art form and explore their commonality. Although the obstacles that prevent such a children's theatre in South Africa are many, it is possible if today's drama and theatre practitioners can rise to the challenges in the way that Celia Evans, Rosalie van der Gucht, Robin Malan, Alwyn Swart, and others did in the past.

BIBLIOGRAPHY

Archive material from the Center for South African Theatre Research of the Human Sciences Research Council.

Bosman, F.C.L. *Drama en Toneel in Suid Afrika, Deel II, 1856–1912*. Pretoria: Van Schaik, 1980.

Bryant, Margot. *Born to Act*. Johannesburg: Ad Donker, 1979.

Greyvenstein, Walter. "The History and Development of Children's Theatre in English South Africa." Ph.D. diss. Rand Afrikaans University.

Storrar, Patricia. *Beginners Please: A History of Children's Theatre in South Africa*. Johannesburg: Children's Theatre, 1968.

NOTES

1. Patricia Storrar, *Beginners Please: A History of Children's Theatre in South Africa* (Johannesburg: Children's Theatre, 1968), 7.
2. Ibid.

Esther van Ryswyk and Patricia Anne Terry

Spain

HISTORY

From the end of World War II until 1964 a number of children's theatre companies played throughout Spain, although without benefit of a national organization to publicize their work. In 1964, however, Spanish representatives attended a meeting in London that promoted the creation of an international association of theatre for children and youth. Spain not only became a founding member of ASSITEJ, but also soon founded a national center that supports all aspects of youth theatre both in the large cities and in the provinces. The major goal of the ASSITEJ Center, located in Madrid, is to develop children's interest in and love of theatre, which then extends to teenage years and to youth in general, and to create for them a specific kind of theatre performed by professional actors or adult amateurs.

A series of national congresses that began in Barcelona in 1967, and now are held in a different city every two years, have made theatre for children and youth better known throughout the country. They consist of open competitions of children's plays as well as seminars dealing with problems faced by the profession. Out of these was launched the National Campaign, which since 1969 has encouraged companies working for young audiences, not only within Spain, but also in thirteen Latin American countries, which since 1981 have created their own ASSITEJ centers. The Campaigns, subsidized by the Ministry of Information and Tourism, have made it possible for as many as eighteen companies to come together to compare their work.

ASSITEJ also publishes the *Iberoamerican Information Bulletin* every three months, which assists centers in Latin America by making available the latest international news. ASSITEJ sends Spanish companies to perform at international festivals, such as the one in Lyon, France, in 1982. The center maintains a library of foreign and national books, magazines, and bulletins that are made available to anyone interested in children's theatre. It also collects videotapes of productions by member groups, making it possible for research to be conducted on the evolution and development of theatre for children and young people.

A typical demonstration of the range of work was seen at the Fourth ASSITEJ Festival held in Madrid in the spring of 1987 under the sponsorship of the Spanish Ministry of Culture. As in previous years, sessions were conducted after every performance among the participating groups and representatives from ASSITEJ International Centers, including Czechoslovakia, Hungary, Denmark, Norway, Israel, Sri Lanka, England, and West Germany. Twelve companies performed before a total audience of 7,000, of whom 6,742 were children from fifty-seven schools. The repertory indicated the wide variety of styles and subject matter available to young audiences in Spain.

THE CURRENT REPERTORY

Company Juanjo Menendez-Ester Gala from Madrid performed *Palabras Solo Palabras* (*Words Only Words*) for thirteen- and fourteen-year-olds, which tells the story of two rogues who arrive in a town and decide to make their fortunes by duping the citizens. They plot a series of adventures that closely parallel scenes from plays by Jacinto Benavente, Lope de Vega, and other Spanish classics with which audiences are already familiar. Company El Compas, also from Madrid, presented *Los Vagabundos (The Tramps)* for ten- to twelve-year-olds, which reveals the imaginations of two vagabonds who, when faced by the barriers of a large city, must survive through fantastic adventures, comical situations, and tragic experiences. Company El Diablo Cojuelo from Madrid appeared in *Entremeses de Cervantes (Interludes of Cervantes)*, for ages twelve to fourteen, which combines four of Cervantes' "Entremeses" (interludes or farces) to make a play on the language of the lie. A light and mocking work, this piece is intended to make audiences hear words written four centuries ago by Spain's most remarkable author.

From Barcelona came Company L'Ocas in *Los Lunastronautas* (*The Moon Astronauts*), for audiences between eight and ten years old. This adventure play concerns three little girls who build a rocket from the debris they find in their local junkyard with the hope that they may travel to the moon. Realizing that they need some hammers and saws for this project, they approach various adults who invariably tell them, "Tools are not for little girls." At the same time, Luis regrets being a little boy because he is always being given tasks to perform by his father, whereas the little girls are free to play. Rosa suggests that they swap clothes so Luis will learn that little girls "don't have it so easy either." When Uncle Juan arrives he assigns the girls (including the imposter) the "feminine" work (dusting and cleaning up but not touching anything that might be heavy), while the boy (Rosa in disguise) must do everything else. Later, when Rosa and Luis exchange clothes again in front of Uncle Juan's eyes, he admits that he has judged people not by their abilities, but by their appearances.

Company Arca of Barcelona presented *Marco & Polo o Viceversa* (*Marco & Polo or Vice-versa*), for nine- to eleven-year-olds, which involves two beggars who perform in the streets. They portray the traditional clown figures, one who is smart and dominating and the other who is stupid but who also sometimes changes roles with his counterpart. An audience participation show, everyone is invited to come on stage and take an active part in the story as the two clowns imagine a great sea voyage. *Mi Ventana da a El Teatro* (*My Window Looks on the Theatre*) was offered by Company Abrego from Santander for audiences from five to seven. Members of the audience are asked to help create a play through improvisation, using costumes and props, and under the direction of a flamboyant director. Soon they are involved in staging three separate scenes that reveal to them how expressive they can be and tell an entertaining story.

From Valencia, Company La Falaguera played *Historias de la Falaguera* (*Stories of the Falaguera*), for children aged five to seven, in which "people come to realize that to be good is not so good, and to be bad is not so bad." This is accomplished through fights, hypnosis, dancing, magic, chases, and other elements of children's stories. Another audience-participation play from Company La Quimers de Plastico, from Vallodolid, titled *Ensalada de Nandidos* (*Bandit Salad*), grew out of actual experiences of teachers in Valladolid when they discovered the powerful results dramatics had on their students. Likewise, Company La Gorgona, from Madrid, presented a participation play for five-to seven-year-olds with its *La Gallina Magica* (*The Magic Hen*), in which the audience helps three clowns in their fight against the Witch of Laughter. The performance combines adventure with music, games, lights, and special effects.

A version of a Grimm fairy tale, here presented so that the characters reveal the reverse of their behavior, was played by La Quebrada, from Madrid: *La Increible Historia de una Reina, su Espejo y Blancanieves* (*The Incredible Story of a Queen, Her Mirror, and Snow White*), for audiences seven to nine years old. Company Cambaleo, from Madrid, performed *En Busca del Tesoro* (*Treasure Hunt*), for ages nine to eleven, in which everyday objects are used to tell a story. Three clowns take the audience on a journey designed to show that clowning and dramatic play are the theatre's fundamental elements. From Madrid, Company Cocktail appeared in *Una del Oeste* (*A Western*), for ages ten to twelve. During the course of filming a third-rate Western the director encounters difficulties from his actors, technicians, and assistants in a comedy that satirizes movies, love stories, and theatre itself.

Most of the plays described here were created by the companies that perform them, but other groups, such as Los Titeres (the National Youth Theatre in Madrid), offer plays by well-known authors, such as Cervantes, Calderon de la Barca, Lope de Vega, and Tirso de Molina. The repertories also include titles that are familiar around the world: *The Adventures of Pinocchio, Peter Pan, The Little Prince* (of Saint-Exupery), *The Wizard of Oz*, and *Amahl and the Night Visitors*. The most performed play in Spain, *Pluft, the Little Ghost*, is by Brazilian author Maria Clara Machado.

Street theatre is also popular; companies play in open spaces before large gatherings of youngsters who otherwise may never see live theatre. Two companies, Els Comediants in Barcelona and La Tartana in Madrid, have won international acclaim for their work.

CATALAN THEATRE FOR YOUNG PEOPLE

A great deal of activity may be found in the Catalan theatre for young people. In Catalonia, as in any other region that has a rich folkloric heritage and is deeply rooted in its past, theatre for young audiences is based on certain celebrations that could be referred to as "paratheatrical." The "Patum," "Mulasses," "Passions," and "Pastorets," which are popular folk events, ethnically well defined, and whose language and meaning are understood by all, represent a theatre for children that is unsophisticated by nature. Despite some changes, they are special occasions held at various times of the year and continue to bear witness to the indestructible nature of Catalan origins.

For many years some theatres included short plays for children between their regular adult performances. As in ancient Greek and Roman theatre, this practice assured the presence of children in the audience. By the end of the past century renowned Catalan writers had begun to write plays for young audiences. Every Thursday afternoon, from 1921 to 1923, children's plays were performed in the center of Barcelona.

Josep-Ma Folch i Torres, an outstanding playwright still unknown outside Spain, first worked as a journalist, then wrote some naturalistic novels that were critically well received, and next went into political exile for several years at the beginning of the twentieth century. He also wrote plays for children and young people, staged some fifty of his works, and co-edited a Catalan-language magazine, *Patufet*, which was published from 1904 until 1938, when Franco forced it to cease operation. Although fifty years have elapsed since the magazine's last issue was published, many Catalans still remember learning to read and write their language (which has been forbidden in schools at various stages throughout Spain's history, the most recent being from 1939 until the 1980s) through the pages of *Patufet*.

The Romea theatre, one of Barcelona's oldest and currently the home of the Catalan Dramatic Center, is the venue in which Folch i Torres' new works were regularly performed. Some of his plays, such as a version of *Cinderella*, are now part of the classic repertory. During Folch i Torres' heyday Catalonia had more than 500 amateur theatre groups, which ensured that his works were widely known. The Romea theatre currently offers a yearly theatre season for youngsters (which has been operational since 1967). Under the sponsorship of the city of Barcelona, plays are presented every Sunday morning from October until March.

In the midst of the Francoist era, when Catalan was not taught in schools and books in the language were not published, this theatre became an important part in the struggle to retain ethnic identity. Versions of classic plays by Molière,

Shakespeare, Goldoni, and even Durrenmatt and Brecht were performed, and although authorities permitted the plays to be seen only by audiences over fourteen years of age, they were, nevertheless, appreciated and enjoyed. Soon the idea spread to numerous cities and villages. Groups emerged that took on the responsibility of organizing performances, and suddenly Catalan-language theatre was everywhere. It was performed throughout Catalonia, reaching schools, streets, and even the marketplaces.

The audiences responded equally as well to the traditional types of theatre (generally proscenium presentations) as to puppet theatre, community/street theatre, musical shows, and clowns, among others. As a matter of fact, when a production is accessible to everyone, when the whole family is able to attend in a happy and natural way, then the show truly becomes a tool for communication and communion with the spirit of a people. Finally, while taking into account a possibly more didactic aspect, the attendance of school audiences has recently increased at special performances and regular theatre productions.

All is not, of course, problem free. In particular, there is a tendency to separate children's theatre, to underestimate it, and even to suppress the memory of all that has been achieved. But the celebrations of the past; the traditional "Pastorets"; Folch i Torres; the classic authors who wrote in Catalan despite the censors; the hundreds of actors and actresses; the Catalan companies whose high standards have been appreciated during International Congresses; the books, photographs, and videotapes; and, most important, the people's unfailing memories will always enable the Spaniards to cherish, know, and promote a Catalan theatre for children, which, although little known worldwide, is as universal in application as the works of Miro, Dali, and Gaudi and the performances of Barraquer, Caballe, and Casals.

Lowell Swortzell
(Prepared from materials submitted by ASSITEJ/Spain.)

The Shoemaker's Feast, a Czech classic comedy with folk songs, was originally written in 1834 for adult audiences but is now presented for viewers ten and older. One of the songs from the play became the national anthem in 1918. This lively entertainment is in the repertory of both the Jiri Wolker Theatre (depicted here) and the National Theatre (Courtesy ASSITEJ/Czechoslovakia).

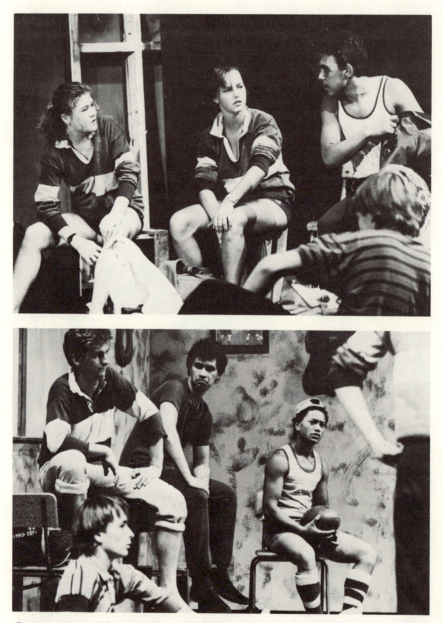

Contemporary problems are investigated in *Tupou*, produced in 1987 by Forum North, Whangarei, New Zealand. This company, composed of young people between 15 and 21 years old, devises plays on subjects of current interest to its members (Courtesy of Sunny Amey).

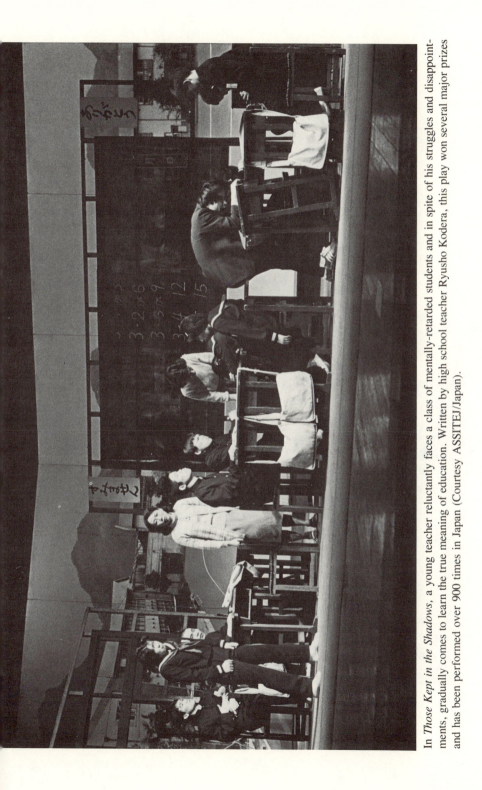

In *Those Kept in the Shadows*, a young teacher reluctantly faces a class of mentally-retarded students and in spite of his struggles and disappointments, gradually comes to learn the true meaning of education. Written by high school teacher Ryusho Kodera, this play won several major prizes and has been performed over 900 times in Japan (Courtesy ASSITEJ/Japan).

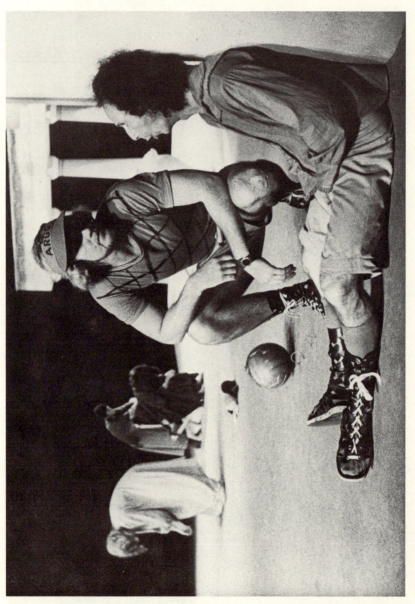

Medea's Children, by Per Lysander and Suzanne Osten, is based on the tragedy of Euripides and takes place both in the classical age and today. The Greek temple in the background suggests antiquity while the children's bedroom and playground in the foreground represent the present. Produced by the Young Klara of Stockholm as well as other theatres throughout the world (Courtesy of Per Lysander).

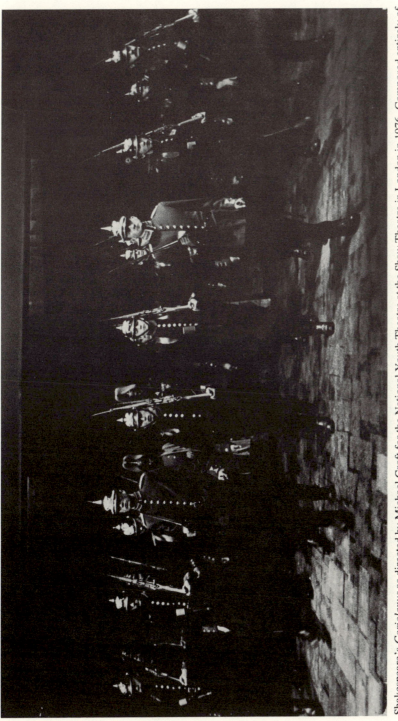

Shakespeare's *Coriolanus* as directed by Michael Croft for the National Youth Theatre at the Shaw Theatre in London in 1976. Composed entirely of teenagers who perform together during summer holidays, the NYT has toured throughout Europe and to New York City, performing both classical and modern works, a number of which have been written specifically for these dedicated young actors (Courtesy of Tony Jackson).

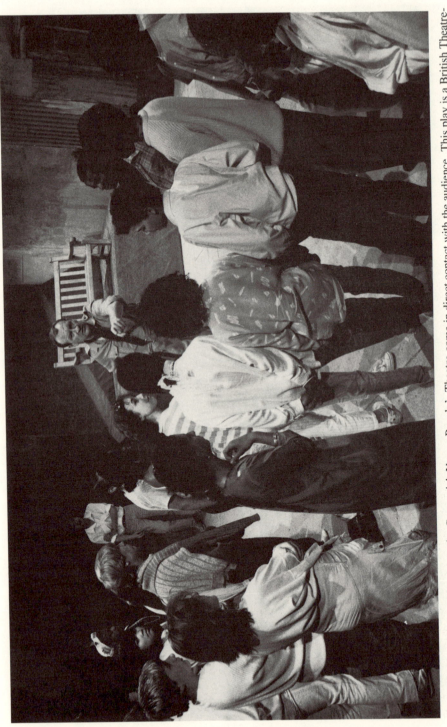

In *Circles of Fire* the performers at the Greenwich Young People's Theatre come in direct contact with the audience. This play is a British Theatre-in-Education production that depends upon discussion of contemporary issues to achieve its effect (Courtesy of Tony Jackson).

Adult actors play pre-school youngsters in this GRIPS Theatre production of *Things that Go Bump in the Night,* which deals with childhood fears and superstitions. The play is directed by Volker Ludwig at this famous theatre in West Berlin (Courtesy GRIPS Theatre).

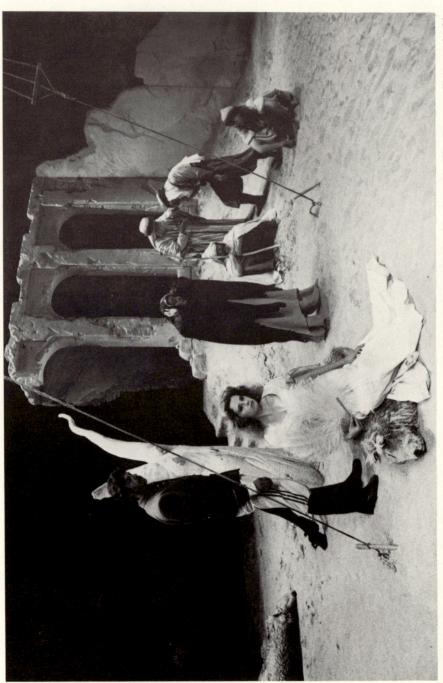

Among the ruins in this corner of the desert are natives and those closely associated with the title character, The Governor Sansame, in this beautifully designed production at the Theatre for Young Spectators in Saint Denis, France. (Courtesy ASSITEJ/France)

The carnival scene from the Children's Theatre Company in Minneapolis, Minnesota, shows a memorable moment in *Hang on to Your Head* by John Clark Donahue. This highly original fantasy employed music by Hiram Titus and design by Jack Barkla (Courtesy The Children's Theatre Company).

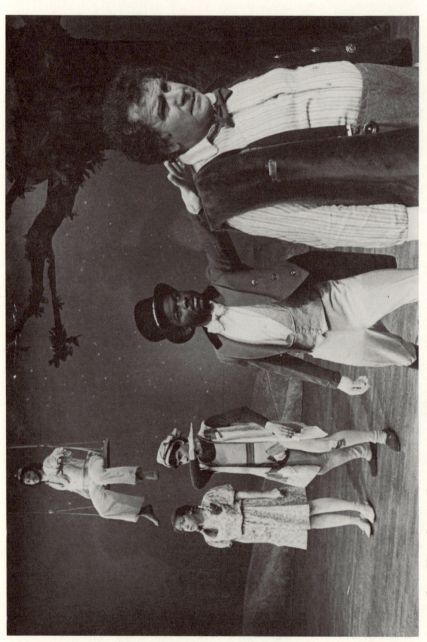

A scene from *The Arkansaw Bear*, by Aurand Harris, in which the bear, far right, turns away from the circus ringmaster who wishes to take him away. Meanwhile, the philosopher looks down from his star-filled perch in this popular play dealing with themes of death. Directed by Nancy Swortzell. (Courtesy The Program in Educational Theatre, New York University)

Sri Lanka

HISTORY

Children's theatre in Sri Lanka has a very short history. Originally, any play acted by children was considered children's theatre; the suitability of its theme, its pedagogical value, and its style and language were not important. The concept and philosophy of children's theatre, as they are thought of today, were not known. Children were also members of the audience at adult theatre, which they attended with their parents. In fact, so many children were present at adult theatre that managements started to present what was called the "school show," adult theatre presentations mounted in the afternoon in performances specifically intended for schoolchildren. These shows were encouraged, since it was believed that they promoted appreciation of theatre in their young spectators and helped them to become intelligent theatregoing adults. The "school show" was one result of a movement that took place after 1956 and called for a revival of Sri Lankan theatre. Modern theatre in Sri Lanka dates from this renaissance.

Theatre performed by children was an early form of children's theatre in Sri Lanka, and it fell into several categories, according to the purpose or occasion on which it was utilized: as an end-of-school term concert, a school play, part of the Interschool Drama Competitions organized by the Ministry of Education and the Arts Council of the Sri Lanka Lion's Club, an offering in the Interschool Shakespeare Competitions organized by the YMCA and the Lion's Club, a play mounted to highlight special causes such as Health Week and World Food Day, or a production by the Montessori schools. Later religious organizations such as the Young Men's Buddhist Association (YMBA) and the Catholic church began to use theatrical performances for the purpose of promoting religious education; they organized interschool Buddhist Drama Competitions and Catholic Children's Theatre Festivals.

These various festivals, both secular and laic, were not run by people trained in children's theatre, and there was little awareness or knowledge of age- and topic-appropriate plays. Children acted in dramas based on folktales and fairy tales, national legends and historical personages, and current social themes; they also mounted Shakespearean productions and translations of recent plays from around the world. In essence, no discrimination was used in choosing works that the children were to perform, for it was largely a case of children performing adult theatre, with proud parents (and other adults) marveling at their talented prodigies who acted as if they were grown-ups.

At the Interschool Drama Competitions one could observe the tendency toward an adult approach in interpreting current social, economic, and political problems. Because many of the pieces performed were written by (or adapted by) the students' teachers, this was not surprising. But attempts were made by some teachers (who were also dramatists), such as Piyasena, Sriyananda, Lionel Ranwela, and Herath, to choose topics suitable for the young performers and language they could realistically speak, although these efforts remained but attempts and cannot be considered as legitimate children's theatre.

In the 1960s two women, Eileen Sarachchandra and Soma Kiriella, gave impetus to the creation of a real children's theatre. Their work with children, using creative dramatics and child drama based on current pedagogical and philosophical theories of children's theatre, reawakened interest in the field.

In the late sixties the faculty of education at the University of Peradeniya, headed by Professor Premadasa Udagama, formed the Lama Natya Mandalaya (Children's Drama Circle). This move was initiated by Bandula Jayewardena and Wimaladharma Diyasena, theatre artists and educators. With the cooperation and support of the Department of Education, the two set up a project in the Kandy schools in which they promoted children's theatre. Seminars and discussions, supported and attended by educators, artists, intellectuals, and the media, were followed by children's theatre competitions that stressed various forms of theatre for children: performances for and by children, theatre-in-education, and creative dramatics. Although the project was well received within the educational and theatrical community, the population at large was not yet convinced of the validity of children's theatre.

In 1967 Gamini Wijesooriya, an actor and teacher attached to the Ministry of Education, organized a drama-in-education workshop for teachers under the sponsorship of UNESCO (United Nations Educational, Scientific, and Cultural Organization) and the Ministry of Education. The workshop was run by Professor David Kemp, a drama-in-education specialist from Canada. The workshops were offered annually through 1972, when they ended because of the lack of funds. Nevertheless, they helped to create an awareness of and interest in contemporary children's theatre, and the Interschool Drama Competitions that followed revealed evidence that ideas investigated and discussed in the workshops had made their way into the classroom.

Of the first group of workshop participants, many (including Chandrasena

Dassanayake, Lionel Ranwela, Piyasena, Daya Alwis, Sriyananda, Sunethra Sarachchandra, Gamini Samarakoon, Gamini Haththotuwa, and Somalatha Subashinghe) made significant contributions to the advancement of children's theatre in Sri Lanka. Popular artists such as Vajira Chitrasena in dance and Nanda Malini in music also made valuable contributions in their specific fields.

Meanwhile folktales such as *Rattaran* and *Elova Gihin Melowa Awa*, by E. R. Sarachchandra, *Nari Bena* and *Goraka Yaka*, by Dayananda Gunawardena, and *Thawath Udesenak*, by Henry Jayasena, which began as plays acted by schoolchildren, were now being presented by adult companies. These works were considered suitable for young audiences and became accepted successes in their new incarnations.

In the early 1970s the Theatre Trust, affiliated with the Ministry of Culture, took up the cause of children's theatre and gave it new life. Under the Trust's patronage an expert in children's theatre from West Germany, Norbert J. Mayer, was invited to Sri Lanka to work with native theatre artists on a project for theatre for children. *Shtokkerlock and Millipilli*, written by Ralner Hachfeld and Volker Ludwig and translated into English by Helen Mayer Hayek, was adapted to Sinhala as *Tikiri Menike* by Chandrasena Dassanayake and directed by Mayer with Dassanayake's assistance. The production was epoch-making in that it was the first contemporary children's theatre presentation in Sri Lanka. Theories and philosophies of children's theatre that had been known mostly through books and in the classroom now were demonstrated on stage. The production was well received by children, artists, educators, the public, and critics alike, and it inspired many people to conduct their own experiments and mount their own children's theatre productions. It also resulted in the formation of several children's and youth theatre organizations.

CHILDREN'S THEATRE TODAY

The Sri Lankan branch of ASSITEJ was founded in 1973, and representatives attended the international Congress held in Berlin in 1975. The organization also published two periodicals, *Theatre News* and *Young Theatre*; unfortunately both publications ceased operations because of financial restrictions. Sri Lanka finds it difficult to attend ASSITEJ Congresses regularly, pay its organizational fees, or even carry out sustained international communication because of its financial situation. Nevertheless, it was represented at the meetings in Moscow in 1984 and in Madrid in 1987.

The establishment of ASSITEJ in Sri Lanka encouraged some teachers and theatre artists to extend their experiments in theatre for children. Only a few of these productions were successful: *Muna Nethi Yaka (Devil Without a Face)*, by Lakmallee Gunawardena; *Indikale*, by Nalini Sandanayake; and *Goni Billa*, which was the result of a competition organized by the Children's Theatre Panel of the Arts Council. In 1977 the Council's theatre-in-education unit produced *Gorodara*.

In 1978 the Lanka Children's and Youth Theatre Association was formed; its objectives were to promote every aspect of children's theatre. The first production, *Kathandara Dekak (Two Tales)*, was based on two popular folktales interpreted to suit a modern child audience. The works were written and directed in the style of traditional Sri Lankan theatre by Somalatha Subashinghe, an actress and teacher who became interested in children's theatre after visits to countries such as England, Czechoslovakia, USSR, and East Germany. She received her training in children's theatre at the Carl Orff Institute in Salzburg, Austria, and her productions in Sri Lanka have been well received by parents, educators, critics, and, most important, children.

Inspired by this response, Subashinghe founded the first institution in Sri Lanka geared solely toward children's theatre, the Playhouse for Children and Youth, which is affiliated with the Lanka Children's and Youth Theatre Association. The Playhouse sponsors several types of theatre activities; it runs sessions for children, using educational approachs to theatre as well as producing works for child audiences with its own professional company. Some of the plays that have been mounted include *Ottooi*, an adaptation of the folktale about a race between the tortoise and the hare; *Ratmalee*, an adaptation of *Little Red Riding Hood*; *Gamarala Going to Heaven*, adapted from a Sinhala folktale; *Walas Pawula*, an adaptation of the tale of the three bears; and *Hima Kumari*, an adaptation of *Snow White and the Seven Dwarfs*.

The Playhouse is also active in research and experimentation in child and youth theatre, educational theatre, creative dramatics, theatre by children, and children's theatre production for television. It has become active in bringing theatre to handicapped children and participates in children's theatre promotional programs organized by various governmental and nongovernmental agencies. The group has sustained regular and ongoing activity since its inception in 1978. In order to do so it has mounted, in addition to its children's productions, presentations for adult audiences that have subsidized its work with children. Although these added adult performances disturb and distract the group from its main purpose, they are necessary if the Playhouse is to survive.

Another company, headed by a young theatre artist named Rohan Welivita, also tried to become established in children's theatre with a performance of *Tom Sawyer*, adapted by Welivita. Although the production was well received, the group was short-lived. The untiring efforts of the company were not enough to make the group financially viable. They played a few more scattered performances at different theatres, each time having a positive impact on the audience, but ultimately had to cease operations. The company did, however, contribute to the cause of children's theatre in Sri Lanka by spreading awareness.

Versatile Sinhala actor Jayasekera Aponso also heads a children's theatre company that travels around the country presenting low-cost plays in classrooms and school halls. Two of the company's well-known productions are *Samanallu (Butterflies)* and *Pata Pata Lokayak (A Colorful World)*. Like the Playhouse, this group also has to mount adult productions in order to support its children's theatre activities.

Notwithstanding the companies above, the primary form of children's theatre in Sri Lanka remains that of plays enacted by student actors under the sponsorship of schools and religious organizations. Programs run by social and religious groups that promote children's and youth theatre are also active. Among the organizations involved are the International Institute for Integral Education, the Jankala Sevena (sponsored by the Christian Education Institute), the Sarvodaya, the YMBA, and the National Youth Council (under the Ministry of Youth Affairs). In addition, the University of Colombo offers drama as a subject for the Diploma in Education in order to encourage further development of children's theatre.

There is currently a promising project under way at the State Museum, where Professor Rudi Corens (from Belgium) began a Puppetry and Puppet Theatre workshop for children. The project has been extended, and now a group of actors under the guidance of Corens is working with children, relating stories and using creative dramatics to "make theatre." The group has produced two plays, *Nephew from Angoda* and *The Prince and the Yaka*, and is now working on a project that would periodically invite guest directors to mount plays for the Museum Children's Theatre. This ambitious project has received some state support because of the interest expressed by Thelma Gunawardena, director of the State Museum.

The projects, workshops, and production companies mentioned herein are sporadic. No regular children's theatre activities take place in Sri Lanka because of a basic lack of funds. In many cases it is the sacrifice of the people involved that produces what is seen. Other major problems include the scarcity of appropriate scripts and a dearth of theatres (a problem that plagues adult theatre as well). Outside the capital city there are no real theatres. Companies must rent school assembly halls and city, town, municipal, or community halls, where facilities are minimum. The economy remains a problem, since the average income of parents is low and admission prices must be kept to a minimum.

Given the financial problems, it is not possible to earn a living solely from children's theatre; company members must also work in adult theatre, a condition that makes it difficult to give proper attention to the cause of children's theatre. There is an immediate need for a centralized organization with state financial support or sustained support from nongovernmental sources. The state currently gives full moral support to efforts to advance children's theatre, but that is not enough: monetary support must be forthcoming. Nongovernmental financial support from, among others, the Lions and Rotary Clubs, school drama associations, voluntary cultural organizations, and philanthropists is encouraging.

The situation has been aggravated by the recent ethnic problems and political disturbances in the country. Many parents and schools are reluctant to bring children to the theatre for reasons of security and safety. Also, roadblocks make it impossible for companies to travel to certain provinces. The situation does not make for a climate receptive to the needs of children's theatre. But the public's awareness of the value of good children's theatre should not be underrated; this awareness is so inspiring that the field continues undaunted in its efforts.

The Arts Council of Sri Lanka is just now becoming interested in fostering more effective theatre for young people. It is attempting to command possible resources from the private sector and to promote sponsorship of companies. This timely endeavor may prove valuable in these times of heightened public awareness of and interest in theatre for the young.

Somalatha Subashinghe

Sweden

THE SWEDISH THEATRE SYSTEM

The Swedish theatre system functions in four sectors:

1. The three national theatres. Dramaten (The Royal Drama Theatre) and Operan (The Royal Opera) exist in old theatres in the capital, Stockholm, while Riksteatern (The National Theatre Center) is based in Stockholm but mounts productions that go on tour all over Sweden. These three theatres obtain most of their money from the central government; box office income is a minimal part of their budgets.

2. Twenty-four city and regional theatres. At the start of the 1960s there were about eight city theatres. Since then it has been a goal of cultural politics to spread theatre (and the other arts) everywhere. These theatres are financed by local and regional authorities, but they do receive certain grants from the central government to cover part of their payrolls. Box office is a minimal part of their budgets.

3. About 120 independent theatre companies. Most of them tour from their bases in major cities. These companies provide a large proportion of the total theatre productions in Sweden; all were formed after the mid–1960s. Forty-five companies receive grants from the National Council for Cultural Affairs and many get money from local authorities. Even the most acknowledged and subsidized have to earn at least half their budget from box office receipts or by selling pre-mounted productions to local theatres and organizations.

4. A few private theatres (mainly in Stockholm). These theatres receive no money from the central government, but when in financial trouble, they often receive help from local authorities.

HISTORY

Children's theatre in Sweden before the mid–1960s was not remarkable. In most of the country it was nonexistent except around Christmastime, when municipal theatres traditionally put their least talented actors into large, flashy productions aimed at family audiences. Time for rehearsals was scarce and texts were stupid, but this made little difference, since in these productions the stage effects mattered most. Smoke and bombs and smart changes of scenery were more important than themes and acting—often the stage manager directed the entire enterprise.

There were some exceptions. Riksteatern was created by the government in 1934 with the aim of touring the entire country with first-class productions. During its first year the theatre attempted to mount special performances for young people in schools. That experiment soon ended when teachers and headmasters showed no interest. A new attempt ten years later met no better response. In the fifties, however, the schools generated more enthusiasm and theatre for children became a steadily growing feature in the repertory of Riksteatern.

By 1929 an association had been formed in Stockholm with the aim of subscribing performances of adult plays for schoolchildren. A few enthusiasts founded Skolbarnsteatern (The Schoolchildren's Theatre) in 1947. The new association, with powerful financial support from the city authorities, performed its own productions in the schools of Stockholm. Many classics were mounted, but The Schoolchildren's Theatre (which existed until the mid–1960s) also tried some new plays.

Michael Meschke, a young marionette player, puppet maker, and director, originated several productions for The Schoolchildren's Theatre in the early fifties. He became the director of a new theatre in 1958 with financial guaranties from the city of Stockholm. One condition for this municipal support for Marionetteatern (The Marionette Theatre) was that Meschke produce theatre for both children and adults. This was an important occasion. Not only did it mean that serious marionette theatre was firmly established in Sweden, but also that a step had been taken toward the general recognition that theatre for young people was of equal importance to that for grown-ups.

However, apart from Meschke, who introduced a new theatre form into Sweden, even the best productions for children in the fifties and the first half of the sixties were far from new in form or content. The repertory consisted of fairy tales, selected classics, and simple adventure stories. An excellent example is the Norwegian play *Klas Klättermus (The Climbing Mouse in the Hackebacke Forest)* that was staged at Kungliga Dramatiska Teatern (The Royal Dramatic Theatre) in 1964. Ingmar Bergman had recently become director of that theatre, declaring his intention to produce first-class children's theatre. In *Klas Klättermus* there was nothing new in Torbjörn Egner's conventional text or in Jackie Söderman's traditional direction. But it was significant that the most renown theatre in Sweden gave all its resources and a score of its best actors to a large, entertaining production for children.

CHANGES IN THEATRE AND SOCIETY

In the middle sixties many changes occurred: experimental theatres were founded that tried new artistic forms, often in cooperation with painters, sculptors, poets, and musicians, mingling drama with the other arts. Visitors from abroad also had great influence—The Living Theatre and La Mama from the United States and Jerzy Grotowski from Poland. There was also a change in the content of the plays, both in new theatres and in the traditional institutions. For example, Bertolt Brecht, who had been produced only a few times in Sweden through the sixties, now became popular. Peter Weiss became the "name of the day." There was also a thorough reorganization of the training of actors, which was moved from the established schools at the four largest theatres to state theatre schools linked to the universities. Actors were now trained for change and development, instead of for maintaining traditions.

In 1964–1965 a large-scale sociological analysis of theatre audiences was published, revealing that mainly upper- and middle-class people went to the theatre. That this was so in a country in which a Social Democrat government had ruled for thirty years and in which great efforts had been made to spread theatre to a broader segment of the population was a shock to many people.

Changes in the theatre coincided with two important changes in Swedish society at large. One was a strongly growing interest in children's issues, especially the culture offered to children. Gunilla Ambjörnsson's 1967 book *Skräp-kultur för barnen (Junk Culture for Children)* was crucial in that debate; she scrutinized one cultural sphere after another and by merely listing objective facts found that most of what was being offered to Swedish children was junk. This book had great influence and mirrored what many people thought. The Swedish economy was flourishing, state and municipal governments had money to spend on culture, and it was generally agreed that it was time to give children more than "junk." Also during these years many reforms of the school system were prepared and widely discussed, with the result that a new curriculum for the elementary school was adopted by Parliament in 1969. One stipulation stated that every child had a right to see good theatre, and that schools had a responsibility to provide such opportunities.

The other change was in the political field. Sweden had been for several decades a stable society with no strikes and few political conflicts. That changed when "consciences were raised" about the enormous contrasts between the wealthy industrialized countries and the poverty in the Third World. The social injustices in Sweden itself became obvious, for in just a few years a new left-wing opposition began that grew strongly, was optimistic, and mainly worked outside the framework of the established political parties.

From this overall context the new children's theatre grew. For the many young directors and actors with new ideas and left-wing sympathies (which in those days meant everyone) it became obvious to turn toward children's theatre. By playing in schools they could break the social isolation of theatre and reach a broad selection of the population. And it was the children who were going to create the society of the future—they were the essential audience for those who wanted to change the world.

From these conditions a revolution began, not a political revolution, but an artistic one that changed the whole outlook of Swedish theatre. In just a few years children's theatre became the avant garde throughout the country and broke all traditions with its overwhelming creative power and variety. In the late sixties a Swedish production could be about anything, it could be performed anywhere, and it could be made in any form. However bold the experiments were, the young audiences answered with delight and enticed the theatre groups into even more reckless, poetic, and scenic adventures.

When in 1974 Parliament passed an act on future cultural policy much of its content was based on what theatre people were already trying to accomplish. The act talked about renewal and decentralization of culture in Sweden by spreading theatre and all other arts to ever broader segments of the population. At the same time, Statens Kulturråd (The National Council for Cultural Affairs) was created.

Riksteatern–The National Theatre Center

In 1966 Riksteatern introduced a School Theatre Department with an artistic director of its own. Its repertory soon turned edgy and contemporary as the department started to find new dramatists. It has encouraged authors from other fields to write for the children's theatre, sometimes by employing playwrights on a yearly basis, but most often by commissioning new plays on very generous terms. Through the years and under changing leaderships the School Theatre Department has managed to maintain reasonably high standards, for of its approximately eight productions each year, there might be one or two disappointments but also many exciting experiments.

Fickteatern

In 1967 four persons left the avant garde theatre Narren to form their own independent group. They wanted to go out and seek their audiences in everyday life milieus, such as schools and libraries. To stress the point that they wanted to create a pure and simple theatre, they proclaimed that they would not use more props and scenery than they could carry in the pockets of their clothing. From this image they took their name, Fickteatern ("ficka" means "pocket" in Swedish).

In truth, Fickteatern used some additional props. A carpet, a keyboard (for music), and costumes that although simple, were carefully selected and designed. But they performed in fully lighted rooms in which the emphasis was always on the actors and their close association with their young audiences. From the start Fickteatern developed methods of involving groups of children in rehearsals; their productions often grew from improvisations that had been initiated by these children. At the same time, the group also worked successfully with eminent authors. Even though Fickteatern was dissolved in 1971, its working methods and high artistic standards had great influence on the further development of children's theatre in Sweden.

During the last years of the sixties many independent groups were formed, most of them with children's theatre as the main part of their repertories. In 1969 there were enough groups to form a common distribution organization: Teatercentrum (The Theatre Center).

The Regional Theatres

In 1967 Norrbottensteatern (The Norrbotten Regional Theatre) was founded in Sweden's northernmost county, a vast, thinly populated territory with approximately 200,000 inhabitants in 27,000 square kilometers. The theatre was financed jointly by state, county council, and municipalities. Its first director was Georg Fant, former director of the Malmö Actor's School, who brought with him a group of his former students. In 1967 the most exciting, honorable, and revolutionary thing a young actor could do was to take theatre to new lands. From the outset Fant declared that one-third of the resources of his theatre should go to productions for children and young people.

In recent years children's theatre has not always been as important as it was during the pioneer years. Indeed, at times the productions for young audiences have been rather insignificant. Still, many of the best productions of Norrbottensteatern have been for children and teenagers, for here it is established that a production for children shall be as ambitious as one for adults.

At the end of the sixties the National Touring Theatre stationed regional companies in Västerås (1968), Skellefteå (1969), and Växjö (1970), and in each, children's theatre was of utmost importance. During the seventies they developed into county theatres. In other counties a regional theatre could be developed from an independent group; today most of the counties in Sweden have their own regional theatres.

SUSANNE OSTEN AND UNGA KLARA

Susanne Osten was one of the founders of Fickteatern, where she not only directed the productions, but also wrote many of the texts. At the same time, she was one of the leaders in the women's liberation movement. She put her artistic talents to political uses and deepened her drama work with political insights. When Fickteatern was dissolved in 1971 Osten joined Stockholm's Stadsteater (The Stockholm City Theatre), where she staged productions for both children and adults. In 1976 Unga Klara (Young Klara; Klara is a parish in central Stockholm) was organized as an independent company within the City Theatre. Its aim was to play for children and young people, and it had financial, technical, and artistic resources equal to that of the adult productions.

Osten has been the artistic director of Unga Klara since its inception. Although many other producers and directors have worked there (several of the actors of

Unga Klara are also good directors), it is mainly her productions that have formed the public image of the theatre. By all standards she is a brilliant director. Bold, creative, and intellectual, she refuses to take anything for granted. She is always experimenting and trying out new ideas, yet she never experiments simply for its own sake; instead, she constantly searches for truth. Nowadays she mounts as many productions for adults as for children, but she claims that she can make more advanced experiments when working for a young audience because they are not as prejudiced.

Unga Klara has a distinct style: its productions have strongly stylized elements with many strange and zany turns; the mood can switch instantly from the hilariously funny to the deeply tragic. Osten works closely with her actors and is good at releasing them from their own inhibitions and habitual straitjackets. Improvisation is used both for training and as a working tool during rehearsals.

Most of Osten's productions have been of new plays, sometimes written by herself, often in collaboration with Per Lysander, who for years was Unga Klara'a dramatist, before becoming director of the theatre department of the Swedish Radio Company. She has continued to use the working methods of Fickteatern, commissioning authors to write plays and then bringing them into rehearsals so that the finished play is a collaboration between author, actors, and director. Like Fickteatern, Unga Klara also uses groups of children and young people during rehearsals for reference and inspiration.

Osten, Lysander, and the other members of the Unga Klara company have an intense and active interest in public discussions on arts, pedagogy, and psychology. Their approach to young audiences was, from the outset, influenced by the theories of the French sociologist Philippe Aries, who after intense historical research viewed childhood less as a matter of biology than as a matter of social and historical circumstances. Another source of inspiration is the American psychologist Bruno Bettelheim, who, in his *The Uses of Enchantment*, digs into the psychoanalytical levels of fairy tales. In later years Unga Klara was also greatly influenced by the theories of the Swiss psychoanalyst Alice Miller. Among many influences from the international theatre, the most important in recent years has been the English-Canadian dramatist-director and teacher Keith Johnstone.

Unga Klara first seeks to find what questions currently are of greatest concern to children and young people and then attempts to recreate these issues on stage with maximum honesty. The theatre is convinced that children have as much right as adults to see their crucial matters artistically formulated. Problems are not solved by pretending that they do not exist; instead, they must be maximally clarified. Unga Klara has dealt with such topics as divorce, alcoholism among parents, and school problems. Of their three latest productions for children one was about Adolf Hitler's childhood, one was about God, and one was a dramatization of Ovid's *Metamorphoses*, which was produced for infants.

Plays created by Unga Klara have been mounted by many other theatres, both in Sweden and abroad; Osten and her collaborators are generous and eager to share their discoveries and experiences. They write articles for the press, participate in seminars, and have recently published a book on their work. The theoretical aspects of their activities have meant much to the Swedish theatre in general.

FINN POULSEN

In 1969 young Danish director Finn Poulsen was so attracted by the dynamic events in Swedish theatre that he moved here. First he worked at Riksteatern's new regional company in Västerbotten; then in 1970 he was one of the instigators of the regional company Växjö. During most of the seventies and early eighties he mainly worked at Folkteatern in Gothenburg (this unique theatre is closely allied to the worker's movement, owned by trade unions and adult education organizations). But he also found time to work in other regional theatres and even directed a few productions of Swedish plays in the United States and West Germany. Although Poulsen has staged many significant plays for adults, it is his work for children and young people for which he is most noted. In recent years he has turned more toward mounting productions that aim at family audiences because he finds it important to give adults and children the chance to share theatrical experiences.

A quiet, poetically minded analyst, he has been strongly influenced by the dramaturgical ideas of Bertolt Brecht (by way of Brecht's pupil Rudi Penka, who has taught widely in Sweden). He is not as wildly experimental as Osten, but his work has as much consistency and he is as concerned about the situation of children today. His productions are often deeply tragic and move into dark and negative areas, for he believes that children must not be told lies, but must be confronted with life and society as they are. Yet even his most tragic productions are filled with love and human warmth, mainly because of the acting. His actors are self-confident and tender in their cooperation both toward one another and toward the audience.

In 1987 Poulsen became the new artistic director of Riksteatern's School Theatre Department. He declared that one of the most important tasks was to find new young dramatists. This is in line with the traditions of the department but also significant for Poulsen, since throughout his career he has been eager to inspire authors to write for children's theatre, often with good results.

STAFFAN GÖTHE

In 1972 the shortage of good texts for children was a problem for the regional company at Växjö. Staffan Göthe, a young man from the Gothenburg actor's school who had written revues and club farces during his student years, tried his hand at a play for elementary schools, *En natt i februari (A Night in February)*. It was a great success. Poulsen, who directed it and the first productions of many other plays by Göthe, has said that Göthe's texts were a turning point in his own career: "He has a new very poetical and a very theatrical language. He spoke directly to the children in the audience, as CHILDREN, not as future adults."

Göthe's plays had a broader appeal and a greater degree of artistic maturity than even the best of the children's plays before them. His language is colorful and poetic, subtle and nuanced. He mixes comedy and seriousness, realism and absurdities. He is a tender pessimist with infinite faith in human possibilities. It is obvious that his plays have been written by an actor because they are singularly playable; every scene is fraught with basic conflicts and constitutes a kind of Chinese box with many bottoms to it. Even the small roles are rich in possibilities and dimensions. His weakness is in the dramatic structure, for although his plays are unusually rich and strong, the whole is not always as strong as the sum of the parts.

Göthe chiefly writes about the exposed position of the child and various ways of either adapting to or revolting against everyday oppression. Much of Göthe's dramatic material is taken from his own childhood and youth. He talks about his "deep urge to describe what I really love and really hate." Although he has written only five plays for children (and seven for adults), he is Sweden's most frequently staged dramatist after Strindberg.

THE GOTHENBURG CITY THEATRE

In the late sixties a special children's theatre troupe was formed within the framework of Stadsteatern i Göteborg (The Gothenburg City Theatre). It mounted many notable productions, but as the years passed interest faded, and in 1978 a new children's theatre group was formed, with the director Eva Bergman and the actor Ulf Dohlsten as artistic directors. After a few years it moved from central Gothenburg to the suburb of Backa and has become known as Backa Teater (The Backa Theatre). It uses one-tenth of the City Theatre's budget and presents one-third of its productions.

Bergman is strongly influenced by directors Ingmar Bergman, Ralf Långbacka (she has been assistant to them both), and Susanne Osten. But her main inspirations come from music and cinema. She is the great showman of the Swedish children's theatre in her playfulness and faultless musicality. Singing, music, and dancing are interwoven with the action and almost always given a crucial dramatic function. Backa Teater employs four full-time musicians, which is unusual for a company with only eight actors, but for all Bergman's showmaking and funny games, there is nothing superfluous about her work. She has deep social concerns and strives to create theatre that is on the child's side, theatre that tries to provide children with deep experiences that will give them the hope and strength to take over the world.

STAFFAN WESTERBERG

Staffan Westerberg began his career in the middle sixties at Marionetteatern, directing and acting in his own plays. Since then he has staged his works at several theatres and created numerous puppet theatre productions for television. Westerberg is a poetic surrealist whose productions always bear his own personal stamp, that of a dark humorist, walking a thin tightrope between anxiety and liberation. He mingles puppets with real actors and other elements because in his hands anything can become a marionette or a puppet. Old stockings, tools, and a needle become exciting personalities through his theatrical skills and imagination.

At first glance it might seem as if Westerberg's theatre differs from the other developments in Swedish children's theatre. However, his work is borne of the same interest and respect for children. The difference is that he is more concerned with the inner life, with irrationality, fantasies, and dreams. Many of his plays have been staged by other directors, such as Finn Poulsen.

MODELLTEATERN—ORIONTEATERN

In 1969 Modellteatern (The Model Theatre) was formed in Eskilstuna (a town in the middle of Sweden with approximately 90,000 inhabitants). During its first years the group shared its time between pedagogical work with children and stage performances, but since the middle seventies it has concentrated on production. Much of its best work at that time was in delightfully zany and poetic outdoor summer productions. There the company developed a playful and comprehensive style that it has managed to maintain even when it has gone into other fields. Its productions possess a rare ability to combine exquisite planning with improvisation.

Modellteatern stayed in Eskilstuna for thirteen years. During that time it built up a sizable and steady audience in and around the town. But even though the group was generally acknowledged as one of the best children's theatre companies in Sweden, it had problems. A theatre of its own was not to be found in Eskilstuna, and the company felt that even though its reputation was known, it was ignored by the media. In 1982 Modellteatern moved to Stockholm, took over an old factory building, turned it into a theatre, and changed its name to Orionteatern. Since then the group has mounted productions for both children and adults and is considered one of the most successful (among both audiences and critics) and publicized independent groups.

BYTEATERN AND TITTUT

Byteatern (The Village Theatre) was founded in 1970 and settled at Kalmar, in southeastern Sweden, in 1974. Many of the people who formed the group had been visual artists, a fact that contributed to the development of Byteatern's special brand of marionette and puppet theatre. The productions are a delight to the eye, with music and image having equal status with dialogue. However, their style is not a matter of beauty for beauty's sake, since Byteatern is as concerned about people and society as any other group. The difference is that it gives its productions an unusually picturesque form. During the winter months Byteatern performs at its theatre in Kalmar and goes on nationwide tours. Every second summer the group tours the whole coast of Sweden in a showboat, the *M.S. Helene.*

Tittut (Peep-bo!), founded in 1977, concentrates on puppet theatre for two- to four-year-olds. Because it strives (most often very successfully) to give this young audience full-fledged theatrical experiences, the performances have a particular charm in their delightful interplay between actors, puppets, and audience.

PROBLEMS TODAY

The well-deserved success of Modellteatern/Orionteatern is telling. The Swedish press today still does not give enough coverage to children's theatre, making it particularly difficult for theatres and groups outside Stockholm. But whereas regional theatres have a rather safe economy, the independent groups depend on selling tickets and getting grants from central and local authorities, so publicity is important to them.

Statistics from 1984–1985 show that the approximately forty-five independent groups that received government grants produced 51 percent of all children's theatre performances. The city and regional theatres accounted for 38 percent; The National Theatre Center, 8 percent; The Royal Drama Theatre, 2.5 percent; and The Royal Opera, 0.5 percent. There are no statistics on the approximately ninety-five groups that do not receive government grants or on the commercial theatres, but these figures provide a helpful general picture and document the fact that independent groups are responsible for a great part of all children's theatre in Sweden.

The grants received are far from being in proportion to that importance. Most of the independent groups today operate on risky budgets, so much so that if a production is not successful, bankruptcy is near. This leaves little room for experimentation. The problem is worsened by a general stagnation in the Swedish economy, for even though the country is still wealthy, there have been drastic cuts in the budgets of the state and local authorities during the late seventies and early eighties. Schools, libraries, and community centers now have much less money to spend on cultural activities.

One result of this situation has been an increase in small productions since the early eighties. A play with two actors is much cheaper to produce and easier to sell than a big production. What Modellteatern did—moving to Stockholm—other groups and individuals are doing more and more. In the capital there is a larger audience, more opportunities for extra work (an actor in even the most successful group makes a considerably smaller salary than his colleagues in the subsidized theatres, and he is probably "on the dole" three or four months of the year), many other groups and theatres to cooperate with, and many critics and journalists who might happen to write about the performances.

Another problem is the strong tendency for the reemergence of bad children's theatre. This started when some private theatres in Stockholm discovered that easy money could be made by staging a production with little rehearsal and by filling a big theatre simply by hiring one or two well-known actors. This formula has become effective, especially as it is more attractive for journalists to write about television personalities than about children's theatre itself.

Worse yet, this formula has spread to government-supported theatres. Since the late sixties The Royal Drama Theatre has produced little theatre for children and young people. Sometimes it opens its doors and budgets to great artists like Staffan Westerberg, but in general, there have been no efforts to create a lasting interest for children's theatre among the directors and actors in the ensemble of the Royal Drama Theatre. And recently the group, the richest and most highly subsidized of all Swedish theatres, has presented several superficial productions for children with trivial content, short rehearsal periods, and several actors who did not put their hearts, minds, or skills into their work. The commerical wave has also begun to spread into some regional theatres and even into some independent groups.

IMPORTANT PLAYS

Medeas Barn (Medea's Children), by Susanne Osten and Per Lysander (1975), is based on Euripides and tells the story from the viewpoint of Jason's and Medea's children. It is an artful intermixture of Greek tragedy and a modern divorce story for ages seven to ten.

In *En Natt I Februari (A Night in February)*, Staffan Gothe's first play (1972), three actors personify the thoughts of a boy after a misadventurous ski trip. The boy himself is never seen on stage; he is sleeping somewhere nearby. The play is for ages seven to nine.

In *Bortbytingen (The Changeling)*, dramatized by Goran Tunstrom after a short story by Selma Lagerlof (1984) and aimed at family audiences, a troll woman exchanges her child for the new baby of a farmer couple. The farmer's wife nurses the ugly and unpleasant changeling as well as she would her own baby. By that, she wins her own child back.

FESTIVAL

In 1981, 1983, 1985, and 1987 a "Week of Children's Theatre" was held in the town of Gävle, whose Cultural Department arranged the festival. During the week the National Theatre Center, many of the best independent groups, and some regional theatres perform their productions for children and young people.

The charm of the festival is that although it is the only theatre festival of importance in Sweden, it is really not a festival. Most of the performances take place in ordinary schools and community centers in the suburbs of Gävle. The theatre people who attend the festival from all over Sweden and abroad travel throughout the town and see the plays along with the audiences at whom they are aimed. The event has become an established and much needed meeting place for journalists and theatre people who are interested in children's theatre. Also, here children's theatre gets the media coverage it deserves (print, television, radio). Even though it's only one week every second year, the festival is a significant advance for children's theatre in Sweden.

BIBLIOGRAPHY

Hägglund, Kent. *Theatre for Children in Sweden* (1985).
Osten, Susanne. *Unga Klara*. A fifty-page account of the work that led up to *Medea's Children*, reprinted from *Children's Theatre in Sweden* (1979).
The Swedish section of ITI (International Theatre Institute) sometimes publishes a multilingual magazine on current theatre in Sweden.

Kent Hägglund

Switzerland

HISTORY

In roles as organizers, managers, administrators, technicians, translators, producers, drivers, and actors more than twenty professional theatre companies currently are touring in Switzerland. They play in big cities and small villages and in removed and isolated areas, and they invite to their performances people who, because of their geographical situation, are prevented from participating in many cultural activities. Only rarely do they perform in large theatres that benefit from regular financial support; instead, they improvise in schools and small theatres. Although they have little money and no continuous financial or popular support, they possess idealism and play with assiduity and great imagination.

How long has their activity been going on? Looking back over fourteen years of children's and youth theatre in Switzerland, one finds clever managers of the Municipal Theatres who produced traditional fairy tales to full houses, while incurring little expense for publicity. Even though these performances were credible, the "freelancers" and dramatists did not approve of this sort of entertainment. Productions often were prepared without feeling and imagination, and actors performed with little pleasure because they were not genuinely interested in young spectators. Plays for children were simply a duty. Independent groups and authors complained about the lack of quality and the pervasive belief that the young audience was a public with no education, no imagination, and no ideas, one readily satisfied by speed and silly tricks. Children and youngsters were generally held in less interest and of less value than adults.

A few large theatres attempted to change this attitude by demonstrating sympathy for the young, and suddenly a new and independent theatre for children and youngsters appeared. An active, innovative, and creative theatre emerged and endured despite difficult financial situations and other problems endemic to freelance groups.

THE FIRST GROUPS IN THE GERMAN-SPEAKING PART

In 1974 Theater Spilkischte, founded in Basel, opened with Paul Maar's *Kikerikischte*; this was the first group to perform expressly for a young public. The famous young Swiss author Hans-Joerg Schneider wrote a play for the company, *Robinson lernt tanzen*, which has become well known abroad. For two years Spilkischte was Switzerland's only professional troupe, and is the only one that owns its theatre today. Spilkischte developed several forms of theatre: fairy tales, performances with imagination, and plays with an educational background. When planning the repertory, members refer to their own experiences, feelings, ideas, wishes, and dreams, which they translate, by means of improvisation, into scenes. They have been popular.

A play of the Rote Grütze in Berlin inspired a group in the German-speaking part of Switzerland to create its own production. Afterward they turned toward the adult theatre. But two members of the original company founded Spatz and Co. in 1976 (in Bremgarten), working in a style similar to that of GRIPS or Rote Grütze in Berlin. Their plays explored problems of children in confrontation with adults. Teachers who became aware of this new form also suggested suitable topics.

However honest and high in quality, sometimes pleasure and joy were missing because the educational and political statements emerged as more important. This type of theatre often walked a fine line between education and art, lesson and game. Nevertheless, Spatz and Co. convinced parents, teachers, and authorities that theatre can appeal to children and adults alike. They also successfully intensified the exchange of information between the few existing theatre companies.

In 1979 Spatz and Co. organized the "First National Meeting" to inform the public about its different activities and to establish the meaning and necessity of this new theatre. It was discovered that different forms, styles, and definitions of theatre existed, and, above all, that adults and children could enjoy the same performance. This conference demonstrated that theatre for a young public could be considered both as an educational instrument and as a medium to express art and culture.

Spatz and Co. created plays that sometimes were played by youngsters. In Berne the first coproduction between the Municipal Theatre and a freelance group, the Zimmertheater Chindlifrässer, began when a social worker and theatre fan wrote stories that the young people performed. In Basel the Basler Jugendtheater, founded in 1977, is composed of professionals and young people who joined the group because they enjoy working together. At first, contact between such groups remained weak, but recently, as new teams are established, a regular exchange of personnel has taken place.

In the eighties new groups emerged: Ond-Drom (1982), Luki-ju (1982), P.Y.J.A.M.A.R.I.A. (1983), Theater Momo (1980), Siebe uf ei Tätsch/Octopus (1984), and Sgaramusch (1982). These companies play not only in cities, but also in remote areas, where they try to develop new audiences. Often they lack financial support, which interferes with their continuity; only three receive regular funding. Nonetheless, their situation improved a great deal between 1974 and 1985, so that now this is a theatre of many shapes, colors, forms, and definitions. Today the plays reflect the daily life of the young audience, their feelings, fears, dreams, joys. Children, youngsters, and adults enjoy the same language now, for didacticism has been replaced by imagination, anger, warmth, and friendliness. Because there are so few interesting plays, companies often write or rewrite scripts or translate them from other languages.

Another trend can be observed in the German-speaking part of Switzerland, where plays attempt more and more independence from education through an artistic and cultural approach.

THE FIRST GROUPS IN THE FRENCH-SPEAKING PART

In 1967 the Théâtre Populaire Romand (TPR) (La Chaux-de-Fonds) presented the first professional play for children and youngsters other than traditional fairy-tale productions at Christmas: *Molière et nous*. TPR also planned a special day for participation in schools, which soon became a regular Monday commitment. TPR extends its efforts to methodical studies, publications, and contact with the Department of Education. After nine years these activities were examined and analyzed, leading, in 1976, to a new era in which voice, movement and expression, choreography, and stage design became increasingly important. Since then TPR has not presented a play exclusively for children but gives performances for everybody, a popular theatre for all ages.

In 1974 Théâtre Am Stram Gram was founded in Geneva. From the beginning, spectacle was important as well as the choice of plays because here children and adults were spectators of equal importance and rights. The repertory reflects the individuality and open-mindedness of the young spectators. Among the companies, Am Stram Gram holds a favored position as far as the financial situation is concerned. In 1988 the group opened a theatre of its own, another tribute to the ongoing financial and popular support of the public of Geneva. With a bus and tent the company tours small productions, even abroad, but always working in close contact with the local Department for Education. Consequently its productions are well introduced into the schools.

The Théâtre pour Enfants de Lausanne (TEPL) started to work with children (workshops, special lessons in schools, and performances) in 1974. TEPL wants to work in spaces in which children and youngsters can express themselves with individual forms (improvisation, expression, or different techniques). Here children and youngsters learn to develop sensitivity, personal perception, and their general personality. Other small groups study different theatrical forms and styles. Both the Théâtre Escarboucle (1981) and La Main dans le Chapeau (1983) conduct programs for children, youngsters, and adults. PATATRA (1983) and Froschtheater (1984) are bilingual groups that are important in Switzerland.

THE FIRST GROUPS IN THE ITALIAN-SPEAKING PART

All companies face the same problems in every section of the country. But in the south the situation is severest. Teatro Panzini in Lugano (1974), despite great difficulties, has realized several interesting productions. Besides conducting special workshops for children, youngsters, and adults, Panzini organizes, every second year, an International Festival for Children and Youth Theatre and keeps in close contact with other groups in Switzerland and, above all, in the south of Europe, where the company often tours.

Collaboration between the local Department of Education and the schools remains a serious problem for most companies. Panzini attempts to please everyone with modern productions, although it constantly struggles to find suitable plays and stories. Today Panzini has been joined in the south by three other companies: the Compagnia Teatro Dimitri, the Compagnia Teatro Paravento, and the Teatro delle Radici. They, too, offer their productions to children, youngsters, and adults.

In the summer of 1987 all the freelance companies that perform for adults and young audiences formed a special organization that in time will take on the responsibilities of a trade union.

PROBLEMS AND GOALS

Those traditional and established institutions in the cultural life of Switzerland, such as large theatres, orchestras, art galleries, and museums, long have received financial support from the national, cantonal, and communal authorities and the population itself. But for the most part theatres for young people do not, and the freelance groups, in particular, lack financial support. Yet these companies, when on tour, reach a public that is not otherwise involved in the country's cultural life because of its geographical location, a fact largely overlooked by financial authorities.

In order to fulfill their artistic goals, continuity is necessary. Only when the experience gained in the process of one production is evaluated and used in the next production will artistic quality improve. But continuity cannot be guaranteed when financial support is missing. Many companies must change teams when members have to look for additional work in other fields, some even canceling performances or curtailing seasons. Other groups work with frequent interruptions because their members require additional jobs in order to survive. Most members never earn living wages from careers in theatre for young people.

Fund raising for productions requires time and special skills that take away from the artistic work: only a few companies can afford an administrator. The groups live from hand to mouth for years, not only in seeking sponsors, but also in confronting problems of space, such as finding rooms for experimentation and rehearsals that provide good working conditions. Mainly they have to look for new space for each production.

The collaboration with different cantonal Departments of Education needs to be strengthened. Sometimes teachers are suspicious perhaps because only a few of them are interested in theatre. The regional and communal authorities also should collaborate more regularly and closely; the two main partners that support companies, the Department of Education and the Department of Cultural Affairs, are under the same roof yet have no strong relationship. One can be certain that in Switzerland, children's and youth theatre as part of cultural life will exist only as long as those diehards who believe in their work do it in spite of difficulties, problems, and bad conditions.

The Swiss are still fighting (and sometimes wonder for how much longer) so that

- the freelance companies will benefit from additional regular financial and popular support and can work in conditions similar to those in the large theatres;
- the authorities on each level will decide on a cultural policy for freelance companies that is committed to continuity and not to the encouragement of a single production or of a single group;
- the work of the companies will be recognized by both authorities and the Swiss population;
- the collaboration between responsible people in the fields of culture, art, and education will become closer and ongoing;
- the critics will report regularly in the press and electronic media about children's theatre work; and
- the dramatists will write plays of quality for young audiences.

ASSITEJ

ASSITEJ is a group of professionals working *for* young audiences. Moreover, amateurs, teachers, libraries, schools, and cultural and leisure centers are also members of ASSITEJ. Switzerland belongs to the international association as one of the forty-five members that work worldwide in this field.

At the beginning of 1985 the structure of ASSITEJ was modified from its founding thirteen years ago when a part-time office was opened in Berne. The Executive Committee was newly composed of eleven members from the three linguistical parts of the country. Although they are theatre professionals, they also belong to other professions. With the new structure, they hope (a) to disseminate information to the members and other interested people; (b) to coordinate existing activities on national and regional levels; (c) to intensify the contacts with organizations working in the field of education, youth training, and culture and also with the authorities on each level; and (d) to participate more actively in political and cultural discussions.

ASSITEJ holds a collection of more than 400 volumes of international and national children and youth theatre literature (plays, and theoretical surveys and papers). This collection is part of the "Swiss Theatre Institute" and is supervised by ASSITEJ. The association owns an exhibition with a survey of the work of the freelance groups; it publishes a *News Letter* five times a year and a *Theatre Calendar* nine times a year. It supports national and regional projects such as festivals and workshops. It maintains records about membership groups and other national and international activities.

Finances are still a problem. The Swiss cannot compare their situation to that of other European countries because they still lack both financial and popular support, although the Federal Office for Cultural Affairs offers ASSITEJ a modest subsidy for its office and projects. There are but two main sources of support: the Federal Office and the annual subscriptions of members. The association's financial situation limits participation in festivals and meetings abroad. International exchange is largely accomplished through individual initiatives and the European Children and Youth Theatre Encounters organized biennially in member countries of the Council of Europe. ASSITEJ collaborates and assumes the organization, administration, and artistic work on behalf of the Federal Office for Cultural Affairs.

Lowell Swortzell
(Based on materials submitted by ASSITEJ/Switzerland and Esther Mischler.)

Thailand

HISTORY

Two factors should be noted for their great impact on the development and trends of theatre in Thailand. First, various regions in the country have not developed at the same pace. Therefore, there is a large difference in material growth between big cities, specifically Bangkok, and the rest of the country. This phenomenon results in a populace with totally different lifestyles. With regard to theatre, there is a question about its function: Who should the theatre serve? The elite few in affluent Bangkok, or the rest of the country? So far, theatre has been produced only for the centralized Bangkok audience. Second, Thailand has never been colonized. The country enjoys its own culture and rich traditions acquired at its own pace. There is no need to search for a national identity; nor is there a need to oppose Westernization as colonist. This phenomenon leads the Thai people to take traditional theatre for granted. At the same time, there are no reservations about accepting Western theatre influences.

Thailand is rich in traditional performing arts, including classic and folk theatre; some of them are the masked play (Khon), classic dance drama (Lakon Jatri, Lakon Nok, and Lakon Nai), shadow and doll puppet play (Nang Yai, Nang Talung, and Hun Krabok), folk dances, martial arts, and instrumental and vocal music (Piphat, Strings, Mahoree, Mohlum, Lamtat, and Likay). The task of preserving these traditional art forms rests with the Fine Arts Department of the Ministry of Education. Research and data collection regarding folk theatre and endangered traditional theatre are complied by teacher-training colleges in various provinces. Throughout its history of development and change traditional theatre has always been in the hands of royal patrons and a handful of experts whose task is to preserve it within modern society.

In contrast, the contemporary theatre movement started with the founding of a drama program at university level (around 1960) by Western-educated professors. They taught theories and practices of Western theatre and translated, adapted, and produced Western plays in Thai languages. University graduates and workshop trainees are currently working in all areas of drama, theatre, television, and the film business in Bangkok. A few also have started a theatre movement in the provinces.

However, among these theatre practitioners there is a rather definite division between people who adhere to the traditional and those who espouse the contemporary. It is hoped that somehow these two groups of "caretakers" will merge and assimilate their knowledge and experience. There is currently a better balance between preservation and creativity. Those in traditional theatre use new approaches and modern techniques of presentation, whereas those in contemporary theatre turn more to traditional arts and cultural heritage for inspiration, content, or styles of presentation.

Theatre activities in Thailand operate through various outlets, including the national theatre, university educational theatre, television theatre, a hotel dinner theatre, one newly formed theatre group, and occasional young enthusiastic groups. All of them operate in Bangkok.

THEATRE FOR THAI CHILDREN

Thai children do not have many choices in terms of recreation. Cultural activities are mainly organized for adults. Children in Bangkok live in the materialistic world of shopping centers, television, and video, while the rest of Thai children face problems such as inadequate housing, malnutrition, lack of education, unemployment, labor abuse, prostitution, crime and violence, and environmental degradation. If there is to be an ideal theatre for these diverse groups of children, it should be a functional theatre whose content touches on social awareness, a theatre that appeals to all as a necessity and not simply as a luxury.

Theatre for children in Bangkok has been promoted in earnest by Chulalongkorn University, using creative drama as the approach. University theatre at first tried to provide a regular theatre program for young audiences. Later several other groups emerged, such as Truck Theatre Project, Children's Theatre to the Provinces, An Hour for Children, and Workshops on Children's Theatre and Creative Drama.

Educational institutions produced graduates in drama and theatre who in turn originated new theatre groups and formed a new wave of young enthusiasts. However, many of them are drawn into the commercial world for financial reasons. Even so, several indications point toward progress in children's theatre in Thailand. Although the country still lacks original scripts, playwrights, and directors, those it has are improving, thanks to exposure, especially in Asian countries. In children's theatre, which is freer from commercial ties than theatre for general audiences, the work is more artistic and experimental, just as it is in university theatre.

Moreover, Thai children are now given a better chance to express themselves in the arts. There are professional children's bands, child singers, and child television actors. There is a newspaper with children as reporters and editors. Many children win international prizes for their artwork. Several projects for youth, such as Youth Music Festival, Youth Painting Workshop and Exhibition, and Travelling Exhibition of Children's Art, are also helping to make impressive progress in the arts.

There has recently been a unique movement of national interest in the general welfare of Thai children. Several volunteer groups and government and non-government organizations are working closely to form interesting projects, such as Mobile Library for Children, Lunch Program for Children, Foundation for Handicapped Children, Foundation for Infants in Slum Areas, Community Sanitation Group, and the Information Center for Child Development.

Many of these groups have obtained financial support from foreign organizations such as the Friedrich-Naumann-Stiftung, Bread for the World, Asian Community Trust, and Japan Center for International Exchange. More and more these groups are using drama and theatre in their approaches to dealing with the problems of their young clientele. Some of the techniques are creative drama, puppetry, storytelling, role-playing, and improvisation. The work of the Maya, in its seventh year, is an example; some of its exciting projects are Mobile Theatre, Media Center for Education, Training Course and Workshop Project, and Mobile Teaching Technique Training Unit Program. The group has steadily gained national and international acclaim while improving its work from both managerial and artistic standpoints.

Out of this movement arise two positive signals. First is the tendency to look within one's own culture for inspiration, content, or styles of presentation, as in the case of the Maya group and Chulalongkorn University drama department's production presented at the Fourth International Workshop on Living Children's Theatre in Asia. Second is the movement toward bringing theatre to the rural areas, thus embracing children in the provinces. There is a strong commitment toward community theatre and creative drama, rather than elaborate productions in Bangkok. It is hoped that a new theatre for all children in Thailand will soon emerge. And although there is no permanent children's playhouse, more than thirty-two volunteer groups and private organizations are working on various projects to help deprived children. Awards are given to groups and corporations that contribute to children, and publications are translated and printed for children of various age levels.

Thailand has enjoyed many outstanding types of traditional performing arts. However, these are overshadowed by the film, television, and video industries and suffer from lack of appeal to younger audiences. Contemporary theatre is struggling for survival and national identity, and children's theatre is slowly emerging. The future of children's theatre depends on contributions from government agencies, private organizations, university theatre, and individuals who are dedicated to the art and to children. Television programs for children provide the only solid ground for professional work. University theatre will continue to be the major surviving contributor to children's theatre in Thailand. However, children's theatre can be fully developed only when it embraces the majority of Thai children and draws on rich traditional sources in order to find its unique national identity.

Lowell Swortzell
(Prepared from materials submitted by Onchuma Yuthavong.)

Turkey

HISTORY

The concept of children's theatre arose in Turkey only at the turn of the past century. Before that time there had existed traditional puppet and *Karagöz* shadow plays, whose audiences were made up of children and adults. In its early stages children's theatre was approached as an element of education, with the first plays being written for school performances. In 1913 Ismail Hakki Balta-cioğlu introduced the idea of school theatre. This renowned pedagogue went on to encourage drama in the schools in which he taught and was an administrator, and in the process staged many children's works.

Baltacioğlu's thoughts on school drama form a systematic theory and are original for his time. He believed that no school should be without a drama program to foster cooperation and the spontaniety of improvised works free from costumes or sets. In his view, this activity would develop not only the child's personality and character, but also his sense of national identity at a time when the idea of "Turkishness" was a recent acquisition.

A set of directives, published by the Ministry of Education in 1915 and titled "Teaching Through School Performances," states that because children are born imitators, it is their natural right to perform. As they do so, they will learn about history, receive moral instruction, and acquire literary values and tastes. The idea of instituting a true children's theatre, as distinct from that which had been merely educational in its aims, was first put forward by Mushin Ertuğrul, who is considered the father of modern theatre in Turkey and who, at the time, headed the Municipal Theatre in Istanbul. On a visit to the Soviet Union, Ertuğrul met with Professor E. Arkin, a pedagogue interested in children's drama; on returning to Turkey, Ertuğrul set up a children's theatre division within the Istanbul Municipal Theatre.

Its first performance, of a play by the actor M. Kemal Küçük titled *A First Drama Lesson for Children*, was given on October 1, 1935. Meanwhile the same institution was publishing a children's drama magazine that was distributed free to young people. In time the Istanbul Children's Theatre diversified, taking account of the children's different ages and offering productions according to age groups, and presenting a greater number of plays each season. Among the dramatists frequently represented were Mümtaz Zeki Taşkin, Sabih Gözen, Akif Obay, and Vecihe Karamehmet. The contribution of Ferih Egemen, both as a writer and as a director, was particularly great.

Turkey's second publicly funded children's theatre was established as a division of the Izmir Municipal Theatre and gave regular performances from 1946 to 1950. Since 1957 plays for children have been presented by the State Theatre Stage in Izmir.

The largest publicly funded theatre in Turkey, the State Theatre in Ankara, has had an active children's division since 1948. At first limiting its performances to Ankara itself, the company went on to present children's plays in Izmir, Bursa, Istanbul, Adana, and Trabzon. In 1984 a Youth and Children's Theatre was established as part of the State Theatre, with the aim of bringing fresh approaches to children's and young adult's drama through the use of young actors in the productions. Among the dramatists who have written for this theatre are actors such as Semih Sergen, Haldun Marlali, Ziya Demirel, and Ferdi Merter; critics like Ergun Sav; and established playwrights such as Ülker Köksal and Dinçer Sümer.

The first private venture in children's theatre came in 1940 when the Ankara Society for Orphaned Children began showing puppet and *Karagöz* shadow plays. Under the guidance of the *Karagöz* master Baltacioğlu, these productions made use of oversized figures, electric lighting to replace the traditional candlelight, and contemporary musical compositions as accompaniment. In the puppet shows an attempt was made to raise a traditional form to the level of a children's theatre that would be both contemporary and national. The appropriateness of this effort was debated in the press of the time.

CHILDREN'S THEATRE TODAY

During the 1950s and 1960s there was an increase in the number of private children's theatres. City banks, in particular, founded many children's theatres, with an eye to their future clientele. There is a long list of other institutions, beginning with the Turkish Trade Bank's Keloğlan Children's Theatre (1961), The Akbank Children's Theatre (1972), and the Business Bank (IsBank) Children's Theatre (1977). Chief among the children's theatres established during the past quarter century are The Thousand and One Nights Children's Theatre (1968), The World Children Players (1969), The Little Rascals Theatre (1969), The Anatolian Children's Playhouse (1978), The Ankara Children's Theatre

(1976), The Anatolian Arts Center Children's Playhouse (1986), and The Bell Theatre (1983). A number of these are still active today.

Of these groups, The Anatolian Children's Playhouse has made a name for itself abroad, with the efforts of Umit Denizer and company reaping praise in the foreign press as well as at home. In 1976 the Playhouse made its mark on the Hamburg International Festival of Children's Theatre with a performance of *Keloğlan*, and has since annually received invitations to perform in various European cities.

The Ankara Children's Theatre, under the direction of Salih Kalyon, has chosen to address the problems of the times through the medium of children's plays. In successfully carrying out this aim they have been abetted by collaborating psychologists and educators.

A number of other professional theatre companies periodically offer productions intended for a younger audience to supplement their adult fare. Such productions primarily aim at being strong box office attractions.

Recent years have seen a blossoming of academic interest in children's theatre. In 1979 the Ankara University drama department held a Symposium on Children's Theatre attended by faculty members, playwrights, and performers. This example has been followed with round table and panel discussions at other cultural institutions. Various government and private organizations hold contests and offer prizes to encourage the writing of children's plays. In 1987 the Ministry of Culture and Tourism allocated a portion of its subsidy for private theatres specifically to children's playhouses.

A substantial amount of air and screen time is devoted to children's plays by Turkish Radio and Television. This tradition was begun by Vedat Demirci at Radio Istanbul and Neriman Hizir at Radio Ankara and continues to be followed by their successors.

Today the debate over children's drama in Turkey revolves around such issues as the encouragement of playwriting for children, the determination of meaningful age groupings, the teaching of drama in places of learning, and the importance of making educators and schools aware of how useful this art can be in developing personality, helping the child to assume various roles in society, and bringing out his or her innate talents.

Sevda Şener

Union of Soviet Socialist Republics

HISTORY

Before the October 1917 Revolution theatre for children held little importance, except perhaps as an educational enterprise, but under socialism it soon acquired an extremely important artistic significance and social perspective.

Natalia Sats organized the first professional theatre for children, which opened in Moscow in 1920 with *Mowghli*, based on Kipling's story. Later, as the Moscow Children's Theatre, she moved her company to the large theatre near the famous Bolshoi Theatre, which today is the home of the Moscow Central Children's Theatre. In exile through much of World War II, Sats returned later to found the first musical theatre for young people, which operated in temporary quarters until its new building opened in the early 1980s. It was here she was honored at the opening ceremony of the Eighth ASSITEJ World Congress in 1984.

Another pioneer, Alexander Bryantsev, opened the Leningrad Theatre for Young Spectators in 1922 and began four decades of notable productions, such as his famous version of *The Little Humpbacked Horse*, which is still one of the most popular plays produced in Russia. He designed his own auditorium in the shape of an amphitheatre instead of following the form of the traditional proscenium in an attempt to bring audiences closer to the performers and to more directly involve them in the action that often takes place in the aisle and throughout the theatre. Bryantsev's work was continued by Zinovi Korogotzki who brought the Leningrad theatre international fame in the seventies and eighties when he took *Our Circus* on tour and when foreign visitors to Leningrad saw his distinguished productions of works such as *The Mountebanks, Spring Turnabouts*, and *Bambi*.

"Theatre for children is a means of communist education"—that was the slogan of the Leningrad Theatre of Young Spectators back in 1932; this great mission of educating the new individual remains the purpose of Soviet theatres for children today. Many factors serve the common aims of providing ideological and aesthetic education for Russian young people and inculcating good taste in them. Among these are the low cost of tickets, annual grants, maintenance of buildings, state-paid wages for the troupes, construction of new theatres, and competitions and festivals. All these serve to raise the level of those engaged in theatre for children and young people. Through theatre the state takes care of the spiritual development of its future citizens, of their moral upbringing, by instilling in them respect for human dignity, love of peace and internationalism, faithfulness of communist ideals, and readiness for an active role in society. The theatres for young people are an important link in the overall system of education in the USSR and a school for future spectators at adult theatres.

There are sixty professional repertory drama theatres for children and young people and one Children's Musical Theatre, the only children's opera and ballet house in the world. The Russian Federation (the republic with the biggest territory and population) alone can boast thirty-three theatres for youth, and twenty-four more are scattered throughout the national Union republics.

A feature that distinguishes them from adult theatres is an obligatory education division headed by an experienced pedagogue whose purpose is to maintain close links with schools and the teaching community in order to draw the theatres into the overall process of helping young people to form their world views and raise their cultural levels. Often a performance seen in a theatre is offered as a theme for an essay at school, or is discussed in a literature or history class. Theatres frequently hold contests for the best essay or the best drawing about their plays. Groups of senior schoolchildren attend rehearsals and help theatres keep in touch with children's tastes and interests.

In keeping with the theory of education, the repertory is selected with a view to satisfying the specific demands of each age group—five-to nine-year-olds, ten- to fifteen-year-olds, and sixteen- to eighteen-year-olds. This results in three theatres in one, each speaking to its audience in a language that is most suitable for the audience's level of development, each conforming with the laws of image-oriented thinking. Naturally each theatre and each director has a unique way of achieving the desired aims, style, and individual dramatic devices. This freedom of creative endeavor, artistic quest,and experimentation is encouraged in every way. Each theatre has its own image and creative program.

"Adult" theatres, too, include an increasing number of children's plays in their repertories. They were inspired to do so by the annual all-USSR theatre week, called "Theatre to Children and Youth," which covers ever wider areas of the Soviet Union and draws a constantly growing audience. The all-Union productions of children's plays contribute to the expansion of children's theatre repertories and introduce the element of creative competition, stimulating artistic quests and new discoveries.

Theatres for children have recently started staging "adult" plays on a wider scale. This trend emerged in order to attract older teenagers into the theatres, not only secondary-school students, but also college students and young workers.

Currently it is the children's theatres in many Soviet cities that lead the popularity lists among both child and adult theatregoers. Plays for children are usually attended by the parents too, while plays intended for older teenagers are played to mixed audiences, as they are preferred by young teenagers—the most troublesome viewers.

The theatre is a game that reflects life and the times; it revives historical personages on the stage, or tells a tale, a legend, or a myth based on the life of past ages. The theatre looks at the present day much like an implacable moral judge who has become the conscience of the age. From the outset the Soviet theatre made a great social and aesthetic impact on life. Having preserved its emotional and spiritual meaning and deep insight into the characters' inner world, the Soviet theatre has become enriched with new subjects and attitudes, closely following current events and issues in the country's life. The theatre has widened young viewers' notions of the past, present, and future, opening as it does a broad panorama of life, which fosters a more emotional and exacting attitude toward life.

Psychologists and sociologists have been aware for quite some time that teenagers' neuroses, the painful transformation of a young person's character on the threshold of adult life, result more often than not from inadequate preparation for real life. Because the new generation of stage directors for children's theatres have not forgotten their own childhoods, their primary concern is to show truth that does not retreat in the face of pain, cruelty, or betrayal. Categorical judgments toward young spectators are intended to rouse them, to lead them out of a passively contemplative attitude toward life. By presenting tragic aspects of life, the theatre speaks of each person's responsibility before all.

Does this orientation toward "adult" truth mean that children's productions have no joyful, festive atmosphere? By no means! Children feel joyous and delighted not only because they are aware that they are taken in full seriousness, not only because of an overall atmosphere of trust and optimism, but also because of the high level of professionalism of the producers of children's plays. Most of the productions for young audiences are good theatre, a festive occasion, and an exciting game—the result of a constant search for new theatrical forms and of new experiments. Oversimplification has no place in today's children's theatre.

Classic repertory (including Russian classics, selected plays from the republics, and world classics) is an important field of experimentation, proof of the maturity of theatres for children and youth and of their high professional standards. From the early days of children's theatre, producers turned to classics because they wanted to draw on rich and vital literary material. "Classical drama staged for young audiences introduces them to the cultural treasure of their people and thus contributes to their cultural education," said Alexander Bryantsev at the 1923 rehearsal of Alexander Ostrovsky's *Poverty Is No Sin* at the Leningrad Theatre for Young Spectators. This was the first classic drama produced for children.

Indeed, classic drama is as necessary for children as it is for directors and actors. Classic drama gives the company a chance to perfect its skills and probe the creative potential of the director while the audience is introduced to eternal humanistic ideals, to the world's inexhaustible treasure trove of ethical and artistic values. Without replacing classroom interpretations of a classic work, both youth and adult theatres discover new depths and find new original solutions to their scenic presentation, thus scraping off their textbook patina. Appealing directly to the feelings and minds of the young audience, theatre shows them new aspects of a familiar classic, arouses their interest, and widens their knowledge about the world of classic literature. Moreover, a profound message presented in perfect form is capable of bringing children closer to an understanding of harmony in art.

Of the Russian classics, A. N. Ostrovsky's plays have probably the greatest vogue at theatres for youth. Bryantsev's *Poverty Is No Sin* was received as a theatrical and pedagogical manifesto, and today it is running once more on the Small Stage of the Children's Theatre in Moscow. *The Power of Darkness*, by Leo Tolstoy, at the Krasnoyarsk Theatre for young spectators was acclaimed as a highlight of the jubilee season dedicated to the great Russian writer. Gogol's *Marriage* in Khabarovsk and *The Inspector-General* in Novosibirsk had an incisively topical ring. Dostoyevsky, too, has been produced for children. One of the oldest children's theatres in the country, the Saratov Theatre, has produced *The Boys*, based on *The Karamazov Brothers*, dramatized by Viktor Rozov, a leading Soviet dramatist writing for young audiences. Dostoyevsky's *Idiot* is running in Perm.

The famous comedy *Wit Works Woe*, by Griboyedov, has been produced in Chelyabinsk, while the children's theatre in Gorky presented Gorky's *The Legend of Danko*, both works being part of the school curriculum. Besides the widely produced Russian classics, there are occasionally pleasant surprises—productions of works that do not yield themselves readily for scenic presentation, although they may be well known and widely read. Such was the dramatization of Saltykov-Shchedrin's *History of a Town* in the Erevan youth theatre, a biting social caricature depicting the tragedy of a people deceived and intimidated by dishonest politicians. It calls to mind some present-day dictatorial regimes and leads the viewer to an understanding of how revolutionary protest is born in the interminable gloom of lawlessness.

Theatres for young people are equal to Chekhov's subtle and complex drama, the highest test for any director. *The Sea Gull* was produced in Saratov (and earlier, in the 1960s, in Omsk and Novosibirsk), *The Three Sisters* is running in Gorky, and *The Cherry Orchard*, in Vladivostok. In some cases it is children's theatre that discovers the dramatic possibilities in a classic that has never been staged before. A good example is *Svetlana*, a production based on Vassily Zhukovsky's ballads and poems, at the Perm Theatre of Young Spectators. Moscow Region Theatre of Young Spectators gave life to the great monument of ancient Russian literature, *The Lay of the Igor's Host*.

Along with the Russian classics, world drama is well represented too. Pride of place belongs to Shakespeare, who has grown much younger at children's theatres. According to sociological research, children are more impressed by characters who are close to them in age, for young spectators identify with them, as was the case with Romeo and Juliet in Rostov-on-Don and with Hamlet in Krasnoyarsk, Leningrad, and in Alma-Ata's Kazakh Children's Theatre. *A Midsummer Night's Dream* is permeated with playful gayety in the beautiful production in Gorky, in which the theme of the rustics' obsession with the theatre itself is emphasized. *The Comedy of Errors* is currently running in Leningrad. During its Moscow tour Oryol Theatre of Young Spectators presented *Twelfth Night* and *Troilus and Cressida* to the Moscow public. The Youth Theatre in Vilnius, Lithuania, has offered its own version of *Romeo and Juliet*, producing it as a musical titled *Love and Death in Verona*.

Other classics, too, come to life on the stages of Soviet children's theatres: Molière's *Le Bourgeois Gentilhomme* (in Gorky) and *Scapin's Tricks* (in Luchaferul Theatre, Moldavia), Goldoni's *Servant of Two Masters* and Calderon's *Open Secret* (in Ryazan), Rostand's *Romantics* (in Tashkent) and *Cyrano de Bergerac* (in Krasnoyarsk), *Les Miserables* adapted from Hugo (in Moscow Central Children's Theatre and in Theatre of Young Spectators in Voronezh), and Brecht's *Mother Courage* (in Vladivostok). Special mention should be given the Riga theatre for children (Latvia), which has presented successful productions of Ibsen's *Peer Gynt* and Kleist's *Prince Friedrich von Homburg*.

Stage adaptations of favorite children's classics from all over the world feature prominently in the repertories of children's theatres: *The Song of Hiawatha, Treasure Island, The Adventures of Tom Sawyer, The Adventures of Huckleberry Finn, Pippi Longstocking, Little Boy and Karlsson Who Lived on the Roof, The Cat That Walked by Himself, Puss in Boots, The Adventures of Cipollino, Alice in Wonderland, Peter Pan, The Little Prince, Mary Poppins*, and many tales by Andersen, Perrault, and the brothers Grimm, to name but a few. Authors from socialist countries produced in Soviet children's theatres include Pancho Panchev and Nedyalko Iordanov of Bulgaria; I. Tyl, I. Kainar, J. Stibor, M. Steglik, and Julius Fucik of Czechoslovakia; Sandor Todd of Hungary; Ion Lucian and V. Popa of Rumania; H. Kalau of East Germany; and Janos Korczak, K. Hoinski, and V. Nizursky of Poland. Their dramatic works not only broaden the child's horizon, but also instill international attitudes.

As for the drama of the Soviet national republics, mention should be made of the position of the national theatres that are to be found all over the Russian Federation and the two other republics. Just as school instruction is offered in two languages (both Russian and the language of the particular republics), children's theatres, too, perform in two languages. Usually there are two companies within one theatre as, for instance, in Ukraine, Byelorussia, Uzbekistan, Kasakhstan, Georgia, Azerbaidjan, Lithuania, Moldavia, Latvia, Tadjikistan, Armenia, Turkmenia, and Estonia.

Theatres for children and youth in national republics vary not only linguistically, but also in their degree of experience. Some of them have marked their half centenary (the theatres in Ukraine, Uzbekistan, Georgia, Azerbaidjan, and

Armenia), whereas others, such as Moldovian theatres, were opened only in the 1960s. The Turkmenian theatres for children will soon turn twenty. The theatres in Estonia and Lithuania have celebrated their fifteenth anniversary. And since the mid–1980s new theatres have sprung up in Kara Kalpakia, Abkhazian Autonomous Republic, and elsewhere. One of the important features of national drama is that none is confined to any one republic. National drama travels all over the country, for interpenetration, interaction, and mutual enrichment of cultures are inherent in socialist internationalism and contribute to the flourishing of nations and to drawing them closer together. Learning in the spirit of internationalism is an important part of the communist education.

The recent decades have seen growing popularity of the national classics and, as a result, a wider exchange of plays between the republics. The children's theatre in the Siberian city of Irkutsk staged *The Forest Song*, by the famous Ukrainian poetess Lesya Ukrainka. At the Central Children's Theatre in Moscow a group of producers from Ufa (the capital of Bashkiria) gave Mustai Karim's *A Long Long Childhood*, a stage adaptation of the celebrated Bashkirian poet's story about a dramatic episode in the history of his people. One of the first productions of the newly formed theatre for children in Tomsk, an old cultural center in Siberia, was the play by the young Lithuanian dramatist Sauljus Saltenis, *Scat, Skinny, Scat!*

Love, Jazz and the Devil, a play by the veteran Lithuanian dramatist Juosas Grusas, had a successful run in Ryazan, Kirov, and Kiev. The play looks at the present-day young people's problems through the eyes of a wise old man. The Youth Theatre of Vilnius (Lithuania) has staged *And the Day Lasts Longer Than the Age*, by the world-famous Kirghizian writer Chingiz Aitmatov. At the Yerevan children's theatre the Byelorussian dramatist Andrei Makayonok's play *The Tribunal* and Estonian author Hans Luik's play *And That Lad Is Me* were staged. The same theatre is also showing the Georgian playwright Shota Rokva's *Beyond the River Is My Village*. At the Lvov Theatre for children and youth (Ukraine) the heroic *Ballad of a Feat of Valor* has been running to full houses for many years now. *Ballad* is the work of Armenian dramatist Armen Yagdzhan.

There is a whole series of productions based on plays from various Soviet republics in Ukraine. Apart from the above-mentioned play by Grusas, they are *Overtaking the Summer*, a fairy tale by the Lithuanian Violetta Palcinskaite; *My Dear Baby*, by the Armenian Azat Shaginyan; *The Choice*, by the Byelorussian Evgeny Shaban; *The Fragrance of the Ripe Quince*, by the most popular of the Moldavian dramatists, Ion Drutse; and *The Drivers of Fire*, by the Lithuanians Saltenis and L. Jacinevicius. The jolly Georgian fairy tale *Chinchrakvella*, by Georgy Nakhutsrichvilli, staged at the Moldovian Luchaferul theatre, was awarded a Diploma of Merit at the All-Union Festival of theatres for children and youth.

Often plays from other republics and those staged by guest directors turn out to be exceptionally successful. It is neither the exotic aspects that attract the audience nor the mere encouragement of experimentation, but the inspiring feeling of freshness from contact with a different poetic vision of the world that results when a director of another nationality ventures into a new cultural area. A creative spark is born at the juncture of two cultures, igniting the flame of inspiration that produces a new work of art with an imprint of cultural fusion— the result of exchange of cultural values.

This brings us back to the principle of equality among theatres, which is coupled with the principle of internationalism. All dramatists and producers in all republics have equal opportunities in every children's theatre in the USSR; quality of writing and directing is the only consideration. All plays—classic, Russian, non-Russian, and foreign—are the common stock from which all theatres, both adult and children's, can draw.

Bold experiments are being conducted with theatrical space. An interesting example is the Riga Theatre production of *Lads from Sunciem* (based on A. Upits), which was staged in the open air. The Tallinn Youth Theatre uses as a stage an old Dominican church, a children's playground in the old part of the city, an old mansion, and even the seashore. It was here on the seashore that Merle Carusoo staged the theatre's most famous production, *I'm Thirteen.*

Some experimental devices are intended to provoke the audience to start a discussion and voice their opinions even during the performance. For example, the motivation of a heroic deed is an exciting topic for debate when the subject of the play is the heroic past. Romantic heroes and romantic stories electrify the audience, excite them, and spur them on to discuss the burning topic right on the spot. But when it comes to a theme from modern life that affords only a short range of vision, romanticism gives way to a sober view and to practical evaluation. An extraordinary occurrence or action in the play can either unite or divide the audience into assenters or dissenters. So, experimenters must be careful.

In the realm of fairy tales, experiments and artistic searches take other forms. Each nationality has its own rich tradition of folk art, its own poetry, rituals, and games. In the friendly family of Soviet republics folklore provides the source of inspiration and a basis for modern parables and fairy-tale plays. Whereas earlier theatres for children preferred tales about everyday life, they now favor performances in the style of a folk festival that involves games, rituals, songs, solo dances, round dances, ditties, and jokes, all this treated on an elevated poetic plane. There are performances wholly made up of folk materials presented in musical-poetic miniature scenes. A production of this sort, based on Pushkin's fairy tales, has been popular at the Moscow Central Children's Theatre. The characters of Samuil Marshak's comedy in verse, *The Cat's House*, produced in Khabarovsk, play musical instruments, and the play is reminiscent of a performance at a fair given by wandering clowns.

The theatre for children and young people is constantly developing, finding ever new expressive means, for audiences in this fast-moving age are rapidly growing up and changing too. How is the theatre to find the most precise and effective ways to reach the young person, the child, the teenager? How does the young spectator of today differ from the one of yesterday? What kind of audience will come to the theatre tomorrow? What will they look for in the theatre? Answers to these questions are essential for further progress by all children's theatres.

Soviet children's theatres (each to the extent of its talent, possibilities, and views, as well as to the individual inclinations of the people actually engaged in it) strive to be in tune with the times and to feel the pulse of the modern day. To introduce a young public to the cultural wealth of its country and of the world, to give it new knowledge made attractive by the magic of the theatre, to turn the young generation toward understanding themselves and learning about the world—these are the main aims of the present-day theatre for children, adolescents, and young people. This drives its artists to search constantly, in rejection of the old and exploration of the new.

Any undertaking, and theatre in particular, needs worthy successors who have to be carefully trained. Directors and actors who work in children's theatre must be artists and pedagogues at the same time. They must be skillfully selected from among the multitude of talented aspiring artists. To meet this demand the drama colleges and conservatories in the national republics have set up special departments that train actors and directors for children's theatre (in addition to similar departments already in existence at the national theatrical institutes, such as the Lunacharsky Institute of Theatrical Arts, the Shchepkin and the Shchukin Drama Schools, the Studio-School of the Moscow Art Theatre, and the Institute of Drama, Music and Cinema in Leningrad). Significantly, teaching at these schools is done not only in classes, but also at theatres, in practical work.

From the first year of studies, students actually take part in performances. Children's theatre companies recruit new actors from graduates of these special departments that exist in all national republics. This is seen as a guarantee of further rapid development of these theatres in the national republics. This country's principle, "Nothing but the best for children," is also the motto of the personnel of the children's theatres. So it comes as no surprise that such outstanding theatre personalities of the Soviet stage as Igor Ilyinsky, Nikolai Cherkasov, Maria Babanova, Boris Chirkov, Maria Knebel, Georgy Tovstonogov, Oleg Yefremov, Anatoly Efros, and many others were at one time or another associated with children's theatre. Anatoly Efros writes in his book, *Rehearsal Is My Love*: "The day I was accepted at the Central Children's Theatre was the happiest day in my life."

If one were to draw a map of all the Soviet children's theatre tours across the country, all the republics would be covered by a web of countless intersecting lines. The companies make tours regardless of distance, from Siberia to Dushanbe, from Riga to Ukraine. The Tbilisi Theatre made a tour of Yerevan, Baku, Astrakhan, Kiev, and Krasnodar. The children's theatres of the Russian Federation give guest performances in all of the national republics. The language barrier is no obstacle either. Public address systems are provided at theatres, and special booklets are published to provide all the necessary information to facilitate appreciation of the play.

A special occasion for regional companies is a guest engagement in Moscow. At such times their work is judged by the capital's critics and colleagues, and reviews and articles appear in the press. Each year Moscow is visited by the more interesting theatres for children around the country. Among the recent tours of special interest were those by theatres of the Russian Federation, Georgia, Azerbaidjan, Lithuania, Turkmenia, Armenia, and Latvia.

Like any theatre organization, children's theatres go through various stages in their development: blossoming and creative stagnation, mustering strength and slumber, striking leaps ahead and hidden "growing pains." But their general atmosphere of creativity reflects exceptionally boisterous activity, inspiration, and complete dedication.

It is to be expected that in any artistic enterprise success depends on the actual people responsible for it. Most companies are made up of people who are utterly dedicated to their work, who see their profession as their life's mission. This is a most gratifying phenomenon. People engaged in these theatres must be "artists with the mental attitude of teachers and teachers with the sensitivity of artists." It is precisely this happy combination of hard work, a real sense of involvement, and talent that marks the work of the USSR's more interesting stage directors in children's theatre.

Children of today are usually described as being well informed from their vast access to the most varied information. At the same time, they are quite experienced theatregoers who often themselves are endowed with many talents. Yet for all their accelerated development, children will be children: naive, sincere, and trustful. They are quite prepared to believe implicitly in what's happening on the stage and to identify themselves completely with it for the duration of the performance. How are they to be freed from inhibitions? Only by the implicit faith that artistic invention on the stage is an expression of the supreme truth. Children's devotion to the theatre begins with that instantaneous flash of spiritual freedom, strength, excitement, and the desire to take part, with the actors, in the creation of the magic world of the theatre.

This direct appeal to childhood and selfless devotion to children's art constitute the romanticism of theatre for children and youth. Both the world outlook (stern and principled as it is) and the theatre's striving to understand the deep-lying processes of the times give birth to emotional dramatic realism in the theatre's work. By awakening kindness, sincerity, and love in children's hearts the theatre creates genuine poetry. This is what children's theatre has in common with the other forms of art, and what makes it unique.

REPRESENTATIVE PLAYS

Victor Rozov, born in 1913 and one of the most popular of Soviet dramatists (*Good Luck to You, In Search of Joy, A Woodgrouse Nest*), wrote *Riders from*

Rosa Station for production at Moscow's Central Children's Theatre in 1978. This two-act play explores conflicts in the consciousness of a child. Seryozha, disturbed because a tutor opened a letter he had written to his father, leaves the pioneer camp at the height of the summer season. At the local station camp officials plead with him to return, while a journalist he befriends urges him to stick to his principles. The play attempts to communicate the boy's psychology as he deals with a dilemma he desparately tries to understand. Even though basically a realistic play, the language at times becomes poetic as the hero reflects:

And here I am, one fine evening, lying down and looking up at the clouds. And up there, I see something flashing, in the clouds. Raising myself on my elbows and fixing my gaze, I see riders in helmets and cloaks, with lances held horizontal, riding galloping horses, the tails and mains flowing. I say in a low voice, ''Riders, drive the clouds away, please.'' I wake in the morning and the first thing I see is a clear sky, blue, and not a single cloud.

Yet It Does Move, by Alexander Khmelik (born in 1925, the author is a famous Soviet screenwriter), was first produced in Moscow in 1981. This two-act farce centers on Vasya, who, reporting that he has met a spaceman from another planet, disrupts his entire school, which is eager for a full account. Instead, the teachers force him to renounce his story as pure fiction, but as he reads their prepared statement the very creature he denies having seen enters the classroom. The dramatist emphasizes the power of fantasy, belief in the improbable—even in the impossible—as Vasya, who is normally late and a nuisance to his teachers because of his overactive imagination, becomes a true dreamer with a lofty and poetical spirit.

Shota Rovka (born 1927) is an Abkhazian poet and playwright whose twelve volumes of poetry are composed in Georgian. His plays largely deal with Abkhazian rural life; they have been translated into Russian and performed in theatres throughout the Soviet Union. Best known are *Moscow Calling, A Hot-Tempered Old Woman*, and *Love Is Like a Rainbow*. *Beyond the River Is My Village*, a dramatic narrative in two acts, was first produced by the Children's Theatre of Kuibyshev in 1982. In it, twelve-year-old Giya has come to spend the summer with his grandfather in a small village where he learns respect for the land on which his ancestors were born. The boy decides to live in the village permanently and to help his grandfather overcome his loneliness. In the portrait of the grandfather the best traits of the Georgian character are shown. That is why the ideas of the succession of generations is so important for the playwright, why he made a small boy the hero and gave him the mission of restoring the ties of time, as exemplified in these lines: ''How long the days are . . . when one is alone. . . . Life is people, and if one is alone for a whole day, then that day will prove to be the longest in one's life. . . . Time never passes slower than when one is without people.''

Some 500 theatres in the Soviet Union have performed more than 25,000 performances of Lev Ustinov's plays, and sixteen have been translated and staged in eighty-eight countries, including the United States, Japan, Finland, Syria, and Cyprus. Born in 1923, he specializes in fairy-tale plays, the first of which was produced in 1951 and which include adaptations of *Snow White and the Seven Dwarfs*, *The Little Organ Grinder*, and *The Glowing Stone*. Perhaps his best-known play, inside and outside Russia, is *A City Without Love*, which, according to a Swedish critic, "is a fairy tale about a world of grownups. It could be our own world, a mad, dull, grey soulless world. A world without laughter, without tears and love. The tale has a happy ending which does not always happen in life, and I think the children realize it. The company is to be congratulated for going against time-worn notions of plays for children and staging this one." After its publication in the United States a number of productions were given by university theatres.

BIBLIOGRAPHY

Ignatieva, M. "Create a Collective Body." *Theatrical Life*, no. 22 (1986): 12–23.
Korogodsky, Z. *Your Theatre*. Moscow, 1984.
Moral and Aesthetical Education of School Children by Means of Theatrical Art. Moscow: Institute of Scientific Research in Artistic Education, Academy of Pedagogical Science, 1984.
"Theatre and Children." *Theatre*, no. 2 (1987): 95–135. The articles include "The Young Spectators's Theatre: To Be or Not To Be," "The Young Theatregoer Needs a Hero," "It Is Necessary to Find a Way Out," "They Need New Forms," "I Stand for an 'Inconvenient' Theatre," "Many Things Alarm," and "The Situation Aggravates."
Voronov, I., and Voronov, N. "Young Spectator's Theatre: Are You Ready?" *Children's Literature*, no. 11 (1984): 57–59, 66–67.

Natalia Sats
(Prepared from materials submitted by ASSITEJ/USSR.)

United States of America

HISTORY

Although there were some productions for children in the United States during the nineteenth century, the first well-recorded children's theatre was not established until 1903. That year, therefore, is accepted as the founding date of what was to become a movement that involved various dramatic activities on professional, community, and educational levels. Unlike theatre for adults, children's theatre in America was born in the ghetto as a social and educational force to help the children of immigrants learn the language of their adopted country, to provide a meeting place for children and their families, and to offer wholesome entertainment to the children of the poor. It is interesting that these three goals have remained constant, although the ranking order varies according to the philosophy and practice of the producing group or company.

This first children's theatre, which functioned successfully for seven years with a regular schedule of performances, was the Children's Educational Theatre, established at the Educational Alliance in New York City in 1903. The founder, Alice Minnie Herts, was a social worker with a strong interest in the performing arts and an equally strong commitment to the children of the ghetto. Noting that of all the activities sponsored by the settlement house, theatre drew the largest number of adults, she surmised that it would have the same appeal for children, were they given the opportunity to experience it. She was correct. Storytelling, story acting, classes in puppetry, and performances of appropriate plays by adult actors immediately drew scores of young people to the center. The first production given by the Children's Educational Theatre was Shakespeare's *The Tempest*, a play that provided exciting entertainment, magic, and a rich visual experience for the spectators. Shakespeare's dialogue offered the words and cadences lacking in the limited vocabulary of the street and the books read in the elementary grades. Moreover, it stimulated a desire to reenact the story and create original plays.

The Tempest was followed by productions of children's classics. Despite the success of the project, funds became increasingly inadequate, causing the theatre to close in 1910. A new group was formed, but meanwhile the concept of a theatre designed specifically for the child audience had caught on, with the result that groups sprang up in poor neighborhoods in Boston, Chicago, San Francisco, Cleveland, Detroit, and Washington, D.C. During the next decade there was a proliferation of community programs throughout the United States as well as occasional productions by professional companies on Broadway and in the more affluent sections of the larger cities. None of the latter survived for any appreciable length of time, however, and few professional actors or playwrights were sufficiently attracted to the field to remain in it. The reason given was lack of money for production and the impossibility of earning a living.

Most of the plays were written by social workers and classroom teachers in an effort to meet the needs of a theatre that was in a formative stage. A few names do stand out, however: among them were Constance D'Arcy Mackay, a keen observer of the scene and author of plays and articles on the subject; Percy Mackaye, playwright for the adult theatre and promoter of the pageant; Stuart Walker, playwright and producer of the Portmanteau Theatre, a small touring company in New York; and Jane Addams and Lillian Wald, directors of settlement houses in Chicago and New York, respectively.

During the twenties a new force appeared with the establishment of pioneering drama programs in the schools. Credit for this must be given to Winifred Ward, former teacher and professor at Northwestern University in Evanston, Illinois. One of her first acts was to differentiate between creative drama (improvisation) *with* children and children's theatre (formal production) *for* children. Ward's other contributions included courses in creative drama for university students planning to teach, a convincing argument for the Evanston Board of Education to add drama to the other arts in the elementary school curriculum, the establishment of a theatre for child audiences in the city, and, in 1944, an invitation to a group of children's theatre leaders to a meeting on the campus of Northwestern University for the purpose of establishing a professional organization. This meeting resulted in the formation of a committee that later became the Children's Theatre Association of America. Ward's four books, *Creative Dramatics, Theatre for Children, Playmaking with Children,* and *Stories to Dramatize,* were not only among the first in the field, but also became standard texts for many years. Although schools across the country did not immediately follow suit by introducing creative drama along with the other arts, the experiment provided a model that, during the next fifty years, was admired and in some cases replicated, in part.

Meanwhile community organizations and institutions were contributing in other ways to the growth of the children's theatre movement. Chief among them was the Association of Junior Leagues of America, a women's service organization with chapters throughout the United States. Many young women, recently graduated from college or prepatory school, selected dramatic activities with children as an area in which to do volunteer work. They went into community centers to lead dramatics classes and, in some of the larger cities, to mount lavish productions of children's plays. Although tickets were sold at high prices, blocks of seats were always reserved for inner-city children. From all reports, these productions were beautiful, although casts were composed entirely of amateur actresses, and only a few performances of a play were given. Later the League shifted its emphasis from the elaborate, large-scale productions to small touring performances of plays designed for trouping. By the seventies many Leagues were sponsoring plays by professional companies rather than performing themselves; after eighty years the Junior League is still serving the community but in a different capacity from its original program.

Another national organization, the Drama League of America, founded in 1910 and dedicated to the development of a strong regional theatre, also had an impact on children's theatre through its publications, community activities, and consulting service. While the major thrust of the Drama League was the promotion and improvement of adult community theatre, it also provided guidance for people working with and for youth. Stimulated by this grassroots activity, little theatres sprang up in all regions of the United States. Large and small towns organized amateur groups and, in some cases, more affluent communities actually built little theatres for the productions of their plays. Some of them developed into fully professional theatres as time went on, and many still are in existence, providing good live theatre in areas far from Broadway and other large city centers. Plays for children followed and, again, in some instances, became a strong ongoing component of the adult organization. As a result, many regional theatres today not only provide entertainment for child audiences, but also offer after-school workshops and weekend classes in creative drama for younger children, acting for teenagers, and workshops in dance, mime, puppetry, and stagecraft.

Despite the success and influence of the Drama League, however, it suspended operations in 1931. Many reasons were given for its closing, but the stated explanation was that it had accomplished its purpose: to decentralize the American theatre and to stimulate local dramatic activities in all parts of the country. So far as children's theatre was concerned, many civic groups established during this period continued, with junior entertainment as an important branch of the adult theatre.

Although it has been stated that there was little interest in children's theatre on the part of commercial theatre during the first decades of the century, there were a few groups that deserve mention. Noted for its longevity and extensive touring program was Clare Tree Major's company, the Threshold Players of New York. Major was a young English actress who emigrated to America in 1916. Early on she perceived the paucity of children's entertainment here, and in accordance with her perception and interests, she launched her own company in 1921. The next year she began a repertory of plays for high school students. For the younger children she produced adaptations of popular fairy tales and for the older ones, Shakespeare and other classics suggested by the National Council of Teachers of English and the New York City Board of Education. She also established classes for her actors at her studio in Pleasantville, New York, where for over thirty years she trained her company and rehearsed and scheduled performances of her plays, which she toured throughout the United States. Her death in 1954 brought the oldest children's theatre in America to an end.

Another company to receive high praise at the time was Junior Programs, Inc. It was established by Dorothy McFadden, a concerned parent in Maplewood, New Jersey, who was dissatisfied with the quality of the productions her children saw. Not a producer or actress herself, McFadden nevertheless proceeded to hire and administer a large company, including actors, directors, choreographers, and musicians, plus a strong public relations and business staff. World War II interrupted this most successful venture after only seven years, during which time McFadden had expanded her enterprise to include three companies offering theatre, dance, and music. But the loss of performers to the armed forces and the rationing of gasoline for her trucks caused a suspension of activities that was never resumed.

A third professional group that was hailed with enthusiasm at the time was the Children's World Theatre, founded in 1947. It also was terminated after only a few years after the death of producer-director Monte Meacham in 1955. Children's World Theatre was established as a small nonprofit corporation with adult professional actor-teachers and clearly stated artistic and educational objectives.

The Goodman Theatre of the Art Institute of Chicago was a well-known institution whose young apprentices performed plays for children on weekends. The Goodman Theatre was a beautifully equipped facility with a stage that could be transformed into every conceivable setting because of its modern technical equipment and fine staff. Noteworthy also is the fact that one of the United States' best children's playwrights, Charlotte Chorpenning, wrote many of her scripts for the Goodman Theatre. Chorpenning was influential in that she observed children's audiences closely and wrote a set of rules for the fledgling playwright wanting to write for this level. Her plays were primarily dramatizations of children's classics and traditional fairy tales; although they tended to be longer than the majority of children's plays written today, they were well constructed and had great appeal. Indeed, most of her plays are still being produced, although other forms have been created since and the folktales and fairy tales have declined in popularity.

There were numerous other companies that were fully or partially professional, but the theatres cited above were among the best known. Some others that survived several seasons with less publicity but with dedication and hard work were the Knickerty Knockerty Players and Grace Price Productions of Pittsburgh, Seattle Junior Program, Inc., The Curtain Pullers of the Cleveland Play House, the Children's Experimental Theatre of Baltimore, the Traveling Playhouse of

New York, and the Karamu Children's Theatre, a community arts center in Cleveland that continues to operate. Other companies came and went, in nearly every instance closing for lack of money.

One group that does not fit into any category was the King-Coit School in New York. This was a school of acting and design directed by Dorothy Coit, who taught acting to children aged five to thirteen, and Edith King, who taught arts and crafts. The two women, both former teachers, worked together in a selective after-school program. Each autumn they chose a story or play of high literary quality with visual appeal on which the children worked until spring, when it was given two or three public performances. There was emphasis on design and painting as well as on performance, and often the children's designs were used in the final production. Although creativity was considered important, technical excellence was stressed, according to all reports. In order to achieve a beautiful effect scene painters and lighting experts were hired to mount and light the shows. Plays presented by the King-Coit School included *Kai Khrosu, Aucassin and Nicolette, The Tempest, The Story of Theseus, The Rose and the Ring, The Image of Artemis*, and *The Golden Cage* (from the poem by William Blake). The school carried on its program until the late fifties and then closed with the retirement of the two directors.

The Great Depression, which followed hard on the demise of the Drama League, proved a boon to the community theatres, particularly those that included plays for children. The financial troubles of the professional theatre had little, if any, effect on children's theatre, for it was in the communities of America rather than on the commercial stage that children's theatre continued to thrive. Indeed, one of the most effective programs to appear during the thirties, as a direct result of the Depression, was the Federal Theatre Project. Established as a temporary relief measure for unemployed actors and technicians in 1935, it was thoroughly professional, although it was nonprofit and independent of the box office for support. One of the most successful branches of the Federal Theatre was the children's program. Within the four-year period of its existence (1935–1939) plays were presented to child audiences in New York; Gary, Indiana; Los Angeles; Seattle; New Haven, Connecticut; Portland, Oregon; Cleveland; Denver; and Tampa. In addition, a few cities featured summer touring productions in parks and playgrounds. In New York City not only did the most extensive work take place, but also the first major research was done on child audiences, their reactions to plays, and age-level programming.

The policy of the Federal Theatre stipulated that plays must provide more than mere amusement; hence entertainment and education were linked in equal ranking order. Although political controversy plagued the Federal Theatre Project from its inception, and caused its termination after only four years, it exerted a far-reaching influence on theatre for young people. Many talented young writers and producers found this area of theatre not only a means of earning a living, but also one that provided personal satisfaction and an opportunity for creativity and experimentation; for those reasons they remained with it after the federal program came to an end. In fact, the children's branch of the Federal Theatre was conceded to be one of the most successful of all the programs launched at the time.

With the educational theatre now firmly established at Northwestern University and in a growing number of other colleges and universities, education in the theatre arts had become a reality. If aesthetic education were to be accepted as an integral part of the school curriculum, however, and if community theatres were to continue producing plays of high quality for the public, knowledge of the child audience and of appropriate material for it were required. Accordingly, in an effort to meet these needs, a group of theatre professors met in the winter of 1936 to lay the cornerstone of a professional association that would serve all sectors. This was the American Educational Theatre Association (AETA).

AETA was organized by regions from coast to coast with the following division for different levels: college and university theatre, secondary-school theatre, children's theatre, community theatre, army theatre, and a student division that was periodically active, depending on its membership. National conventions brought all divisions together annually, with special programs planned for each as well as some sessions for all. In addition, during the year, most regions held their own conferences. These were frequently augmented by local activities such as showcases and workshops on specific topics. Later the word "Education" was dropped from the title of the association, as the intent to identify with the American theatre took precedence over the more parochial implication of the original name. During the sixties and seventies the American Theatre Association (ATA) boasted a membership of more than 6,000, with some members belonging to two or three divisions. In the 1980s, however, rising costs, problems affecting all nonprofit organizations, and drastic budget cuts that decimated arts programs in many schools and community centers throughout the nation resulted in fewer job opportunities for teachers and drama leaders. All of this dealt ATA a staggering blow from which it could not recover. In the spring of 1986, after fifty years of service, this first professional association ceased operation.

ATA had accomplished several important goals, however. It brought practitioners together for the first time; it raised standards on all levels; it published journals, newsletters, books, and materials for members; and it listed employment opportunities for members seeking positions. When ATA ceased operation in 1986 some of the divisions quickly re-formed and incorporated so that by the next year they were again functioning independently, although on a smaller scale and without a large, central office. The children's theatre division was the first to recover, and a year later it was joined by the secondary school association, thus shifting the former emphases from two age levels to the concept of a single developmental program that recognized a kindergarten-through-twelveth-grade curriculum.

This joining of forces created a stronger organization than the former separation between the elementary and the high school. Although members acknowledged major differences in the interests and needs of younger children and adolescents, they also recognized the scope and sequence of a carefully planned arts curriculum that included the theatre experience. With teachers, producers of professional theatre for young people, and community theatres now working more closely together, there was a greater understanding of student needs and the responsibility of outside groups to meet them. It was to take time, however, before this awareness developed into clear and effective action, but by the eighties definite changes in American children's theatre had become visible.

ASSITEJ/USA

In 1964 the international organization ASSITEJ was founded at a meeting in England. The Children's Theatre Association of America (CTAA) was one of the original thirty-three founding members, voting it a committee of the association in the beginning. A few years later it separated from CTAA and became an independent entity: ASSITEJ/USA. This new organization of professional theatres for children offered a unique opportunity for Americans to learn about and see theatre in other parts of the world. A congress is held every three years in a different country, which members are invited to attend. By 1984 there were forty-three member countries in the association. In June of that year ASSITEJ/ USA and the Louisiana World's Fair presented a World Festival of Theatre for Young Audiences in New Orleans as a special feature of the event. Included among the fifteen companies selected to appear were Theatreworks/USA of New York, The Sheffield Ensemble Company of Biloxi, Mississippi, The Honolulu Theatre for Youth, and the Young ACT Company of Seattle. Although ASSITEJ is not an American organization, it is an important part of the scene, invigorating, educating, and influencing children's theatre producers in all sectors and in all parts of the United States. It has shown what can be accomplished artistically with sufficient subsidy to attract the best writers, actors, directors, designers, and dramaturgs. Although they do not yet have the financial support needed to reach the standard to which they aspire, there has been improvement in both script and performance skills. The fact that Arts Councils were established in all fifty states at the time the United States joined ASSITEJ made more funding available than had previously been possible.

CHILDREN'S THEATRE TODAY

Today children's theatre in America differs in many important respects from its progenitors in the early part of the century, although a few of the major problems remain. The objectives, to entertain and educate, are still the stated goals of nearly every group performing for children. Productions continue to come from three sources—the professional or commercial theatre, the community theatre, and the educational theatre—with some very good work to be found in each. Whereas the professional theatre has a pool of skilled actors on which to draw, the community theatre often has many experienced men and women, and in some cases even children, among its membership. The fact that the adults are employed and the children attend school means, however, that the actors seldom are available for touring engagements or extensive performances. The educational theatre, on the other hand, has the advantage of the university as producer, often with enviable facilities and experienced directors. The disadvantages, however, are the changing student population and the limits set by academic priorities of time and student work loads.

The greatest problem, particularly for the professional companies, continues to be financing. Producers are often dedicated, idealistic men and women, sacrificing time and money to work in a field that promises little beyond the satisfactions of doing a good job and enjoying it. It is true that more funding sources are available now that every state has an arts council. The National Endowment for the Arts extends support on occasions, and corporations may be generous, especially when their products are related to children. Even with this help, children's theatre is far behind adult theatre in budget, staffing, and public respect. The Actor's Equity contract (the professional performer's union) has brought better salaries and benefits, at the same time forcing some companies out of business. The result is that there are fewer but better groups in the eighties than there were in the sixties and seventies. Whereas the community and university groups enjoy the luxury of large casts, the majority of professional companies must still work within the confines of the four- or five-member company.

Higher fees for sponsors is a concern that has been met by increased school performances and with workshops for both teachers and students after the play. Some companies offer residencies of from a day to a semester in what is termed an "educational component." This is of particular value to schools with no drama specialist on the staff, as well as a welcome source of income for actors.

A popular way for sponsors to see the productions of available touring companies is the "showcase." By holding a spring conference at which a number of companies who have already been screened are presented, sponsors can plan ahead for their individual schools and communities. The first to introduce this idea was the New York metropolitan area CTAA in the early sixties. Today many regions present local companies, both professional and educational. One large showcase comprising Equity actors is presented in New York City in March; the other important showcase is sponsored by the American Alliance for Theatre and Education, which is also held every spring in a large city such as Philadelphia, Cleveland, or Detroit. Both showcases feature straight plays, musicals, dance groups, and puppet companies, all of which are available for booking the next year. In this way, both the presenter's and the sponsor's needs are met. Different styles of production, as well as of content, may be found in the selections.

Plays that simply entertain, usually in proscenium style, and theatre-in-education (TIE) scripts currently predominate. Participation plays, popular a few years ago, seem to have peaked, although they are still to be found, particularly in a repertory designed for younger children. The participation technique, however, is frequently used in TIE plays in which directors want the audience to become actively involved in the issues. Many of these plays are purposely left open-ended so as to encourage discussion and classroom activities afterward. Companies working in this genre prepare study guides that they send to schools in advance so that teachers can prepare their classes for the performance and be ready to follow up suggestions after seeing it. Often actors go into classrooms to work with students and teachers in order to ensure the fullest response. This means that actor-teachers must have special preparation, for they are essentially handling two roles. This technique can be extremely effective, and more and more companies are dealing with subject matter that a generation ago would have been considered inappropriate, now put into a form that would have seemed unfinished to producers of the well-made play.

PLAYS AND PLAYWRIGHTS

Because of the origin of children's theatre in America, few scripts of professional quality were to be found before the thirties and forties. Most of the early plays were written by social workers and teachers in an effort to meet immediate needs. Playwrights for the adult theatre did not write for the child audience, and the lack of financial reward did not attract authors of children's books. Charlotte Chorpenning, playwright and educator, was one of the first people to make a serious effort to write well-structured plays that respected the child's intelligence and interests. She also laid down a set of rules for other playwrights to follow that had evolved from her own experience and observation. She was a friend and colleague of Winifred Ward and taught a playwrighting course at Northwestern University, where she influenced many student playwrights.

One playwright who was there at the time and who today expresses gratitude for his education at Northwestern is Aurand Harris, often described as America's "most produced children's theatre playwright." Harris taught in the elementary school for many years during which time he wrote constantly. He is currently retired from teaching, devoting himself entirely to writing with classes and residencies on various campuses and in communities, where he works with teachers in the schools.

Harris, like Chorpenning, largely prefers to write adaptations rather than to create original plots. He has been successful with the latter but believes that he does a better job starting with a familiar story. Most of his plays are longer than the typical school assembly play because of his choice of plot and his insistence on character development and appropriate dialogue. The hundreds of performances of his works annually attest to his popularity, and the fact that his *Androcles and the Lion*, for example, has been translated into nine languages proves his ability to reach children of many lands and cultural backgrounds. He is one of the few children's theatre playwrights to receive a Creative Writing Fellowship from the National Endowment for the Arts, and in 1987 he was invited by the People's Republic of China to direct one of his plays in Shanghai.

There he worked with a Chinese director on a production of *Rags to Riches*, a play based on the American success story of a boy who rose from poverty to wealth through his own hard work and ambition.

Another popular children's playwright is Joanna Kraus, whose subject matter differs from Harris' in her concern for the social problems many children confront. Her *Ice Wolf* is based on an Eskimo legend in which racial prejudice leads to the persecution and death of a child before the people of the village realize that they were responsible through their own bigotry and ignorance. This play was followed by others such as *Circus Home*, the story of a "freak" as protagonist; *Mean to Be Free*, a Civil War story; and some works based on curricular subject matter.

The work of Flora Atkin, on the other hand, is divided between folktales and problem plays written to meet the specific needs of the small touring company performing in schools. Suzan Zeder is a playwright whose works address the more personal situations faced by children today: broken homes, divorce, and psychological problems. These are only a selected few of the men and women who are now in the field, writing plays for children as a serious profession.

From the themes cited it is obvious that children's plays have gone far beyond the familiar folktales and fairy tales with happy endings once assumed to be the only suitable material for young audiences. Today one finds, in addition to the problems already mentioned, subjects such as death, intergenerational conflicts, and handicapping conditions, including those of the learning disabled. A few years ago there was a move away from fairy tales; today they have regained some of their popularity, but there is now a balance between traditional and contemporary fare in the lists of plays that companies announce for a season of children's entertainment. Proof of the growing number of good scripts is to be found on the title pages of the catalogues of play publishers. Although a number of publishers handle some plays for children's audiences, the major houses are Anchorage Press, New Plays, Inc., Samuel French, Inc., Baker's Plays, Coach House, Pioneer Press, and the University of Texas Press at Austin.

A genre that does not fit any of the categories described is the TIE program, developed by the company or written by a playwright-in-residence. These scripts deal with social problems and are often left open-ended. Few of these plays are to be found in the catalogues from the publishing houses because they are either commissioned or written for a particular company. Best known among American TIE companies is the Creative Arts Team (CAT), based at New York University.

REPRESENTATIVE COMPANIES

The Creative Arts Team

CAT was formed in 1974 by Professor Nancy Swortzell and a group of graduate students who had studied in the New York University Summer Abroad program at Bretton Hall College in England. Although their inspiration came from the

British model, the students adapted it to American needs and problems. The group was highly successful and within a few years became professional. Today it is composed of sixty members who participate in performing and workshop troupes under the direction of professional directors, administrators, and educators. The separate companies are as follows: Arts Partners (for the New York City Board of Education), The Reading Support Program, Conflict Resolution Through Drama, Drama for the Child with Special Needs, and Youth Employment Video Series. Although CAT is still affiliated with the university, it is a separate entity, autonomous and self-supporting through grants and contracts with school districts and other outside groups.

Originally, programs were developed by the company as a whole. Today a playwright-in-residence is responsible for scripts, with the various troupes working on special projects. Commissioned performances in the schools deal with current issues such as child abuse, racial conflicts, and drugs. Thousands of students in the New York metropolitan area alone have been reached by CAT. In addition to regular scheduled appearances in the city, the company has been featured in special performances at the Kennedy Center, the Lincoln Center, and the New York Shakespeare Festival Public Theatre, and scenes from some current works have been shown on television. Recipient of several awards and honors, CAT continues to be a leader in TIE in America.

The Paper Bag Players

A form that defies categorization is the children's revue—an original format created by the Paper Bag Players of New York City in 1958. It has been called by some enthusiasts ''America's Best Children's Theatre,'' and indeed, it has the distinction of surviving for one of the longest periods of time under the same leadership. Judith Martin, founder, director, and performer, holds high standards for her company of five (four actors and one musician, who is also the composer of their original music, which is an integral part of the performance). The Paper Bag Players maintain a consistent policy of creating short, original sketches in a fifty-minute presentation that is amusing, mildly satiric, and professionally performed. One feature of the group that has been imitated by others is the uniform costume. It consists of tights or pants, a top or leotard, with bits of costumes added when needed. The only scenery used is that brought on by the actors: cardboard boxes, signs, two-dimensional props, fabrics, and other pieces found in any home or disposal area of a supermarket. Indeed, one of the points the Paper Bag Players make is that children can create their own plays with simple materials at home or at school. The challenge is to the imagination; by offering short sketches with minimal dialogue, they demonstrate the possibilities of creative drama and dramatic play. Many of the ideas for the sketches come from children and are translated into the unique Paper Bag format.

The Honolulu Theatre for Youth

The Honolulu Theatre for Youth was founded in 1955 to meet the needs of the island children and to build audiences for the future. It was unique at the time in that all previous theatre productions had been the province of the wealthy and were only for adults. The Theatre for Youth, on the other hand, was established in connection with the Department of Parks and was meant for all children. By 1970 it had become Hawaii's largest theatre, winning not only audiences, but also state and national awards for its excellence. Today it is considered one of America's outstanding children's theatre companies. As a policy, plays are carefully selected for both their entertainment and their educational values. Workshops are offered for both children and teachers, and packets containing teacher's guides are prepared as an added service for schools. The season's announcements show a diversity of offerings and a concern for a wide age range.

Financial support comes from the Department of Parks, foundations, government, and individual contributions as well as from the box office. According to its brochure, the Theatre for Youth strives to stimulate the imagination, develop communication skills, maintain a high standard of entertainment, develop an appreciation of theatre as an art form, broaden intercultural understanding, and "allow every child to recognize within himself the qualities of a hero." The diversity of the population of Hawaii has made for an unusual degree of sensitivity to children of many cultural backgrounds.

The Empire State Institute for the Performing Arts

The Empire State Institute for the Performing Arts (ESIPA) has the distinction of being the only state-mandated theatre in the United States. Founded in 1976 by Patricia Snyder of the State University of New York in Albany, it has one of the few facilities built for children in the country. A magnificent building with rehearsal space, two auditoriums, classrooms, and costume, scenery, and office space, it provides ESIPA a place to operate a large-scale program of workshops and in-service training courses are offered at the Institute. As an added feature, interns receive instruction and experience in a special program.

Plays are selected for their literary quality with an eye toward the family audience. Announcements for the season list plays and programs that are equally appropriate for both children and adults (*The Miracle Worker*, Ballet Hispanico, *Peter Pan*). The aesthetic aspect of the production is also stressed. Budgets take into account the artistic mounting of plays, orchestral music when called for, publicity, and public relations. The company has performed twice in the Soviet Union, as well as in Europe, and Natalia Sats has made two trips to Albany with her Moscow Musical Theatre for Children in exchange visits. Ten years after its founding, ESIPA has become one of America's best known theatres for youth.

Other Forms of Children's Theatre

Showcases intersperse plays and TIE programs with other types of entertainment—music, dance (some of which approaches theatre in its subject matter and style of movement), mime, storytelling, puppetry, and, recently, clowning and circus skills. A few years ago improvisational theatre was popular; although it is still shown, it appears to have lost interest for sponsors, who are seeking more structured and substantive programs. Occasionally one sees a company combine several art forms successfully, particularly human actors and puppets. The musical for children, like the adult musical, is extremely popular, and because of the demands it makes on the cast, it reveals a general improvement in all performance skills.

PLAYHOUSES

Despite the growth of children's theatre in America, few playhouses have been constructed for its exclusive use. Among the first were the Palo Alto Children's Theatre in California, a community theatre operating year round, and the Nashville Academy Theatre in Tennessee. Others include the Wichita Children's Theatre, the Minneapolis Children's Theatre, and the Institute for the Performing Arts, in New York. Most professional companies tour and perform for part of the season in small adult theatres on weekends. Universities sponsor plays by students in their child drama programs, giving performances for the public on campus and taking student actors to community centers, schools, and hospitals. Most Americans acknowledge the progress that has been made, largely through the efforts of idealistic and dedicated leaders, but they look forward to the time when the best they have now will be multiplied and made available in all its diversity to the children of every community in the United States.

BIBLIOGRAPHY

Books

Davis, Jed, and Mary Jane Evans. *Theatre, Children and Youth*. New Orleans: Anchorage Press, 1987.

Goldberg, Moses. *Children's Theatre: A Philosophy and a Method*. Englewood Cliffs, N.J.: Prentice-Hall, 1974.

Landy, Robert. *A Handbook of Educational Drama and Theatre*. Westport, Conn.: Greenwood Press, 1982.

McCaslin, Nellie. *Children and Drama*. Lanham, Md.: University Press of America, 1985.

———. *Historical Guide to Children's Theatre in America*. Westport, Conn.: Greenwood Press, 1987.

Swortzell, Lowell. *All the World's a Stage*. New York: Delacorte Press, 1972.

————. *Six Plays for Young People from the Federal Theatre Project*. Westport, Conn.: Greenwood Press, 1986.
Way, Brian. *Audience Participation*. Boston: Walter Baker, 1981.

Plays

Goldberg, Moses. *The Wind in the Willows*. New Orleans: Anchorage Press, 1974.
Harris, Aurand. *Androcles and the Lion*. New Orleans: Anchorage Press, 1964.
————. *The Arkansaw Bear*. New Orleans: Anchorage Press, 1980.
Koste, Virginia. *The Adventures of Tom Sawyer*. New Orleans: Anchorage Press, 1978.
Kraus, Joanna H. *The Ice Wolf*. Rowayton, Conn.: New Plays, Inc., 1963.
Wolak, Camilla Howes. *The Wizard of Oz*. Rowayton, Conn.: New Plays, Inc., 1971.
Zeder, Suzan. *Step on a Crack*. New Orleans: Anchorage Press, 1976.

Nellie McCaslin

Vietnam

HISTORY

In March 1985 the ASSITEJ Center of Vietnam was officially opened in Hanoi. This ceremony took place in the presence of the president of the National Assembly of the Vietnam Socialist Republic, Nguyen Huu Tho, and representatives of the Ministries of Culture and Education, the Ho Chi Minh Communist Youth League of the Pioneer and Children's Committee, various international organizations, and several embassies in Vietnam. The elected Executive Committee of the Center consists of fifteen members who represent all aspects of theatrical work: playwrights, composers, musicians, directors, actors and actresses, teachers, pedagogues, and children's artistic training instructors.

In 1985 the Festival of Scenic and Choreographic Arts was held in Vietnam. Participating companies from the Center were awarded gold and silver medals for the high quality of the performances for children and the remarkable skills of the performers, including those from the Young People's Theatre and the Young Performers' Company. These performances were given not only for children and young people living in the cities and towns, but also for those living in the remotest areas: mountainous regions, tablelands, and coastal islands. For example, on the occasion of the recent Tet Festival (beginning of 1987) the Young People's Theatre spent two months touring the High Tablelands to perform for local compatriots.

In accordance with a resolution adopted by the Executive Committee at its meeting of June 1, 1986, professional companies began touring small troupes of actors who performed in school playgrounds. In regular theatres the price of tickets is reduced by at least 50 percent for school students and young children, whereas it can be reduced by 70 to 75 percent when actors perform in local venues, for example, in schools. The pertinent artistic content of the themes chosen by the professional companies proves to be interesting for both children and young people, and therefore makes a considerable contribution to the development of their aesthetic sensibilities.

The ASSITEJ Center decided to organize a seminar every year on the theme "Theatre and School." The first sessions, held in 1985, were attended by some 200 persons in charge of art and education. Thirty papers of the highest theoretical and practical interest were delivered by teachers, scholars, science doctoral candidates, playwrights, composers, and theatre and film directors. The magazine *La Scene*, in which members of the Theatre Actors Association share ideas and information, published a selection of these papers. In particular, the Minister for Education's paper was published, in which ASSITEJ was praised for its positive activity in providing valuable assistance to education, especially in the area of aesthetics. In the years to come the Center will continue to organize these seminars aimed at discussing issues such as "Arts Serving Children." To celebrate the founding of the Vietnam Center, which is mainly concerned with the inner life of children, a week of performances by a number of theatre groups was organized. These performances were of many types: theatre, pantomime, songs and music, dance, circus, puppets, popular theatre, and even puppet shows on water. They took place in playhouses, out of doors, and on the lakes. Tens of thousands of children and young people shared in an atmosphere of sheer happiness. The slogan of "Humanity—Progress—Peace" was very much publicized. More than ten newspapers reported on the artistic program, the founding of the Vietnamese ASSITEJ Center, and its activities.

THE CURRENT SITUATION

The Center has seen a continuous growth in membership. There are currently fourteen collective members and some thirty individual members. Leading actors, pedgogues, and playwrights form the majority of the members. The Vietnamese Center is involved, together with the Association of Theatre Actors, in the organization of camps devoted to the writing of plays for children. Thirty playwrights attended the 1985 camp and produced a total of twenty-six scenarios, six of which were staged in 1986. The other scenarios in turn were broadcast over the radio or put into print.

Theatre groups that belong to the Center give regular performances for children (millions of spectators each year), including special programs by circus troupes (animal acts, conjuring tricks); puppet shows such as *Meat Feather, Plastic Ball, Snow White and the Seven Dwarves, Dam Noi, The Brave Fighter and the Sea Monster, and Kim Dong the Child Hero*, which were staged by the Puppet Theatre and by puppet companies; and plays staged by the Young People's Theatre and the Ho Chi Minh City Young Performers' Company, such as *Tam and Cam (Cinderella), The Last Lie, The Little Humpbacked Horse, The Mountain of Dreams, The Blue Bird*, and *Love Story*.

The Pioneers' Houses and Palaces in the capital city and in several provincial cities also produced lively synthesized artistic programs, including songs, music, circus, and pantomime. In addition, the work of the ASSITEJ Center of Vietnam inspired and encouraged professional theatre companies to perform plays specifically designed for children. A festival for children was staged in Ho Chi Minh City at the end of 1985; this was held in a venue usually reserved for adult productions. Sixteen companies performed plays selected for children: *The Jade Hare, The Flowered Hill of a Thousand Good Deeds, The Young Tran Quoc Toan, The Very Young Fighter*, and *The Fox and the Stork*.

As a result of exchanges and cooperation between theatres belonging to the Vietnam Center and the Leningrad Youth Theatre, the Russian folktale *The Little Humpbacked Horse* was staged and produced in collaboration with the director Zinovi Korogotzki and the designer Dagnile Dagniline. In 1986 the Youth Theatre performed *The Lark*, by Jean Anouilh, as part of the theatrical cooperation between Vietnam and France; this was directed by J. C. Bourbauld. At the end of 1987 the Youth Theatre performed *The King Drostenberg*, a work based on Grimms' fairy tales, in collaboration with a director from East Germany and with the technical support of the Halle Young Guard Theatre. Some of the five Australian plays that were brought to us by Roger Chapman and Michael FitzGerald will be staged for young Vietnamese audiences in the future. In addition to classic works that have been and are still performed using puppets or live theatre (*Romeo and Juliet, The Bourgeois Gentilhomme, The Blue Bird*), the audience was able to discover other works, such as *Puss in Boots, Goldilocks, May and Li, The Elder Son*, and *The Seven-hued Flower*.

The Vietnamese ASSITEJ Center was pleased to welcome foreign performing groups such as the Halle Young Guard Theatre (East Germany), the Nombre d'Or Theatre, the French Puppet Group, the Czechoslovakian Music and Singing Youth Ensemble, and the Japanese Puppet Troupe, whose tours have been a complete success. The Center is looking forward to welcoming other companies to its country.

In the autumn of 1986 a delegation from the Australian ASSITEJ Center led by President Michael FitzGerald visited Vietnam. FitzGerald wanted to see the preparations for the Vietnamese ASSITEJ Center's Congress, and he was accompanied by Roger Chapman, director of the Carclew Youth Performing Arts Center. Both were impressed by the devotion shown by the people active in the field of theatre for children and young people and by the lack of resources that still affects the work of the actors and actresses.

The Center publishes a regular newsletter in order to keep the other ASSITEJ Centers informed of its activities. A pantomime, song, and theatre training course is offered at the Youth Theatre. Trainees are selected from the mass movement, and the curriculum is defined by the Ministry of Culture. This initiative enables professional actors to train talented young people who are capable of working efficiently among young spectators. In 1985 construction of a rehearsal space at the Youth Theatre commenced. This also will be used as a theatre. Completion is envisaged for the late 1980s or early 1990s. The space will consist of four large rehearsal rooms and a 600-seat theatre. It will be a meeting place for all young people who enjoy the performing arts. The Australian delegation visited the site and expressed its admiration for the efforts displayed by the Vietnamese Center and the support provided by the government of the Socialist Republic of Vietnam; it promised to provide a lighting system for the theatre and to approach various agencies in order to find necessary resources.

Lowell Swortzell
(Prepared from materials submitted by ASSITEJ/Vietnam.)

Yugoslavia

HISTORY

The earliest instance of theatre for children and youth is found in performances given in Jesuit grammar schools. In Zagreb in 1607 an allegory was enacted to honor the opening of a school. First performed in Latin, presentations were being given in Croatian by 1618. In Zagreb, Varaždin, Požega, and Osijek school-children acted in church and secular performances from the beginning of the seventeenth century, and in 1732 the School Theatre (Skolsko pozoriste) was founded in Sremski Karlovci.

By the mid-nineteenth century children's theatre drew some sporadic interest from professional groups, who mounted holiday productions, mostly historical and didactic, from time to time, but it was not until 1904 that Branislav Nišić, a well-known Yugoslav comedy writer, founded an independent theatre for children, The Little Theatre (Malo pozorište), in Belgrade. Between the two world wars theatres for children and youth developed in Zagreb, Centinje, Novi Sad, Subotica, and Belgrade, but often they lasted for only short periods. The most important of these was The Stork's Theatre (Rodino pozorište), established in 1938 by Nušić, his daughter, Gita Predić-Nušić, and two playwrights for children, Milivoj Predić and Živojin Vukadinović. This theatre was significant because it allowed child roles to be played by children; adult roles were performed by eminent Belgrade actors. The same concept was tested at The Children's Empire (Dječje carstvo), founded in Zagreb by the famous Croatian actor-director Tito Strozzi. Although the theatre proved successful, it, along with most other theatres, closed at the outbreak of World War II.

At the height of World War II and the Yugoslav people's war for liberation another theatre was founded, this one on foreign soil. The Pioneer Theatre (Pionirsko kazalište) was established in a refugee camp in the African desert of El Shatt. It grew out of the drama and dance groups organized to keep the children busy, and it developed from their creative play. The theatre's activities were carried on through exceptionally difficult living conditions and offered spiritual comfort to both children and adults. After the war some members of The Pioneer Theatre went on to organize another children's group called Tito's Sailors (Titovi mornari).

The period after liberation was one of great growth and development. Pioneer theatres, supported by the government and the Socialist Youth Organization, were founded across the country: Belgrade, 1944; Subotica and Pančevo, 1946; Rijeka, 1947; Zagreb, 1948; Sarajevo and Osijek, 1950; Titograd, 1951; Karlovac, 1952; Ljubljana, 1955; and Šibenik, 1956. Those in Titograd, Rijeka, and Zagreb, in particular, became noteworthy for their work, which included instruction and participation by local children in dancing, improvisation, and other theatrical activities. In turn the Pioneer theatres have fostered professional theatres throughout the country. The Children's Theatre "Boško Buha" opened in 1950 in Belgrade, performing traditional works as well as those of contemporary authors, both native and foreign. This company has been acclaimed on tours outside the country with such productions as *The Adventures of Tom Sawyer* and *Mida Trojanović*.

CHILDREN'S THEATRE TODAY

A popular style of theatre peculiar to Yugoslavia brings together poetry, music, dancing, and stage lighting in performances titled "Poetski recital." Beginning in 1950 as an amateur theatre in Sarajevo, the Pozoriste za mlade (now The Youth Theatre) turned professional twenty years later. Actors from this theatre visit schools to augment literature courses by inspiring students to respond to poetry through improvisation and the performance of such classics as Shakespeare's *The Tempest*. Likewise, the Dramatic Studio in Karlovac performs traditional plays such as *Puss in Boots* and contemporary works such as *First Love and Everything Else*. The Slovenian Youth Theatre in Lubljana performs musicals and plays such as *Gulliver's Travels*, which combined puppets and live actors, and *Suku and the Flying Princess*.

An outstanding event takes place in June each year when the Children's Festival is held in Šibenik before an international audience. Here children's theatre groups gather to perform and exchange ideas. "The Festival," according to one little girl, "is when children gather together to show their parents they, too, have rights." Founded in 1958, the Festival has continued to encourage experimentation to broaden the definition of children's theatre. During its twelve days of performances the Festival turns Sibenik into a city of children living and performing together. Everywhere, on stages and in the streets, performers and spectators from throughout Yugoslavia and the world meet and become friends in a celebration of theatrical art.

To one eight-year-old boy the Festival is "a lot of children and a fireworks display in the sky." The Festival includes puppets, music, film, art exhibitions, literary and panel discussions, and creative workshops. Many performances take place in front of the Town Hall, performed on an open-air stage, while others fill theatres throughout the city. No prizes are given, since the Festival refuses to be competitive; just to be invited to participate means recognition of achievement, according to the administrators.

The Yugoslav Center of ASSITEJ is approaching its twentieth anniversary and counts among its members professional companies along with amateur, as well as those institutions that in any way deal with children and creativity. The Zagreb Youth Theatre performed at the ASSITEJ Congress held in Venice in 1964; officers of the Yugoslavia ASSITEJ executive committee have actively participated in every Congress since. A goal of the Center is to foster and develop new theatres throughout the country. Twenty companies currently perform regularly: three in Belgrade, four in Zagreb, others in Dubrovnik, Mostar, Pula, Rijika, Split, Subotica, and Tuzla.

Today the theatres are confronted with youth influenced more and more by the mass media, which necessarily reflects on the way they see their surroundings and themselves. The modern child matures by the television set, so his spiritual rhythm and development are influenced by cartoons, commercials, and pop music; thus he desires the same stimulus in the theatre. Stimulating creativity in the theatre is now a major concern of all companies who want their productions not to remind spectators of the classroom, but to be ennobled entertainment. Through competitions and national festivals the results of these endeavors confirm that they are finding interesting initiatives and innovative attempts not only in the institutional theatres, but also within the semi-professional companies throughout the country.

REPRESENTATIVE COMPANIES

The Children's Theatre "Boško Buha"

The first professional children's theatre, founded in 1950, "Boško Buha" performs works for adolescents and children. In the children's repertory the group presents all styles of theatre, playing mostly works by modern Yugoslav writers. It also performs internationally recognized children's plays, world classics, and works adapted from world and Yugoslav literature. The plays presented to the older audience consist of modern pieces that address the problems of youth. Included in the current repertory are *Captain John Peoplefox*, by Dušan Radović, directed by Miroslav Belvoić; *The Fairytale About the King and the Shepherd*, by Boško Trifunović, directed by Belović; and *The Adventures of Tom Sawyer*, by Mark Twain, directed by Minja Dedić.

The company has participated in many national theatre festivals, such as Sterijino pozorje, The Festival of Small and Experimental Scenes in Sarajevo, the Dubrovnik Summer Festival, and the Child Festival in Šibenik, and it has won many prizes. The group also took part in the Biennales in Venice in 1963 and 1969, in the International Child Festival in Palermo in 1960, and in the International Festival in Lyon.

Mladinsko Gledalishche Ljubljana

Mladinsko Gledalishche Ljubljana is a professional group that, in addition to its resident company, hires many eminent Croatian performers and student actors. Its repertory mainly consists of adaptations of world classics, musicals, and new plays by Yugoslav writers. During the season the company presents five premieres and 150 performances. In 1987 they participated in the Festival in Cardiff and before that were seen in Hamburg. Dušan Jovanović, the artistic leader of the company, is considered one of the country's most important author-directors. The current repertory includes *Perzani*, by Ajshil; *The Persians*, by Aeschylus; *Fear and Bravery (Strah in pogum,)* by Edvard Kocbek; *Ana*, by Rudi Šeligo; *Pinocchio (Ostrežel),)* adapted by Carlo Collodi and Ivo Svetina; and *Alice's Adventures in Wonderland (Alica v čudežni dezeli),)* by Lewis Carroll, adapted by Vito Taufer.

Drama Studio Karlovac

Founded in 1950, The Drama Studio Karlovac serves important social and cultural functions. Since its inception it has presented more than 100 Yugoslav and world theatre pieces, many of them premieres. In addition to its presentations, the group also runs workshops in drama, dance, and creative dramatics. Berislav Frkić, the artistic director, believes in offering creative performances in which the audience participates. The high quality of both the studio work and the performances rank this as one of the best and most significant theatres in the country.

The Zagreb Youth Theatre

Formerly the Zagreb Pioneer Theatre, this company was founded in 1948 for two purposes: to perform plays for children and youth and to develop their creativity. The company has two components: studio and performance group. The goal of the studio is to develop the general creative capabilities of children and youth through the synthesis of poetry, speech, movement, music, and art expression. In the theatre's forty-year history the professional ensemble has presented more than 6,000 performances comprising more than 200 drama, musical, and dance pieces by foreign and Yugoslav authors. These have included poems, fairy tales and stories, classic plays, and modern pieces by such authors as Sofoklo, Shakespeare, Twain, Držić, Mihalkov, Arbuzov, Lorca, Parun, GRIPS Theatre, and Bakarić.

The group has participated in many international festivals (Palermo, Nurberg, Berlin, and Venice) and won many prizes. It has also toured throughout Yugoslavia and to many foreign countries, including Italy, East Germany, West Germany, Poland, Czechoslovakia, France, Sweden, Austria, and Hungary. The current repertory includes *Captain John Peoplefox*, by Radović; *The Hedgehog's Little House*, by B. Ćopić; *Little Apprentice Hlapić*, by Mažuranić; *Puss Gingiskan and Puss Miki Trasi*, by Parun; and *Who Does This Child Take After?* by Eva Janikowsky.

BIBLILOGRAPHY

Books

Čečuk, Slavenka, Durdica Devič, and Zvjezdana Ladika. *Drama Games*. Zagreb.
Dokić, Ljubiśa, Divna Jovanović, and Vukosava Nikolin-Nikolić. *Dramatic Work in School*.
Ladika, Zvjezdana. *The Child and Dramatic Art*. Zagreb.
Nikolić, Staniša. *The Scenic Expression and Psychoanalysis*. Zagreb.
Nola, Danica, Rude Supek, Boris Sorokin, et. al. *The Child and Creativity*. Zagreb.
Supek, Rudi. *Fancy*. Zagreb.

Plays

Brenkova, Kristina. *The Blue Rose for Princes*.
Erić, Dobrica, and Konstantin Babić. *The Cake with Five Floors*.
Parun, Vesna, and Ladislav Tulać. *Puss Gingiskan and Puss Miki Trasi*.
Radović, Dušan. *Captain John Peoplefox*.
Stanislavljević, Miodrag. *Animal Language*.
Timotijević, Božidar. *The Fairy Mountain*.

Zvjezdana Ladika

Zimbabwe

HISTORY

Zimbabwe became independent in 1979 after nearly a century of British rule. During the colonial period all indigenous forms of art were suppressed by both the Christian church and the government because they were considered primitive and heathen. English theatre was brought into the country by the very first settlers, but it was exclusively for white people.

Nearly all dramatization involving local adults was steeped in ritual and condemned by the colonial masters and the church. Virtually all education was in the hands of the churches, which made sure that none of the native people's performances were allowed into the schools. As a result, by 1979, ritual dramatization was practiced only by communities in remote parts of the country that had remained virtually untouched by outside influences. The small percentage of children who attended school dramatized religious plays like *Everyman* and English legends such as *Robin Hood*.

Since independence, however, children's theatrical activities have grown. Many of the activities in the book *Mitambo Yavasikana Navakomana Pasichigare (Traditional Pastimes for Boys and Girls)*, by Aaron Hodza, have all the earmarks of theatre. They range from games in which children perform various activities by following a leader to dramatizations of social and political issues. Popular themes for dramatization include courtship games, parodies of irresponsible family leaders, criticism of rulers, and the condemnation of such anti-social behavior as laziness and excessive drunkenness. Although the children mostly dramatize these issues for their own amusement, it is not uncommon for elders to request special performances at social gatherings. Children use these performances to express their feelings about the adult world.

The courtship games in Hodza's book are also important for children. In one, "Sarura Wako" ("Choose Your Partner"), teenage and post-teenage boys and girls indicate the partners they prefer to marry in response to singing that describes in turn each member of the opposite sex. At the end of the performance those with anti-social behavior who fail to gain partners are jeered by the others. Parents are deeply interested in the outcome of these apparently ''innocent'' games, using the lessons taught by them to correct their errant children. As a result, many marriages have evolved from the games.

Other works on children's theatre in Zimbabwe include *Mukuwasha Abe Nyama (The Greedy Son-in-Law)* and *Sungai Mbabvu (Humorous Sketches)*, by Mordikai Hamutyinei; "The Talking Calabash," by Thompson Tsodzo, in T. O. MacLoughlin's *New Writing in Rhodesia*; and the plays included in the two Shona textbook series for primary and secondary schools, *ChiShona Chakanaka (Good Shona)* and *Rurimi Rwaamai (Mother Tongue)*, both edited by Tsodzo. These collections of children's plays contain both traditional and modern themes, published in English and broken into acts and scenes. Because they deal with current issues, these plays have gained more popularity than Hodza's collection, which today is mostly used by researchers.

Children's drama in Zimbabwe is more prominent on the stage than it is in writing. With the inclusion of culture into the curriculum since independence, most schools hold drama competitions. Because there is a shortage of scripted plays, children improvise works with the help of their teachers. To promote this developing theatre, regional trophies and prizes have been provided in three of the country's eight educational regions. In addition, winning plays from the Manicaland, Mashonaland East, and Harare regions have been shown on national television.

Radio and television programs that feature children's drama have been broadcast by the late Mrs. Munyati (former Deputy Minister of Education) and Mrs. Mlambo, popularly known as "Mbuya Va17 Year Old" ("Seventeen-Year-Old Grandmother"). These programs were so popular with children that their hosts became household names. Before independence the two women endeared themselves to the masses by subtly including in their programs revolutionary ideas under the guise of children's programming.

Perhaps the person who has done the most for children's theatre in Zimbabwe is Ben Sibenke. A talented actor himself, Sibenke, now a school headmaster, entered the Zimbabwean stage in the early 1970s with his farce *Chidembo Chanhuhwa (The Skunk's Smell)*. With a group of unpaid volunteers, Sibenke toured schools in 1974, giving free performances to loudly cheering children. When independence came Sibenke formed the People's Theatre Company with such theatrical celebrities as Steve Chigorimbo, Charles Tom, and Godwin Mawuru. Sibenke has since formed the Tafara Drama Group (in 1986), and in only two years this company has already toured to schools in Harare (the capital city) and appeared on national television with two of its plays.

There are no registered theatre groups for children in Zimbabwe, but church, government, and voluntary youth organizations hold annual festivals sponsored by the National Arts Council that include dramatic activities for youth. Prominent among the church youth groups is the Catholic Youth Association, which began staging children's plays in African townships in the 1960s. Among its current leaders are Brother Fidelis Mukonori, Charles Mavengere, and Charles Sekete, all of whom are well known for promoting youth theatre in the nation. Charles Sekete was also featured in the television play *Babamunini Francis*, by Tsodzo, whose theme is the plight of children of divorced parents.

In the Youth Department of the Ministry of Youth Sport and Culture officers organize variety shows for youth throughout the country. These shows offer sketches with themes based on national development. Voluntary organizations include the Boy Scouts and Girl Guides, which occasionally dramatize the activities of the organization's founders.

The National Arts Council and commercial theatres did little to promote children's theatre during the era of British rule. Formed in 1971, the Council (then called the National Arts Association of Rhodesia) promoted theatre among white schools, holding annual theatre festivals around the country. In the early seventies Goromonzi Secondary School became the first black school to participate in the festivals, on the eve of national independence. Goromonzi became the first black school to win the competition.

One serious defect concerning children's theatre in Zimbabwe is the lack of programs for formal study. Only recently have the first steps been taken to address this situation, with Kedmon Hungwe and Thompson Tsodzo being sent to America to study all forms of theatre and to make recommendations for the enhancement of Zimbabwean theatre. Hungwe, whose study included extensive immersion in children's theatre, has returned to Zimbabwe and is promoting theatre for young people through educational channels.

Like the rest of Zimbabwean theatre, children's theatre is still in its formative stages. Although various efforts are now being exerted, no new trends have yet been noted. The developments of the next several years will determine in what direction youth theatre ultimately will move.

Thompson Tsodzo

Bibliography

BOOKS

Allen, John. *Drama in Schools: Its Theory and Practice*. London: Heinemann, 1979.

Bedard, Roger L., ed. *Dramatic Literature for Children: A Century in Review*. New Orleans: Anchorage Press, 1984.

Bettelheim, Bruno. *The Uses of Enchantment: The Meaning and Importance of Fairy Tales*. New York: Alfred A. Knopf, 1976.

Birner, William B., ed. *Twenty Plays for Young People*. New Orleans: Anchorage Press, 1967.

Boal, Augusto. *Theater of the Oppressed*. New York: Urizen Books, 1979.

Bolton, Gavin. *Towards a Theory of Drama in Education*. London: Longman, 1980.

———. *Drama as Education*. London: Longman, 1984.

Broadman, Muriel. *Understanding Your Children's Entertainment*. New York: Harper & Row, 1977.

Chorpenning, Charlotte. *Twenty-One Years with Children's Theatre*. Anchorage, Ky.: Anchorage Press, 1955.

Coming to Our Senses: The Significance of the Arts for American Education. A panel report, David Rockefeller, Chairman. New York: McGraw-Hill, 1977.

Cook, H. Caldwell. *The Play Way*. London: Heinemann, 1917.

Corey, Orlin. *Theatre for Children: Kid Stuff or Theatre?* New Orleans: Anchorage Press, 1974.

Courtney, Richard. *Play, Drama and Thought*. New York: Drama Book Specialists, 1974.

Davis, Jed, and Mary Jane Evans. *Theatre, Children and Youth*. New Orleans: Anchorage Press, 1982.

Directory of Operas/Musicals for Young Audiences. New York: Central Opera Service, 1984.

Donahue, John Clark. *The Cookie Jar and Other Plays*. Minneapolis: University of Minnesota Press, 1976.

———. *Five Plays from the Children's Theatre Company of Minneapolis*. Minneapolis: University of Minnesota Press, 1976.

Doolittle, Joyce, and Zina Barnieh. *A Mirror of Our Dreams: Children and the Theatre in Canada*. Vancouver, B.C.: Talonbooks, 1979.

Flanagan, Hallie. *Arena*. New York: Duell, Sloan & Pearce Co., 1940.

Foundation of the Dramatist's Guild. *Young Playwrights Festival*. Preface by Gerald Chapman. New York: Avon Books, 1983.

Goldberg, Moses. *Children's Theatre: A Philosophy and a Method*. Englewood Cliffs, N.J.: Prentice-Hall, 1974.

Green, Roger Lancelyn. *Fifty Years of Peter Pan*. London: Peter Davies, 1954.

Heniger, Alice Herts. *The Kingdom of the Child*. New York: E. P. Dutton, 1918.

Herts, Alice Minnie. *The Children's Educational Theatre*. New York: Harper & Brothers, 1911.

Hodgson, John. *The Uses of Drama*. London: Methuen, 1975.

Hodgson, John, and Martin Banham, eds. *Drama in Education, The Annual Survey* (1). London: Pitman, 1972.

———. *Drama in Education, The Annual Survey* (2). London: Pitman, 1973.

———. *Drama in Education, The Annual Survey* (3). London: Pitman, 1975.

Jackson, Tony, ed. *Learning Through Drama*. Manchester, England: Manchester University Press, 1980.

Jennings, Coleman A., ed. *Six Plays for Children by Aurand Harris, Biography and Play Analyses*. Austin: University of Texas Press, 1977.

Jennings, Coleman, and Gretta Berghammer, eds. *Theatre for Youth: Twelve Plays with Mature Themes*. Austin: University of Texas Press, 1986.

Jennings, Coleman, and Aurand Harris, eds. *Plays Children Love: A Treasury of Contemporary and Classic Plays for Children*. New York: Doubleday, 1981.

———, eds. *Plays Children Love, Volume II: A Treasury of Contemporary and Classic Plays for Children*. New York: St. Martin's Press, 1988.

Klein, Jeanne, ed. *Theatre for Young Audiences: Principles and Strategies for the Future*. University Theatre, The University of Kansas, 1988.

Korty, Carol. *Plays from African Folktales*. New York: Charles Scribner's Sons, 1976.

Landy, Robert. *A Handbook of Educational Drama and Theatre*. Westport, Conn.: Greenwood Press, 1982.

Levy, Jonathan. *A Theatre of the Imagination: Reflections on Children and the Theatre*. Rowayaton, Conn.: New Plays Inc., 1987.

Lifton, Betty Jean, ed. *Contemporary Children's Theatre*. New York: Avon Books, 1974.

Linnell, Rosemary. *Approaching Classroom Drama*. London: Edward Arnold, 1982.

McCaslin, Nellie. *Children's Theatre in the United States: A History*. Norman: University of Oklahoma Press, 1971.

———. *Theatre for Young Audiences*. New York: Longman, Inc., 1978.

———. *Historical Guide to Children's Theatre in America*. Westport, Conn.: Greenwood Press, 1987.

———, ed. *Children and Drama*. 2nd ed. Lanham, Md.: University Press of America, 1985.

McGregor, Lynn, Maggie Tate, and Ken Robinson, eds. *Learning Through Drama*. London: Heinemann, 1977.

Masters, Simon. *The National Youth Theatre*. London: Longman's Young Books, 1969.

Morton, Miriam. *The Arts and the Soviet Child*. New York: Free Press, 1972.

———, ed. *Through the Magic Curtain: Theatre for Children, Adolescents, and Young Adults in the U.S.S.R.* New Orleans: Anchorage Press, 1979.

————, ed. and trans. *Russian Plays for Young Audiences: Five Contemporary Selections*. Rowayaton, Conn.: New Plays, Inc., 1977.

Moses, Montrose J., ed. *A Treasury of Plays for Children*. Boston: Little, Brown, 1921.

————, ed. *Another Treasury of Plays for Children*. Boston: Little, Brown, 1926.

O'Toole, John. *Theatre in Education*. London: Hodder & Stoughton, 1976.

Piaget, Jean. *The Language and Thought of the Child*. New York: New American Library, 1974.

Postman, Neil. *The Disappearance of Childhood*. New York: Delacorte Press, 1982.

————. *Amusing Ourselves to Death*. New York: Viking Press, 1985.

Robinson, Ken. *Exploring Theatre and Education*. London: Heinemann, 1980.

Rosenberg, Helane, and Christine Prendergast. *Theatre for Young People: A Sense of Occasion*. New York: Holt, Rinehart & Winston, 1983.

Siks, Geraldine Brain, and Hazel Brain Dunnington, eds. *Children's Theatre and Creative Dramatics*. Seattle: University of Washington Press, 1961.

Slade, Peter. *Introduction to Child Drama*. London: University of London Press, 1958.

Special Edition of ASSITEJ/USA, edited by Kenneth McLeod and C. J. Stevens, for ASSITEJ World Congress held in Lyons, France, June 1981. Nashville, Tenn. Entire issue devoted to children's theatre in the United States.

Spolin, Viola. *Improvisation for the Theatre*. Evanston, Ill.: Northwestern University Press, 1963.

Swortzell, Lowell, ed. *All the World's a Stage*. New York: Delacorte Press, 1972.

————, ed. *Six Plays for Young People from the Federal Theatre Project (1936–1939): An Introductory Analysis and Six Representative Plays*. Westport, Conn.: Greenwood Press, 1986.

Wagner, B. J., and Dorothy Heathcote. *Drama as a Learning Medium*. Washington, D.C.: NEA, 1976.

Walker, Stuart. *Portmanteau Plays*. Cincinnati: Stewart Kidd Co., 1913.

————. *More Portmanteau Plays*. Cincinnati: Stewart Kidd Co., 1919.

————. *Portmanteau Adaptations*. Cincinnati: Stewart Kidd Co., 1921.

Ward, Winifred. *Theatre for Children*. New York: D. Appleton Century Co., 1939. 3rd rev. ed. Anchorage, Ky.: Children's Theatre Press, 1958.

Way, Brian. *Development Through Drama*. London: Longman's, 1967.

Webster, Clive. *Working with Theatre in Schools*. London: Pitman, 1975.

Whitton, Patricia, ed. *Outstanding Plays for Young Audiences: International Bibliography*, Vol. 1. ASSITEJ/USA, 1984.

————, ed. *Six Adventure Theatre Plays*. Rowayaton, Conn.: New Plays, Inc., 1987.

Wright, Lin, ed. *Professional Theatre for Young Audiences*. Tempe: Arizona State University, 1984.

Zipes, Jack. *Breaking the Magic Spell: Radical Theories of Folk and Fairy Tales*. London: Heinemann, 1979.

————, ed. *Political Plays for Children*. St. Louis: Telos Press, 1976.

ARTICLES

"The ASSITEJ Ninth World Congress/The Adelaide Report." *Theatre for Young Audiences Today* 3, no. 1 (Winter 1988):1–48.

Barrager, Pam. "Comedie de Lorraine: Children's Theatre in France." *Children's Theatre Review* 26, 3 (1977):6–13.

———. "The Yugoslav Festival." *Children's Theatre Review* 28, no. 1 (Winter 1979):9.

Barty, Margaret. "Children and the Post-war Theatre." *Theatre World* 39 (August 1943):7–8.

Berghammer, Gretta. "Drama Goes to School: An Examination of Theatre-in-Education." *Youth Theatre Journal* 2, no. 3 (Winter 1988):3–8.

Broadman, Muriel. "Children's Theatre—Who Needs It?" *Backstage* 27, no. 8, sec. 2 (February 21, 1986):1, 22, 31.

Chancerel, Léon. "Youth and the Theatre." *World Theatre* 2 (December 1952):3.

Corey, Orlin. "Report from Bulgaria: Theatre Is Beyond Politics." *Children's Theatre Review* 18, no. 1 (1969):4–5.

Crawford, Dorothy, and Jeanne Hall. "Report on the British National Festival of Theatre for Young People, Summer 1973." *Children's Theatre Review* 22, no. 4 (1973):6–8.

Davis, Jed H. "Prospectus for Research in Children's Theatre." *Children's Theatre Review* 13, no. 4 (December 1961):274–277.

Dezseran, Catherine, and Barbara Myerson Katz. "Theatre-in-Education and Child Sexual Abuse: A Descriptive Study." *Children's Theatre Review* 34, no. 4 (1985):7–13.

Ebsen, Nancy. "A Quick Look Abroad." *Children's Theatre Review* 30, no. 1 (1971):32–34.

Elvgreen, Gillette, Jr. "Children's Documentary Theatre in Nottingham." *Children's Theatre Review* 22, no. 1 (1973):11–13.

Furman, Lou. "Child Drama in Israel: Two Perspectives." *Youth Theatre Journal* 1, no. 4 (1987):9–11.

Goldberg, Moses. "International Children's Theatre: A Challenge to America." *Children's Theatre Review* 30, no. 1 (1971):15–20, 41–43.

Hall, Robin. "East Is East—And West: Children's Theatre in Japan." *Children's Theatre Review* 18, no. 1 (Winter 1979):6–8.

———. "Educational Drama in England." *Children's Theatre Review* 22, no. 1 (1973):16–23.

Hansen, Holden. "Fairy Tales on Stage: A Need for New Adaptations." *Youth Theatre Journal* 1, no. 4 (1987):12–14.

Heining, Rut Beall, and Wanda Herman. "Black Magic: New Techniques in Czech Theatre." *Children's Theatre Review* 28, no. 2 (Spring 1979):12–13.

Heniger, Alice Herts. "The Drama's Value for Children." *Good Housekeeping* 57 (November 1913):636–43.

Henry, William A. III. "Voices from the Inner Depths." *Time* 133, no. 15 (April 10, 1989):112–115.

Herring, J. Daniel, and Debra Humes. "Keeping the Door Open: A Soviet-American Exchange." *Youth Theatre Journal* 3, no. 2 (1988):14–16.

Herts, Alice Minnie. "The Children's Educational Theatre." *The Atlantic Monthly* 100 (December 1907):798–806.

———. "Making Believe." *Good Housekeeping* 66 (March 1917):22–23.

Hill, Ann S. "ASSITEJ Assembly in Venice—Highlight for Children's Theatre Buffs." *Children's Theatre Review* 30, no. 1 (1971):5–14, 43–44.

Hodgson, John. "Theatre in Education." *Theatre Quarterly* 1, no. 1 (1971):57–60.

"The Jiriho Wolkra Children's Theatre in Prague Celebrates Its Fortieth Anniversary." *Children's Theatre Review* 24, no. 4 (1975):12–13.

Johnson, Scott. "Britain's Educational Drama." *English Journal* 76, no. 5 (September 1987):72–74.

Jones, Pamela L. " 'Vår Teatre'—A Pioneer Turns 40." *Children's Theatre Review* 33, no. 1 (January 1984):7–9.

Kauffman, John. "Perestroika and Youth Theatre in the Soviet Union." *Youth Theatre Journal* 3, no. 2 (1988):12–13.

Kilker, M. J. "Children's Theatre in France." *Children's Theatre Review* 23, no. 4 (1974):14–16.

Kohan, John. "Freedom Waiting for Vision." *Time* 135, no. 15 (April 10, 1989):108–109.

Koltai, Judith. "Toward an Integrated Movement—Training for Actors in Children's Theatre." *Creative Drama* (Birmingham, England, n.d.) 4, no. 4:16–22.

Koste, Virginia. "The Old Country's Young Vic: A Personal View." *Children's Theatre Review* 30, no. 1 (1971):25–31, 36.

Kraus, Joanna. "Taking Children's Theatre to the Moon." *Players Magazine* 45 (April-May 1970):186–187.

Kurland, Barbara. "Children's Theatre in the People's Republic of China." *Children's Theatre Review* 26, no. 2 (1977):6–7.

Landy, Robert J. "Measuring Audience Response to Characters and Scenes in Theatre for Children: A Developmental Approach." *Children's Theatre Review* 26, no. 3 (1977):10–13.

Lewis, George. "Children's Theatre and Teacher Training." *Players Magazine* 27 (October 1950):11.

McCaslin, Nellie. "The Yugoslav Festival of the Child." *Children's Theatre Review* 31, no. 4 (October 1982):9–11.

———. "Aurand Harris: Children's Theatre Playwright." *The Children's Literature Association Quarterly* 9, no. 3 (Fall 1984):114–116.

McFadden, Dorothy. "Europe Challenges American Parents." *National Parent-Teacher Magazine* 21 (June 1937):10–11.

Mackay, Constance D'Arcy. "Children's Theatre in America." *Woman's Home Companion* 54 (June 1927):22.

Matassarin, Kate. "Jane Addams of Hull House: Creative Drama at the Turn of the Century." *Children's Theatre Review* 32 (October 1983):13–15.

Meserve, Walter J., and Ruth I. Meserve. "China's Children's Theatre: Education and Propaganda." *Children's Theatre Review* 22, no. 2 (1973):3–10.

Molloy, Toni. "The Fairy-Folk Tale in Media Art Reflections of Disney and Duvall." *Youth Theatre Journal* 3, no. 1 (1988):16–20.

Moses, Montrose J. "Children's Plays." *Theatre Arts Monthly* 8 (December 1924):831–835.

Oaks, Harold R. "Political Trends in Western European Children's Theatre." *Children's Theatre Review* 31, no. 1 (Fall 1981):3–7.

"On a Fox Chase in South Africa—a Report; An Analysis and Conclusions." *Children's Theatre Review* 14, no. 5 (1965):4–9.

Page, Anita. "Some New Aspects of Children's Theatre in West Germany." *Children's Theatre Review* 21, no. 1 (1976):6–7.

Pillai, Janet. "Children's Theatre in Malaysia." *Children's Theatre Review* 34, no. 1 (January 1985):7–10.

Raichle, Marilyn, and Kathie Vitz. "The Making of the Seattle International Children's Theatre Festival." *Youth Theatre Journal* 2, no. 3 (Winter 1988):12–14.

Regan, F. Scott. "A Preliminary Investigation of Current Practices in American Youth Theatre." *Children's Theatre Review* 32, no. 3 (Summer 1983):13–15.

Richards, Stanley. "450,000 Miles of Children's Theatre." *Players Magazine* 31 (December 1954):66–67.

Ritch, Pamela. "Children's Drama in Mexico: An Interview with Socorro Merlin." *Children's Theatre Review* 34, no. 3 (1985):15–18.

Rosenberg, Helane S. "The Actor/Teacher at the Belgrade." *Children's Theatre Review* 22, no. 2 (1973):11–13.

Shail, George. "A Meeting with Zinovy Korogodsky at the Leningrad Theatre of Young Spectators." *Children's Theatre Review* 25, no. 3 (1976):2–5.

Shaw, Ann M., and Orlin Corey. "World Festival of Theatre for Young Audiences." *Children's Theatre Review* 33, no. 4 (October 1984):19–21.

Siks, Geraldine Brain. "A View of Current European Theatre for Children and a Look Ahead in the United States." *Educational Theatre Review* 19 (May 1967):191–197.

Spencer, Sara. "A Decade of Children's Theatre." *Theatre Arts Monthly*, 38 (November 1954):84.

Sucke, Greer. "Inside the Fantasy: How Audiences Function in Participation Plays for Young People." *Children's Theatre Review* 30, no. 2 (1981):5–10.

Swortzell, Lowell. "England's National Youth Theatre Celebrates Its Twentieth Anniversary." *Children's Theatre Review* 26, no. 3 (1977):4–5.

———. "Strindberg's Legacy to Drama for Young People." *The Children's Literature Association Quarterly* 9, no. 3 (Fall 1984):119–121.

———. "Broadway Bound? Or Beyond?" *English Journal* 76, no. 5 (September 1987):52–54.

Swortzell, Lowell, and Nancy Swortzell. " 'Right On, Today!' A Note on Relevancy in Children's Theatre." *Children's Theatre Review* 22, no. 2 (1973):18–20.

Tukesbury, Beatrice L. "Emma Sheridan Fry and Educational Dramatics." *Educational Theatre Journal* 16, no. 4 (December 1964):341–348.

Twomey, Rosemary. "A Visit to the Ion Creanga Theatre of Bucharest, Roumania." *Children's Theatre Review* 22, no. 3 (1973):15–17.

Van Tassel, Wesley. "Differences in Contemporary Views of Theatre for Children." *Educational Theatre Journal* 21, no. 4 (December 1969):414–425.

Whitten, Pat Hale. "ASSITEJ/Lyon/1981." *Children's Theatre Review* 30, no. 4 (October 1981):13–14.

Worrell, Estelle Ansley. "Caracas Venezuela's Teatro Telingo." *Children's Theatre Review* 30, no. 1 (1971):35–36.

Wright, Lin, and Rosemary Willenbrink. "Child Drama 1982: A Survey of College and University Programs in the United States." *Children's Theatre Review* 32, no. 1 (1983):3–18.

Zipes, Jack. "Emancipatory Children's Theatre in the Year of the Child." *Theatre* 11, no. 1 (1979):85–97.

DISSERTATIONS

Abookire, Norena. "Children's Theatre Activities at Karamu House in Cleveland, Ohio, 1915–1975." Ph.D., New York University, 1982.

Adubato, Robert A. "A History of the WPA's Negro Theatre Project in New York City, 1935–39." Ph.D., New York University, 1978.

Anderson, Deborah Dorothy. "Story Theatre: Its Development, Implementation and Significance as a Theatrical Art Form and a Performance Technique." Ph.D., University of Minnesota, 1982.

Badal, Robert Samuel. "Kate and Ellen Bateman: A Study in Precocity." Ph.D., Northwestern University, 1971.

Bedard, Roger Lee. "The Life and Work of Charlotte B. Chorpenning." Ph.D., University of Kansas, 1979.

Berger, Lois Lee Stewart. "John Donahue and the Children's Theatre Company and School of Minneapolis, 1961–1978." Ph.D., Florida State University, 1985.

Bethea, Sara Kathryn. "Opera for Children: An Analysis of Selected Works." Ph.D., University of Kansas, 1971.

Cooper, Janet Louise. "A Study of the Effects of Pre-Performance Materials on the Child's Ability to Respond to Theatrical Performance." Ph.D., University of Georgia, 1983.

Cornelison, Gayle Lynn. "Death and Childhood: Attitudes and Approaches in Society, Children's Literature and Children's Theatre and Drama." Ph.D., University of Kansas, 1975.

Davis, Jed Horace, Jr. "The Art of Scenic Design and Staging for Children's Theatre." Ph.D., University of Minnesota, 1958.

Dodd, Dorothy Verne. "Children's Theatre for the Deaf: A Guide to Production." Ed.D., New York University, 1970.

Franklin, Roger. "The Adaptation of Wagner's 'The Ring of the Nibelung' for Young Audiences." Ph.D., New York University, 1975.

Friedman, Lenemaja von Heister. "Children in Eighteenth Century Dramatic Literature." Ph.D., Florida State University, 1969.

Gamble, Michael Wesley. "Clare Tree Major: Children's Theatre, 1923–1954." Ph.D., New York University, 1976.

Goldberg, Moses Haym. "A Survey and Evaluation of Contemporary Principles and Practices at Selected European Children's Theatres." Ph.D., University of Minnesota, 1969.

Goldberg, Patricia Davis. "Development of a Category System for the Analysis of the Response of the Young Theatre Audience." Ph.D., Florida State University, 1977.

Grabish, Richard Frank. "Montrose Jonas Moses: Critic of American Drama." Ph.D., Kent State University, 1979.

Graham, Kenneth L. "An Introductory Study of Evaluation of Plays for Children's Theatre in the United States." Ph.D., University of Utah, 1947.

Gremore, Constance Fritz. "Characteristics of Stage Adaptations of Works of Children's Literature." Ph.D., University of Minnesota, 1984.

Guffin, Jan A. "Winifred Ward: A Critical Biography." Ph.D., Duke University, 1976.

Hecht, Stuart Joel. "Hull-House Theatre: An Analytical and Evaluative History." Ph.D., Northwestern University, 1983.

Helstein, Melvyn Biron. "A Preliminary Investigation of Some Aspects of the Environment for Children's Theatre." Ph.D., University of Minnesota, 1962.

Herget, Patsy Joan. "A History and Evaluation of the Children's Theatre in Cedar Rapids." Ph.D., University of Iowa, 1957.

Hicks, John Vernon. "The History of the Children's Theatre Company and School of Minneapolis 1961–1981." Ph.D., University of Wisconsin-Madison, 1982.

Jennings, Coleman Alonzo. "The Dramatic Contributions of Aurand Harris to Children's Theatre in the United States." Ed.D., New York University, 1974.

Jones, Charles A. "An Evaluation of the Educational Significance of the Children's Theatre in Evanston." Ph.D., Northwestern University, 1953.

Kingsley, William Harmstead. "Happy Endings, Poetic Justice and the Depth and Strength of Characterization in American Children's Drama: A Critical Analysis." Ph.D., University of Pittsburgh, 1964.

Knobloch, Cassandra Louise. "The Cockpit Theatre and Arts Workshop: A Study of the Youth Arts Centre Concept Within the Inner London Education Authority." Ph.D., Florida State University, 1967.

Kottke, Theodore George. "The Writing and Analysis of a Formal Children's Play by Using a Children's Improvisational Theatre Group Working with an Original Scenario." Ed.D., Columbia University, 1972.

Kraus, Joanna Halpert. "A History of the Children's Theatre Association of Baltimore, Maryland from 1943–1966." Ed.D., Columbia University, 1972.

Kreizenbeck, Alan Dennis. "The Theatre Nobody Knows: Forgotten Productions of the Federal Theatre Project, 1935–1939." Ph.D., New York University, 1979.

Leech, Robert Milton. "Education Through Theatre for Children." Ph.D., University of Denver, 1955.

McCaslin, Nellie. "A History of Children's Theatre in the United States." Ph.D., New York University, 1957.

McGowan, Maureen Ann. "An Analysis of the Fantasy Plays of James M. Barrie Utilizing Vladimir Propp's Structural Model of the Fairy Tale." Ph.D., New York University, 1984.

McGraw, William Ralph, Jr. "The Theatricality of James M. Barrie: An Analysis of His Plays to Determine the Source of Their Effectiveness in the Theatre." Ph.D., University of Minnesota, 1958.

MacKinnon, Theresa Lucina. "Theatre for Young Audiences in Canada." Ph.D., New York University, 1974.

Mashiach, Sellina. "Allegory in Children's Theatre and Drama." Ph.D., University of Kansas, 1975.

Meek, Beryl. "The Establishment of a Children's Theatre in a Teacher Training Institution." Ph.D., New York University, 1942.

Mendoza, Barbara Murphy. "Hallie Flanagan: Her Role in American Theatre, 1924–1935." Ph.D., New York University, 1976.

Muschamp, George Morris. "The Honolulu Theatre for Youth, 1955–1973: A Case Study of Government-Related Theatre in the Primary and Secondary Schools of Hawaii." Ph.D., University of Minnesota, 1974.

Parchem, Georgia Larsen. "The Paper Bag Players, A Theatre for Children, 1958–1982: Development, Creative Process, and Principles." Ph.D., Ohio State University, 1983.

Polsky, Milton Eugene. "Oh, Freedom: Theoretical and Practical Problems in the Transformation of Three American Slave Narratives into Original Plays for Young People." Ph.D., New York University, 1973.

Radliff, Suzanne Patricia. "A Study of the Techniques of Adapting Children's Literature to the Stage." Ph.D., Bowling Green State University, 1969.

Regan, Frederick Scott. "The History of the International Children's Theatre Association from Its Founding to 1975." Ph.D., University of Minnesota, 1975.

Rodman, Ellen Rena. "Edith King and Dorothy Coit and the King-Coit School and Children's Theatre." Ph.D., New York University, 1980.

Rosenberg, Helane Susan. "Theatre in Education at the Belgrade: A Study of Its Origins and Evolution from 1965 to 1974." Ph.D., Florida State University, 1975.

Rubin, Janet Elaine. "The Literary and Theatrical Contributions of Charlotte B. Chorpenning to Children's Theatre." Ph.D., Ohio State University, 1978.

Salazar, Laura Gardner. "The Emergence of Children's Theatre and Drama, 1900 to 1910." Ph.D., University of Michigan, 1984.

Sgrio, Carol Thompson. "The Louisville Children's Theatre: A History." Ph.D., Southern Illinois University at Carbondale, 1979.

Shail, George Ellsworth. "The Leningrad Theatre of Young Spectators, 1922–1941." Ph.D., New York University, 1980.

Sosin, Gene. "Children's Theatre and Drama in the Soviet Union (1917–1953)." Ph.D., Columbia University, 1958.

Stephenson, Robert Rex. "White Column Mansions: Three Original Plays Based on Local History and Folklore: A Process for Developing Local American Historical Materials in Theatrical Productions." Ph.D., New York University, 1984.

Sucke, Greer Woodward. "Participation Plays for Young Audiences: Problems in Theory, Writing and Performance." Ph.D., New York University, 1980.

Swortzell, Lowell Stanley. "Five Plays: A Repertory of Children's Theatre to Be Performed by and for Children (Parts I and II)." Ph.D., New York University, 1963.

Van Tassel, Wesley Harvey. "Theory and Practice in Theatre for Children: An Annotated Bibliography of Comment in English Circulated in the United States from 1900 Through 1968." Ph.D., University of Denver, 1969.

Wood, Ronald D. "The Evolution of Brian Way's Participational Theatre." Ph.D., Florida State University, 1976.

Zeder, Suzan Lucille. "A Character Analysis of the Child Protagonist as Presented in Popular Plays for Child Audiences." Ph.D., Florida State University, 1978.

Index

About the Editor and Contributors

ARUN AGNIHOTRI is the Artistic Director of the Playhouse Theatre Group, a children's theatre/drama/TIE company in Baroda, India.

LUBNA ALAMAN works at the Children's Cultural House in Baghdad.

SUNNY AMEY is a member of the QEII Arts Council, New Zealand.

ZINA BARNIEH co-authored *A Mirror of Our Dreams —Children and Theatre in Canada* (1979) and contributed to the *Oxford Companion to Canadian Theatre*.

HÉLÈNE BEAUCHAMP is a professor in the Theatre Department at the University of Quebec at Montreal. She has written extensively about theatre for children and adolescents in French-speaking Canada.

HILDEGARD BERGFELD is the President of ASSITEJ.

KATHLEEN CIOFFI is a doctoral candidate in the Program in Educational Theatre at New York University and recently lived in Poland for three years.

MARIELLE CREAC'H is a noted expert in French children's theatre.

DENISE CRISPUN, a playwright, has a B.A. in History from the University of Rio de Janiero. Her first play, *Strawberries and Telescopes* (1984), written with her brother, Beto Crispun, opened in Rio in 1985. She has since written and adapted several plays for Brazilian youth audiences.

SULAMITA SCHARFSTEIN DONNOLO lived in Brazil for many years. She recently completed her M.A. in the Program in Educational Theatre at New York University.

STIG ERIKSSON is on the faculty of the Drama Department at Bergen College of Education, Norway.

JIA FEI is Deputy Chief Editor and Deputy Director-General of the Seeing and Hearing Center of *Dramatist* magazine, and Deputy Director of the Dramatic Workshop of Heilongjiang Province, China.

MICHAEL FITZGERALD is the Director of the ASSITEJ Center in Australia. He was also the Director of the 1987 ASSITEJ World Congress and General Assembly, held in Adelaide.

ELIZABETH GAY received her Ph.D. in Educational Theatre from New York University. She is an actress and drama specialist.

BEHROUZ GHARIBPOUR is the ASSITEJ representative in Iran. He also writes plays and directs productions for children.

KENT HÄGGLUND is a teacher of Drama at the Stockholm Institute of Education. He also works as a theatre critic for the Swedish Broadcasting Corporation and contributes articles to a number of newspapers and journals on different aspects of culture for children.

TONY JACKSON is a Lecturer in Drama at Manchester University. He has written many articles and book chapters on children's theatre and drama, educational theatre, theatre-in-education, and theatre history, and his most recent book is *Learning Through Theatre: Essays and Casebooks on Theatre in Education* (1980).

MARC JANOVER is a doctoral candidate in Educational Theatre at New York University and a teacher in New York City.

MILADA KADEŘÁBKOVÁ is the Executive Secretary of the ASSITEJ Center in Czechoslovakia.

XENIA KALOGEROPOULOU is an actress, a director, and a producer, as well as a member of the ASSITEJ Center in Greece.

DAISY KANGHELLARI is a theatre historian and Treasurer of the ASSITEJ Center in Greece.

MARLA KLEINE is the Program Director for Stichting Jeugdtheater Amsterdam. She has worked in children's theatre since 1976 as an administrator, a designer, and a writer.

ZVJEZDANA LADIKA is President of the ASSITEJ Center in Yugoslavia. In addition, she is Director of the Zagreb Youth Theatre and teaches at the Teacher's Training College.

BAN LEE is a Vice-President of the ASSITEJ Center in Korea and a Professor at Sung Eui Women's College in Seoul.

CASEY MAN KONG LUM teaches media studies at the New School for Social Research in New York City.

NELLIE McCASLIN, Professor of Educational Theatre at New York University, is a past President of the Children's Theatre Association. She is the author of numerous children's books and college textbooks, as well as general works about children's theatre and dramatics, including *Creative Drama in the Classroom, Theatre for Children in the United States, Theatre for Young Audiences*, and, most recently, *Historical Guide to Children's Theatre in America*.

ZAKES MDA is the Director of the Theatre-for-Development Project of the National University of Lesotho.

SOCORRO MERLIN is the President of the ASSITEJ Center in Mexico.

ESTHER MISCHLER is the Secretary General of the ASSITEJ Center in Switzerland.

MAYRA NAVARRO is a specialist in theatre for children and an Adjunct Professor on the Faculty of Theatre Arts at the Institute of High Arts, Cuba.

LIN TAO PEI is the Director of the Heilongjiang Provincial Drama Workshop, China, Deputy Chief Editor of *Dramaturge* magazine, and Deputy Council-General of the Heilongjiang Province Drama and Inventive Center.

JANET PILLAI is on the faculty of the University Sains Malaysia.

NONNITA REES is Manager of Theatre Programs for the QEII Arts Council, New Zealand.

ELISA DE LA ROCHE is a graduate student in the Program in Educational Theatre at New York University.

ILSE RODENBERG is President of the ASSITEJ Center in East Germany and a past President of ASSITEJ.

ESTHER VAN RYSWYK was formerly a Professor at the University of Cape Town. She now works as a freelance director in community-based theatre, as well as children's theatre and educational theatre and drama.

FAROUK SALLOUM is the Director General of the Children's Culture House in Baghdad.

NATALIA SATS founded the first children's theatre in Moscow and through her productions, tours, and long service to ASSITEJ became an international leader in theater for young people.

SEVDA ŞENER is the Head of the Drama Department of the Faculty of Letters at the University of Ankara, Turkey.

FRANCES SEY is a member of the Arts Council of Ghana.

SOMALATHA SUBASHINGHE is President of the ASSITEJ Center in Sri Lanka, Deputy Director of the State Institute of Theatre Arts, and Director of the Lanka Children's and Youth Theatre Organization and the Playhouse for Children and Youth.

LOWELL SWORTZELL is Professor of Educational Theatre at New York University where he teaches courses in children's theatre, playwriting, the theatre of Eugene O'Neill, musical theatre, and American drama. He is the author of twelve published plays for young people and the editor of *All the World's a Stage*, which was named an "Outstanding Book of the Year" by the *New York Times Book Review*. His last book was *Six Plays for Young People from the Federal Theatre Project (1936–1939): An Introductory Analysis and Six Representative Plays* (Greenwood Press, 1986).

NANCY SWORTZELL is Director of the Program in Educational Theatre at New York University where she has directed many productions for young audiences, most recently *The Arkansaw Bear*, by Aurand Harris, and an adaptation of *Gulliver's Travels*, by Lowell Swortzell, designed by Ralph Lee.

PATRICIA ANNE TERRY is Senior Researcher at the Center for South African Theatre Research.

THOMPSON TSODZO is a native of Zimbabwe, studied in the United States, and received his M.A. in Theatre from the University of Ohio.

SHOSHANA WEITZ is Chairperson of the Educational Theatre Program in the Theatre Department at Tel-Aviv University.

LUO YING is a member of the Children's Art and Culture Committee of the Ministry of Culture of the People's Republic of China.

ONCHUMA YUTHAVONG is an Associate Professor in the Department of Dramatic Arts at Chulalongkorn University in Kuala Lumpur.